The CHRIST *of the* MIRACLE STORIES

The CHRIST *of the* MIRACLE STORIES

Portrait through Encounter

WENDY J. COTTER, CSJ

Baker Academic

a division of Baker Publishing Group
Grand Rapids, Michigan

© 2010 by Wendy J. Cotter

Published by Baker Academic
a division of Baker Publishing Group
P.O. Box 6287, Grand Rapids, MI 49516-6287
www.bakeracademic.com

Printed in the United States of America

Library of Congress Cataloging-in-Publication Data
Cotter, Wendy, 1946–
   The Christ of the miracle stories : portrait through encounter / Wendy Cotter.
       p. cm.
   Includes bibliographical references (p.   ) and indexes.
   ISBN 978-0-8010-3950-8
       1. Jesus Christ—Miracles. 2. Jesus Christ—Character.
   3. Jesus Christ—Person and offices. I. Title.
   BT366.3.C68 2010
   232.9´55—dc22   2010017451

10   11   12   13   14   15   16   7   6   5   4   3   2   1

For my community,
the Sisters of St. Joseph of the Diocese of London,
Ontario, Canada

In honor of our one hundred and fortieth year in the London Diocese

1868–2008

Congregavit Nos in Unum Christi Amor

Contents

PART IV
Petitioners Who Are Jesus' Disciples

Acknowledgements

I would like to thank Loyola University of Chicago for fostering my research for this book by generously supporting a semester sabbatical and later a summer of study. I thank my colleagues in the Department of Theology at Loyola for their interest and encouragement during the development of this book. I am greatly indebted to Dr. Gregory W. Dobrov, Associate Professor of Classical Studies at Loyola University for his erudite translation of the several passages of Artemidorus, featured in this book. I am grateful for the doctoral students who have greatly assisted me in research over the years: Mr. Paul Voelker, ABD, Mr. Jeremy Miselbrook, ABD, Ms. Teresa Calpino, ABD, and also Sister Lisa Marie Belz, OSU, ABD, with special thanks for her helpful suggestions and initial editing of the chapters. My sincerest thanks to Shirley Decker-Lucke, former editorial director of Hendrickson Publishers, for her patient guidance, and to Allan Emery, Senior Editor, for his kind counsel throughout the preparation of the manuscript. I would like to thank Sister Mary Norita Keenan, CSJ, and Mrs. Jean Galán for the many intense and stimulating conversations about the material over these years as the chapters moved on one by one. My thanks to all my dear Sisters, to whom this book is dedicated, the Sisters of St. Joseph of London, Ontario, Canada, whose lively interest, cheerful encouragement, and kindly prayers have meant so much to me.

I wish to thank the President and Fellows of Harvard College for permission to reprint the following portions of the Loeb Classical Library.

p. 6. Reprinted by permission of the publishers and the Trustees of the Loeb Classical Library from Plutarch, *Alexander. Plutarch's Lives,* Loeb

pp. 31, 67. Reprinted by permission of the publishers and the Trustees of the Loeb Classical Library from Theophrastus, *Characters,* Loeb Classical Library Volume 225, translated by Jeffrey Rusten, Cambridge, Mass.: Harvard University Press © 1993, by the President and Fellows of Harvard College. Loeb Classical Library ® is a registered trademark of the President and Fellows of Harvard College.

p. 31. Reprinted by permission of the publishers and the Trustees of the Loeb Classical Library from Martial, *Epigrams,* Loeb Classical Library Volume 95, translated by Walter C. A. Ker, Cambridge, Mass.: Harvard University Press © 1920, by the President and Fellows of Harvard College. Loeb Classical Library ® is a registered trademark of the President and Fellows of Harvard College.

pp. 37, 63. Reprinted by permission of the publishers and the Trustees of the Loeb Classical Library from Epictetus, *The Discourses as Reported by Arrian, the Manual, and Fragments,* Loeb Classical Library Volume 218, translated by W. A. Oldfather, Cambridge, Mass.: Harvard University Press © 1928, by the President and Fellows of Harvard College. Loeb Classical Library ® is a registered trademark of the President and Fellows of Harvard College.

pp. 59, 64. Reprinted by permission of the publishers and the Trustees of the Loeb Classical Library from Sophocles, *Oedipus the King,* Loeb Classical Library Volume 1, translated by F. Storr, Cambridge, Mass.: Harvard University Press © 1913, by the President and Fellows of Harvard College. Loeb Classical Library ® is a registered trademark of the President and Fellows of Harvard College.

p. 63. Reprinted by permission of the publishers and the Trustees of the Loeb Classical Library from Plato, *Laws,* Loeb Classical Library Volume 192, translated by R. G. Bury, Cambridge, Mass.: Harvard University Press © 1926, by the President and Fellows of Harvard College. Loeb Classical Library ® is a registered trademark of the President and Fellows of Harvard College.

p. 63. Reprinted by permission of the publishers and the Trustees of the Loeb Classical Library from Plautus, *Trinummus,* Loeb Classical Library Volume 328, translated by Paul Nixon, Cambridge, Mass.: Harvard University Press © 1938, by the President and Fellows of Harvard

Cambridge, Mass.: Harvard University Press © 1927, by the President and Fellows of Harvard College. Loeb Classical Library® is a registered trademark of the President and Fellows of Harvard College.

p. 117. Reprinted by permission of the publishers and the Trustees of the Loeb Classical Library from Tacitus, *Histories, Books 4–5; Annals, Books 1–3,* Loeb Classical Library Volume 249, translated by C. H. Moore and J. Jackson, Cambridge, Mass.: Harvard University Press © 1931, by the President and Fellows of Harvard College. Loeb Classical Library® is a registered trademark of the President and Fellows of Harvard College.

p. 119. Reprinted by permission of the publishers and the Trustees of the Loeb Classical Library from Plutarch, *Ceasar: Plutarch's Live,* Loeb Classical Library Volume 99, translated by Bernadotte Perrin, Cambridge, Mass.: Harvard University Press © 1919, by the President and Fellows of Harvard College. Loeb Classical Library® is a registered trademark of the President and Fellows of Harvard College.

pp. 120, 150. Reprinted by permission of the publishers and the Trustees of the Loeb Classical Library from Juvenal, *The Satires,* Loeb Classical Library Volume 91, translated by G. G. Ramsey, Cambridge, Mass.: Harvard University Press © 1918, by the President and Fellows of Harvard College. Loeb Classical Library® is a registered trademark of the President and Fellows of Harvard College.

p. 122. Reprinted by permission of the publishers and the Trustees of the Loeb Classical Library from Cicero, *De Haruspicum Responsis,* Loeb Classical Library Volume 158, translated by N. H. Watts, Cambridge, Mass.: Harvard University Press © 1923, by the President and Fellows of Harvard College. Loeb Classical Library® is a registered trademark of the President and Fellows of Harvard College.

p. 150. Reprinted by permission of the publishers and the Trustees of the Loeb Classical Library from Lucian, *The Parliament of the Gods,* Loeb Classical Library Volume 302, translated by A. M. Harmon, Cambridge, Mass.: Harvard University Press © 1936, by the President and Fellows of Harvard College. Loeb Classical Library® is a registered trademark of the President and Fellows of Harvard College.

pp. 151, 237, 238. Reprinted by permission of the publishers and the Trustees of the Loeb Classical Library from Plutarch, *Moralia,* Loeb

pp. 166, 200. Reprinted by permission of the publishers and the Trustees of the Loeb Classical Library from Dio Cassius, *Roman History,* Loeb Classical Library Volume 176, translated by Earnest Cary, Cambridge, Mass.: Harvard University Press © 1925, by the President and Fellows of Harvard College. Loeb Classical Library ® is a registered trademark of the President and Fellows of Harvard College.

p. 169. Reprinted by permission of the publishers and the Trustees of the Loeb Classical Library from Flavius Josephus, *Against Appius, vol. I,* Loeb Classical Library Volume 186, translated by H. St. J. Thackeray, Cambridge, Mass.: Harvard University Press © 1926, by the President and Fellows of Harvard College. Loeb Classical Library ® is a registered trademark of the President and Fellows of Harvard College.

pp. 169, 239. Reprinted by permission of the publishers and the Trustees of the Loeb Classical Library from Philo of Alexandria, *On the Embassy to Gaius,* Loeb Classical Library Volume 379, translated by F. H. Colson, Cambridge, Mass.: Harvard University Press © 1962, by the President and Fellows of Harvard College. Loeb Classical Library ® is a registered trademark of the President and Fellows of Harvard College.

p. 216. Reprinted by permission of the publishers and the Trustees of the Loeb Classical Library from Theocritus, "The Hymn to the Dioscuri," Loeb Classical Library Volume 28, translated by J. M. Edmonds, Cambridge, Mass.: Harvard University Press © 1912, by the President and Fellows of Harvard College. Loeb Classical Library ® is a registered trademark of the President and Fellows of Harvard College.

p. 217. Reprinted by permission of the publishers and the Trustees of the Loeb Classical Library from Lucian, "On Salaried Posts in Great Houses," Loeb Classical Library Volume 130, translated by A. M. Harmon, Cambridge, Mass.: Harvard University Press © 1921, by the President and Fellows of Harvard College. Loeb Classical Library ® is a registered trademark of the President and Fellows of Harvard College.

p. 227. Reprinted by permission of the publishers and the Trustees of the Loeb Classical Library from Herodotus, *The Persian Wars,* Loeb Classical Library Volume 119, translated by A. D. Godley, Cambridge, Mass.: Harvard University Press © 1922, by the President and Fellows of Harvard College. Loeb Classical Library ® is a registered trademark of the President and Fellows of Harvard College.

p. 254. Reprinted by permission of the publishers and the Trustees of the Loeb Classical Library from Tacitus, *Annals, Books 4–6, 11–13,* Loeb Classical Library Volume 312, translated by J. Jackson, Cambridge, Mass.: Harvard University Press © 1937, by the President and Fellows of Harvard College. Loeb Classical Library ® is a registered trademark of the President and Fellows of Harvard College.

pp. 94, 254. Reprinted by permission of the publishers and the Trustees of the Loeb Classical Library from Suetonius, *Lives of the Caesars,* Loeb Classical Library Volume 31, translated by J. C. Rolfe, Cambridge, Mass.: Harvard University Press © 1915, rev. 1951, by the President and Fellows of Harvard College. Loeb Classical Library ® is a registered trademark of the President and Fellows of Harvard College.

p. 256. Reprinted by permission of the publishers and the Trustees of the Loeb Classical Library from Dio Cassius, *Roman History,* Loeb Classical Library Volume 175, translated by Earnest Cary, Cambridge, Mass.: Harvard University Press © 1924, by the President and Fellows of Harvard College. Loeb Classical Library ® is a registered trademark of the President and Fellows of Harvard College.

Abbreviations

ANCIENT TEXTS, TEXT TYPES, AND VERSIONS

LXX	Septuagint
MT	Masoretic Text

MODERN VERSIONS

NETS	New English Translation of the Septuagint
NIV	New International Version
NJB	New Jerusalem Bible
NRSV	New Revised Standard Version
RSV	Revised Standard Version

APOCRYPHA AND SEPTUAGINT

Sir	Sirach
Tob	Tobit
Wis	Wisdom of Solomon

OLD TESTAMENT PSEUDEPIGRAPHA

Jub.	*Jubilees*
T. Naph.	*Testament of Naphtali*

DEAD SEA SCROLLS AND RELATED TEXTS

1QHᵃ	1QHodayotᵃ

MISHNAH, TALMUD, AND RELATED LITERATURE

b.	Babylonian Talmud
t.	Tosefta
y.	Jerusalem Talmud
'Abod. Zar.	*'Abodah Zarah*
Bek.	*Bekorot*
Ber.	*Berakot*
B. Qam.	*Baba Qamma*
Ḥal.	*Ḥallah*
Meg.	*Megillah*
Mo'ed Qaṭ.	*Mo'ed Qaṭan*
Ned.	*Nedarim*
'Ohol.	*'Oholot*
Šabb.	*Šabbat*
Ṭohor.	*Ṭohoroth*

OTHER RABBINIC WORKS

Midr.	*Midrash* (+ biblical book)
Pirqe R. El.	*Pirqe Rabbi Eliezer*
Rab.	*Rabbah* (+ biblical book)
Tanḥ.	*Tanḥuma*

GREEK AND LATIN WORKS

Achilles Tatius
Leuc. Clit.	*Leucippe et Clitophon* (*The Adventures of Leucippe and Cleitophon*)

Aelius Aristides
Serap.	*Regarding Serapis*

Appian
Hist. rom.	*Historia romana* (*Roman History*)

Apuleius
Metam.	*Metamorphoses* (*The Golden Ass*)

Aristophanes
Plut.	*Plutus* (*The Rich Man*)

Artemidorus Daldianus
Onir.	*Onirocritica* (*The Interpretation of Dreams*)

Athenaeus
   Deipn.   *Deipnosophistae*
Celsus
   Med.   *De medicina (On Medicine)*
Chariton
   Chaer.   *De Chaerea et Callirhoe (Chaereas and Callirhoe)*
Cicero
   Har. resp.   *De haruspicum responses*
   Phil.   *Orationes philippicae*
   Rosc. Amer.   *Pro Sexto Roscio Amerino*
Columella
   Rust.   *De re rustica (On Agriculture)*
Cornelius Nepos
   Exc. duc.   *Liber de excellentibus ducibus exterarum gentium*
                 (Eminent Foreign Leaders)
Dio Cassius
   Hist.   *Roman History*
Dio Chrysostom
   3 Regn.   *De regno iii (Or. 3) (Kingship 3)*
   Troj.   *Trojana (Or. 11) (Trojan Discourse)*
   Ven.   *Venator (Or. 7) (The Hunter) (Euboean Discourse)*
Diodorus Siculus
   Hist.   *Bibliotheca historica*
Diogenes Laertius
   Vit. phil.   *Vitae philosophorum (Lives of Eminent Philosophers)*
Epictetus
   Diatr.   *Diatribai (Dissertationes)*
Eunapius
   Phil. soph.   *Vitae sophistarum (Lives of the Sophists)*
Florus
   Hist. rom.   *Epitomae historiae romanae (Epitome of Roman*
                 History)
Heliodorus
   Aeth.   *Aethiopica (An Ethiopian Story)*
Herodotus
   Hist.   *Historiae (Histories)*
Hesiod
   Op.   *Opera et dies (Works and Days)*

Hippocrates
   Aff.   *De affectionibus (Affections)*
   Morb.   *De morbis (Diseases)*
Homer
   Od.   *Odyssea (Odyssey)*
Horace
   Carm.   *Carmina (Odes)*
   Sat.   *Satirae (Satires)*
Iamblichus
   Vit. Pyth.   *Vita Pythagorae (Life of Pythagoras)*
Josephus
   Ag. Ap.   *Against Apion*
   Ant.   *Jewish Antiquities*
   J.W.   *Jewish War*
   Life   *The Life*
Juvenal
   Sat.   *Satirae (Satires)*
Livy
   Hist.   *History of Rome (Ab urbe condita libri)*
Lucan
   Bell. civ.   *Bellum civile (Civil War)*
Lucian
   Deor. conc.   *Deorum concilium (Parliament of the Gods)*
   Merc. cond. *De mercede conductis (Salaried Posts in Great Houses)*
Martial
   Ep.   *Epigrammata (Epigrams)*
Ovid
   Metam.   *Metamorphosis*
Pausanias
   Descr.   *Graeciae descriptio (Description of Greece)*
Persius
   Sat.   *Satirae (Satires)*
Philo
   Embassy   *On the Embassy to Gaius*
Philostratus
   Vit. Apoll.   *Vita Apollonii (Life of Apollonius)*
Plato
   Gorg.   *Gorgias*
   Leg.   *Leges (Laws)*

Phaed.	*Phaedo*
Resp.	*Respublica (Republic)*
Plautus	
Trin.	*Trinummus*
Pliny the Elder	
Nat.	*Naturalis historia (Natural History)*
Plutarch	
Caes.	*Caesar*
Comp. Cim.	*Comparatio Cimonis et Luculli*
Luc.	
Alex.	*Alexander*
Luc.	*Lucullus*
Lys.	*Lysander*
Mor.	*Moralia*
Porphyry	
Vit. Pyth.	*Vita Pythagorae (Life of Pythagoras)*
Sophocles	
Aj.	*Ajax*
Oed. col.	*Oedipus coloneus (Oedipus at Colonus)*
Oed. tyr.	*Oedipus tyrannus (Oedipus the King)*
Phil.	*Philoctetes*
Strabo	
Geogr.	*Geographica*
Suetonius	
Cal.	*Gaius Caligula*
Jul.	*Divus Julius*
Tib.	*Tiberius*
Tacitus	
Ann.	*Annales (Annals)*
Hist.	*Historiae (Histories)*
Theocritus	
Id.	*Idylls*
Theophrastus	
Char.	*Characteres (Characters)*
Valerius Maximus	
Fact. dict.	*Factorum et dictorum memorabilia (Memorable Doings and Sayings)*
Vegetius	
Epit. mil.	*Epitoma rei militaris (Epitome of Military Science)*

Virgil
  Georg.   *Georgica*
Xenophon
  Mem.   *Memorabilia*

SECONDARY SOURCES

AB	Anchor Bible
AGJU	Arbeiten zur Geschichte des antiken Judentums und Urchristentums
AJP	*American Journal of Philology*
AnBib	Analecta biblica
ANRW	*Aufstieg und Niedergang der römischen Welt: Geschichte und Kultur Roms im Spiegel der neueren Foschung.* Edited by H. Temporini and W. Haase. Berlin, 1972–
AUS	American University Studies
BAGD	Bauer, W., W. F. Arndt, F. W. Gingrich, and F. W. Danker. *Greek-English Lexicon of the New Testament and Other Early Christian Literature.* 2d ed. Chicago, 1979
BETL	Bibliotheca ephemeridum theologicarum lovaniensium
BNTC	Black's New Testament Commentaries
BZ	*Biblische Zeitschrift*
BZNW	Beihefte zur Zeitschrift für die neutestamentliche Wissenschaft
CBC	Cambridge Bible Commentary
CBQ	*Catholic Biblical Quarterly*
CBQMS	Catholic Biblical Quarterly Monograph Series
CGTC	Cambridge Greek Testament Commentary
EHPR	Études d'histoire et de philosophie religieuses
EKKNT	Evangelisch-katholischer Kommentar zum Neuen Testament
ETL	*Ephemerides theologicae lovanienses*
ETR	*Études théologiques et religieuses*
ExpTim	*Expository Times*
FCNTECW	Feminist Companion to the New Testament and Early Christian Writings

FRLANT	Forschungen zur Religion und Literatur des Alten und Neuen Testaments
GR	*Greece and Rome*
GRBS	*Greek, Roman, and Byzantine Studies*
HNT	Handbuch zum Neuen Testament
HTKNT	Herders theologischer Kommentar zum Neuen Testament
HTR	*Harvard Theological Review*
ISBE	*International Standard Bible Encyclopedia.* Edited by G. W. Bromiley. 4 vols. Grand Rapids, 1979–1988
IBC	Interpretation: A Bible Commentary for Teaching and Preaching
ICC	International Critical Commentary
IG	*Inscriptiones Graecae.* Editio minor. Berlin 1924–
Int	*Interpretation*
JBL	*Journal of Biblical Literature*
JHT	*Journal of Hispanic Theology*
JR	*Journal of Religion*
JRS	*Journal of Roman Studies*
JSNT	*Journal for the Study of the New Testament*
JSNTSup	Journal for the Study of the New Testament: Supplement Series
JTS	*Journal of Theological Studies*
KEK	Kritisch-exegetischer Kommentar über das Neue Testament
KTVÜ	Kleine texte für Vorlesungen und Übungen
KUT	Kohlhammer Urban-Taschenbücher
LCL	Loeb Classical Library
LD	Lectio divina
LS	*Louvain Studies*
LSJ	Liddell, H. G., R. Scott, and H. S. Jones, *A Greek-English Lexicon.* 9th ed. with revised supplement. Oxford, 1996.
MM	Moulton, J. H., and G. Milligan. *The Vocabulary of the Greek New Testament.* London, 1930. Reprint, Peabody, Mass., 1997
NAC	New American Commentary
NICNT	New International Commentary on the New Testament

NIGTC	New International Greek Testament Commentary
NovT	*Novum Testamentum*
NovTSup	Supplements to Novum Testamentum
NThT	*Nieuw Theologisch Tijdschrift*
NTL	New Testament Library
NTM	New Testament Message
NTR	New Testament Readings
NTS	*New Testament Studies*
ÖTK	Ökumenischer Taschenbuch-Kommentar
PC	Proclamation Commentaries
PEQ	*Palestine Exploration Quarterly*
PGC	Pelican Gospel Commentaries
PNTC	Pillar New Testament Commentary
PRSt	Perspectives in Religious Studies
RA	Revealing Antiquity
RNT	Regensburger Neues Testament
SANT	Studien zum Alten und Neuen Testament
SBEC	Studies in the Bible and Early Christianity
SBLDS	Society of Biblical Literature Dissertation Series
SCJ	Studies in Christianity and Judaism
SJLA	Studies in Judaism in Late Antiquity
SNTSMS	Society for New Testament Studies Monograph Series
SSG	Studies in the Synoptic Gospels
Str-B	Strack, H. L., and P. Billerbeck. *Kommentar zum Neuen Testament aus Tamud und Midrasch.* 6 vols. Munich, 1922–1961
SUNT	Studien zur Umwelt des Neuen Testaments
SWR	Studies in Women and Religion
TAPA	*Transactions of the American Philological Association*
THKNT	Theologischer Handkommentar zum Neuen Testament
TTH	Translated Texts for Historians
WestBC	Westminster Bible Companion
WUNT	Wissenschaftliche Untersuchungen zum Neuen Testament
ZNW	Zeitschrift für die neutestamentliche Wissenschaft

Introduction

The history of scholarship on the miracle stories has largely focused on the "miracle" itself, the type of power that Jesus exhibits there and what that power claims about his person. It was Rudolf Bultmann[1] who led the way in categorizing the types found in the Synoptic tradition (healings, exorcisms, raisings from the dead, and nature miracles) by noting similar types of miracle stories, both Jewish and non-Jewish, in the world of Greco-Roman antiquity. Subsequently, other scholars, notably Gerd Theissen, further subdivided these classifications and recatalogued them. His analysis results in seven main kinds of characters (demon, sick person, companion, opponent, crowd, disciples, and miracle worker) and thirty-three motifs.[2] Such conscious classification of the miracle story "form" and its kinds, however, belong only to our side of the timeline, for there is no evidence of any awareness of a "miracle story" form in the ancient

---

[1] Rudolf Bultmann, *The History of the Synoptic Tradition* (trans. John Marsh; Peabody, Mass.: Hendrickson, 1963 [German original, 1921]).

[2] Gerd Theissen, *The Miracle Stories of the Synoptic Tradition* (trans. Francis McDonagh; Philadelphia: Fortress, 1983). The thirty-three motifs include (1) arrival of miracle worker, (2) appearance of the crowd, (3) appearance of the distressed person, (4) appearance of representatives, (5) appearance of embassies, (6) appearance of opponents, (7) reasons for appearance of "opposite numbers" (petitioners), (8) description of the distress, (9) difficulties in the approach, (10) falling to the knees, (11) cries for help, (12) pleas and expression of trust, (13) misunderstanding, (14) skepticism and mockery, (15) criticism from opponents, (16) resistance and submission of the demon, (17) pneumatic excitement, (18) assurance, (19) argument, (20) withdrawal of miracle worker, (21) setting the scene, (22) touch, (23) healing substances, (24) miracle-working word, (25) prayer, (26) recognition of miracle, (27) demonstration, (28) dismissal, (29) command to secrecy, (30) wonder, (31) acclamation, (32) rejection, and (33) spread of the news; and six themes: (1) exorcisms, (2) healings, (3) epiphanies, (4) rescue miracles, (5) gift miracles, and (6) rule miracles (pp. 45–114).

world. Therefore, we cannot project our categories and their criteria backwards onto the first-century narrators, who were unaware of them.

As it happens, it is Martin Dibelius's more general category of story, "tale," that comes closer to the free composition of the narrator, as Bultmann's classification does not. Only two elements are necessary for one of these miracle stories: the miracle as climax and the story that gives the context to it. Whether the introduction was to be long or short, the dialogue to be brief or more developed, the conclusion to contain or lack an "acclamation" was not a case of following a "form" or not. As with any story, all that mattered was the message. To understand that message, both elements have to be contextualized within their world. The miraculous deed needs a backdrop of similar miracles performed by gods and/or heroes, traditions well known to the ordinary person, Jewish or non-Jewish, who lived in the Mediterranean world. From that set of stories and the significances regularly claimed for them it is possible to create a set of meanings against which the Jesus miracle can be placed to understand the parameters of his power and the meaning of that power. This is the backdrop that I tried to reconstruct in some way with my book *Miracles in Greco-Roman Antiquity*.[3]

This book, *The Christ of the Miracle Stories: Portrait through Encounter*, addresses the second element, the encounter between Jesus and the petitioner. A cultural contextualization is required to understand that element as well. Miracle stories, however, are not apophthegms, where the focus is on Jesus' defense or his instruction, and where, as Jerome Neyrey notes, Jesus' honor is at stake. In that contest, Jesus' answers always show him to be the wisest.

> Like most honorable people in antiquity, he [Jesus] is a skilled combatant! He accepts challenges (i.e., questions) and parries them expertly by asking counter-questions. No turning of the cheek here! If questions are weapons, then Jesus deserves an Olympic medal for prowess in asking questions which silence his opponents. The few instances of Jesus' asking a question which begins an episode indicate that the evangelist was presenting him not simply as a defensive expert who fends off challenges but also as someone who initiates conflict. If this conflict is read in the light of honor and shame, it functions to shame his opponents and win him further honor.[4]

---

[3] Wendy Cotter, *Miracles in Greco-Roman Antiquity: A Sourcebook* (London: Routledge, 1999).

[4] Jerome H. Neyrey, "Questions, *Chreiai*, Honor: The Interface of Rhetoric and Culture in Mark's Gospel," *CBQ* 60 (1998): 680.

What the reader probably expects me to write here is that unlike the apophthegm, the miracle story focuses on the action of Jesus, a difference underlined by Bultmann. In fact, close attention to the miracle story shows that the encounter built around the miracle, and the way Jesus responds to the petitioner with his miracle, effects something of a portraiture of him, his power, and the lessons that accompany his expression of divine power to help. This idea that the miracle story acts as a revelation of Jesus' person, his portrait, would seem to contradict Bultmann, for the one element that he claimed to be similar to both the miracle stories and apophthegms was their lack of portraiture: "The style of the miracle story is related to that of the apophthegm to this extent—the 'absence of portraiture' (Dibelius) and all that it involves is characteristic of both. Here as there *nothing but the point matters*—there is a saying of Jesus, *here a miracle*."[5]

For Bultmann, then, the point of the miracle story is the working of the miracle, while the story is ancillary. To be fair, when both Bultmann and Dibelius used "portraiture," they were referring to the explicit essays on a hero's character such as one finds in Cicero's *Orations*, Plutarch's *Lives*, Tacitus's *Annals of Imperial Rome*, Suetonius's *Lives of the Caesars*, Dio Cassius's *Roman History*, and the like. Dibelius paralleled the narrative details of the miracle stories to those adventure stories so popular to the pagans in the "foreign," "secular" world:[6] "The breadth of style of the Tale, on the contrary [as opposed to paradigms], is in no wise 'didactic' or otherwise conditioned in some way by the praxis of preaching. On the contrary the living realism of the narrative loves *secular motives*."[7] He explains further, "They are not conditioned by thoughts found in the preaching of salvation and so do not touch the question of the relationship of man to God, or what man enters the Kingdom of Heaven and what is God's real requirement of man. Rather they are dominated by

---

[5] Bultmann, *Synoptic Tradition*, 220 (my italics).

[6] Dibelius's tales in the Markan Gospel include: the healing of the leper (Mark 1:40–45); the stilling of the storm (Mark 4:35–41); the Gerasene demoniac (Mark 5:1–20); the woman with the hemorrhage and the raising of Jairus's daughter (Mark 5:21–43); the feeding of the five thousand (Mark 6:35–44); the walking on the water (Mark 6:45–52); the deaf man with the speech impediment (Mark 7:32–37); the blind man of Bethsaida (Mark 8:22–26); and the possessed boy (Mark 9:14–29) (Martin Dibelius, *From Tradition to Gospel* [trans. Bertram Lee Woolf; 1934; repr., Cambridge: J. Clarke, 1971], 78, 93–95, 103).

[7] Ibid., 78.

the effort to make plain the greatness of a miracle, to show the impossibility of human aid, and to depict the nature of Jesus' intervention."[8] As a result, he concluded that the sole purpose of the miracle story is "to prove the miracle-worker was an epiphany of God, and this was done by the Tale as such apart from inclusion in a sermon."[9] A comparison of these miracle narratives to the Greco-Roman "tales," however, only serves to emphasize how different both types of narrative are, both in size and in character. The miracle stories are dwarfed by the lengthy tales. Moreover, the miracle stories are focused not on a series of adventurous actions but on a single encounter between Jesus and petitioners. In fact, miracle stories do not imitate "the broad style of the tale." Rather, the story is small and singly focused on the encounter. Where there is a story—that is, where there is not simply the statement that Jesus cured someone, but the relating of an encounter between Jesus and petitioners—the "form" is better understood as a kind of anecdote.

I consider it extremely significant that Vernon Robbins chose to include miracle stories in his collection *Ancient Quotes and Anecdotes*.[10] It means that for this erudite analyst of the sayings tradition, miracle stories fulfilled his definition of the anecdote, one closely based on the entry in the *Oxford English Dictionary*:[11] "This book contains stories that reach their high point in a striking saying *or action*."[12] With respect to the criteria of an anecdote, Richard Saller is more particular: "Two elements of the definition should be given particular emphasis. First, an anecdote must have some narrative elements: thus simple apophthegms

---

[8] Ibid., 93.

[9] Ibid., 95.

[10] Vernon Robbins, *Ancient Quotes and Anecdotes: From Crib to Crypt* (Sonoma, Calif.: Polebridge Press, 1989). If we use Bultmann's classification, we find among the anecdotes one exorcism (the man in the synagogue [Mark 1:21–28 // Luke 4:31–37]); six healing stories (the paralytic [Mark 2:1–12 // Matt 9:1–8 // Luke 5:17–26]; the centurion's servant [Matt 8:5–13 // Luke 7:2–10]; the crippled woman at the synagogue [Luke 13:10–17]; the man with dropsy [Luke 14:1–6]; the ten lepers [Luke 17:11–19]; the crippled man at the pool of Bethesda [John 5:1–9]); and three nature miracles (Peter's walking on the sea [Matt 14:28–33]; the withering of the fig tree [Matt 21:18–22]; the changing of water into wine at the wedding at Cana [John 2:1–11]).

[11] "The narrative of a detached incident, or of a single event, told as being in itself interesting or striking" (*Oxford English Dictionary* [2d ed., 1989]).

[12] Robbins, *Ancient Quotes and Anecdotes*, xi (my italics).

do not meet the definition, though Roman anecdotes may include them. Secondly, an anecdote must be a detached incident: longer historical narratives do not qualify." He then adds a third: "Anecdotes must contain a sequence of at least two narrative elements."[13]

Miracle stories seem a much better fit as anecdotes than as "tales." If so, then the function of an anecdote has to be carefully considered, for this goes to the intent of the narrator, who chose anecdote form. Saller notes that anecdotes are found serving six purposes: (1) the report of gossip; (2) entertainment at dinner parties; (3) oratorical examples to support an argument; (4) *exempla*, stories that provide some virtue to be admired and imitated; (5) demonstration of erudition; and (6) characterization of emperors in biographies.[14] With respect to the Jesus' miracle stories, categories 1 and 2 are inappropriate, nor does 5 apply. The stories could be used as in category 3, to support an argument, as the miracle stories are called upon in ordinary Christian rhetoric today. I propose that the narrator of the miracle stories had in mind the usage defined in category 4, *exempla*, because the story attested Jesus' divine power but models an attitude and virtue revealed in the encounter with the petitioner. Thus, the miracle stories serve also to uncover the character of Jesus, as in category 6, characterization.

Plutarch is the master in the use of anecdote to characterize by means of small stories with a striking point. In his preface to the life of Alexander the Great he writes,

> For it is not Histories that I am writing, but Lives; and in the most illustrious deeds there is not always a manifestation of virtue or vice, nay, a slight thing like a phrase of a jest often makes a greater revelation of character than battles where thousands fall, or the greatest armaments, or sieges of cities. Accordingly, just as painters get the likenesses in their portraits from the face and the expression of the eyes, wherein the character shows itself, but make very little account of the other parts of the body, so I must be permitted to devote myself rather to the signs of the souls in men, and by means of these to portray the life of each, leaving to others the description of their great contests. (*Alex.* 1.2–3)[15]

---

[13] Richard Saller, "Anecdotes as Historical Evidence for the Principate," *GR*, 2d series, 27, no. 1 (1980): 69.

[14] Ibid., 70–73. Each of these is fully discussed with several appropriate examples from antiquity.

[15] Plutarch, *Alexander*, in vol. 7 of *Plutarch's Lives* (trans. Bernadotte Perrin; LCL; Cambridge, Mass.: Harvard University Press, 1967), 225.

More recently, Joel Williams (*Other Followers of Jesus*)[16] and Elizabeth Struthers Malbon (*In the Company of Jesus*)[17] have provided a close reading of the Markan miracle narratives with attention to how the petitioners, the "minor characters," act as "exemplars of faith" in service of the Gospel. Although they do not actually identify the miracle stories as anecdotes, their examination shows that Jesus' act of power is not the only point of the account. They both recognize the importance of the contexualizing narrative as one that provides an *exemplum* to the listener in the petitioners' faith.

My research differs from theirs in two ways. First, my investigation addresses the function of the miracle stories prior to their incorporation into the Gospels. This means that prior to any discussion of the Markan accounts, a preliminary redactional analysis is necessary to identify the most obvious signs of his hand, so that the account may be discussed apart from these additions. Here let us swiftly admit that it is impossible to claim with certainty that the vocabulary remaining is not Mark's. He is the writer of the Gospel and was free to use authorial preference for these traditional stories, or so we may assume. Yet, most Markan scholars would agree that Mark seems rather conventional in his presentation of the traditional stories, apart from his obvious interventions, for his presence is usually detected in redundant remarks, clumsy interventions and explanations, or conclusions that result in a contradictory ending. In any case, the study of the miracle story that remains depends not on the precise vocabulary but on the narrative elements of the anecdote. The special attention to the discrete miracle story that survived until the Markan Gospel makes the petitioners not "minor characters," then, but major characters together with Jesus. (Let me add that this exploration of pre-Gospel miracle narratives includes a study of the Q account of the centurion and his servant boy [Q {Luke} 7:1–10], again apart from the influence of the surrounding Q material).

The second way in which my research differs is that I have contextualized the behavior and, where applicable, the speech of petitioners against the backdrop of conventional good manners as understood in the Greco-Roman world, only to find that while some of these petition-

---

[16] Joel F. Williams, *Other Followers of Jesus: Minor Characters as Major Figures in Mark's Gospel* (JSNTSup 102; Sheffield: JSOT Press, 1994).

[17] Elizabeth Struthers Malbon, *In the Company of Jesus: Characters in Mark's Gospel* (Louisville: Westminster John Knox, 2000).

ers are meant to be *exempla* of faith, they provide a very challenging ideal to the ordinary person. Interestingly, the narrator/s seem to choose bold, brash, outrageous, rude petitioners to approach Jesus. And one must ask why this is so if the whole point is to feature only the power of Jesus in the miracle, this is so. The answer is that the situation, the encounter, is not simply a vehicle to hurry us to the amazing miraculous action at all. Rather, it must be that the narrator, having caught the listener's attention with the presence of these bold petitioners, now illustrates Jesus' view of them and his response. It is in this response by Jesus that the would-be follower would find the *exempla*. First is the example that Jesus provides in his response to these persons who, convention would conclude, deserved a good rebuke. Second is the example provided by the faith of the petitioner, as directed by Jesus, another challenge that demands of the follower the abandonment of usual criteria of what is "worthy," to focus on the quality of faith, regardless of status or class. Here I include the healing of the leper (Mark 1:40–45); the healing of the paralytic (Mark 2:1–12); the Syrophoenician mother (Mark 7:24–30); the father of the demonized boy (Mark 9:14–29); the healing of Bartimaeus (Mark 10:46–52); and, from Q, the healing of the centurion's boy (Q [Luke] 7:1, 3, 6b–9).

I have also included the two miracle stories where Jesus tends to the needs of his apostles: the stilling of the storm (Mark 4:35–41) and the walking on the water (Mark 6:45–52). Here the disciples do not emulate the hardy, stalwart sort of ideal disciple brimming with courage and initiative, but are panic-stricken followers as seen in both miracle stories. The fact that Jesus performs an unnecessary miracle in the first case and refrains from continuing one in the second case has its own special message to the community.

In all these responses, the narrator has taken pains to provide situations where the encounter with petitioners will allow Jesus to reveal not only his power, but also his "soul," as Plutarch would say.

This identification of problematic petitioners is only further affirmed if one examines the manner in which Matthew redacts these anecdotes so that petitioners are no longer the brash characters found in the Markan material: petitioners now bow to Jesus, address him as "Lord," and fashion more respectful pleas. In fact, the function of the miracle story that featured Jesus' example in handling such persons no longer seems important, as Matthew deletes the narrative elements of the miracle stories that appeared distracting to the miracle itself and its lesson (e.g., Mark 2:4–5) and removes any provocative speech that might be unworthy of Jesus' dignity (e.g., Mark 9:22–24) or action that might be considered too overt (e.g., Mark 10:49b–50a).[18] This emphasis on the miracle of Jesus and on the conventional, faithful petitioners is understandable in the particular christological focus of Matthew's Gospel. Indeed, once the miracle stories were incorporated into Mark's Gospel, their earlier function would be subordinated to the larger christological agenda of the evangelist and of those evangelists after him who would use his Gospel as a source.

Yet before the first Gospel was written, the miracle stories were serving the Christian communities. This book intends to illustrate that their purpose was not simply one of engendering amazement in pagan converts with these claims of Jesus' power, as Bultmann and Dibelius had assumed. The pattern seen in the stories where narrators deliberately present outrageous petitioners, whose behavior and speech would offend any proper Greco-Roman person, being received by Jesus with understanding and respect, their boldness being complimented by him as "faith" shows that these stories held an important example of virtue to be emulated by a would-be follower.

Such miracle stories reveal a portrait of Jesus himself as cannot be derived from the parables and apophthegms, the wisdom and teachings of Jesus. These forms represent the ideas of Jesus, not his behavior with ordinary flawed people. It seems as if the narrators of the miracle stories have gone out of their way to increase the rough-and-ready character of the petitioners who approach Jesus. Against the cultural backdrop of "proper" manners, these petitioners are forward, pushy, and insistent. This is meant to introduce a tension in the listener, who wonders how Jesus will deal with this person. Surely these rude people deserve to be corrected. Instead, and certainly surprisingly, Jesus does not seem to pay any attention to their behavior, but he rather sees past it to the desperation that brings them to him, and to the unshakeable confidence that explains their determination, a confidence that astonishes Jesus. The response of Jesus shows that his is more than gentlemanly politeness, but a deep understanding and attention to the heart, if we may express it this way. The first-time listener awaits some reproof, but instead sees Jesus move over to the side of the petitioner and answer not only with the mir-

---

[18] See the classic treatment by Heinz Joachim Held, "Matthew as Interpreter of Miracle Stories," in *Tradition and Interpretation in Matthew*, by Günther Bornkamm, Gerhard Barth, and Heinz Joachim Held (trans. Percy Scott; Philadelphia: Westminster, 1963), 165–301.

acle, but in a way that shows deep recognition of the person's need. Thus the miracle story acts as an anecdote to reveal something of the face of Jesus to those who long to know what he was like, and to those followers who would strive to be like him. This must be the reason for these stories, the function of the encounter that is the context of the act of power.

What I want to put forward is this: Just as form critics agree, in the case of the apophthegms, that the context of the question and the relation of the answer to the questioner reveals the *Sitz im Leben* of the community, the same holds true for the miracle stories. Once we recognize that the miracle story is not simply the attestation of a work of power by Jesus, but that it is placed in a context designed to reveal something of Jesus' virtue, his soul, then we can say that this effort of the narrators addresses and serves a community *Sitz im Leben*. The various petitioners who approach Jesus are those who belong to the world of his followers, and mirror the range of petitioners who will come to them for help, care, and intercession in their problems, or maybe just for alms. These stories address the rude, brusque, importunate, and insistent persons who will come to them, with a rough, and even rude, manner of request. The portrait of Jesus in the miracle-story encounters calls for the abandonment of judgment, rejection, reproof, or denial on any grounds, and call the followers to look beneath the externals to the desperate need, the anxiety, the shame, the abuse, and the social rejection that explain their externals. It calls on the followers to feel compassion, understanding, and more. The confidence that impels these petitioners is nothing short of a great faith, which should be recognized humbly by Jesus' followers, as his example shows them he did.

So, these stories were not only meant to reveal the remembered face of Jesus but also to inspire his followers in their own responses. The fact that these stories survived until the gospel accounts were written shows how effective they were, both in asserting the great divine power of Jesus in his miraculous acts and in modeling his great virtues for the edification and imitation by the community.

THE VIRTUES OF THE CHRIST OF THE MIRACLE STORIES

As my analysis of these miracle stories proceeded, the response of Jesus to these forward petitioners clearly demonstrated to me certain virtues, and it was very clear that the narrator(s) intended this, but my question was how to know which virtues would come to the minds of a listener in the culture of the Greco-Roman world of the first century. If there were a study which isolated the main virtues that were considered most admirable in heroes of that world, I could compare them to the presentation of Jesus' portrait in the miracle stories. The search for such a study was finally rewarded with the discovery of the erudite work of Jacqueline de Romilly, *La douceur dans la pensée grecque,*[19] in which she conducts a minute examination of the qualities most praised in Greek heroes from Homer to the early Fathers of the Church. She notes that two virtues emerge as preeminent throughout the ages: *philanthrōpia* and *praotēs.*

Philanthrōpia, that loving concern for others had already received a full definition, prior to de Romilly's work in an article by Hubert Martin Jr.[20] where he draws on Plutarch's "Lives". He brings attention to the several aspects of *philanthrōpia* as understood in the Greco-Roman world: "affability, courtesy, liberality, kindness, clemency, etc. The *philanthrōpos* is gracious and considerate towards all with whom he associates, he is generous towards the needy, he is also merciful and clement towards his enemies."[21]

Similarly, and quite significantly given the results of de Romilly's findings, Martin had even earlier recognized the prominence of *praotēs* as well and had explored the aspects of this virtue, again as manifest in Plutarch.[22] He describes it as "inner restraint."[23] Where ordinarily, offended persons would be tempted to repudiate those who have slighted them, the person of πραότης is composed and even kind. Martin sees

---

[19] Jacqueline de Romilly, *La douceur dans la pensée grecque* (Paris: Société d' Édition, "Les Belles Lettres," 1979). For this reference I am indebted to Tim Duff, *Plutarch's Lives: Exploring Virtue and Vice* (Oxford: Clarendon Press, 1999).

[20] Hubert Martin, Jr., "The Concept of *Philanthrōpia* in Plutarch's Lives," *AJP* 82 (1961): 164–75.

[21] Ibid., 174. This virtue receives its own contextualization for Jesus in Titus 3:4–5 where it expresses his loving kindness and mercy: "But when the goodness and loving kindness [φιλανθρωπία] of God our Savior appeared, he saved us, not because of any works of righteousness that we had done, but according to his mercy, through the waters of rebirth and renewal by the Holy Spirit."

[22] Hubert Martin, Jr., "The Concept of *Praotes* in Plutarch's Lives," *GRBS* 3 (1960): 65–73.

[23] Ibid., 66.

the real root of πραότης in the stoic virtue of *sōphrosynē:* "The intimate connection between *sōphrosynē* and *praotēs* . . . is apparent and serves to emphasize the notion of self-control which is perhaps the basic idea contained in every usage of *praotēs.*"[24] With respect to the gospel of Matthew, Jesus uses *praos* to describe himself in Matt 11:28–29. Yet the understanding of the virtue has been clouded as Dierdre J. Good has shown in her monograph, *Jesus the Meek King.*[25] Certain translations into English use "meek," which conveys something of a lowliness. Good sees this translation as a sign of influence from the LXX. For example, in Job 24:4, 36:15, *praos* translates the Hebrew עָנִי where the context describes someone economically and socially humbled. Yet other translators of the LXX passages involving economic deprivation use ταπεινός, (humbled or brought down), not, *praos* (such as Ps 81:3 [LXX 82:3]; Isa 11:4; 14:32; 32:7; 49:13; 54:11; Jer 22:16; and Amos 2:7). In fact, sometimes the translators of the LXX do use *praos* according to Hellenistic usage, which is never used to describe a situation of lowly acceptance of a hardship, but the decision to be kind and gentle when one has the right to be angry or even punitive, as in Num 12:3; and especially when it occurs in the psalms.[26] It is this Hellenistic sense that is intended for Matt 11:28–29, where Jesus exhorts,

> Come to me all you that are weary and carrying heavy burdens, and I will give you rest. Take my yoke upon you, and learn from me, for I am gentle [*praos*] and humble in heart, and you will find rest for your souls.

Jesus is contrasting his behavior with that of earthly Lords with their haughty disdain for underlings. This understanding needs to be carried over to the second beatitude in Matthew (Matt 5:5), one found only in his gospel, where *hoi praeis* is translated into English as "the meek": "Blessed are the meek [*hoi praeis*], for they will inherit the earth." The ordinary sense of meekness conveys the sense of a lowliness, a humility, a readiness to be subordinate, obedient, compliant, and without resistance. Yet if one is consistent with the Hellenistic usage found in Matt 11:28–29, the beatitude rather is enjoining the listener to abandon retaliation, and instead to treat offenders kindly. De Romilly herself

---

[24] Ibid., 68.

[25] Dierdre J. Good, *Jesus the Meek King* (Harrisburg, Pa: Trinity Press International, 1999), esp. 61–93.

[26] E.g., Ps 36:11 [MT 37:11]; 75: 10 [MT 76:9]; 146:6 [MT 147:6]; 149:4.

makes this point, noting that the very psalm upon which the Matthean beatitude draws, Ps 37:11 (LXX 36:11), has a context in which the offended are counseled to let go of their anger (LXX v. 8). "Refrain from anger, and forsake wrath. Do not fret—it only leads to evil."[27] So, the importance of *praotēs* as a fitting description of Jesus' responses to others affirms what de Romilly has shown to be a virtue that was important in a hero who is to be claimed preeminent and singularly worthy of love and admiration.

De Romilly also found that beyond the two main virtues of *philanthrōpia* and *praos* a cluster of virtues appear in combinations, all portraying aspects of these two main virtues and contributing to the "sweetness" of the hero, as de Romilly expresses it, "*la douceur.*" More than simply acting in a gentle way, it is the hero's perception, his regard for others, that gives rise to the gentle response, that is virtue truly possessed. The use of *hēmeros* conveys the idea of the cultivated person, that aspect of *praos* which underlines the sense of one who is in control of the passions and never violent. A very common addition is *epiekeia* an explicit focus on the understanding of others that removes any harsh judgment on them, and *syngnōmē,* the particular merciful aspect of *praos* that results in a generous and swift pardoning of others.

The description of these virtues of *philanthrōpia* and *praos* and the ancillary virtues that often accompany them, as elucidated by Martin and de Romilly, seem to mirror those that were deliberately intended by the narrators of these encounters between Jesus and the unruly petitioners. There, never commenting, never noticing the behavior that the first-time listener would find so objectionable, Jesus sees beneath the offensive behavior of the petitioner to the person's need, and to their unshakeable confidence, their "faith" as he will call it, that amazes and moves him. This is the revelation of the soul of Jesus, his "sweetness" as de Romilly would express it.

Variations on this pattern do occur, as in the accounts where parents petition Jesus on behalf of their demonized children. Jesus' initial response is shown to be disapproving and he seems at first to carry the image of the righteous prophet, holding the parents' lack of faith in God responsible, as seen in Chapter 5 ("Jesus and the Syrophoenician Mother, Mark 7:24–30") and Chapter 6 ("Jesus and the Father of a Demonized Boy, Mark 9:14–29"). Where Jesus' soul is revealed in these

---

[27] De Romilly, *La douceur,* 313.

stories is in his *praos* in listening closely to each parent's response, recognizing the truth in their words, and immediately granting the miracle for which they ask. Jesus is also able to be instructed against a home visit to cure a servant boy as he is by the petitioning Centurion in the Q material best represented in Matt 8:5–13. There, as shown in Chapter 4, the soldier points out to Jesus that his authority is sufficient, and the visit would be inappropriate given his exalted rank. Interestingly, where it is the disciples who are petitioners, or the needy, Jesus' virtue is shown in his merciful miracles to calm them, despite the fact that, unlike the strangers who petition Jesus, they lack faith.

These stories that reveal not only Jesus' power, but also his person, are meant to inspire great confidence and love for Jesus, but they also instigate in his followers, as we have stated, a striving for emulation in the concrete examples. They challenge a community living in a very stratified society to confront the social criteria of "acceptability" and to abandon any notion of personal or religious superiority. They ask the follower to learn from these petitioners, and to emulate the adamantine character of their faith.

In the conclusion of her treatment, de Romilly adds a chapter concerning the Christian introduction of the virtue *agapē,* the special love that is the fountainhead for all the other virtues that Jesus would reveal to his listeners.[28] We may say that these stories reveal how the virtues of Jesus are profound expressions of the *agapē* enjoined on all his followers.

THE TITLE OF THE BOOK

In the title of this book I use "Christ," even though the stories identify Jesus with his own name, to signal that this book does not pretend to address the issues of the quest for the historical Jesus. The study here more modestly treats the compositions of a community from their faith, and, using evidence from the first-century world, attempts to "hear" what the narrator wished to convey about Jesus' encounter in the miracle and how it revealed his face.

I use miracle "stories" rather than miracle "anecdotes" in the title of this book because the former is more familiar, and I do not want to suggest to the reader that my focus in this book is an argument about

---

[28] Ibid., 312–13.

form. In the book, however, I will use "anecdote" because these stories are in fact anecdotes, something that was common in the first century. There was no conscious literary form called "miracle story" in antiquity.

My study tries to illustrate the role that the encounter plays in a revelation of Jesus' persona, his portrait. The many descriptions of *praos* and *philanthrōpia* have seemed to me exactly those demonstrated by Jesus in these miracle stories. But I welcome my scholarly reader to suggest other virtues that first-century listeners would have immediately recognized. I do not consider this to be a final statement, but rather a beginning.

THE ORGANIZATION OF THE BOOK

Since this study focuses on Jesus' encounter with petitioners, I have organized it according to the relationship of the petitioners to the needy person: (1) petitioners who must ask for themselves; (2) petitioners who ask on behalf of others; (3) petitioners who ask on behalf of their child; (4) petitioners who are Jesus' disciples.

PART I
Petitioners Who Must Ask for Themselves

Chapter 1: Jesus and the Leper (Mark 1:40–45)

Chapter 2: Jesus and Bartimaeus (Mark 10:46–52)

PART II
Petitioners Who Ask on Behalf of Others

Chapter 3: Jesus and the Friends of the Paralytic (Mark 2:1–12)

Chapter 4: Jesus and the Centurion (Q [Luke] 7:1, 3, 6b–9)[29]

---

[29] Although the order of the Q text is given in accord with the placement in the Lukan Gospel, the reconstruction relies on Matthew. See James M. Robinson, Paul Hoffmann, and John S. Kloppenborg, eds., *The Critical Edition of Q: Synopsis Including the Gospels of Matthew and Luke, Mark and Thomas with English, German, and French Translations of Q and Thomas* (Minneapolis: Fortress, 2000), 102–17.

PART III
Petitioners Who Ask on Behalf of Their Child

Chapter 5: Jesus and the Syrophoenician Mother (Mark 7:26–30)

Chapter 6: Jesus and the Father of a Demonized Boy (Mark 9:14–29)

PART IV
Petitioners Who Are Jesus' Disciples

Chapter 7: Jesus and His Storm-Tossed Disciples (Mark 4:35–41)

Chapter 8: The Sea-Walking Jesus and His Disciples (Mark 6:45–52)

METHOD AND PROCEDURE

Each anecdote is first analyzed for the most obvious signs of redaction, so that the discrete and independent account can be studied for its message. There will be a significant portion of each chapter given to the description afforded the petitioner/s. Characterization of the petitioner and Jesus as presented by the narrator and seen against the backdrop of cultural sources will be discussed step by step. The chapter will conclude with the way in which Jesus' virtue, his "portrait," is shown by the narrator.

Part I

*Petitioners Who Must
Ask for Themselves*

I

Jesus and the Leper (Mark 1:40–45)

"And Aaron said to Moses, 'Oh, my lord, do not punish us because we have done foolishly and sinned. Let her [Miriam, struck by God with leprosy] not be as one dead, of whom the flesh is half consumed when he comes out of his mother's womb.'" (Num 12:11–12 RSV)

"But seeing another person who has this (scabies, leprosy, elephantiasis or a similar disease, such as psoriasis or mentagra) signifies grief and worry, for everything that appears repugnant and hideous is heart-breaking and depressing to look at." (Artemidorus Daldianus, *Onir.* 3.47)[1]

I. MARK 1:40–45: SIGNS OF MARKAN REDACTION

⁴⁰καὶ ἔρχεται πρὸς αὐτὸν λεπρὸς παρακαλῶν αὐτὸν [καὶ γονυπετῶν] καὶ λέγων αὐτῷ ὅτι ἐὰν θέλῃς δύνασαί με καθαρίσαι. ⁴¹καὶ σπλαγχνισθεὶς ἐκτείνας τὴν χεῖρα αὐτοῦ ἥψατο καὶ λέγει αὐτῷ· θέλω, καθαρίσθητι· ⁴²καὶ εὐθὺς ἀπῆλθεν ἀπ' αὐτοῦ ἡ λέπρα, καὶ ἐκαθαρίσθη. ⁴³καὶ ἐμβριμησάμενος αὐτῷ εὐθὺς ἐξέβαλεν αὐτόν ⁴⁴καὶ λέγει αὐτῷ· ὅρα μηδενὶ μηδὲν εἴπῃς, ἀλλὰ ὕπαγε σεαυτὸν δεῖξον τῷ ἱερεῖ καὶ προσένεγκε περὶ τοῦ καθαρισμοῦ σου ἃ προσέταξεν Μωϋσῆς, εἰς μαρτύριον αὐτοῖς. ⁴⁵ὁ δὲ ἐξελθὼν ἤρξατο κηρύσσειν πολλὰ καὶ διαφημίζειν τὸν λόγον, ὥστε μηκέτι αὐτὸν δύνασθαι φανερῶς εἰς πόλιν εἰσελθεῖν, ἀλλ' ἔξω ἐπ' ἐρήμοις τόποις ἦν· καὶ ἤρχοντο πρὸς αὐτὸν πάντοθεν.

---

[1] Translation by Dr. Gregory W. Dobrov, Loyola University, Chicago, Illinois. For the Greek text, see Artemidori Daldiani Onirocriticon libri V (ed. Roger A. Pack; Leipzig: Teubner, 1963), 224.

⁴⁰A leper came to him begging him, [and kneeling] he said to him, "If you choose, you can make me clean." ⁴¹Moved with pity, Jesus stretched out his hand and touched him, and said to him, "I do choose. Be made clean!" ⁴²Immediately the leprosy left him, and he was made clean. ⁴³After sternly warning him he sent him away at once, ⁴⁴saying to him, "See that you say nothing to anyone; but go, show yourself to the priest, and offer for your cleansing what Moses commanded, as a testimony to them." ⁴⁵But he went out and began to proclaim it freely, and to spread the word, so that Jesus [he] could no longer go into a town openly, but stayed out in the country; and people came to him from every quarter.

Since the special focus of this study is trained on the function of the pre-Gospel miracle stories, it is necessary to recognize the most obvious signs of Markan redaction so that the story may be considered without those additions (Mark 1:40–42).

⁴⁰καὶ ἔρχεται πρὸς αὐτὸν λεπρὸς παρακαλῶν αὐτὸν [καὶ γονυπετῶν] καὶ λέγων αὐτῷ ὅτι ἐὰν θέλῃς δύνασαί με καθαρίσαι ⁴¹καὶ σπλαγχνισθεὶς ἐκτείνας τὴν χεῖρα αὐτοῦ ἥψατο καὶ λέγει αὐτῷ, θέλω, καθαρίσθητι· ⁴²καὶ εὐθὺς ἀπῆλθεν ἀπ' αὐτοῦ ἡ λέπρα, καὶ ἐκαθαρίσθη.

⁴⁰A leper came to him begging him, [and kneeling] he said to him, "If you choose, you can make me clean." ⁴¹Moved with pity, Jesus stretched out his hand and touched him, and said to him, "I do choose. Be made clean!" ⁴²Immediately the leprosy left him, and he was made clean.

Most scholars today agree that Mark 1:40–42 is a unitary composition, although there is some dispute over possible redaction with respect to the man's "kneeling" (καὶ γονυπετῶν) and Jesus' response, "moved with pity" (σπλαγχνισθεὶς). Since the argument over these requires a view of the entire pericope, they will be discussed later. Where clear disjuncture occurs is in vv. 43–45.

⁴³ἐμβριμησάμενος αὐτῷ εὐθὺς ἐξέβαλεν αὐτόν, ⁴⁴καὶ λέγει αὐτῷ, ὅρα μηδενὶ μηδὲν εἴπῃς, ἀλλὰ ὕπαγε σεαυτὸν δεῖξον τῷ ἱερεῖ καὶ προσένεγκε περὶ τοῦ καθαρισμοῦ σου ἃ προσέταξεν Μωϋσῆς, εἰς μαρτύριον αὐτοῖς. ⁴⁵ὁ δὲ ἐξελθὼν ἤρξατο κηρύσσειν πολλὰ καὶ διαφημίζειν τὸν λόγον ὥστε μηκέτι αὐτὸν δύνασθαι φανερῶς εἰς

πόλιν εἰσελθεῖν, ἀλλ' ἔξω ἐπ' ἐρήμοις τόποις ἦν· καὶ ἤρχοντο πρὸς
αὐτὸν πάντοθεν.

⁴³After sternly warning him he sent him away at once, ⁴⁴saying to
him, "See that you say nothing to anyone; but go, show yourself to
the priest, and offer for your cleansing what Moses commanded, as
a testimony to them." ⁴⁵But he went out and began to proclaim it
freely, and to spread the word, so that Jesus [he] could no longer
go into a town openly, but stayed out in the country; and people
came to him from every quarter.

As early as 1901, Johannes Weiss conjectured that in this miracle
story two narratives had been joined: a miracle story (vv. 40–42) and
other remnants (vv. 43–44).² Vincent Taylor agreed, but unlike Weiss,
who saw no particular form in vv. 43–44, Taylor saw a pronouncement
story. In fact, Taylor includes vv. 43–44 in the block of pronouncement
stories that follow this anecdote, Mark 2:1–3:6, "in which the interest
centers on questions of religious importance to the community connected with significant acts and words of Jesus."³ Taylor did admit that
v. 45 must belong to the miracle story of vv. 40–42, because otherwise,
it would mean that the man's proclamation of the miracle of Jesus would
be a direct disobedience of Jesus' command in v. 44. This would not be
something that the church intended.⁴

⁴³καὶ ἐμβριμησάμενος αὐτῷ εὐθὺς ἐξέβαλεν αὐτόν. ⁴⁴καὶ λέγει αὐτῷ
ὅρα μηδενὶ μηδὲν εἴπῃς, ἀλλὰ ὕπαγε σεαυτὸν δεῖξον τῷ ἱερεῖ καὶ
προσένεγκε περὶ τοῦ καθαρισμοῦ σου ἃ προσέταξεν Μωϋσῆς, εἰς
μαρτύριον αὐτοῖς.

⁴³After sternly warning him he sent him away at once. ⁴⁴And he said
to him, "See that you say nothing to anyone; but go, show yourself
to the priest, and offer for your cleansing what Moses commanded,
as a testimony to them."

---

² Johannes Weiss, *Das älteste Evangelium: Ein Beitrag zum Verständnis des
Markus-Evangeliums und der ältesten evangelischen Überlieferung* (Göttingen:
Vandenhoeck & Ruprecht, 1903), 153.
³ Vincent Taylor, *The Gospel according to St. Mark: The Greek Text with
Introduction, Notes, and Indexes* (London: Macmillan; New York: St. Martin's
Press, 1955), 185.
⁴ Ibid., 185, 190.

The NRSV translation does not pick up the roughness conveyed here. What has been rendered "sternly warning" represents the participle ἐμβριμησάμενος, which literally means "snorting" as horses do. The translation of ἐξέβαλεν αὐτόν with "sent him away" does not convey the harshness of "threw him out." Then there is the vehemence of Jesus' warning that the man must remain silent about his cure. How does this behavior qualify as expressions of Jesus "being moved with pity"?

The answer is found when one recognizes that the order to remain silent belongs to the Markan "Messianic Secret" theme. Such commands to silence about Jesus' identity are a well-known feature of the Markan Gospel. Once that theme is recognized as a Markan insertion and thus removed from the pre-Markan anecdote, all disjuncture disappears. There is no vehement warning or rough treatment of the man.

⁴⁵ὁ δὲ ἐξελθὼν ἤρξατο κηρύσσειν πολλὰ καὶ διαφημίζειν τὸν λόγον, ὥστε μηκέτι αὐτὸν δύνασθαι φανερῶς εἰς πόλιν εἰσελθεῖν, ἀλλ᾽ ἔξω ἐπ᾽ ἐρήμοις τόποις ἦν· καὶ ἤρχοντο πρὸς αὐτὸν πάντοθεν.

⁴⁵But he went out and began to proclaim it freely, and to spread the word, so that Jesus [he] could no longer go into a town openly, but stayed out in the country; and people came to him from every quarter.

Just as vv. 43–44 are recognized as Markan, v. 45 is likewise seen as another piece in that theme underway here. First, of course, Mark wants it made clear that the fame of Jesus and the gathering of crowds were not due to his efforts but quite the contrary. Despite Jesus' commands for silence about healings and exorcisms, the word about him spread, precisely by people like this man cured of leprosy and unable to obey Jesus' order.⁵ Second, this conclusion brings to the fore the victim Jesus of Mark's Gospel. A reversal in freedom occurs in that now it is Jesus who must remain in the desert places, while the man cured of leprosy may openly enter the towns and villages at will.

Summary: The anecdote shows itself to have been redacted by Mark in the insertion of the Messianic Secret theme in vv. 43, 44b, 45. With

---

⁵Weiss (*Das älteste Evangelium*, 152) identifies v. 45 as secondary due to the contradiction with v. 43, which he considers tradition. The possibility that Mark himself had created this situation of disobedience in service of his own themes was not yet part of the scholarship of Weiss's day.

these elements removed, the following elements appear to have featured in the pre-Markan anecdote.

II. THE PRE-MARKAN ANECDOTE: JESUS AND THE LEPER

⁴⁰καὶ ἔρχεται πρὸς αὐτὸν λεπρὸς παρακαλῶν αὐτὸν [καὶ γονυπετῶν] καὶ λέγων αὐτῷ ὅτι ἐὰν θέλῃς δύνασαί με καθαρίσαι. ⁴¹καὶ σπλαγχνισθεὶς ἐκτείνας τὴν χεῖρα αὐτοῦ ἥψατο καὶ λέγει αὐτῷ· θέλω, καθαρίσθητι· ⁴²καὶ εὐθὺς ἀπῆλθεν ἀπ' αὐτοῦ ἡ λέπρα, καὶ ἐκαθαρίσθη. . . . ⁴⁴καὶ λέγει αὐτῷ· . . . ὕπαγε σεαυτὸν δεῖξον τῷ ἱερεῖ καὶ προσένεγκε περὶ τοῦ καθαρισμοῦ σου ἃ προσέταξεν Μωϋσῆς, εἰς μαρτύριον αὐτοῖς.

⁴⁰A leper came to him begging him, [and kneeling] he said to him, "If you choose, you can make me clean." ⁴¹Moved with pity, Jesus stretched out his hand and touched him, and said to him, "I do choose. Be made clean!" ⁴²Immediately the leprosy left him, and he was made clean. . . . ⁴⁴And he said to him, . . . "Go, show yourself to the priest, and offer for your cleansing what Moses commanded, as a testimony to them."

The Presentation of the Petitioner: A Leper

⁴⁰καὶ ἔρχεται πρὸς αὐτὸν λεπρὸς παρακαλῶν αὐτὸν [καὶ γονυπετῶν] καὶ λέγων αὐτῷ ὅτι ἐὰν θέλῃς δύνασαί με καθαρίσαι.

⁴⁰A leper came to him begging him, [and kneeling] he said to him, "If you choose, you can make me clean."

What Is Meant by "Leper"?

Hendrik van der Loos is one scholar who claims that the man suffers from leprosy as we know it today—that is, Hansen's disease.[6] He is relying on Pliny the Elder's description of *elephantiasis*, however, and there has been some confusion whether that is the illness from which

---

[6] Hendrik van der Loos, *The Miracles of Jesus* (NovTSup 9; Leiden: Brill, 1965), 464–79. See Pliny the Elder, *Nat.* 26.5.

the man suffers, since among the Greeks, *elephantiasis* was simply called "leprosy." As a general term for skin ailments Greeks used *lepra*.[7] When W. H. S. Jones, translating Pliny's description of *elephantiasis*, came to Pliny's use of that word, he chose to use "leprosy," which increases the confusion.

The Markan anecdote describes the petitioner as λεπρός, the singular substantive adjective for someone who has *lepra*, the skin ailment, and not the disease *elephantiasis*. The two are quite different, and *elephantiasis* is far more devastating. The description of *elephantiasis* by Pliny is as follows (here we follow Jones's translation, recalling that he chooses to represent Pliny's word *elephantiasis* as "leprosy"):

> I have said that leprosy [*elephantiasis*] did not occur in Italy before the time of Pompeius Magnus [106–48 B.C.E.], and that though the plague usually begins on the face, a kind of freckle on the tip of the nose, yet presently the skin dries up over all the body, covered with spots of various colors, and uneven, in places thick, in others thin, in others hard as with rough itch-scab [scabies], finally however going black, and pressing the flesh on to the bones, while the toes and the fingers swell up. This plague is native to Egypt. When kings were attacked, it was a deadly thing for the inhabitants, because the tubs in the baths used to be prepared with warm human blood for its treatment. This disease indeed quickly died out in Italy, as also did that called by the ancients *gemursa* which appeared between the toes, the very name being now obsolete. (*Nat.* 26.5)[8]

In the Markan anecdote, the man who is cured of his ailment is told to go and show himself to the priests and to offer the gift that Moses commanded (v. 44). This is an appeal to Lev 14:1–32, which concerns the obligations on those who are found to be clean of *lepra*, the skin ailment described in Lev 13:1–37. That skin ailment is very different from *elephantiasis*.

Four main details of the *lepra* described in Lev 13 distinguish it from *elephantiasis*:

1. "If the hair in the diseased area has turned white and the disease appears to be deeper than the skin of his body, it is a leprous disease" (Lev 13:3).

---

[7] Jacob Milgrom, *Leviticus 1–16* (AB 3; New York: Doubleday, 1964), 816, with reference to J. G. Anderson, "Studies in the Medical Diagnosis of Leprosy in Denmark," *Danish Medical Bulletin* 16, supplement 9 (1969): 6–142.

[8] Pliny the Elder, *Natural History* (trans. H. Rackham et al.; 10 vols.; LCL; Cambridge, Mass.: Harvard University Press, 1966), 7:271.

2. "If there is a white swelling in the skin that has turned the hair white, and there is quick raw flesh in the swelling it is a chronic leprous disease in the skin of his body. The priest shall pronounce him unclean" (Lev 13:10b–11).

3. "If raw flesh ever appears on him, he shall be unclean; the priest shall examine the raw flesh and pronounce him unclean. Raw flesh is unclean, for it is a leprous disease" (Lev 13:14–15).

4. "But if the raw flesh again turns white, he shall come to the priest; the priest shall examine him, and if the disease has turned white, the priest shall pronounce the diseased person clean. He is clean" (Lev 13:16–17).

One obvious difference is that *elephantiasis* turns the skin black, whereas *lepra* results in white scaling on sores. Curiously, van der Loos himself notes the "white" of Miriam's leprosy in Num 12:10 ("And the cloud departed from off the tabernacle; and behold, Miriam became leprous, white as snow; and Aaron looked upon Miriam and, behold, she was leprous").[9] This is the *lepra* described in Lev 13–14.

Jacob Milgrom explains that further confusion was set up in the ninth century C.E. when John of Damascus, an Arabian physician, began to use the term *lepra* for the Greek "leprosy" (i.e., *elephantiasis*), and as Milgrom notes, "his mistake persists till this day."[10]

Why the Proper Understanding of *Lepra* Matters

If this petitioner were suffering from *elephantiasis*, the horror of that disease would completely overpower the story and result in the listeners immediately forgiving any violation of social rubrics demanding distance and polite address to Jesus.[11] The entire focus would be on the

---

[9] Van der Loos, *Miracles of Jesus*, 475.

[10] Milgrom, *Leviticus 1–16*, 816.

[11] Pliny (*Nat.* 20.52) claims that Pompey the Great discovered that wild "pennyroyal" (*menastrum*), if chewed and applied topically, cures *elephantiasis*, but the first-century physician Celsus is far from agreeing that a cure is possible. Some of his description seems appropriate here in view of this discussion on the differences between *elephantiasis* and *lepra*: "The surface of the body presents a multiplicity of spots and swellings, which, at first red, are gradually changed to be black in colour. The skin is thickened and thinned in an irregular way, hardened and softened, roughened in some places with a kind of scales; the trunk wastes, the face, calves and feet swell. When the disease is of long standing, the fingers and toes are sunk under the swelling: feverishness

cure itself. Someone suffering from *lepra* is in a different situation. Although the ailment is painful and disfiguring, and without any known cure, it was a nonfatal condition and could suddenly disappear, as the stipulations of Lev 14 indicate. Even in Greek medicine, Hippocrates notes *lepra* among the ailments that can be cured[12] and stipulates that it is not really a disease at all but rather a "disfigurement."[13]

In that case, the story of a person suffering from *lepra* does not engender horror at the very mention of it. What were the reactions that one could expect in listeners to a story about a man suffering from *lepra*? Here, it is most helpful to review the set of other "disfigurements" with which it is grouped by Hippocrates: "*Lepra, prurigo, psora, lichen, alphos,* and *alopecia* arise because of phlegm. These are disfigurements rather than diseases" (*Aff.* 35).[14]

Prurigo (κνισμός in Greek, from the word for "tickle" or "itch") was colloquially referred to as "the itch."[15] Psora (from the Greek ψάω, "to rub away") is "mange" or "scabies."[16] Celsus, a first-century medical practitioner, offers this comment: "Scabies is harder: the skin is ruddy, from which pustules grow up, some moist, some dry. From some of these sanies escapes; and from them comes a persistent itching ulceration, which in some cases rapidly spreads. . . . The rougher the skin, and the more the itching, the more difficult is its relief" (*Med.* 5.28).[17] Lichen (from the Greek λειχήν, "tree moss") is ringworm,[18] thought to begin on the chin and from there to spread contagiously. Alphos is a white, scaly condition very much like leprosy but seeming to break out on the face,[19] and alopecia (from the Greek ἀλώπηξ, "fox") is another type of mange, named "the fox" because the resulting baldness was the same for humans as for foxes.[20]

---

supervenes, which may easily destroy a patient overwhelmed by such troubles" (*Med.* 3.25) (*De Medicina* [trans. W. G. Spencer; 3 vols.; LCL; Cambridge, Mass.: Harvard University Press, 1960–1961], 1:343).

[12] Hippocrates, *Morb.* 1.3.

[13] Hippocrates, *Aff.* 35.

[14] Hippocrates, *Affections; Diseases I; Diseases II* (trans. Paul Potter; LCL; Cambridge, Mass.: Harvard University Press, 1988), 59 (my italics).

[15] Pliny the Elder, *Nat.* 25.87; 27.5; 28.18.

[16] Ibid., 20:2, 20; 22:32.

[17] Celsus, *De Medicina* (trans. Spencer), 2:167.

[18] Pliny the Elder, *Nat.* 23.63; 26.10.

[19] Galen, *Opera Omnia*, vol. 6 (trans. C. G. Kühn; Hildesheim: Georg Oms, 1965), 243.

[20] Pliny the Elder, *Nat.* 20.20, 87.

Leviticus 13 shows something of a similar grouping as that proposed by Hippocrates where along with leprosy other ailments were grouped into the reference "the itching disease" (Lev 13:29–37).[21]

This group of ailments—scabies, ringworm, mange, and generally "the itch"—helps to establish the context for *lepra*. In all of them there is the suspicion of lack of hygiene and thus a certain degree of disgust. One could say that the ordinary response would be fear of contagion, which was not unfounded in some of these, and a general revulsion.

Lepra from the Perspective of the Victim

It is also necessary to recognize the pathos of the condition of *lepra* for the sufferer. The fear and disgust on the faces of people and the expectation for distance would have resulted in certain loneliness, the end of intimate relationships, and for the Jew, the separation from one's community for prayer and simple social intercourse. It was common for lepers to try to remove the sores, even if in doing so the sufferer was left with scars. This must have been common practice, since Pliny the Elder reports usual recourses for people. The inner bark of the elm tree "relieves leprous sores,"[22] as does the sorrel root;[23] and wild lupins, "if they are boiled down to the consistency of honey, . . . cure even black eruptions and leprous sores."[24] A popular salve was made from a burnt shellfish called "myax," mixed with honey and applied to heal multiple skin conditions, "the bites of dogs and men, leprous sores, and freckles."[25] Saliva from a fasting person was thought to keep the leprous sores from spreading.[26]

---

[21] Jacob Milgrom comments, "The most recent, comprehensive medical analysis of *ṣāraʿat* reaches the following conclusion: psoriasis is the disease that fulfills most of the characteristics of *ṣāraʿat*, with two exceptions: *neteq* (13:30–39) resembles *favus*, a fungus infection of the skin, and the pure skin-condition called *bōhaq* (13:39) resembles vitiligo [a chronic depigmentation of the skin]" (*Leviticus 1–16*, 817). Milgrom references E. V. Hulse, "The Nature of Biblical 'Leprosy' and the Use of Alternative Medical Terms in Modern Translations of the Bible," *PEQ* 107 (1975): 87–105.

[22] Pliny the Elder, *Nat.* 24.33.

[23] Ibid., 20.86.

[24] Ibid., 22.74.

[25] Ibid., 32.31.

[26] Ibid., 28.7.

Pliny notes that sometimes lepers used caustic mixtures to burn off the leprous sores, and then again to heal the painful scars:

> Dittander (pepperwort) is considered to be one of the caustic plants. So it clears the complexion, but produces sores on the skin, which, however, are easily cured with wax and rose oil. Thus used, it always removes leprous sores and psoriasis as well as the sores left by the scars. (*Nat.* 20.70)[27]

These efforts could not prevent the return of the sores, as the precautions of Lev 13:24–28 prove: the supposedly "clean" person was placed in quarantine for a week.[28]

The mention of a person suffering from *lepra*, then, would have brought to mind the mental picture of lepers with signs of those scars on their exposed skin, and the new outbreak of the white scaley sores. Even without these measures, *lepra* resulted in "disfigurement," but around it, the suspicion that it was the result of one's own crude habits.

Levitical Rules for Separation of Lepers

Most commentaries provide the ruling of Lev 13:45–46: "The leper who has the disease shall wear torn clothes and let the hair of his head hang loose, and he shall cover his upper lip and cry, 'Unclean, unclean.' He shall remain unclean as long as he has the disease; he is unclean; he shall dwell alone in a habitation outside the camp" (Lev 13:45–46).

Van der Loos makes the argument that outside of Jerusalem, the holy city, treatment of lepers was much less stringent than within the city, and although a certain degree of separation was expected, they still had a place in society.[29] This probably is true. The fact that in Mark 1:44b, Jesus commands the leper to go and show himself to the priest

---

[27] Pliny the Elder, *Natural History* (trans. Rackham et al.), 6:105–7.

[28] Leviticus also mentions precautions to test for the "itching disease" whereby the supposedly cured person undergoes two one-week quarantine periods, with inspections after each one (Lev 13:29–37). Notice how the topics of leprosy and the "itching disease" are handled one after the other, for as Hippocrates also groups such ailments, they are skin disfigurements akin to each other.

[29] See van der Loos, *Miracles of Jesus*, 481. Carl Kazmierski notes that Torah observance in the matter of leprosy was much more stringent for cities like Jerusalem than what would be the case in the country. Citing the research of van der Loos, he concludes that just because lepers had to maintain some separation

and offer the gift that Moses prescribed conveys to the listener that Jesus both knows and respects Torah's regulations about a person's reentry into the society. This will work to highlight the degree of compassion and "meekness" that Jesus shows in reaching out to touch the man while he is still in a leprous state (v. 41).

Societal Expectations for Lepers to Keep Their Distance

Aside from the issue of Torah observance, the distance to be observed by lepers was clearly expected in society.

The effect of the sight of a leper or any person with such skin disfigurements and diseases is shown by Artemidorus Daldianus, a second-century C.E. man of letters who gathered dream interpretations from across the empire. His appeal to common responses and associations makes his collection especially helpful in reconstructing the culture of Greco-Roman antiquity. In his reference to leprosy, he distinguishes *lepra* from scabies and *elephantiasis* but groups them as those diseases that "make their victims conspicuous."[30] This aspect of conspicuousness is so prominent that if it is a dreamer who contracts the diseases, it is a portent of coming wealth and fame if the dreamer is poor, and public office if the dreamer is wealthy and influential. If, however, a dreamer dreams of another person afflicted with these diseases, it is a portent of coming grief and anxiety: "But seeing another person who has this (scabies, leprosy, elephantiasis or a similar disease, such as psoriasis or mentagra) signifies grief and worry, for everything that appears repugnant and hideous is heart-breaking and depressing to look at." (*Onir.* 3.47).[31]

Thus, the story of a leper coming right up to Jesus can be expected to create in the listener a certain revulsion even in the imagining of it. The general expectation that persons with such skin disorders keep their distance is brought out in Theophrastus's *Characters* in his treatment of the squalid person. His use of the leprous condition is in the context of the person with a disgusting lack of personal hygiene:

---

there, they were still considered part of the society (Carl Kazmierski, "Evangelist and Leper: A Socio-Cultural Study of Mark 1:40–45," *NTS* 38 [1992]: 43).

[30] Artemidorus Daldianus, *Onir.* 3.47. Translation by Dr. Gregory W. Dobrov, Loyola University, Chicago, Illinois. For the Greek text, see *Artemidori Daldiani Onirocriticon libri V* (ed. Roger A. Pack; Leipzig: Teubner, 1963), 224.

[31] Ibid., 73 (my italics).

Squalor is a neglect of one's body which produces distress [in others]. The squalid man is the sort who goes around in a leprous and encrusted state [οἶος λέπραν ἔχων καὶ ἀλφὸν], with long fingernails, and says these are all inherited illnesses; he has them like his father and grandfather before him, so it won't be easy to smuggle an illegitimate child into *their* family! You can be sure he is apt to have sores on his shins, whitlows [abscesses] on his fingers, which he doesn't treat but lets fester. (*Char.* 19.1–3)[32]

This is the second text to identify the reaction of distress caused by the very presence of the leper. Far from the more genteel presentation by Artemidorus, in which the sight of such persons "pulls at the heart," here there is ridicule of the person unaware that filthy personal habits have resulted in this revolting personal state.

Juvenal could be cited as another voice from the first century complaining over lack of distance for persons with disgusting skin diseases. His satire mentions persons with "lichens," one of the "disfigurements" with which *lepra* is grouped by Hippocrates. With his usual appeal to the extreme, Juvenal presents the case of the infected person who insists on kissing him:

'Tis impossible Flaccus, to get free from kissers; they press on you, stay you, follow you up, meet you, and from this side and that, no matter when, wherever. No malignant ulcer or inflamed pustules, nor diseased chin and dirty scabs [nec triste mentum sordidique *lichenes*], nor lips smeared with oily salve, nor icicle on a frozen nose, will protect you. (Martial, *Ep.* 98)[33]

These texts show that for the listener to this account, it would have been not only the Torah regulations that the leper defied in approaching Jesus, but also the social expectations of distance, which this man overturns in his aggressive appeal to Jesus.

III. THE LEPER PETITIONS JESUS

⁴⁰καὶ ἔρχεται πρὸς αὐτὸν λεπρὸς παρακαλῶν αὐτὸν [καὶ γονυπετῶν] καὶ λέγων αὐτῷ ὅτι ἐὰν θέλῃς δύνασαί με καθαρίσαι.

---

[32] Theophrastus, *Characters* (trans. Jeffrey Rusten; LCL; Cambridge: Mass.: Harvard University Press, 1993), 19.3, pp. 118–19.

[33] Martial, *Epigrams* (trans. Walter C. A. Ker; 2 vols.; LCL: London: Heinemann, 1919–1920), 2:305 (my italics).

⁴⁰A leper came to him begging him, [and kneeling] he said to him, "If you choose, you can make me clean."

Does the Leper Present Himself Kneeling?

There is a textual dispute over whether the leper kneels before Jesus, and it matters. If he does, then something of his boldness is mitigated. If he does not, then the sense is that the man came up to Jesus and faced him squarely, a rather bold action.

Why is there even a question about this? Surveying the manuscripts that attest the man kneeling, we find Codex Sinaiticus, a strong Alexandrian text-type witness, and also Codex Koridethi.³⁴ This is a strong attestation because both of these texts resist embellishments. Codex Ephraemi, another Alexandrian text-type witness, makes the action even more full, indicating that the man kneels "to him" (καὶ γονυπετῶν αὐτόν). Not so strong is the agreement of Codex Alexandrinus and the Byzantine lectionaries, since both are Byzantine in text type and regularly introduce improvements and corrections on texts.

Curiously, there is an omission of the man kneeling in Codex Vaticanus, which is considered something of a twin of Codex Sinaiticus. But here they diverge. One might consider that the copyist accidentally overlooked the participle, except that the man's kneeling is also missing from Codices Bezae and Washingtonensis. This is significant because these texts witness to a Western text type usually considered to be the opposite of the conservative Alexandrian style found in Codex Sinaiticus. How is it, then, that the copyists from two such different text traditions, and text circles, managed to "omit" an action as deferential, and important to the story, as the man kneeling?

Besides the manuscript signs that the participle was not in the earliest manuscript, there is the compositional evidence, which seems to support that conclusion. Ordinarily, the action of the man would be described before his act of speaking, so that one would expect this: "And a leper came to him, kneeling, and beseeching him, saying to him, 'If you choose, you can make me clean.'" But in this case the description of the man's kneeling is placed between his "beseeching" and his "saying":

---

³⁴ For a review of the codices and text-type families, see Bruce M. Metzger, *The Text of the New Testament: Its Transmission, Corruption, and Restoration* (3d ed.; New York: Oxford University Press, 1992), esp. 42–47, 56–57.

And a leper came to him, beseeching him, and kneeling, saying to him . . .

The kneeling appears to be a secondary insertion.

Perhaps Christian copyists were influenced to add the kneeling by Mark 10:17, where the man who asks what he must do to enter the kingdom kneels before Jesus, for this is the only Markan pericope where the verb γονυπετέω ("kneel") appears. In the versions of the leper story in Matthew (Matt 8:1–4) and Luke (Luke 5:12–16), both evangelists show their desire to make the man's behavior more respectful. Both add the respectful title κύριος, and while neither has the man kneeling (which suggests that their copy of Mark did not have that description), each in his own way brings the man to the ground before Jesus. Matthew chooses his favorite προσκυνέω (προσελθὼν προσεκύνει αὐτῷ [Matt 8:2]),[35] while Luke omits the man's close proximity altogether and has the leper fall on his face when Jesus enters the city and sees him (ἰδὼν δὲ τὸν Ἰησοῦν, πεσὼν ἐπὶ πρόσωπον [Luke 5:12]).[36]

---

[35] Matthew's Gospel has eleven other occurrences of προσκυνέω. Two of these occur in the Q temptation narrative: Satan asks Jesus to prostrate himself before him (Matt 4:9 // Luke 4:7), and Jesus quotes Deut 6:13, which commands that one should prostrate oneself only before God (Matt 4:10 // Luke 4:8). But Matthew shows that he favors the idea of a prostration before Jesus as the only proper expression of reverence in his redaction of four Markan pericopae: (1) in the story of Jesus' raising Jairus's daughter, Matthew changes the father's approach so that he prostrates himself (Matt 9:18); (2) in the miracle of Jesus' walking on the water, the disciples prostrate themselves before Jesus when he enters the boat (Matt 14:33); (3) the Canaanite mother petitioning for an exorcism prostrates herself before Jesus (Matt 15:25); (4) the mother of James and John prostrates herself before Jesus as she asks for a special place for her sons when Jesus comes in his glory (Matt 20:20). Besides these, Matthew uses the reverential act four times more in two pericopae exclusive to his tradition: (1) in the narrative of the magi (Matt 2:1–12), the magi say that they wish to prostrate themselves before Jesus (Matt 2:2), and they do (Matt 2:11); and Herod says that he wishes to prostrate himself (Matt 2:8); (2) in the parable of the unforgiving servant, the servant in debt prostrates himself before the servant who has just been forgiven by the king (Matt 18:26).

[36] This sensitivity to the proper distance maintained by the leper may be due to Luke's possession of the tradition of the ten lepers (Luke 17:11–19), where they stood "far off" (Luke 17:12). The action of falling on one's face before Jesus recalls the action of the healed leper from that Lukan tradition, where the healed Samaritan who returns to thank Jesus is described as "falling on his face at his [Jesus'] feet" (ἔπεσεν ἐπὶ πρόσωπον παρὰ τοὺς πόδας αὐτοῦ [Luke 17:16]). But this proximity is only proper because now the man is cured.

These separate redactions of Matthew and Luke underline the otherwise bold behavior of the man as found in the Markan text.

Conclusion: The manuscript evidence, the compositional awkwardness, and the separate redactions of Matthew and Luke make it more probable that the leper was described as approaching Jesus without kneeling before him.

Characterization of the Leper by His Actions

The foregoing research makes it plain that this leper defies both Torah regulations and social expectations as he approaches Jesus. Any first-century listener imagining the leper's aggressive proximity to Jesus would find the thought revolting.

Characterization of the Leper by His Speech

> παρακαλῶν αὐτὸν καὶ λέγων αὐτῷ ὅτι ἐὰν θέλῃς δύνασαί με καθαρίσαι.

> Begging him, he said to him, "If you choose, you can make me clean."

The multiple interpretations for the leper's petition signals its unconventional character. First there is the question of how "to be made clean" should be interpreted. Ordinarily, the literal translation, "Should you want to, you could cleanse me," is understood as a request for healing. Recently, however, Carl Kazmierski has revived the theory of Johannes Weiss that since the literal meaning of the verb καθαρίζω is "to cleanse" and not "to cure," the petition of the leper should be understood as a request for Jesus to pronounce the man free to enter society once more.

> Is Jesus willing to break the official boundaries within which human intercourse is permitted within the official interpretation of the Tradition, and to accept the leper into community as he has perhaps been accepted by his own? To concentrate on the cure-miracle aspect is to miss this basic cultural dynamic which, we would argue, is the central concern of this part of the story in Mark.[37]

---

[37] Kazmierski, "Evangelist and Leper," 45 (see esp. 44–46).

To the question as to why then Jesus would send the man to the priests (v. 44) if they no longer have any real authority, Kazmierski replies that Jesus is asking the leper to face the social realities in which he must live.

> The fact that he (and Jesus!) must live with that social reality causes a tension that cannot be overcome except that it must be met with an outward submission, if not in fact, then inward. The conflict, then, is between the world of the community created by Jesus' healing activity and the world "out there" to which the man must return.[38]

This answer, however, does not explain why Jesus would ask the man to offer the gift that Moses commanded for those free of the disease, if the man was still leprous. Moreover, how likely is it that the narrator would intend to communicate to the audience that Jesus would allow a person still leprous to enter society and freely associate with others?

Kazmierski's readiness to interpret this story as an attestation of Jesus' greater authority would be better supported through the argument of C. H. Cave and Werner Kelber concerning εἰς μαρτύριον αὐτοῖς (v. 44e). They hold that the usual translation, "as a witness *to* them," should treat the εἰς as adversative, as it is found so often in the LXX.[39] In that case, the meaning would be "as a witness *against* them."[40] According to Cave, Jesus is asking the cured man to go back and offer the sacrifice demanded by Moses just to show up the oppressive priesthood. But Cave accepts that the man is actually cured, and he holds that if the εἰς is adversative, the whole phrase was added by Mark. The conflictual relationship between the authorities and Jesus begins in Mark 2:1–3:6 and is answered here by Jesus.[41] So Cave would not assign it to the pre-Markan stratum.

In the end, the proposal of Weiss and of Kazmierski, that καθαρίζω should be understood in a literal way, must bypass the allusions to Lev 14 in v. 44, where the stipulations for a person cured of leprosy are found, and the fact that Lev 13–14 use καθαρίζω in the sense of "to cure."

---

[38] Ibid., 48.

[39] Deut 31:19; Josh 24:27; Job 16:8; Hos 2:12; Amos 1:11; Mic 1:2, 7:18; Zeph 3:8.

[40] C. H. Cave, "The Leper: Mark 1:40–45," *NTS* 25 (1978–1979): 245–50 (see esp. 249–50).

[41] Ibid.

ἐὰν θέλῃς . . .

"If you should choose . . ."

The leper's initial condition has been variously interpreted as an expression of desperation, an admission of sinfulness, or a christological witness. Douglas Hare is one of the scholars who observe that since leprosy is frequently a punishment for sin in the Jewish Scriptures (Num 12:9–12; 2 Kgs 5:27; 15:5; 2 Chr 26:19–21), the man's "if you should choose" is a recognition of his sinful condition. Hare writes, "There was a natural analogy between ritual impurity, which separated a person from the worship of God, and sin, which separated one from God in a profounder sense. If this is the basis of the words 'If you choose,' the leper is implicitly requesting the forgiveness of sins."[42]

Hare supports his conclusion in the Markan Gospel by referring to what he sees as a similar connection in the healing of the paralytic in Mark 2:1–12, the miracle anecdote found immediately following this one in the narrative. He notes that when the friends of the paralytic lower him, Jesus' forgives the man's sins: "Son, your sins are forgiven" (Mark 2:5).[43] Thus, the idea is that the man's sins are related to his paralysis.

The evidence of the story does not support that conclusion, however, because even after Jesus forgives the man's sins, he remains in a paralyzed state. If the point were that the paralysis was connected to the sins, the man would then jump up, healed. As it is, he must wait until Mark 2:11, when Jesus gives the command for healing: "I say to you, stand up, take your mat and go to your home." In the same way, the story of the leper makes no mention of any sin, so the listener has no indication that this affliction is the result of divine punishment.

A second interpretation is given by Michal Wojciechowski, who claims that the emphasis on Jesus' will suggests a connection with the divine will. Here he refers to the importance of God's will as expressed in Wis 12:18, "Although you are sovereign in strength, you judge with mildness, and with great forbearance you govern us; for you have power to act whenever you choose [πάρεστιν . . . σοι ὅταν θέλῃς τὸ δύνασθαι]," and he points to this theme in Ps 115:3 (113:11

---

[42] Douglas R. A. Hare, *Mark* (WestBC; Louisville: Westminster John Knox, 1989), 34.
[43] Ibid.

LXX), "Our God is in the heaven above the heavens, and in all the earth he does whatever he pleases [ὅσα ἠθέλησεν ἐποίησεν]," as well as Ps 135:6 (134:6 LXX), "Whatever the LORD pleases he does [πάντα ὅσα ἠθέλησεν ὁ κύριος ἐποίησεν], in heaven and on earth in the seas and in all the deeps."[44] Thus, Wojciechowski concludes that the man wishes to identify Jesus' power with that of God.[45] The question is whether the formulation ἐάν θέλῃς would be sufficiently particular to use in the LXX and unfamiliar in ordinary speech to warrant that connection.

As early as the mid-eighteenth century, Jacob Wettstein discovered a similar petition in one of Epictetus's essays, "How Ought We to Bear Our Illnesses?"[46] There, the philosopher uses it in a reproof to would-be disciples: "Why, then, do you wheedle your physician? Why do you say, 'If *you* wish, Master, I shall get well' [τί λέγεις, ἐὰν σὺ θέλῃς, κύριε, καλῶς ἕξω]?"[47] He further comments, "Why do you give him occasion to put on airs [τί παρέχεις αὐτῷ ἀφορμὴν τοῦ ἐπᾶραι ὀφρῦν]?" (*Diatr.* 3.10.15).[48]

Epictetus deliberately intends to create an obsequious plea, of course. We notice his care to have the patient address the doctor with

---

[44] Michal Wojciechowski, "The Touching of the Leper (Mk 1:40–45)," *BZ* 33 (1989): 114–19. See also Rudolf Pesch, *Das Markusevangelium* (3d ed.; 2 vols.; HTKNT; Freiberg: Herder, 1984), 1:143.

[45] Simon Légasse, however, goes even further than Wojciechowski, citing other texts that, for him, indicate that the man is identifying Jesus as divine: Isa 55:11 (where God says, "So shall my word be that goes out from my mouth; it shall not return to me empty, but it shall accomplish that which I propose, and succeed in the thing for which I sent it"); Job 42:2, (where Job says to God, "I know that you can do all things, and that no purpose of yours can be thwarted"); Wis 11:23 (where the writer says of God, "But you are merciful to all, for you can do all things, and you overlook people's sins, so that they may repent"). See Simon Légasse, *L'Évangile de Marc* (LD 5; Paris: Cerf, 1997), 150–57, esp. 151.

[46] Jacob Wettstein, *Novum Testamentum Graecum* (2 vols.; Amsterdam: Ex officina Dommeriana, 1752; repr., Graz: Akademische Druck, 1962), 1:557.

[47] I have italicized "you" in the translation to indicate the emphasis created in the Greek. The sick person's statement suggests special honor being given to the physician.

[48] Epictetus, "How Ought We to Bear Our Illnesses?" in *The Discourses as Reported by Arrian, the Manual, and Fragments* (trans. W. A. Oldfather; 2 vols.; LCL; Cambridge, Mass.: Harvard University Press, 1959–1961), 2:77.

the respectful "Master,"[49] and to emphasize the importance of the doctor by the emphatic insertion of σύ. This mockery of Epictetus addresses what he sees as a common abandonment of one's fortitude and readiness to believe in the rightness of what providence brings. On the one hand, it shows that the use of ἐὰν θέλῃς would not be associated with the LXX.

Here is a comparison of the two pleas:

ἐὰν σὺ θέλῃς, κύριε, καλῶς ἕξω. (Epictetus)

"Should *you* want, *Master*, I will get well." (my translation)

ἐὰν θέλῃς δύνασαί με καθαρίσαι. (Mark 1:40)

"Should you want, you can make me clean." (my translation)

The plea of the leper is much more direct, devoid of obsequious embellishments. He is not flattering Jesus, but stating a fact of which he is completely certain. His point is that the transformation of his life from this terrible existence is completely dependent on whether Jesus wants to do it. As John Painter states, "The 'ἐὰν θέλῃς' makes Jesus' *willingness* as the issue."[50] And here, the very emphasis voiced to Jesus that everything depends on his will suggests the possibility that he will not feel like doing it. It is a statement that witnesses to the possibility of caprice on Jesus' part.

Summary: If the narrator had wanted to present a conventionally pious petitioner, a docile sort of person, he would not have allowed so many signs of the man's intentional proximity to Jesus while in a leprous state. Signs of reverence would be in evidence, such as the kneeling, which a later copyist inserted, and an address to Jesus that employed the reverential title "Lord," which Matthew and Mark included. For as it is, the overall impression of the leper in this little anecdote is of a man desperate and past following all the restrictions, as is shown by his actions and by the edge in his statement of petition.

---

[49] Both Matthew and Luke add κύριε (Matt 8:2; Luke 5:12) to the leper's petition as well as a prostration before Jesus to inject unmitigated awe and reverence into the characterization of the leper.

[50] John Painter, *Mark's Gospel: Worlds in Conflict* (NTR; London: Routledge, 1997), 49.

IV. THE RESPONSE OF JESUS

⁴¹καὶ σπλαγχνισθεὶς ἐκτείνας τὴν χεῖρα αὐτοῦ ἥψατο καὶ λέγει αὐτῷ· θέλω, καθαρίσθητι·

⁴¹Moved with pity, Jesus stretched out his hand and touched him, and said to him, "I do choose. Be made clean."

Did the Text Say "Moved with Pity" or "Moved with Anger" or Either?

There is a textual disagreement over the identification of Jesus' emotional response to the leper. Most texts hold σπλαγχνισθεὶς ("moved with pity"). Codex Bezae, a major witness to the Western text-type family, holds ὀργισθείς ("moved with anger"), but the reason is not hard to discern. The Markan insertions of vv. 43–44a, in which Jesus, "snorting," throws the man out and warns him to say nothing to anyone, probably led the copyist of Codex Bezae to conclude that the earlier copyist had piously replaced ὀργισθείς ("moved with anger") with σπλαγχνισθεὶς ("moved with pity").

Characterization of Jesus by His Actions

καὶ ἐκτείνας τὴν χεῖρα αὐτοῦ ἥψατο.

And extending his hand, he touched him.

The action of Jesus in touching the man is unique to this Gospel. In all other anecdotes of the Markan tradition, when Jesus touches someone, he is said to "grasp" (κρατέω) the hand (Mark 1:31; 5:41; 9:27).[51] This story alone carries the LXX expression "extending his hand."[52] This

---

[51] The verb ἐκτείνω is found twice (Mark 3:5) in the account of the man with the withered hand (Mark 3:1–6), where Jesus orders the man to extend his hand, and the man obeys. Jesus does not extend his own hand.

[52] Matthew uses the expression in Matt 12:13 (as in Mark 3:5, Jesus tells the man with the withered hand to extend it); 12:49 (Matthean redaction on Mark 3:33); 14:31 (special Matthean insertion on Mark 6:45–52, where Jesus extends his hand to Peter when he sinks into the sea); 26:51 (Matthean redaction on Mark 14:47 to describe the striking of the high priest's servant during Jesus' arrest).

phrasing helps to focus on the action, prolongs it in the imagination, so that the listener can imagine Jesus reaching out and then touching the leper. This touch is not necessary. Contact with Jesus' hand is not connected with healing as it is in the cure of Peter's mother-in-law (Mark 1:29–31) and of the formerly demonized boy who requires healing after the demon's savage departure (Mark 9:26–27). This anecdote could have had Jesus cure the leper without any touching, by a word of healing, such as when he heals the paralytic (Mark 2:10–11) and restores the sight of Bartimaeus (Mark 10:52). Only in the raising of Jairus's daughter does Jesus combine touch and the command of restoration (Mark 5:41), but that story employs the usual grasping of the hand (Mark 5:41: καὶ κρατήσας τῆς χειρὸς τοῦ παιδίου).

In this story, Jesus does not grasp the hand of the leper, but reaching out his hand, he touches him. This is his first response to the man, and it shows Jesus going farther than the leper did. Jesus responds to the man's approach by reaching out to effect the contact between them. In effect, he moves in exactly the opposite direction that society moves in. The man is met and received. Jesus joins the man in overturning the Torah rules, and even more so, by establishing the touch. This is the first expression of his *praos*, his *philanthrōpia*.

Characterization of Jesus by His Speech

καὶ λέγει αὐτῷ· θέλω, καθαρίσθητι.

And he said to him, "I do choose! Be made clean."

The fact that Jesus begins his answer with θέλω ("I do want to") shows that the narrator intended the issue of Jesus' wanting to help as the challenge leveled at him by the leper. Using the leper's own words (ἐὰν θέλῃς δύνασαί με καθαρίσαι), Jesus responds in his two-word reassuring reply: θέλω, καθαρίσθητι. This answer again emphasizes Jesus union with the man, his attention to him and his desire to communicate his sincere caring.[53] The edge in the man's statement to Jesus is answered with sincerity, and no indication of its, perhaps, bitterness and resent-

---

[53] Scholarly translations of the Greek result in rather stiff renderings such as "I am willing. Be clean" (NIV, NJB), less stiff offerings such as "I do choose! Be made clean" (NRSV). But this leaves out the frankness of the verb θέλω ("to want"), used by the leper and by Jesus in reply to him. Does Jesus "want to"?

ment is in view at all. The man is addressed with a compassionate and concerned directness, physically and verbally. This is established before Jesus then pronounces the word of command, "Be cleansed."

⁴²καὶ εὐθὺς ἀπῆλθεν ἀπ' αὐτοῦ ἡ λέπρα, καὶ ἐκαθαρίσθη.

⁴²Immediately the leprosy left him, and he was made clean.

This verse attests the efficacy of Jesus' command. Certain allusions to Elisha's healing of the Syrian general Naaman (2 Kgs 5:1–14) have been suggested, but the differences are more substantial. Most importantly, Elisha never personally encounters the sufferer, Naaman, but works through a messenger. That story, then, works to reveal the prophet's virtue not in the context of an encounter but through the efficacy of his miracle. Elisha keeps his distance; he does not reach out to Naaman in a reassuring way. The prophet sends word to the general to dip himself in the Jordan seven times. The Markan story features the immediate departure of the disease at the word of Jesus. So many elements of these two stories are distinct that it is difficult to suggest that the narrator had 2 Kgs 5:1–14 in mind.

⁴⁴καὶ λέγει αὐτῷ· . . . ὕπαγε σεαυτὸν δεῖξον τῷ ἱερεῖ καὶ προσένεγκε περὶ τοῦ καθαρισμοῦ σου ἃ προσέταξεν Μωϋσῆς, εἰς μαρτύριον αὐτοῖς.⁵⁴

⁴⁴And he said to him, ". . . Go, show yourself to the priest, and offer for your cleansing what Moses commanded."

So perhaps the Phillips translation best captures Jesus' reply: "Of course I want to—be clean!"

⁵⁴ The objection by Morna Hooker (*A Commentary on the Gospel according to St. Mark* [BNTC; London: A & C Black, 1991], 80) that the leprosy could not have been healed immediately but rather took place later, such as in the case of Luke's ten lepers who are healed "on the way" (Luke 17:14), misses the narrator's intent. When Jesus commands the man to go and show himself to the priests, it signals to the reader that the former leper was now ready for reentry into the community, completely free of his disfigurement. William Hendriksen (*New Testament Commentary: Exposition of the Gospel according to Mark* [Grand Rapids: Baker, 1975]) observes the intent to state that the cure is immediate occurs also in the healing of Peter's mother-in-law (Mark 1:29–31), where she is able to get up immediately and serve her company (Mark 1:31), of the paralytic who is able to immediately pick up his mat and walk out (Mark 2:12), and of Jairus's daughter, who is able to get up and walk as a sign of her return to life (Mark 5:42).

The narrator closes the story with Jesus' command, and this serves the listener in two important ways. First, and most obviously, since there are no observers in the story, the man's instant cure is witnessed by Jesus, who would not send the man to the priests if the healing had not taken place. The second function is to clarify to the listener that Jesus' breech of Torah in touching the man was not due to ignorance of or disrespect for Torah regulations. It is clear from the specificity of Jesus' command to the man that Jesus both knows and respects the Torah. Thus, this conclusion sends the listener back to the reception that Jesus gave the leper, to recognize the choice that Jesus made for compassion and understanding over strict observance of the Torah.

CONCLUSION

If the narrator of this account was concerned only with the power of Jesus to cure leprosy immediately, why did he not create a conventional encounter instead of this meeting between Jesus and this bold leper? Why not have the leper "stand from afar" and call out to Jesus as Luke shows that it is proper to do (Luke 17:11–19)? Then the full focus would be on the cure.

Rather, to place the cure of leprosy in an anecdote where the petitioner is problematic, testy, and aggressive allows the anecdote to do more than attest to the miracle, which of course it does. It allows the interested listener to see Jesus up close as he deals with an imperfect and testy petitioner who shows himself frustrated with rules that keep him distant. This is the situation where the attitudes of heart and the practice of virtue can be seen. In this little anecdote, Jesus reveals not only his supernatural power in commanding the leprosy to leave, but also something of his "soul," as Plutarch would have said. What virtues would come to the mind of the listener or the group of Christians who used this anecdote for their own discussions? Would it be *syngnōmē*, the willingness to overlook a provocation? Certainly, Jesus invites the description of *praos* ("meekness"). Jesus, instead of taking offense at the man's proximity and demanding more distance, or challenging his insinuation of a capricious ministry, sees only the man's terrible need and shows him that compassion and *ēpios* ("gentleness") which become this anecdote's lesson for the listener.

2

Jesus and Bartimaeus (Mark 10:46–52)

"The LORD will afflict you [those who break the covenant] with madness, blindness, and confusion of mind; you shall grope at noon as blind people grope in darkness, but you shall be unable to find your way; and you shall be continually abused and robbed, without anyone to help."
(Deut 28:28–29)

"In this respect beggars are most repugnant and helpless. There is nothing wholesome about them and they block the course of every undertaking."
(Artemidorus Daldianus, *Onir.* 3.53)[1]

The story of the healing of Bartimaeus is the second of the two pre-Gospel miracle stories (the other being the healing of the leper in Mark 1:40–45) in which a petitioner must ask for himself. Like the leper, the blind beggar Bartimaeus has no one to intercede for him. In this story, he is shown without any friends or family, and he carries the stigma of the parasite on society.

This account stands apart from all others on four counts. First, it is the only miracle in the Synoptic Gospels where the recipient is personally named (Bartimaeus son of Timaeus [v. 46]), and second, the only one where Jesus is identified as "Son of David" (vv. 47–48). The irony in contrasting their sonship cannot be missed. Third, in no other miracle story does the petitioner hold the spotlight. As Sophie Schlumberger notes, it is Bartimaeus rather than Jesus who is at the center of the narrative.[2] Finally, there is no other story that features such a lengthy account of the petitioner's efforts to reach Jesus. When one considers that all

---

[1] Translation by Dr. Gregory W. Dobrov, Loyola University, Chicago, Illinois.

[2] Sophie Schlumberger, "Le récit de la foi de Bartimée (Marc 10,46–52)," *ETR* 68 (1993): 75. See also Vincent Taylor, *The Gospel according to St. Mark:*

that is necessary for a healing story is the indication of the problem, the action of Jesus, and some sign or statement of the efficacy of the miracle, the detail in this anecdote is notable. Martin Dibelius concludes that miracles of such length as this are clear signs of their use for the amazement and entertainment of the coarse Gentiles being addressed in the Gentile mission. But is the bulk of material merely entertaining, or does it serve other, deeper, paraenetic purposes? To address the signs of such a story's service before its inclusion into the Gospel, it is necessary to review the story for any obvious signs of Markan intervention, so that any such added narrative elements might be excluded from our examination of the signs of service that this story held in the pre-Markan community.

I. MARK 10:46–52: SIGNS OF MARKAN REDACTION

⁴⁶καὶ ἔρχονται εἰς Ἰεριχώ. καὶ ἐκπορευομένου αὐτοῦ ἀπὸ Ἰεριχὼ καὶ τῶν μαθητῶν αὐτοῦ καὶ ὄχλου ἱκανοῦ ὁ υἱὸς Τιμαίου Βαρτιμαῖος, τυφλὸς προσαίτης, ἐκάθητο παρὰ τὴν ὁδόν. ⁴⁷καὶ ἀκούσας ὅτι Ἰησοῦς ὁ Ναζαρηνός ἐστιν ἤρξατο κράζειν καὶ λέγειν· υἱὲ Δαυὶδ Ἰησοῦ, ἐλέησόν με. ⁴⁸καὶ ἐπετίμων αὐτῷ πολλοὶ ἵνα σιωπήσῃ· ὁ δὲ πολλῷ μᾶλλον ἔκραζεν· υἱὲ Δαυίδ, ἐλέησόν με. ⁴⁹καὶ στὰς ὁ Ἰησοῦς εἶπεν· φωνήσατε αὐτόν. καὶ φωνοῦσιν τὸν τυφλὸν λέγοντες αὐτῷ· θάρσει, ἔγειρε, φωνεῖ σε. ⁵⁰ὁ δὲ ἀποβαλὼν τὸ ἱμάτιον αὐτοῦ ἀναπηδήσας ἦλθεν πρὸς τὸν Ἰησοῦν. ⁵¹καὶ ἀποκριθεὶς αὐτῷ ὁ Ἰησοῦς εἶπεν· τί σοι θέλεις ποιήσω; ὁ δὲ τυφλὸς εἶπεν αὐτῷ· ῥαββουνί, ἵνα ἀναβλέψω. ⁵²καὶ ὁ Ἰησοῦς εἶπεν αὐτῷ· ὕπαγε, ἡ πίστις σου σέσωκέν σε. καὶ εὐθὺς ἀνέβλεψεν καὶ ἠκολούθει αὐτῷ ἐν τῇ ὁδῷ.

⁴⁶They came to Jericho. As he and his disciples and a large crowd were leaving Jericho, Bartimaeus son of Timaeus, a blind beggar, was sitting by the roadside. ⁴⁷When he heard that it was Jesus of Nazareth, he began to shout out and say, "Jesus, Son of David, have mercy on me!" ⁴⁸Many sternly ordered him to be quiet, but he cried out even more loudly, "Son of David, have mercy on me!" ⁴⁹Jesus stood still and said, "Call him here." And they called the blind man, saying to him, "Take heart; get up, he is calling you." ⁵⁰So throwing off his cloak, he sprang up and came to Jesus. ⁵¹Then Jesus said to

---

The Greek Text with Introduction, Notes, and Indexes (London: Macmillan; New York: St. Martin's Press, 1955), 447.

him, "What do you want me to do for you?" The blind man said to him, "My teacher, let me see again." [52]Jesus said to him, "Go; your faith has made you well." Immediately he regained his sight and followed him on the way.

Several important articles have contributed significantly to this study, but I am most indebted to Earl S. Johnson[3] and Ernest Best.[4]

[46]καὶ ἔρχονται εἰς Ἰεριχώ. καὶ ἐκπορευομένου αὐτοῦ ἀπὸ Ἰεριχὼ καὶ τῶν μαθητῶν αὐτοῦ καὶ ὄχλου ἱκανοῦ ὁ υἱὸς Τιμαίου Βαρτιμαῖος, τυφλὸς προσαίτης, ἐκάθητο παρὰ τὴν ὁδόν.

[46]They came to Jericho. As he and his disciples and a large crowd were leaving Jericho, Bartimaeus son of Timaeus, a blind beggar, was sitting by the roadside.

Signs of Markan redaction are seen first of all in the awkward introduction. Jesus is said to enter the city ("they came to Jericho" [v. 46a]) only to exit ("and as he was leaving Jericho" [v. 46b]). It is best explained if the pre-Markan story began with Jesus leaving the city along with the crowd, but once inserted into the narrative of the Gospel, it required a notification of his entry.[5] Compositional features support this conclusion. Notice in v. 46a the plural pronoun, "*they* came to Jericho," which presumes the disciples accompanying Jesus, whereas v. 46b, the pre-Markan introduction, uses the singular for Jesus alone ("and as *he* was leaving"). Then Mark has been impelled to insert "with his disciples" between Jesus and the large crowd (καὶ τῶν μαθητῶν αὐτοῦ καὶ ὄχλου ἱκανοῦ) because it is his Gospel placement of the story that necessitates their mention, although they have no part to play here.

Excursus: The Spiritually Blind Disciples in Mark

The story of Jesus and Bartimaeus holds an important place in the Markan Gospel structure, as it brings to a close a special mid-

---

[3]Earl S. Johnson, "Mark 10:46–52," *CBQ* 40 (1978): 191–204.

[4]Ernest Best, *Following Jesus: Discipleship in Mark* (JSNTSup 14; Sheffield: JSOT Press, 1981); "Miracles," in *Disciples and Discipleship: Studies in the Gospel according to Mark* (Edinburgh: T & T Clark, 1986), 177–96.

[5]Walter Schmithals, *Das Evangelium nach Markus* (2 vols; ÖTK; Gütersloh: Mohn, 1979), 2:472; Best, *Following Jesus*, 139 n. 2, 143.

section of the book (Mark 8:22–26) that might be entitled "The Spiritually Blind Disciples." Throughout the section, Jesus tries to prepare his disciples for both his coming passion, death, and resurrection (Mark 8:31; 9:31; 10:33–34) and to impart to them the special demands of discipleship that will necessitate the surrender of their personal ambitions in a leadership characterized by service to the most needy. Mark achieves this by creating successions of chreiai where the disciples manifest their ambition and desire to control only to be counseled by Jesus that their leadership must be expressed in serving others, not dominating them (e.g., Mark 8:31–33; 9:28–29, 33–37, 38–50; 10:13–16, 32–40, 41–45). The continued expressions of their ambition show that they do not understand or accept Jesus' teachings. Jesus' last attempt in that section is to have his disciples note how he himself models this service: "For the Son of Man came not to be served but to serve" (Mark 10:45). The section concludes with another story of a blind man, just one such story (the blind man of Bethsaida [Mark 8:22–26]) begins the section. Between these narrative markers the evangelist has situated a section that signals the theme of spiritual blindness. The irony of the whole section is that Jesus can give physical sight to the physically blind but is unable to give spiritual sight to his own disciples.[6]

The account of Bartimaeus has been cleverly placed at the very end of the section so that the blind man's petition to Jesus operates as a sad contrast with the ambitious request of James and John. After Jesus' third and most detailed passion prediction, the two brothers show that they have paid attention only to Jesus' promise that he will rise again, and they take him aside. Jesus asks them, "What do you want me to do for you?" (τί θέλετέ με ποιήσω ὑμῖν), to which they answer, "Grant us to sit, one at your right hand and one at your left, in your glory." Mark knew that in the story of Bartimaeus, Jesus asks the blind man, "What do you want me to do for you?"

---

[6] The symbolic use of physical blindness for ignorance is ancient, as shown by Eleftheria A. Bernidaki-Aldous, "Blindness as Ignorance: Seeing as Light, Truth, Moral Goodness," in *Blindness in a Culture of Light: Especially the Case of "Oedipus at Colonus" of Sophocles* (AUS 17/8: New York: Peter Lang, 1990), 49–55. Her references include Plato, *Resp.* 6.506c, 508de; 7.514a–517c, 518a–d, 521c; *Gorg.* 479b; *Phaed.* 96c; Sophocles, *Aj.* 51–52; 59–60; Aristophanes, *Plut.* 86–89; 90–91; Plutarch, *Lys.* 18.4–5; *Mor.* 1095a.

(τί σοι θέλεις ποιήσω), and Bartimaeus answers, "Rabbouni, that I might see again!" Mark closes the section with the Bartimaeus story because when the listener hears the same question from Jesus to the blind man, they realize how truly blind James and John really are. They have not recognized their own spiritual blindness but rather make their ambitious, power-hungry request from their lack of spiritual insight. This explains, then, why, as I will explain below, it is Mark's hand that inserts the conclusion that Bartimaeus, upon receiving his sight, followed Jesus along the way (v. 52d). It is a negative, ironic portent about the blind disciples for the listener: since the disciples remain spiritually blind, they will not be able to see where Jesus is going, and will not be able to follow him.

ὄχλου ἱκανοῦ

a sizeable crowd

Earl Johnson proposes that it is Mark who has introduced the crowd so that they will be the same ones who welcome Jesus into Jerusalem (Mark 11:1–11.)[7] This is not so clear, since Mark 11:1–7 seems to be a private session between Jesus and his disciples, preparing for the entrance by sending them to find the colt. There is no sense that he is doing this in the middle of a clamoring crowd wanting to proclaim him king. Rather, the crowd seems to gather as soon as Jesus mounts the colt.

Certainly, Mark is known to use crowds in his introductions (e.g., Mark 1:21, 29; 2:1; 3:1a, 31; 4:1; 5:1; 6:45; and they are mentioned with disciples in Mark 8:34; 9:14; 10:1) as they are in this narrative. What is unusual, however, is that Mark usually uses πολύς ("large"), such as in his summaries (Mark 5:21, 24), introductions (Mark 6:34; 8:1; superlative πλεῖστος in 4:1), and his own conclusion in Mark 12:37. Here in v. 46b, the word ἱκανός ("large enough" or "sizeable") is not typical of his style and is found again only in a pre-Markan passion account where it is part of an idiom (τὸ ἱκανὸν ποιεῖν) used to describe Pilate's desire to placate the crowd (τῷ ὄχλῳ τὸ ἱκανὸν [Mark 15:15]). So the phrasing is unlike Mark. Moreover, the narrative element of a crowd shows no sign of an artificial insertion, but is a necessary element to the story itself. Since Jericho was no little town, the crowd pouring out of the gates would necessitate the blind beggars situated there to yell over the

---

[7] Johnson, "Mark 10:46–52," 193.

noises of the people. The mention of the crowd here prepares for the "many" who rebuke Bartimaeus for his shouting (v. 48). It also explains why Jesus will have to order the people to call to Bartimaeus, who is located behind him, since with the flow of a crowd leaving the gates, it would be easier for the blind man to follow that flow up to Jesus than for Jesus to try to work his way back. The notification of a crowd with Jesus is more probably a basic introduction to the story of a crowd scene, not a Markan insertion.

ὁ υἱὸς Τιμαίου Βαρτιμαῖος

the son of Timaeus, Bartimaeus

Is it Mark who provided the translation of the man's name? The issue has raised scholarly debate. When Mark does supply a translation, he places the Greek after the Aramaic with ὅ ἐστιν (Mark 3:17; 5:41; 7:11, 34; 12:42; 15:22, 34), but here the pattern is in reverse order. Ernest Best concludes that it suggests a Greek-speaking community unfamiliar with Aramaic[8]—that is, the pre-Markan community.

The name itself is a hybrid of Aramaic "bar" ("son") and Greek "Timaeus" ("of honor"). Vincent Taylor makes the plausible case that in an earlier version the entire name might have been in Aramaic: "Bartamea." Since Aramaic "tamea" means "uncleanness," the man's name (or epithet) would have been "son of uncleanness."

Taylor supposes that a Greek translator misunderstood "tamea" for "timaios" ("honored"), and thus the hybrid occurred. Taylor also suggests that the translation was inserted after the Markan Gospel had circulated, since neither Matthew nor Luke carries that translation.[9] Burton Mack agrees with Taylor that the full Aramaic name, "Bartamea" ("son of defilement"), belonged to the earliest Aramaic version of this anecdote, not only because it is a more believable name for someone of his condition, but also because there is another example of Aramaic in the anecdote, where the blind man addresses Jesus as "Rabbouni" (v. 51), a title found nowhere else in the Markan gospel.[10] The "hybrid" translation that now appears in the Markan Gospel reflects the pre-Markan rendering of the story. There is no need to assign the translation to a

---

[8] Best, *Following Jesus*, 141.
[9] Taylor, *St. Mark*, 448.
[10] Burton L. Mack, *A Myth of Innocence: Mark and Christian Origins* (Philadelphia: Fortress, 1988), 297 n. 2.

later copyist inserting it into the Markan Gospel, simply because that translation does not appear in the versions of this account in Matthew and Luke because none of Mark's translation notes appear in either of those Gospels. Both Matthew and Luke seem to have avoided these signs of foreignness.

τυφλὸς προσαίτης ἐκάθητο παρὰ τὴν ὁδόν

a blind beggar, was sitting by the roadside

The remainder of the verse must belong to the pre-Markan tradition, since it contains the information necessary for this miracle story. The man's problem is his blindness, and thus he must sit at the side of the road, out of the stream of people pushing their way out of the city.

⁴⁷καὶ ἀκούσας ὅτι Ἰησοῦς ὁ Ναζαρηνός ἐστιν ἤρξατο κράζειν καὶ λέγειν· υἱὲ Δαυὶδ Ἰησοῦ, ἐλέησόν με. ⁴⁸καὶ ἐπετίμων αὐτῷ πολλοὶ ἵνα σιωπήσῃ· ὁ δὲ πολλῷ μᾶλλον ἔκραζεν· υἱὲ Δαυίδ, ἐλέησόν με. ⁴⁹καὶ στὰς ὁ Ἰησοῦς εἶπεν· φωνήσατε αὐτόν. καὶ φωνοῦσιν τὸν τυφλὸν λέγοντες αὐτῷ· θάρσει, ἔγειρε, φωνεῖ σε.

⁴⁷When he heard that it was Jesus of Nazareth, he began to shout out and say, "Jesus, Son of David, have mercy on me!" ⁴⁸Many sternly ordered him to be quiet, but he cried out even more loudly, "Son of David, have mercy on me!" ⁴⁹Jesus stood still and said, "Call him here." And they called the blind man, saying to him, "Take heart; get up, he is calling you."

υἱὲ Δαυὶδ Ἰησοῦ

Son of David, Jesus

Josef Ernst argues that the choice of "Son of David" belongs to Mark because it so clearly prepares for the revelation of Jesus as Son of God by the centurion in Mark 15:39.[11] Christoph Burger also holds for Markan redaction here, but his reason depends on the presupposition that Mark received the Aramaic version and was the first to translate it.[12] For his part, Vernon Robbins argues for three stages in the account, the third

---

[11] Josef Ernst, *Das Evangelium nach Markus* (RNT; Regensburg: Pustet, 1981), 314.

[12] Christoph Burger, *Jesus als Davidssohn: Eine traditionsgeschichtliche Untersuchung* (FRLANT 98; Göttingen: Vandenhoeck & Ruprecht, 1970), 59–63.

being the redaction of Mark. He claims that Mark introduced the "Son of David" title to create a Christology in which that title would be linked to healing.[13] For Robbins, the fact that Mark situated the healing of Bartimaeus between the discipleship teaching of the middle section (Mark 8:27–10:45) and the entrance of Jesus into Jericho (Mark 11:1–10) is especially significant because a reference to "our ancestor David" occurs in the latter in v 10: "Blessed is the coming kingdom of our ancestor David!"[14]

The question is whether Mark has a special desire to press home the "Son of David" title. Why is it that only Bartimaeus uses the title "Son of David" and not the crowd that acclaims Jesus when he enters Jerusalem? Instead, the crowd cries out, "Blessed is the coming kingdom of our ancestor David!" (Mark 11:10). Matthew is the one who redacts Mark 11:1–10 so that people welcome not the kingdom of their ancestor David but rather the person of Jesus as "Son of David": "Hosanna to the Son of David! Blessed is the one who comes in the name of the Lord. Hosanna in the highest heaven!" (Matt 21:9). Notice that Matthew also redacts Mark's version of Jesus' protest in the temple so that it becomes something of a royal visitation in which the children cry out, "Hosanna to the Son of David" (Matt 21:15). It is Matthew, not Mark, who emphasizes this royal title for Jesus.[15] In fact, Mark regards the title "Son of David" as inadequate, as can be seen in Mark 12:35–37a:

---

[13] Vernon Robbins, "The Healing of Blind Bartimaeus (Mk 10:46–52) in the Markan Theology," *JBL* 92 (1972): 234–35.

[14] Ibid., 237.

[15] Matthew's Gospel opens with the announcement of the genealogy of Jesus Christ, the son of David, the son of Abraham (Matt 1:1), and the genealogy is divided so that David is the midway marker in the chronology (Matt 1:17). This idea is further emphasized when Joseph is addressed as "son of David" (Matt 1:20). Special Matthean insertions can be seen in Matthew's version of the Q story of the exorcism performed on the demoniac who was blind and mute (Matt 12:22–24 // Luke 11:14–16), where Matthew adds this acclamation by the people: "Can this be the Son of David?" (Matt 12:23). Likewise, in his redaction of the Markan account of the Syrophoenician mother (Matt 15:21–28 // Mark 7:24–30), Matthew introduces an address to Jesus by the woman: "Have mercy on me, Lord, Son of David" (Matt 15:22). To this we may add Matthew's insertions into the Markan text about Jesus' entrance into Jerusalem (Matt 21:1–9 // Mark 11:1–10), where he has the crowds directly acclaim Jesus: "Hosanna to the Son of David!" (Matt 21:9). He also inserts the narrative element of the children inside the temple who cry, "Hosanna to the Son of David!" (Matt 21:15). This evidence makes it clear that it is Matthew who longs for Jesus' identity as Son of David to be impressed upon his audience.

"While Jesus was teaching in the temple, he said, 'How can the scribes say that the Messiah is the son of David? David himself, by the Holy Spirit, declared, "The Lord said to my Lord, 'Sit at my right hand, until I put your enemies under your feet.'" David himself calls him Lord; so how can he be his son?' And the large crowd was listening to him with delight" (Mark 12:35–37a).

If Mark wished to augment the title "Son of David," the rest of his Gospel offers no evidence of it. Most tellingly in this pericope, when the blind man's shouts of "Son of David, Jesus, have mercy on me!" are finally heard by Jesus, and Bartimaeus is asked what he wants, he addresses Jesus with the very simple title "Rabbouni" (v. 51a).[16] If Mark were the one to introduce the title "Son of David" as a link to healing, as Robbins proposes, this would be the pertinent time to make that identity clear. Rather, the cumulative evidence leads to the opposite conclusion. The pre-Markan community likely appreciated the irony that Bartimaeus's efforts to gain Jesus' attention were actually true; he shows that he has no idea that Jesus is this royal prince, since his address to Jesus is so sincerely affectionate, respectful, and simple: "Rabbouni."

[48]καὶ ἐπετίμων αὐτῷ πολλοὶ ἵνα σιωπήσῃ· ὁ δὲ πολλῷ μᾶλλον ἔκραζεν· υἱὲ Δαυίδ, ἐλέησόν με.

[48]Many sternly ordered him to be quiet, but he cried out even more loudly, "Son of David, have mercy on me!"

Robbins's argument for the Markan insertion of "Son of David" notes that it is unlike Mark for anyone other than Jesus to order anything to be silent (i.e., nature in Mark 4:35–42). From this order to be silent, Robbins concludes that Mark's hand is in evidence.[17] But v. 48 stands apart from the Markan pattern precisely because it is not Jesus who commands the silence but rather the "many" who are bothered by Bartimaeus's shouts. Robbins, however, because he proposes that the "Son of David" title is part of Mark's Messianic Secret motif, sees this urging from the crowd as part of the attempt to prevent Jesus' true identify from being exposed in public.[18] The problem is that Bartimaeus ignores their rebuke and proves his decision right, for Jesus does hear him and commands those near him

---

[16] See the masterful argumentation by Robert H. Gundry, *Mark: A Commentary on His Apology for the Cross* (Grand Rapids: Eerdmans, 1993), 600–601.

[17] Robbins, "Blind Bartimaeus," 233.

[18] Ibid.

to call him over, and the people congratulate Bartimaeus: "Take heart; get up, he is calling you." Moreover, if Bartimaeus were identifying Jesus' special identity as Son of David, this would be the only time in the gospel when Jesus encourages someone making his identity known in such a public manner. Then, of course, as mentioned above, why does Bartimaeus drop the title "Son of David" when he finally reaches Jesus and address him instead as "Rabbouni"? So Robbins's theory does not seem to be supported here. There simply is not the same concern about the title "Son of David" that one finds when Peter identifies Jesus as the Messiah (Mark 8:30) or when a healing is followed by Jesus ordering silence about the miracle (Mark 1:44; 8:26; 9:25). Throughout this Gospel then, Jesus discourages public promulgation of his miracles and power, as he does titles that are Messianic. The reason for the crowd scolding Bartimaeus has to be sought elsewhere, in the pre-Markan stratum.

⁵⁰ὁ δὲ ἀποβαλὼν τὸ ἱμάτιον αὐτοῦ ἀναπηδήσας ἦλθεν πρὸς τὸν Ἰησοῦν. ⁵¹καὶ ἀποκριθεὶς αὐτῷ ὁ Ἰησοῦς εἶπεν· τί σοι θέλεις ποιήσω; ὁ δὲ τυφλὸς εἶπεν αὐτῷ· ῥαββουνί, ἵνα ἀναβλέψω.

⁵⁰So throwing off his cloak, he sprang up and came to Jesus. ⁵¹Then Jesus said to him, "What do you want me to do for you?" The blind man said to him, "My teacher, let me see again."

These verses are the center of the miracle story and must be identified as traditional. There is nothing particularly Markan to this element.

⁵²καὶ ὁ Ἰησοῦς εἶπεν αὐτῷ· ὕπαγε, ἡ πίστις σου σέσωκέν σε. καὶ εὐθὺς ἀνέβλεψεν καὶ ἠκολούθει αὐτῷ ἐν τῇ ὁδῷ.

⁵²Jesus said to him, "Go; your faith has made you well." Immediately he regained his sight and followed him on the way.

The order of Jesus to the former blind man to depart and the compliment about his "faith," together with the notification that he immediately received his sight, is generally accepted as the pre-Markan conclusion.[19] Notice that Jesus' words to Bartimaeus, ὕπαγε, ἡ πίστις σου σέσωκέν σε ("Go; your faith has made you well"), repeat Jesus' response to the woman who was healed of the twelve-year hemorrhage (Mark 5:34) and support the pre-Markan character. Nothing particular to Markan themes can be found there.

---

[19] Best, *Following Jesus*, 141.

καὶ ἠκολούθει αὐτῷ ἐν τῇ ὁδῷ

and he followed him on the way

This final clause has divided scholars. On the one hand, it could be argued from a form-critical view that Bartimaeus's following Jesus is the necessary "demonstration" that fulfills the third part of the usual healing miracle story (problem, the healer's action, the demonstration or acclamation). Second, this final clause results in a literary inclusio because it recalls the first mention of road in v. 46, where Bartimaeus is described sitting by the side of the road.

On the other hand, it must be noted that Bartimaeus's following Jesus constitutes a disjuncture with Jesus' order to him, "Go." So this ending has Bartimaeus disobeying Jesus. It has already been noted in the excursus on Mark 10:46–52 how Bartimaeus's following Jesus serves as the final, ironic ending of the section on the disciples' spiritual blindness (Mark 8:22–10:56). Mark wants to prepare his listeners for the fact that because the disciples remain blind, they will not see where Jesus is going or be able to follow him. So, this last clause of Mark 10:52 provides a problem of disjuncture for the discrete anecdote but provides a powerful conclusion when situated by Mark in this section. Disobedience to Jesus' orders belong to Markan redaction in the healing of the leper (Mark 1:45) as well, and disjuncture is seen elsewhere when Mark redacts an account, as in Mark 1:21–28.[20] These observations make it much more probable that Mark created the disjuncture with the man's disobedience than that it was part of the pre-Markan anecdote.

Summary: The Markan additions to this account occur only where "they" enter the city (v. 46), where Mark must add "with his disciples"

---

[20] In Mark 1:23–28, the introduction, which stipulates that Jesus was teaching, heads an exorcism story in which there actually is no teaching. The artificiality becomes noticeable when, after the successful exorcism, the people exclaim, "What is this? A new teaching—with authority! He commands even the unclean spirits, and they obey him" (v. 27). The mention of the teaching does not match with the authoritative exorcism, but only with the Markan introduction (vv. 21–22). In the same account, Mark adds to the demon's scream, "Have you come to destroy us?" an identification of Jesus, "I know who you are, the Holy One of God" (v. 24). Then Jesus silences the demon (v. 25), certainly a redaction by Mark, for when he continues with the pre-Markan anecdote, the demon does not obey Jesus' order to be silent, but instead, it comes out, "crying with a loud voice" (v. 27).

(v. 46), and where Bartimaeus disobeys Jesus' order to depart and instead "followed him along the way" (v. 52).

If one considers the anecdote without these narrative additions, the following anecdote with its narrative elements can be seen.

II. THE PRE-MARKAN ANECDOTE: JESUS AND BARTIMAEUS

⁴⁶ᵇκαὶ ἐκπορευομένου αὐτοῦ ἀπὸ Ἰεριχὼ . . . καὶ ὄχλου ἱκανοῦ ὁ υἱὸς Τιμαίου Βαρτιμαῖος, τυφλὸς προσαίτης, ἐκάθητο παρὰ τὴν ὁδόν. ⁴⁷καὶ ἀκούσας ὅτι Ἰησοῦς ὁ Ναζαρηνός ἐστιν ἤρξατο κράζειν καὶ λέγειν· υἱὲ Δαυὶδ Ἰησοῦ, ἐλέησον με. ⁴⁸καὶ ἐπετίμων αὐτῷ πολλοὶ ἵνα σιωπήσῃ· ὁ δὲ πολλῷ μᾶλλον ἔκραζεν· υἱὲ Δαυίδ, ἐλέησόν με. ⁴⁹καὶ στὰς ὁ Ἰησοῦς εἶπεν· φωνήσατε αὐτόν. καὶ φωνοῦσιν τὸν τυφλὸν λέγοντες αὐτῷ· θάρσει, ἔγειρε, φωνεῖ σε. ⁵⁰ὁ δὲ ἀποβαλὼν τὸ ἱμάτιον αὐτοῦ ἀναπηδήσας ἦλθεν πρὸς τὸν Ἰησοῦν. ⁵¹καὶ ἀποκριθεὶς αὐτῷ ὁ Ἰησοῦς εἶπεν· τί σοι θέλεις ποιήσω; ὁ δὲ τυφλὸς εἶπεν αὐτῷ· ῥαββουνί, ἵνα ἀναβλέψω. ⁵²καὶ ὁ Ἰησοῦς εἶπεν αὐτῷ· ὕπαγε, ἡ πίστις σου σέσωκέν σε. καὶ εὐθὺς ἀνέβλεψεν.

⁴⁶ᵇAnd as he . . . and a large crowd were leaving Jericho, Bartimaeus son of Timaeus, a blind beggar, was sitting by the roadside. ⁴⁷When he heard that it was Jesus of Nazareth, he began to shout out and say, "Jesus, Son of David, have mercy on me!" ⁴⁸Many sternly ordered him to be quiet, but he cried out even more loudly, "Son of David, have mercy on me!" ⁴⁹Jesus stood still and said, "Call him here." And they called the blind man, saying to him, "Take heart; get up, he is calling you." ⁵⁰So throwing off his cloak, he sprang up and came to Jesus. ⁵¹Then Jesus said to him, "What do you want me to do for you?" The blind man said to him, "My teacher, let me see again." ⁵²Jesus said to him, "Go; your faith has made you well." Immediately he regained his sight.

Excursus: The Pre-Markan Account as a "Call Story"

Before discussing the elements of the anecdote and its revelation of Jesus' virtue, I must address a prominent proposal concerning the pre-Markan anecdote. Paul Achtemeier and Michael Steinhauser[21] have argued that from a form-critical perspective, this pericope should be regarded as a "call story." Steinhauser provides six parallels between this anecdote and the call stories of Gideon and Moses:

1. *The Divine Confrontation*: Judg 6:11–12 (Gideon); Exod 3:1–3a–4 (Moses);

Mark 10:46–47b (Bartimaeus hears that Jesus is passing by)

2. *The Introductory Word*: Judg 6:12b–13 (Gideon); Exod 3:4–9 (Moses);

Mark 10:47b (Bartimaeus cries, "Jesus, Son of David, have Mercy on me!")

3. *The Objection*: Judg 6:15 (Gideon); Exod 3:11 (Moses);

Mark 10:48 (the "many" tell Bartimaeus to be silent)

4. *The Commission*: Judg 6:14 (Gideon); Exod 3:10 (Moses);

Mark 10:49a (Bartimaeus is called by Jesus)

5. *The Reassurance*: Judg 6:16 (Gideon); Exod 3:12 (Moses);

Mark 10:49b (the "many" now say, "Take heart, arise, he is calling you")

6. *The Sign*: Judg 6:17 (Gideon); Exod 3:12 (Moses);

Mark 10:51–52 (Jesus gives Bartimaeus his sight)[22]

Besides the parallel elements of the progression, Steinhauser also notes another parallel element found in Bartimaeus's throwing off his cloak (Mark 10:50). This is the sign of starting a new life. Just as Peter and Andrew, James and John, leave their boats (Mark 1:17, 20) and Levi

---

[21] Paul J. Achtemeier, "'And He Followed Him': Miracles and Discipleship in Mark," *Semeia* 11 (1978): 115–45; Michael G. Steinhauser, "Part of a Call Story," *ExpTim* 94 (1982–1983): 204–6; "The Form of the Bartimaeus Narrative," *NTS* 32 (1986): 583–95.

[22] Steinhauser, "Bartimaeus Narrative," 584–87.

leaves his tax collecting booth (Mark 2:17b) to follow Jesus, so too Bartimaeus throws off his only possession.[23]

These parallels would appear quite compelling except that Bartimaeus is not called to follow Jesus; he is told to depart (v. 52). The narrative has Jesus order the people near to him to call Bartimaeus only because the man is too far away for Jesus to ask him what he can do for him. When Jesus asks him at last, "What is it you want me to do for you?" this shows that Jesus simply did not know how he could help the man.

A less strong argument one could insert here is that in the Gospel tradition, Jesus never calls anyone who has been marginalized by sickness or possession to become a disciple. Such persons always are told to depart so that they can return to their families (Mark 1:44; 2:11; 5:19, 34; 7:29). Even when the former Gerasene demoniac wants to follow Jesus, he is told, "Go home to your friends, and tell them how much the Lord has done for you, and what mercy he has shown you" (Mark 5:19). In the story of the call of the rich man (Mark 10:17–22), Jesus addresses someone who has no illness, and he is told to divest himself of his possessions, give to the poor, and follow Jesus (Mark 10:21–22). Bartimaeus's story belongs with the other healing stories where the cured person is told to depart.

For Steinhauser, Jesus' command "Go" is a mandate for Bartimaeus to leave his beggar's life and become a disciple. That is why he follows Jesus. This is an unusual way for Jesus to call anyone to discipleship, since none of the other orders to depart appear meant to be understood in this way. Luke's response is rather enlightening. He sees a contradiction in Bartimaeus's behavior and avoids the embarrassing disobedience by removing Jesus' order to depart (Luke 18:42–43).

The argument that this is a pre-Markan call story misses the main feature in that Jesus never asks Bartimaeus to follow him. In fact, Jesus orders him to depart.

Bartimaeus's following Jesus is understood once it is connected to Mark's usage of the story, as explained above. It is a portent of the disciples' inability to stay with Jesus during his passion and death. In a spiritual sense, since they did not want to receive their sight, they did not want to see where Jesus was going, and they could not follow him down that road.

---

[23] Steinhauser, "Call Story," 205.

The Presentation of the Petitioner: A Blind Beggar

⁴⁶ᵇκαὶ ἐκπορευομένου αὐτοῦ ἀπὸ Ἰεριχὼ . . . καὶ ὄχλου ἱκανοῦ ὁ υἱὸς Τιμαίου Βαρτιμαῖος, τυφλὸς προσαίτης, ἐκάθητο παρὰ τὴν ὁδόν.

⁴⁶ᵇAnd as he . . . and a large crowd were leaving Jericho, Bartimaeus son of Timaeus, a blind beggar, was sitting by the roadside.

ὁ υἱὸς Τιμαίου Βαρτιμαῖος

the son of Timaeus, Bartimaeus

Although this man's name in an earlier Aramaic version might well have been "Bartamea," meaning "son of defilement," as explained earlier, the pre-Markan text now presents him as "the son of Timaeus, Bartimaeus." If one hears the play on words, "son of Timaeus/honor," the irony could not be greater.

To Be Physically Blind

τυφλός

a blind man

To be physically blind was a suffering worse than public dishonor, as Eleftheria Bernidaki-Aldous notes.

> In a shame-culture, in which honor is the highest good, utter dishonor is the supreme misfortune. Blindness (lack of *light*) which, at all times, vies with dishonor to win the title of "the worst of sufferings," is another condition which (for the Greeks) leaves no room for happiness.[24]

The comment of the chorus in Sophocles' *Oedipus the King* as they mourn the king's blindness is especially telling: "Thou wert better dead than living and blind" (*Oed. tyr.* 1360).[25] Artemidorus Daldianus, a second-century C.E. man of letters and compiler of dream interpretations across the Mediterranean world, writes this: "Someone dreamt

---

[24] Bernidaki-Aldous, *Blindness in a Culture of Light*, 103.

[25] Sophocles, *Oedipus the King*, in vol. 1 of *Sophocles* (trans. F. Storr; LCL; Cambridge, Mass.: Harvard University Press, 1962), 125. For this reference I am indebted to Bernidaki-Aldous, *Blindness in a Culture of Light*.

that he was told: 'do not fear that you will die; but you will not be able to live, either.' The man lost his sight—an outcome that accords exactly with the prediction: he did not die inasmuch as he continued to live; but he was not living, either, inasmuch as he could not see the light."[26] In a later Jewish text, Rabbi Joshua ben Levi is claimed to have said, "Four are accounted as dead: A poor man, a leper, a blind person, and one who is childless" (*b. Ned.* 64b).[27] Bernidaki-Aldous adds, "The blind share in the characteristic most characteristic of the dead (Hades), namely, darkness."[28] More specifically, she states, "The way in which blindness is described in Greek literature and depicted on the Greek stage supports this interpretation: physical dependence on others, lack of control over one's environment, uncertainty in direction are always emphasized. In short, the helplessness which blindness brings was an extreme misery to the Greeks, worse, perhaps, than the darkness of death itself."[29]

Besides the suffering of blindness, there was also a social stigma, a shadow that connected blindness with divine displeasure. The blind person quite possibly had merited this "worst of sufferings" somehow. In the Greek world, this connection is frequently demonstrated in myth and saga. A striking example is found in Teiresias, the prophet said to be blinded for hubris by an outraged Athena when he accidentally saw her bathing while he was hunting in the woods.[30] Most famously, King Oedipus blinds himself as he discovers that he has committed incest

---

[26] Artemidorus Daldianus, *Onir.* 5.77. Translation by Dr. Gregory W. Dobrov, Loyola University, Chicago, Illinois.

[27] "Nedarim," *The Babylonian Talmud* (ed. I. Epstein; trans. H. Freedman; 6 vols.; London: Soncino, 1936), 5.3:206. The context concerns the situations in which one might be freed from a vow. The situations of these persons constitute grounds for release from vows made beforehand, for just as a death removes a person's obligation to fulfill a vow, so too these situations renders these persons incapable.

[28] Bernidaki-Aldous, *Blindness in a Culture of Light*, 99.

[29] Ibid., 36.

[30] Perhaps the best-known version is Callimachus's poem "Hymn to the Baths of Pallas." Although Callimachus dates only to the third century B.C.E., he is known to be dependent upon Pherecydes, a mythographer circa 450s B.C.E. In that version, Teiresias's prophecy is a compensation given to him when his mother, the nymph Chariclo, and maid of Athena plead with the goddess to show mercy. Another version of his blinding begins with Teiresias's prophetic powers: Zeus strikes him with blindness for revealing the secrets of the deities. See a fuller treatment in Bernidaki-Aldous, *Blindness in a Culture of Light*, 63–65. In both cases, the blinding is punishment for an offense against the divine.

with his mother and murdered his father. As the blinded king comes onto the stage he cries,

> Dark, dark! The horror of darkness, like a shroud,
> Wraps me and bears me on through mist and cloud.
> Ah me, ah me! What spasms athwart me shoot,
> What pangs of agonising memory! (*Oed. tyr.* 1310)[31]

In the Jewish religious tradition, too, blindness is often a punishment from God for offense against his majesty. At the Babylonian conquest, for example, God blinds the priests and prophets of Jerusalem for their sins.

> This was for the sins of her prophets and the iniquities of her priests, who shed in the midst of her the blood of the righteous. They wandered, blind, through the streets, so defiled with blood that none could touch their garments. (Lam 4:13–14 RSV)

Again, one of the warnings against breaking the covenant of the Lord is the curse of blindness by God, as stipulated in Deuteronomy:

> The LORD will afflict you with madness, blindness, and confusion of mind; you shall grope about at noon as blind people grope in darkness, but you shall be unable to find your way; and you shall be continually abused and robbed, without anyone to help. (Deut 28:28–29)

In the New Testament, two references to the continued connection between blindness and sin occur in John 9:1–41, the story of the man born blind. Jesus' disciples assume that the man's condition is punishment for sin ("Rabbi, who sinned, this man or his parents, that he was born blind?" [v. 2]), and the Pharisees are convinced of it ("You were born entirely in sins, and are you trying to teach us?" [v. 34]).

Within Jewish observance, the blind person belongs to the category of persons who are "blemished." Notice the reason given for why the blind person may not serve as a priest: "For no one who has a blemish shall draw near, one who is blind or lame, or one who has a mutilated face or a limb too long, or one who has a broken foot or a broken hand, or a hunchback, or a dwarf, or a man with a blemish in his eyes or an itching disease or scabs or crushed testicles. . . . He shall not come near the curtain or approach the altar, because he has a blemish, *that he may*

---

[31] Sophocles, *Oedipus the King* (trans. Storr), 121–23.

not profane my sanctuaries; for I am the LORD; I sanctify them" (Lev 21:18–23 [my italics]). Notice that the impediment is not the practical difficulties involved with a blind person's service at the altar; it is because the person is imperfect and therefore must not be allowed to "profane" the sanctuary.

This combination of (1) physical suffering and constant difficulty, (2) the shadow of sin, and (3) for the Jewish person, belonging among the oddities and freaks, a ritually "blemished" person, conveys something of the miserable situation of the person who was blind.

To Be a Beggar

προσαίτης

a beggar

While scholars often note the poverty of a beggar, there has been less attention to the social reaction to them, which amounted to disgust, especially toward those who were insistent, loud, and impertinent.

It is his being a beggar that distinguishes Bartimaeus from the blind man of Bethsaida (Mark 8:22–26), who has friends to intercede for him. Bartimaeus is without such friends to petition for him. Like the leper of Mark 1:40–44, who is also outside society's circles, he must fend for himself.

Without friends or caring family, a blind person's natural recourse would be to begging. A society that offered no financial help of any kind left the person dependent on alms. The social perception of beggars was that they were parasites. As early as the *Odyssey*, the rough manner in which beggars were treated is seen in the way the disguised Odysseus, dressed as a beggar, enters his own banquet hall where the many suitors of his wife, Penelope, dine: "Clad in mean raiment, in the likeness of a woeful and aged beggar, leaning on a staff, and miserable was the raiment that he wore about his body; and . . . even those that were older men, . . . assailed him with evil words and with missiles" (Homer, Od. 24.155). [32]

Plato's *Laws* reason that no beggar deserves pity, but only a virtuous person struck by some calamity. Then the state should give assistance.

---

[32] Homer, *Odyssey* (trans. A. T. Murray; 2 vols.; London: Heinemann, 1919), 2:413.

The man who suffers from hunger or the like is not the man who deserves pity, but he who, while possessing temperance or virtue of some sort, or a share thereof, gains in addition evil fortune; wherefore it would be a strange thing indeed if in a polity and State that is even moderately well organised, a man of this kind (be he slave or free man) should be so entirely neglected as to come to utter beggary. Wherefore the Lawgiver will be safe in enacting for such cases some such law as this:— There shall be no beggar in our State; and if anyone attempts to beg, and to collect a livelihood by ceaseless prayers, the market-stewards shall expel him from the market, and the Board of city-stewards from the city, and from any other district he shall be driven across the border by the country-stewards, to the end that the land may be wholly purged of such a creature. (Plato, *Leg.* 11.936b–c)[33]

In his comedy *Trinummus*, Plautus skewers the uncompassionate wealthy persons of Athens through his character Philto, a wealthy father who rebuffs his softhearted son, Lysiteles, for wanting to give money to a beggar. When the young man explains that the man lost his money through a combination of kindheartedness and self-indulgence, the father replies, "You do a beggar bad service by giving him food and drink; you lose what you give and prolong his life for more misery. I say this not because I am unwilling to do what you wish and do it gladly: but when I apply these words to that somebody of yours, I forewarn you to pity others in such a way as not to let others pity you." When Lysiteles answers, "But I should feel disgraced to desert him in misfortune and be a helpgrudger," Philto replies, "Better to feel disgraced than disgusted" (*Trin.*, act 2, scene 2, lines 339–46).[34]

In the first century, the social attitude toward beggars is shown in Epictetus's criticism of Cynics who reduce themselves to destitution: "But a Cynic who excites pity [literally, 'mercy'] is regarded as a beggar; everybody turns away from him, everybody takes offence at him" (*Diatr.* 3.22.89).[35] As a second witness, Artemidorus comments, "In this respect beggars are most repugnant and helpless. There is nothing

[33] Plato, *Laws* (trans. R. G. Bury; 2 vols.; LCL; London: Heinemann, 1926), 2:465.

[34] Plautus, *Trinummus*, in vol. 5 of *Plautus* (trans. Paul Nixon; LCL; London: Heinemann, 1912), 131.

[35] Epictetus, "On the Calling of a Cynic," in *The Discourses as Reported by Arrian, the Manual, and Fragments* (trans. W. A. Oldfather; 2 vols.; LCL; Cambridge, Mass.: Harvard University Press, 1959–1961), 2:161–63.

wholesome about them and they block the course of every undertaking." (*Onir.* 3.53).[36]

Is this ignominy of the beggar the reason why, when he joins Mark's two stories about blind men—the man from Bethsaida (Mark 8:22–26) and Bartimaeus (Mark 10:46–52)—Matthew removes "beggar"? Does Matthew want to forestall the negative reaction of his listeners to these petitioners?

ἐκάθητο παρὰ τὴν ὁδόν

was sitting by the roadside

Beggars must choose sites in the city that experience the most traffic, such as bridges if there are any,[37] the marketplaces, and certainly the city gates. For the blind beggars, the city gates are a sensible choice because they could stay just to one side of the traffic, where they would be visible and near enough to receive alms but still removed from the danger of being struck by pedestrians carrying bundles, litters being carried in the streets, and carts moving merchandise to market. Their own movement was very constricted. Here we recall Teiresias's description of the blind Oedipus, "feeling the ground before him with his staff" (*Oed. tyr.* 450). This certainly would be true with regard to the city of Jericho, which was a larger city by first-century standards.[38]

III. BARTIMAEUS PETITIONS JESUS

The Characterization of Bartimaeus

[47]καὶ ἀκούσας ὅτι Ἰησοῦς ὁ Ναζαρηνός ἐστιν ἤρξατο κράζειν καὶ λέγειν· υἱὲ Δαυίδ Ἰησοῦ, ἐλέησόν με.

---

[36] Artemidorus Daldianus, *Onir.* 3.53. Translation by Dr. Gregory W. Dobrov, Loyola University, Chicago, Illinois.

[37] See references in Martial, *Ep.* 12.32.25.

[38] In fact, Josephus describes Jericho's warm climate being such that Herod the Great chose to pass the winters there, away from the damp and cold of Jerusalem. Upon returning from Rome, Herod had erected a number of buildings in Jericho so that it bore something of the appearance of Pompeii. Jericho also was wealthy because the oasis provided abundant fruit, balsam in particular. This made Jericho a center for both medicine and beauty products (Josephus, *J.W.* 4.459–75).

⁴⁷When he heard that it was Jesus of Nazareth, he began to shout out and say, "Jesus, Son of David, have mercy on me!"

The particular characterization of Bartimaeus begins with his raucous yelling to Jesus. He must remain stationary because unlike sighted beggars, who can target people and follow them to wheedle alms, blind beggars cannot see who is passing and must remain out of the way so as not to be injured. Thus, the blind beggar at the side of the road must scream to catch the attention of the passersby if they hope to be heard above the noise and be seen by the distracted travelers.

What Does Bartimaeus Intend by "Son of David"?

υἱὲ Δαυίδ Ἰησοῦ

"Jesus, Son of David"

Bruce Chilton proposes that Bartimaeus's epithet for Jesus, "Son of David," is a reference to Solomon, who was known for his successful exorcisms and in time took on the reputation of as healer as well. Jesus as Son of David, then, suggests that he is the new Solomon, certainly in the Davidic line.³⁹ Chilton is largely dependent on the work of Dennis Duling, whose article on ancient references to Solomon and the "Son of David" title⁴⁰ concludes with an appeal to scholars not to banish the possibility that just such a reference is intended here. Where Duling differs from Chilton, however, is in his admission that "never is 'Son of David' used here [i.e., for Solomon] absolutely or as a form of address in the New Testament; rather it appears more as an additional clarification of descent, as in the wisdom literature and some passages of the Testament of Solomon."⁴¹ Moreover, and very importantly, he sees the pattern that whenever Solomon is called "Son of David" in Jewish sources, it is always with his own name accompanying it, modifying it.⁴² Thus, if "Son of David" was intended to mean that Jesus was like

---

³⁹ Bruce Chilton, "Jesus ben David: Reflections on the Davidssohnfrage," *JSNT* 14 (1982): 88–112. See also Paul J. Achtemeier, *Mark* (PC; Philadelphia: Fortress), 44–45.

⁴⁰ Dennis Duling, "Solomon, Exorcism and the Son of David," *HTR* 68 (1975): 235–52.

⁴¹ Ibid., 247.

⁴² Ibid.

Solomon, there are not enough cues to the listener. But Chilton's point that the story places Jesus in the Davidic line is well noted, and it may well be that the pre-Markan community intended the listeners familiar with Jewish Scriptures to recall God's promise to David in 1 Chr 17:14.

Robert Gundry has objected to this interpretation because if we excise Solomon, we have here a military reference, and there are no obvious political markers on the story.[43] One could observe, however, that David represents more than only the political. Ancient sagas underline God's love of him and a covenant of blessing for his offspring due to that mutual love.

It is plain from the narrative here that Bartimaeus is not supposed to notice how true his epithet of honor really is, for when he reaches Jesus, the "Son of David" title disappears, and, as we have noted, he addresses Jesus simply as "Rabbouni." This means that the listener is to understand Bartimaeus's shouts of "Son of David" in another way.

Beggars as Flatterers

Sighted or not, beggars were notorious for their outrageous flattery. Dio Chrysostom reports what he has heard, since, of course, he would not be mingling with the riff-raff on the street: "Beggars of the present time, however, tell nothing but lies, we are told, and nobody would accept the evidence of any of them on any matter whatsoever or receive their praise as sincere. *For everyone knows that they are compelled to cajole in all they say*" (*Troj.* 15–16).[44]

This is just the sort of behavior that the narrator presents here. All Bartimaeus is told is that "Jesus of Nazareth" passing by. This title for Jesus represents the simplest identification.[45] When the blind beggar Bartimaeus begins shouting, "Jesus, Son of David, have mercy on me!" the first-time listener would be quick to identify him with the usual unsavory crowd of beggars continually assaulting ordinary people with their raucous praises. Of course, the irony not to be missed is that the royal epithet that he has chosen happens to be true.

---

[43] Gundry, *Mark*, 601.

[44] Dio Chrysostom, *The Eleventh, or Trojan, Discourse*, in *Discourses 1–11* (trans. J. W. Cohoon; LCL; London: Heinemann, 1932), 457 (my italics).

[45] Matt 26:71; Mark 1:24 // Luke 4:34; Mark 10:47 // Luke 18:37; Mark 16:6; Luke 24:19; John 18:5, 7; 19:19; Acts 2:22; 6:14; 10:38; 22:8; 26:9.

Robert Gundry understands Bartimaeus's call to Jesus as the narrator's effort to allude to the psalms: "Bartimaeus uses an OT-like plea to God for mercy, but redirects it to Jesus."[46] But Gundry is unable to explain why Bartimaeus drops the title when he finally reaches Jesus and there addresses him with the simple "Rabbouni."

The presentation of Bartimaeus is meant to present to the listener the usual loud and raucous, flattering and pestering beggar.

ἐλέησόν με.

"Have mercy on me."

Most listeners would understand Bartimaeus's shouts for "mercy" as shouts for money. Epictetus's description of Cynics making themselves so destitute as to make people think they are beggars was presented above to establish the fact of social scorn of beggars. The Greek text reads ἐλεούμενος δὲ Κυνικὸς ἐπαίτης and is, as we saw above, translated by W. A. Oldfather as "a Cynic who excites pity." The participle ἐλεούμενος, which Oldfather translates as exciting "pity," actually indicates exciting "mercy." The idea here is that arousing mercy will result in alms, handouts. The first-time listener has every reason to conclude that Bartimaeus is targeting Jesus for alms.

[48]καὶ ἐπετίμων αὐτῷ πολλοὶ ἵνα σιωπήσῃ· ὁ δὲ πολλῷ μᾶλλον ἔκραζεν· υἱὲ Δαυίδ, ἐλέησόν με.

Many sternly ordered him to be quiet, but he cried out even more loudly, "Son of David, have mercy on me!"

In this verse, the response of the "many" reflects the normal reaction of people raised with social grace. Those loud screams of Bartimaeus together with the embarrassing flattery shouted out in the open street are irksome. Theophrastus's treatment of "The Boorish Person" includes the example "he talks in too loud a voice" (*Char.* 4.1),[47] and in "The Obnoxious Person," "he calls out by name to someone in the crowd with whom he is not acquainted" (*Char.* 11.4).[48]

---

[46] Gundry, *Mark*, 600.

[47] Theophrastus, *Characters* (trans. Jeffrey Rusten; LCL; Cambridge: Mass.: Harvard University Press, 1993), 64–65.

[48] Ibid., 94–95.

In such a stratified society, not all boorish and/or obnoxious persons could be rebuked, and certainly not in public if they came from important families or were accompanied by prestigious friends. Bartimaeus can be rebuked in public because he is a person without honor and behaving in a shameless way.[49]

ὁ δὲ πολλῷ μᾶλλον ἔκραζεν· υἱὲ Δαυίδ ἐλέησόν με.

But he cried out even more loudly, "Son of David, have mercy on me!"

Here is the place where Bartimaeus shows his disregard of the niceties of social conventions in his fierce determination for Jesus to hear him before he is too far away. Bartimaeus does not reply to the crowd's obstructive rebukes, but simply ignores them. Knowing that with every second, Jesus moves farther away from him, and not knowing how far that is, Bartimaeus increases the volume of his screams, which include his princely title for Jesus. This movement of the anecdote is designed to reinforce the first-time listener's aversion to incorrigible beggars, and, in this case, one who insists on his high-flown flattery.

The Characterization of Jesus

[49]καὶ στὰς ὁ Ἰησοῦς εἶπεν· φωνήσατε αὐτόν. καὶ φωνοῦσιν τὸν τυφλὸν λέγοντες αὐτῷ· θάρσει, ἔγειρε, φωνεῖ σε.

Jesus stood still and said, "Call him here." And they called the blind man, saying to him, "Take heart; get up, he is calling you."

καὶ στὰς ὁ Ἰησοῦς εἶπεν· φωνήσατε αὐτόν.

Jesus stood still and said, "Call him here."

The story shows that Bartimaeus was right to increases the volume of his shouts, because otherwise Jesus would not have heard him. It also

---

[49] Euripides, in his play *Helen*, attests the disrespectful way in which beggars were treated, when Menelaus, shipwrecked and destitute, arrives at the rich house of Helen only to be refused entrance by the old lady who is the gatekeeper. He tells Helen, "I was driven from them [the gates of the house] like a beggar" (*Helen; Phoenician Women; Orestes* [vol. 5 of *Euripides*; trans. David Kovacs; LCL; Cambridge, Mass.: Harvard University Press, 2002], 709).

explains why Bartimaeus did not receive an immediate reply from Jesus, something that otherwise might have been assumed by the listener to be the result of the beggar's coarse shouts. That Jesus responds once he has passed the man is unique. Robert Gundry surely is right that Jesus' decision to stop and have the people call Bartimaeus is a clear sign of his own regard for the man's needs,[50] and this indeed does stand in absolute contradiction to the way ordinary society regarded and treated beggars. I have never found any instance in ancient storytelling where anyone, having already passed the site of beggars, stopped upon hearing their cries and commanded those nearby to summon one of them. This would be quite astonishing for the first-time listener, as the social views of beggars shown above make plain.

The large flow of traffic coming out of the city makes it simpler for Bartimaeus to follow the flow to Jesus than for Jesus to try to go against it. Thus, he asks the people around him to call the man to come through to him. No one can miss the irony in the fact that those who represent social propriety and tried to silence Bartimaeus will play the role of intermediary between Bartimaeus and Jesus precisely because the man did not listen to their annoyed rebukes, and because Jesus was not annoyed at all, as he shows.

καὶ φωνοῦσιν τὸν τυφλὸν λέγοντες αὐτῷ· θάρσει, ἔγειρε, φωνεῖ σε.

And they called the blind man, saying to him, "Take heart; get up, he is calling you."

Robert Gundry has proposed that Jesus' command to the people imposes his authority on them to accept Bartimaeus.[51] What is being presented here by the people's response is not a reluctant people under orders, but rather a surprised and excited group. Indeed, they probably mirror the surprise of the first-time listener. In all ancient writings, crowds are thought to be fickle, changeable, and that is what we see here. One minute following the conventions of excluding people such as Bartimaeus, the next minute they are exuberant as Jesus shows that he is not at all offended and wants to see this man. Their θάρσει ("take heart") at the very beginning of their address conveys sincere happiness at Bartimaeus's amazing good fortune.

---

[50] Gundry, *Mark*, 594.
[51] Ibid.

Building the Characterization of Bartimaeus

⁵⁰ὁ δὲ ἀποβαλὼν τὸ ἱμάτιον αὐτοῦ ἀναπηδήσας ἦλθεν πρὸς τὸν Ἰησοῦν.

⁵⁰So throwing off his cloak [*himation*], he sprang up and came to Jesus.

What Significance Is There in Bartimaeus's Throwing Off His Himation?

The *himation* is an outer garment, with dimensions very much like those of a sheet for a single bed, that was worn over the tunic when men or women were in public. The usual manner was to loop it diagonally across the body from the left shoulder.[52] Vincent Taylor is puzzled by Bartimaeus's throwing off his *himation* to leap up because "the man would not be wearing his garment but using it to spread out on the ground to receive alms."[53] Taylor's report of this ancient custom has been footnoted by many scholars, but its actual source has proved untraceable. But Taylor's solution to the problem was to suggest that the use of ἀποβαλὼν was meant to indicate "pushing aside." Thus, Bartimaeus "pushed aside" his *himation*, which was spread out in front of him, "and indeed on this interpretation his action is more decisive and dramatic."[54]

Taylor probably was encouraged by the fact that there is a variant for ἀποβαλών ("throwing off") in codex 565 and a few Latin versions, where ἐπιβαλών ("throwing on") occurs. Nevertheless, the lack of more external attestation for ἐπιβαλών leaves ἀποβαλών the reading best attested.

My own suggestion is that Taylor did read that beggars spread out their *himation* around them, but that they were sighted beggars. The blind need to feel the money in their hand or in a receptacle that they

---

[52] For a treatment of the *himation* (= Roman *pallium*) and its presence in Jewish representation from the Greco-Roman period, see Alfred Rubens, "Biblical and Talmudic Periods," in *A History of Jewish Costume* (New York: Funk & Wagnalls, 1967), 5–28, esp. 13–18, and fig. 13.

[53] Taylor, *St. Mark*, 449. See also Morna D. Hooker, *A Commentary on the Gospel according to St. Mark* (BNTC; London: A & C Black, 1991), 253; Gundry, *Mark*, 602.

[54] Taylor, *St. Mark*, 449.

hold. They cannot rely on knowing when a coin might fall on a *hima-tion* spread out in front of them, and one cannot discount the possibility of other needy, sighted persons pouncing on the alms and running off through the crowds. The narrator gives us the impression that as Barti-maeus sat, he was wearing his *himation*.

Ancient paintings and sketches of men wearing a *himation* while sitting or reclining show that the garment was allowed to open more loosely in the front, with folds falling naturally across the body.[55] If pass-ersby threw coins onto those folds, the beggar would feel it.

The Interpretation of the Himation *as Symbolic*

Some scholars see Bartimaeus's flinging off his *himation* as a sign of his readiness to give up all that he has to follow Jesus, just as Simon and Andrew, James and John had left their boats (Mark 1:16–20), and Levi his tax booth (Mark 2:14). For example, J. Dupont brings out the singular importance of Bartimaeus's *himation* by noting that Exod 22:25–26 and Deut 24:12–13 forbid anyone taking a person's *himation* as surety on a loan. For Dupont, Bartimaeus is throwing away a sym-bol of everything important that he owns. Second, the *himation* is also symbolic of "the old man," as Paul would say it, and thus the action is a kind of baptism:

> Comment ne serait-on frappé par ce geste du mendicant qui commence par se débarrasser de ce qui constitue son unique bien?... Cet "abandon" avait déjà été souligné par l'évangéliste dans son récit de la vocation des premiers disciples (1:18, 20). Un rapprochement s'impose aussi avec la catéchèse baptismale qui soulignait le symbolisme du fait qu'on devait quitter ses vétements pour entrer dans l'eau du baptême (Rm 13,12; Ep 4,22.25; Col 3,8; He 12,1; Jc 1,21; 1 P 2,1; 2 P 1,14). Dans ce contexte, le geste de Bartimée deviant une illustration du dépouillement du "vieil homme" que réclame la condition du disciple.[56]

---

[55] See, for example, an illustration of a man seated whose *himation* is al-lowed to drape around his body (David J. Symons, *Costume of Ancient Greece* [London: Batsford, 1987], 36–37, esp. 37, fig. 56).

[56] J. Dupont, "L'aveugle de Jericho recouvre la vue et suit Jesus (Marc 10,46–52)," *Revue Africaine de théologie* 8, no. 16 (1984): 176. See also Christo-pher D. Marshall, *Faith as a Theme in Mark's Narrative* (SNTSMS 84; Cam-bridge: Cambridge University Press, 1988), 141. Note also Morna Hooker's comment, "Like others who are called by Jesus, he abandons everything he has (cf. 1:18, 20; 2:14; 10:21, 28)" (*St. Mark*, 253).

Dupont's theory is based on this narrative being a call story, and the problem is that the internal evidence to support such a theory is lacking, as discussed above.

The Himation *as Proper Dress for a Man in Public*

The meaning of Bartimaeus's action is actually explained in relation to his other bold and irrepressible behavior. In both Hellenistic and Roman cultures, it was expected that once in public, a proper man was to wear a *himation* over his tunic. In fact, both Greek and Latin describe a man's failure to do so as rendering him γυμνός/*nudus* ("naked").[57] The wearing of a tunic alone was acceptable when working in a shop or on the land.[58] It does not require an explanation of how impractical the *himation* would be in these circumstances. In public, however, the tunic was insufficient. This was the same for Jews as well as Gentiles. Lucille Roussin notes, "Worn over the man's tunic was a mantle, the *tallit*, equivalent to the Roman *pallium* and the Greek *himation*. The sources describe proper dress for going out in public, 'Dressed in *haluq* [tunic] and wrapped in a *tallit* [*himation*].'"[59] Here it is perhaps pertinent to

---

[57] See the treatment of *nudus*/γυμνός in William Smith, *Dictionary of Greek and Roman Antiquities* (Boston: Little, Brown, 1859), 409. There, Smith refers to Hesiod's description of a farmer plowing, sowing, and reaping while being γυμνός (Hesiod, *Op.* 391), the phrase repeated in Latin by Virgil (*Georg.* 1.299), not that the man is working in the fields without wearing any clothes, but rather clad only in a tunic. Smith notes the usage in the account of Cincinnatus learning that he had been named dictator by the senate. He was found by the messenger, plowing his four-acre farm "nudo," and he was asked to clothe and present himself to the senate, whereupon he put on his toga (Livy, *Hist.* 3.26.9; Pliny the Elder, *Nat.* 18.4). Smith provides a sketch from an ancient Roman carving that depicts a man wearing only a tunic as he uses a plow drawn by two oxen. See also "γυμνός," BAGD 167, where, after the first meaning, "stripped bare," the second reads, "without an outer garment, without which a decent person did not appear in public." Note also: "the familiar sense of γυμνός = 'with only the χιτών' comes out well in the PMagd 6.7 (iii/B.C) ὡς ἤμην γυμνὸς ὑπ' αὐ[τῶν: the complainant had been stripped of his ἱμάτιον" ("γυμνός," MM 33).

[58] For example, Odysseus, in recounting his adventures says, "Thoas, son of Andraimon, threw off his *himation* and set out running to the ships whereupon I took the *himation* and lay in it comfortably till morning" (Homer, *Odyssey* 14.500 [London: Heinemann, 1919], 2:71).

[59] Lucille A. Roussin, "Costume in Roman Palestine: Archeological Remains and the Evidence from the Mishnah," in *The World of Roman Costume*

notice that Jesus' attire in public references the *himation* (Mark 5:27, 28, 30; 6:56; 9:3; 15:20, 24).[60]

In the light of this social custom, the narrator's detail that Bartimaeus "threw off" his *himation* is intended to bring out how Bartimaeus refused to allow social niceties to obstruct him. Instead of leaping up and adjusting his *himation* so that he could present himself to Jesus properly, he chose to be free of its hobbling effects and reach Jesus as soon as he could. So, this boldness fits in with every other manifestation of Bartimaeus's character.

ἀναπηδήσας ἦλθεν πρὸς τὸν Ἰησοῦν.

He sprang up and came to Jesus.

Beggars' clothes are described, conventionally, as filthy rags and disgusting.[61] The imagination of the listeners would supply the image

---

(ed. Judith Lynn Sebesta and Larissa Bonfante; Madison: University of Wisconsin, 1994), 182–90, esp. 184. Roussin references *t. Ṭohor.* 8:13.

[60] This also helps to explain the dramatic statement being made when men remove their *himation* to place it along the way where a hero will travel. One has stripped, so to speak, in order to accommodate the passage of one who is exalted. In 2 Kgs 9:13, the people take off their outer garments and lay them on the steps where the Lord's newly appointed king, Jehu, will pass. In Plutarch's *Life of Cato the Younger*, the soldiers spread their cloaks on the passageway where their much beloved and retiring leader Cato will pass (Plutarch, *Life of Cato the Younger* 8.12). This also helps to contextualize the degree of honor afforded Jesus when the people lay down their outer garments along the road before him as he enters Jerusalem (Mark 11:8).

[61] The conventional appearance of a beggar in any of the literature always stipulates rags for clothes, and often there is direct reference to filth. In Homer's *Odyssey*, Athena disguises Odysseus as a beggar: "She withered the fair skin on his supple limbs, and destroyed the flaxen hair from off his head, and about all his limbs she put the skin of an aged old man. And she dimmed his two eyes that were before so beautiful, and clothed him in other raiment, a vile ragged cloak and a tunic, tattered garments and foul, begrimed with filthy smoke. And about him she cast the great skin of a swift hind, stripped of the hair, and she gave him a staff, and a miserable wallet, full of holes, slung by a twisted cord" (*Od.* 13.431–38) (Homer, *Odyssey* [trans. A. T. Murray; 2 vols., LCL; London: Heinemann, 1931], 2:33). And again, as one of several more references, Odysseus responds to the insulting servant Melantho, "Is it because I am foul and wear mean raiment on my body, and beg through the land?" (*Od.* 19.72–73) (Homer, *Odyssey* [trans. Murray], 2:233–35). As a second example, in Sophocles' *Oedipus at Colonus*, Polyneices, Oedipus's son, upon arriving and seeing his

of a man presenting himself to Jesus γυμνός, in nothing but a tunic, in disgusting condition.

IV. THE RESPONSE OF JESUS

Jesus and Bartimaeus Meet

⁵¹καὶ ἀποκριθεὶς αὐτῷ ὁ Ἰησοῦς εἶπεν τί σοι θέλεις ποιήσω; ὁ δὲ τυφλὸς εἶπεν αὐτῷ· ραββουνί, ἵνα ἀναβλέψω.

⁵¹Then Jesus said to him, "What do you want me to do for *you?*"[62] The blind man said to him, "My teacher,[63] let me see again."

A Further Characterization of Jesus

This moment of the encounter holds a great deal of teaching value for the would-be follower of Jesus. In front of Jesus is the bold Bartimaeus, γυμνός in his filthy rag of a tunic. Most listeners would presume that his shouts for mercy are now going to result in a plea for alms. Jesus' question shows that he does not share any such presumption. His

---

father's condition laments, "Ah me, my sisters, shall I first lament / My own afflictions, or my aged sire's, / Whom here I find a castaway, with you, / In a strange land, an ancient beggar clad / In antic tatters, marring all his frame, / While o'er the sightless orbs his unkempt locks / Float in the breeze; and, as it were to match, / He bears a wallet against hunger's pinch" (*Oed. col.* 1254–60) (*Oedipus at Colonus*, in vol. 1 of *Sophocles* [trans. F. Storr; LCL; Cambridge, Mass.: Harvard University Press, 1962], 265). Ragged clothing on beggars is so common as to be suitable for a metaphor, as shown in Sophocles' *Philoctetes* where Philoctetes, describing the sailors' abandonment of him, says that they "sailed away, flinging me, as they went, some cast-off rags, a beggar's alms" (*Phil.* 270) (*Philoctetes*, in vol. 2 of *Sophocles* [trans. F. Storr; LCL; London: Heinemann; New York: Macmillan, 1913], 389).

[62] My italics are to emphasize that the Greek word σοι ("for you") is not grammatically necessary. Its presence results in a special emphasis on the person of Bartimaeus.

[63] "Rabbouni" is an affectionate form of the Hebrew word *rabbi*, "my teacher." The rabbinical movement did not begin until after the fall of Jerusalem in 70 C.E., and this story predates that event by at least twenty years. No "rabbis" as post–70 C.E. Judaism would develop the title were known at the time of the composition of this account.

question to Bartimaeus is phrased so that he asks what the man wants him to *do*, and there is the inclusion of the unnecessary σοι ("for you"), which emphasizes the particular importance of Bartimaeus's wishes. Jesus has not been offended by Bartimaeus's shouting or by his appearance. Jesus is concerned only about the reason for his shouts, the desire to do whatever he can for him. Already this reception of the man shows Jesus' *praos* ("meekness") and *epieikia* ("understanding").

The Final Piece in the Characterization of Bartimaeus

51bὁ δὲ τυφλὸς εἶπεν αὐτῷ· ῥαββουνί, ἵνα ἀναβλέψω.

51bThe blind man said to him, "My teacher, let me see again."

True to his characterization throughout the anecdote, Bartimaeus shows that same boldness and direct focus, but with no more overt behavior. Instead, his request is simple and astonishing: ῥαββουνί, ἵνα ἀναβλέψω ("My teacher, let me see again").

The use of the address "Rabbouni" for Jesus is unique in this Gospel. The honorific "Rabbi," another form of "my teacher" (διδάσκαλος), is twice used by Peter to address Jesus (Mark 9:5; 11:21), and once by Judas as he pretends a disciple's reverence but betrays his master (Mark 14:45). But in all of the New Testament canon, "Rabbouni" is found again only in Mary Magdalene's greeting to the resurrected Jesus (John 20:16). There seems to be no firm agreement on whether the title is Aramaic or just a variation of "Rabbi." Does this form suggest endearment? Robert Gundry has proposed that since rabbinic documents largely reserve the title for God, the use of it here may be an attestation to Jesus' divinity.[64] Bartimaeus's actions, however, do not lead to that conclusion. Surely, the narrator would have Bartimaeus prostrate himself and would include some epithet greater than "Rabbouni" if the listener were meant to understand that address as a more overt indication of the divinity of Jesus. Rather, the title "Rabbouni" seems better connected to the simple "Jesus of Nazareth" title. Both of these seem to fit together quite well. Bartimaeus seems confident that Jesus has the gift of healing, and he has confidence in Jesus' care. Dupont effectively captures the aura of the address when he describes it as one of "un pro-

---

[64] Gundry, *Mark*, 602.

found respect mais se colore d'une nuance d'intimité." The enormity
of what Bartimaeus asks for is contained in one verb: ἀναβλέψω ("I
might see again"). Again Dupont's comment seems to express best the
narrator's intention: "le ton est devenu celui d'une confiance humble
et audacieuse."[65] Humble confidence and audaciousness combine. He
is indeed "audacious," since medical texts of the day have no remedies
for loss of sight.[66] This was an extraordinary request indeed. The gift of
sight, or restored sight, does belong to those who have a divine power,
of course. In the Greek world, it is Asclepius who is most frequently
associated with a miracle of this kind.[67]

In the Jewish traditions, the only story of miraculous restoration of
sight occurs in the book of Tobit, where, through the agency of God's
angel Raphael, the cure is effected by a special mixture applied to the
eyes of Tobit (Tob 11:7, 9–15; 14:2).[68] This request by Bartimaeus is
breathtaking in its boldness.

---

[65] Dupont, "L'aveugle de Jericho," 175.

[66] To keep away opthamalia, Pliny the Elder reports that applying saliva
every morning as an eye ointment is employed (*Nat.* 28.7), and another cure
for dry opthamalia is to place a burnt loin of pork on the eye, or to follow the
custom of she-goats and gazelles, which never suffer from dry opthamalia, and
consume herbs or pellets of their dung coated in wax (*Nat.* 28.47).

[67] "To Valerius Aper, a blind soldier, the god revealed that he should go
and take the blood of a white cock along with honey and compound an eye
salve and for three days should apply it to his eyes. And he could see again
[ἀνέβλεψεν] and went and publicly offered thanks to the god" (*IG* 14.966 [second century C.E.]) (Emma J. Edelstein and Ludwig Edelstein, *Asclepius: Collection and Interpretation of the Testimonies* [Baltimore: Johns Hopkins University
Press, 1998], 250 n. 438). Other examples include Ambrosia, who doubted the
god's power, and then in her dream was visited by Asclepius, who demanded
a silver pig as an offering for her offense. Then, in the dream, he cut out her
eyeball and applied medications, and she awoke with full sight (*IG* 4.1.121–22)
(Edelstein and Edelstein, *Asclepius*, 230 n. 4). Alcetas of Haleis was visited in a
dream by the god, who opened his eyes with his fingers (*IG* 4.1.121–22) (Edelstein and Edelstein, *Asclepius*, 233 n. 18.). Aside from certain diverse oracles that
communicate the way the sufferer is to be healed (e.g., Herodotus, *Hist.* 2.111),
intervention by a deity for miraculous healing rests with Asclepius.

[68] "Raphael [God's angel] said to Tobias, before he had approached his
father, 'I know that his eyes will be opened. Smear the gall of the fish on his
eyes; the medicine will make the white films shrink and peel off from his eyes
and your father will regain his sight and see the light.' . . . Then Tobit [Tobias's
blinded father] got up and came stumbling out through the courtyard door.
Tobias went up to him with the gall of the fish in his hand, and holding him

The Final Piece in the Characterization of Jesus

⁵²καὶ ὁ Ἰησοῦς εἶπεν αὐτῷ· ὕπαγε, ἡ πίστις σου σέσωκέν σε. καὶ εὐθὺς ἀνέβλεψεν.

⁵²And Jesus said to him, "Go; your faith has made you well." And immediately he regained his sight.

The astonishing request made by Bartimaeus is swiftly, easily granted to him by Jesus. He modestly attributes this enormous miracle to the strength of Bartimaeus's faith. "Faith" is how Jesus sees the blind man's readiness to endure the displeasure of the crowds, to ignore those who tried to silence him, to increase his call to Jesus, to be determined to reach Jesus as soon as possible, to throw off the confining *himation* deemed proper by society. In a way, then, Bartimaeus is the incongruous ideal for the listener. The narrator is saying that Jesus saw in Bartimaeus the most admirable conviction and unshakeable resolve. Yet, the behavior that expressed it completely conflicts with what is considered refined and worthy of praise. Even Bartimaeus himself, from the bottom rung of society, is held up by Jesus as a model.

This story shows a Jesus who sees through social strata and social convention and looks straight through to the heart. Bartimaeus holds Jesus' admiration.

CONCLUSION

It is indisputable that Bartimaeus overpowers this story, and this study has shown the ways in which he offended social sensibilities over and over again. The narrator has presented him in such a way as to engage stereotypical judgments on blind beggars. The actions of Jesus directly challenge the attitudes of the conventional first-century listener.

---

firmly, he blew into his eyes, saying, 'Take courage, father.' With this he applied the medicine on his eyes, and it made them smart. Next, with both his hands he peeled off the white films from the corners of his eyes. Then Tobit saw his son and threw his arms around him, and the wept and said to him, 'I see you, my son, the light of my eyes!' The he said, 'Blessed be God, and blessed be his great name, and blessed be all his holy angels. May his holy name be blessed throughout all the ages. Though he afflicted me, he has had mercy upon me. Now I see my son Tobias!'" (Tob 11:7, 9–15).

His behavior teaches *epieikia*, a true fairness and understanding, and profound *philanthrōpia*. More, Jesus holds up Bartimaeus's determination and readiness to ignore social rules if they obstruct anyone in the way to God. To hold up Bartimaeus's courage and faith as a model is also to reject stratification of persons and prejudicial judgments on those who are reduced to live in filth and poverty. Thus, it is not only Jesus' *philanthrōpia*, *praos*, and *epieikia* that are modeled here for the would-be follower, but also the boldness of Bartimaeus in the actual practical ramifications of them.

Part II

*Petitioners Who Ask
on Behalf of Others*

3

Jesus and the Friends of the Paralytic (Mark 2:1–12)

"Those who are gravely paralyzed in all their limbs are as a rule quickly carried off, but if not so carried off, some may live a long while, yet rarely however regain health. Mostly they drag out a miserable existence, their memory lost also." (Celsus, *Med.* 3.27)

In the Markan Gospel, the story of Jesus' healing of the paralytic, with its internal controversy defending his authority to forgive sins, is the first unit of a cluster of controversies (Mark 2:1–3:6) in which Jesus is challenged by the authorities for his behavior and his permissions: (1) Jesus' authority on earth to forgive sins shocking the scribes (Mark 2:1–12); (2) Jesus' call of a tax collector, Levi, to discipleship and then eating with tax collectors and sinners challenged by the "scribes" of the Pharisees (Mark 2:13–17); (3) Jesus' failing to teach his disciples to fast questioned by an unnamed group (Mark 2:18–22); (4) Jesus' allowing his disciples to make a path through the grain questioned by the Pharisees (Mark 2:23–28); (5) Jesus' restoration of a man's withered hand on the Sabbath condemned by the Pharisees (Mark 3:1–6).[1]

---

[1] It is by no means certain that Mark 3:1–6 belongs to the pre-Markan stratum. Unlike the other controversy stories of the collection, the form in this account is irregular: (1) The activity of healing on the Sabbath is not described but is raised as a possibility by Jesus' foes (v. 1). (2) The enemies, the Pharisees, are not identified until v. 6, but must be deduced from the previous account of Mark 2:23–28 as the referent for "they." Thus, the account relies on the previous story and cannot be considered a discrete pronouncement story. (3) The question is posed not by the enemies but by Jesus (v. 4). (4) There is no pronouncement. The Pharisees maintain a silence that proves their bad faith: they do not actually care if the Sabbath is violated. Rather, the focus is

To examine the pre-Markan account of the healing of the paralytic in Mark 2:1–12 separately from the light cast on it by its place in the Markan Gospel, as well as the influence of the cluster that it now heads, it is necessary first to examine the text for signs of internal Markan redaction.

I. MARK 2:1–12: SIGNS OF MARKAN REDACTION

¹καὶ εἰσελθὼν πάλιν εἰς Καφαρναοὺμ δι' ἡμερῶν ἠκούσθη ὅτι ἐν οἴκῳ ἐστίν ²καὶ συνήχθησαν πολλοί ὥστε μηκέτι χωρεῖν μηδὲ τὰ πρὸς τὴν θύραν, καὶ ἐλάλει αὐτοῖς τὸν λόγον. ³καὶ ἔρχονται φέροντες πρὸς αὐτὸν παραλυτικὸν αἰρόμενον ὑπὸ τεσσάρων. ⁴καὶ μὴ δυνάμενοι προσενέγκαι αὐτῷ διὰ τὸν ὄχλον ἀπεστέγασαν τὴν στέγην ὅπου ἦν, καὶ ἐξορύξαντες χαλῶσι τὸν κράβαττον ὅπου ὁ παραλυτικὸς κατέκειτο. ⁵καὶ ἰδὼν ὁ Ἰησοῦς τὴν πίστιν αὐτῶν λέγει τῷ παραλυτικῷ· τέκνον, ἀφίενταί σου αἱ ἁμαρτίαι. ⁶ἦσαν δέ τινες τῶν γραμματέων ἐκεῖ καθήμενοι καὶ διαλογιζόμενοι ἐν ταῖς καρδίαις αὐτῶν· ⁷τί οὗτος οὕτως λαλεῖ; βλασφημεῖ· τίς δύναται ἀφιέναι ἁμαρτίας εἰ μὴ εἷς ὁ θεός; ⁸καὶ εὐθὺς ἐπιγνοὺς ὁ Ἰησοῦς τῷ πνεύματι αὐτοῦ ὅτι οὕτως διαλογίζονται ἐν ἑαυτοῖς λέγει αὐτοῖς· τί ταῦτα διαλογίζεσθε ἐν ταῖς καρδίαις ὑμῶν; ⁹τί ἐστιν εὐκοπώτερον, εἰπεῖν τῷ παραλυτικῷ· ἀφίενταί σου αἱ ἁμαρτίαι, ἢ εἰπεῖν· ἔγειρε καὶ ἆρον τὸν κράβαττόν σου καὶ περιπάτει; ¹⁰ἵνα δὲ εἰδῆτε ὅτι ἐξουσίαν ἔχει ὁ υἱὸς τοῦ ἀνθρώπου ἀφιέναι ἁμαρτίας ἐπὶ τῆς γῆς – λέγει τῷ παραλυτικῷ· ¹¹σοὶ λέγω, ἔγειρε ἆρον τὸν κράβαττόν σου καὶ ὕπαγε εἰς τὸν οἶκόν σου. ¹²καὶ ἠγέρθη καὶ εὐθὺς ἄρας τὸν κράβαττον ἐξῆλθεν ἔμπροσθεν πάντων, ὥστε ἐξίστασθαι πάντας καὶ δοξάζειν τὸν θεὸν λέγοντας ὅτι οὕτως οὐδέποτε εἴδομεν.

¹When he returned to Capernaum after some days, it was reported that he was at home. ²So many gathered around that there was no longer room for them, not even in front of the door; and he was speaking the word to them. ³Then some people came, bringing to

---

on their hatred of Jesus. If only Jesus can be accused of wrongdoing, they will be pleased. When Jesus does restore the man's hand, they go out to collude with the Herodians about how to destroy Jesus (v. 6). These irregularities, all of which serve the Markan themes of Jesus' coming crucifixion, point to Markan redaction rather than pre-Markan material. See the thorough discussion in Robert H. Gundry, *Mark: A Commentary on His Apology for the Cross* (Grand Rapids: Eerdmans, 1993), 155–56.

him a paralyzed man, carried by four of them. ⁴And when they could not bring him to Jesus because of the crowd, they removed the roof above him; and after having dug through it, they let down the mat on which the paralytic lay. ⁵When Jesus saw their faith, he said to the paralytic, "Son, your sins are forgiven." ⁶Now some of the scribes were sitting there, questioning in their hearts, ⁷"Why does this fellow speak in this way? It is blasphemy! Who can forgive sins but God alone?" ⁸At once Jesus perceived in his spirit that they were discussing these questions among themselves; and he said to them, "Why do you raise such questions in your hearts? ⁹Which is easier, to say to the paralytic, 'Your sins are forgiven,' or to say, 'Stand up and take your mat and walk'? ¹⁰But so that you may know that the Son of Man has authority on earth to forgive sins"—he said to the paralytic—¹¹"I say, to you, stand up, take your mat and go to your home." ¹²And he stood up, and immediately took the mat and went out before all of them; so that they were all amazed and glorified God, saying, "We have never seen anything like this!"

¹καὶ εἰσελθὼν πάλιν εἰς Καφαρναοὺμ δι' ἡμερῶν ἠκούσθη ὅτι ἐν οἴκῳ ἐστίν.

¹When he returned to Capernaum after some days, it was reported that he was at home.

Although Rudolf Bultmann believes that "here the editorial work can no longer be clearly distinguished from the tradition,"² the fact that these narrative elements are not necessary to the account presumes the Markan placement of the pericope. The notice that Jesus entered Capernaum "again" refers to his first reported visit in Mark 1:23–38, after which Jesus leaves to preach in the synagogues and to perform miracles throughout the countryside (Mark 1:39–45). Second, the idea of the word spreading that Jesus is "at home" belongs to the flow of the Gospel narrative, since Mark has presented the scene of Jesus becoming known to the people of Capernaum in the block of Mark 1:21–34. While Mark usually uses εἰς τὴν οἰκίαν (Mark 1:29; 7:30; 10:10) or ἐν τῇ οἰκίᾳ (Mark 2:15; 6:4; 9:33; 14:3), these other usages describe Jesus entering a house or being in a house, whereas the formulation ἐν οἴκῳ, lacking the article,

---

²Rudolf Bultmann, *The History of the Synoptic Tradition* (trans. John Marsh; Peabody, Mass.: Hendrickson, 1963), 14.

is an expression to indicate that Jesus has been away and is now back, settled in his own quarters.

²καὶ συνήχθησαν πολλοί ὥστε μηκέτι χωρεῖν μηδὲ τὰ πρὸς τὴν θύραν, καὶ ἐλάλει αὐτοῖς τὸν λόγον.

²So many gathered around that there was no longer room for them, not even in front of the door; and he was speaking the word to them.

This verse shows more Markan composition. The gathering of crowds is a feature of Markan redaction,[3] especially in Markan introductions (e.g., Mark 2:13; 3:20; 4:1; 5:21; 6:34; 8:1; 10:1). It might be argued that here the mention of the crowd is necessary because the many people in the house force the paralytic's friends to find another way to Jesus, but that narrative element is already found in v. 4. Moreover, other vocabulary in v. 2a is Markan, such as the use of πολύς in introduction (Mark 6:34; 8:1; superlative πλεῖστος in 4:1), summary (Mark 5:21, 24), and conclusion (Mark 12:37). The detail is is unnecessary, given the pre-Markan core.

καὶ ἐλάλει αὐτοῖς τὸν λόγον

and he spoke the word to them

This expression is Markan, as evinced in his summation of the parable chapter, Mark 4:33: καὶ τοιαύταις παραβολαῖς πολλαῖς ἐλάλει αὐτοῖς τὸν λόγον καθὼς ἠδύνατο ἀκούειν ("and with many such parables *he spoke the word to them* as they were able to hear it"); and again in reporting the first passion prediction, he adds a summary statement, Mark 8:32: καὶ παρρησίᾳ τὸν λόγον ἐλάλει ("and he spoke the word openly"). Mark 2:3–11 holds narrative elements necessary to the logic of the story and give no signs of Markan redaction.

¹²καὶ ἠγέρθη καὶ εὐθὺς ἄρας τὸν κράβαττον ἐξῆλθεν ἔμπροσθεν πάντων, ὥστε ἐξίστασθαι πάντας καὶ δοξάζειν τὸν θεὸν λέγοντας ὅτι οὕτως οὐδέποτε εἴδομεν.

¹²And he stood up, and immediately took the mat and went out before all of them; so that they were all amazed and glorified God, saying, "We have never seen anything like this!"

---

[3] Ibid., 343.

Verse 12a holds the proof of the man's cure. Verse 12b, the exultation of the people, uses a Markan verb, ἐξίστημι ("to be amazed"). It carries the idea of being outside oneself with astonishment, and it may be this excessive character that explains why Matthew deletes every instance of its usage in the Markan Gospel.[4] But the presence of "and glorified God" is not usual to Mark, and it is more likely that Mark inserted ἐξίστημι into a response that featured an acclamation by the people who witnessed the healing: "And the people glorified God, saying, 'We have never seen anything like this.'"

Summary: This review of the text indicates very little redaction on the part of Mark. He contextualized the miracle in vv. 1–2 and inserted his familiar ἐξίστημι into the final acclamation.

II. THE PRE-MARKAN ANECDOTE: JESUS AND THE PARALYTIC

Once these few Markan additions are removed from the anecdote, one could say that the resulting narrative elements would be as follows:

³καὶ ἔρχονται φέροντες πρὸς αὐτὸν παραλυτικὸν αἰρόμενον ὑπὸ τεσσάρων. ⁴καὶ μὴ δυνάμενοι προσενέγκαι αὐτῷ διὰ τὸν ὄχλον ἀπεστέγασαν τὴν στέγην ὅπου ἦν, καὶ ἐξορύξαντες χαλῶσι τὸν κράβαττον ὅπου ὁ παραλυτικὸς κατέκειτο. ⁵καὶ ἰδὼν ὁ Ἰησοῦς τὴν πίστιν αὐτῶν λέγει τῷ παραλυτικῷ· τέκνον, ἀφίενταί σου αἱ ἁμαρτίαι. ⁶ἦσαν δέ τινες τῶν γραμματέων ἐκεῖ καθήμενοι καὶ

---

[4] Where Mark uses ἐξίστημι to represent the opinion of Jesus' relatives about him (Mark 3:21), notice that the comment is absent from the gospels of Matthew and Luke. This likely is due to their understanding of the verb as a description of someone "outside oneself," which would be a denigrating statement about Jesus and would cause confusion to the listener familiar with their infancy narratives. In both these gospels, Jesus' mother knows that he is divine; there would be no such negative opinion of Jesus' state. Matthew also removes it from the disciples' response to Jesus walking on the sea (Mark 6:51), since the disciples in his Gospel recognize the significance of Jesus' action and appropriately adore him (Matt 14:33). Luke too avoids ἐξίστημι where Mark uses it except in the one instance of Mark 5:42 // Luke 8:56 where it is used to describe the reaction of the parents to the raising of their daughter from the dead by Jesus. In his own traditional material, Luke uses it for the response of the elders in the temple upon hearing the wisdom of the twelve-year-old Jesus (Luke 2:47).

διαλογιζόμενοι ἐν ταῖς καρδίαις αὐτῶν· ⁷τί οὗτος οὕτως λαλεῖ; βλασφημεῖ· τίς δύναται ἀφιέναι ἁμαρτίας εἰ μὴ εἷς ὁ θεός; ⁸καὶ εὐθὺς ἐπιγνοὺς ὁ Ἰησοῦς τῷ πνεύματι αὐτοῦ ὅτι οὕτως διαλογίζονται ἐν ἑαυτοῖς, λέγει αὐτοῖς· τί ταῦτα διαλογίζεσθε ἐν ταῖς καρδίαις ὑμῶν; ⁹τί ἐστιν εὐκοπώτερον, εἰπεῖν τῷ παραλυτικῷ· ἀφίενταί σου αἱ ἁμαρτίαι, ἢ εἰπεῖν· ἔγειρε καὶ ἆρον τὸν κράβαττόν σου καὶ περιπάτει; ¹⁰ἵνα δὲ εἰδῆτε ὅτι ἐξουσίαν ἔχει ὁ υἱὸς τοῦ ἀνθρώπου ἀφιέναι ἁμαρτίας ἐπὶ τῆς γῆς – λέγει τῷ παραλυτικῷ· ¹¹σοὶ λέγω, ἔγειρε ἆρον τὸν κράβαττόν σου καὶ ὕπαγε εἰς τὸν οἶκόν σου. ¹²καὶ ἠγέρθη καὶ εὐθὺς ἄρας τὸν κράβαττον ἐξῆλθεν ἔμπροσθεν πάντων, ὥστε ... πάντας ... δοξάζειν τὸν θεὸν λέγοντας ὅτι οὕτως οὐδέποτε εἴδομεν.

³Then some people came, bringing to him a paralyzed man, carried by four of them. ⁴And when they could not bring him to Jesus because of the crowd, they removed the roof above him; and after having dug through it, they let down the mat on which the paralytic lay. ⁵When Jesus saw their faith, he said to the paralytic, "Son, your sins are forgiven." ⁶Now some of the scribes were sitting there, questioning in their hearts, ⁷"Why does this fellow speak in this way? It is blasphemy! Who can forgive sins but God alone?" ⁸At once Jesus perceived in his spirit that they were discussing these questions among themselves; and he said to them, "Why do you raise such questions in your hearts? ⁹Which is easier, to say to the paralytic, 'Your sins are forgiven,' or to say, 'Stand up and take your mat and walk'? ¹⁰But so that you may know that the Son of Man has authority on earth to forgive sins"—he said to the paralytic—¹¹"I say, to you, stand up, take your mat and go to your home." ¹²And he stood up, and immediately took the mat and went out before all of them; so that ... they all ... glorified God, saying, "We have never seen anything like this!"

The Complex Form of the Pre-Markan Story: A Controversy Apophthegm Inside a Miracle Story

The form of the remaining story shows the presence of a controversy apophthegm inside a miracle story.

Healing Miracle

1. Description of the Illness

> "Then some people came, bringing to him a paralyzed man, carried by four of them. And when they could not bring him to Jesus because of the crowd, they removed the roof above him; and after having dug through it, they let down the mat on which the paralytic lay" (vv. 3–4).

2. Jesus' Response

> "When Jesus saw their faith, he said to the paralytic . . ." (v. 5a).

Apophthegm

> (a) Provoking Word
>
> > "Son, your sins are forgiven" (v. 5b).
>
> (b) Challenge
>
> > "Now some of the scribes were sitting there, questioning in their hearts, 'Why does this fellow speak in this way? It is blasphemy! Who can forgive sins but God alone?'" (vv. 6–7).
>
> (c) Pronouncement
>
> > "At once Jesus perceived in his spirit that they were discussing these questions among themselves; and he said to them, 'Why do you raise such questions in your hearts? Which is easier, to say to the paralytic, "Your sins are forgiven," or to say, "Stand up and take your mat and walk"? ¹⁰But so that you may know that the Son of Man has authority on earth to forgive sins'—he said to the paralytic—" (vv. 8–10).
> >
> > "I say to you, stand up, take your mat and go to your home" (v. 11) (both the healing command of the miracle and the conclusion of Jesus' pronouncement).

Healing Miracle, continued

3. Demonstration and Acclamation of the Miracle

> "And he stood up, and immediately took the mat, and went out before all of them; so that . . . they all . . . glorified God, saying, 'We have never seen anything like this!'" (v. 12).

These two forms, miracle story and apophthegm, are linked by the repetition of "he said to the paralytic" in v. 5 and v. 10.

A miracle story requires, first, the special problem, in this case the paralytic's condition (vv. 3–4); second, it requires the miracle in response, in this case Jesus' command that the man stand up, pick up his mat, and go home (v. 11); and finally, it is satisfying to have a demonstration that the miracle was successful, in this case the paralytic walking (v. 12a) and an acclamation from the witnesses (v. 12b). A controversy apophthegm requires, first, some provoking action or word from Jesus, here his pronouncement of forgiveness of sins (v. 5); second, it requires some opposition on the part of opponents, here charges of blasphemy from the scribes (vv. 6–7); and finally, there is the pronouncement that proves the rightness of Jesus' actions or teachings, in this case Jesus' argument that it is harder to pronounce sins forgiven than to heal, but to prove one by the other, he performs the healing (vv. 9–12a).

Which Is Primary: the Apophthegm or the Miracle Story?

Under the influence of Martin Albertz, Vincent Taylor proposed that this account, attached as it is to the other controversy stories of the unit, Mark 2:1–3:6, suggests that it began as a controversy story, and then "the original beginning and end of the Pronouncement-Story were cut away and replaced by the fuller details of the Miracle-Story."[5] The best evidence against this proposal is Taylor's own admission that "if we bring the sundered phrases together, and reduced them to one, we gain a perfect Miracle-Story."[6] Moreover, if the context of the apophthegm

---

[5] Vincent Taylor, *The Formation of the Gospel Tradition* (2d ed.; London: Macmillan, 1949), 68. See also Martin Albertz, *Die Synoptischen Streitgespräche: Ein Beitrag zur Formengeschichte des Urchristentums* (Berlin: Trowitzsch, 1921), 6.

[6] Taylor, *Gospel Tradition*, 67. Cf. Bultmann, *Synoptic Tradition*, 47 ("the insertion into an alien narrative is quite plain").

(i.e., the present miracle story) had been a replacement for something earlier, one has to ask why such distracting features as the four men opening the roof to let down the paralytic would have been chosen. The focus is meant to be on Jesus' authority to forgive sins. Why not eliminate the elements of the crowd-filled house and the outrageous act of the friends digging through the roof? Why not just have the paralytic brought forward to Jesus by his friends in the open, where Jesus could forgive his sins and scribes might overhear him. In fact, that is precisely the way Matthew deals with this mixed story. In Matt 9:2–8, the paralyzed man is brought out from his house as Jesus is there in the street, and Jesus, noting their faith, pronounces the forgiveness of sins. Given that public venue, the presence of scribes is believable, as though they were passing by.

This does mean that Jesus' reference to the faith of the friends is newly focused on their obvious belief in bringing out their friend to him. This is a marked difference from the Markan tradition, where the idea is that Jesus is responding not just to the friends bringing the paralytic, but to their being so determined that they unroof the roof, digging a hole through it in order to lower him in front of Jesus. By eliminating that extreme action, Matthew leaves as the most startling feature of the story Jesus' pronouncement of forgiveness of sins. Matthew's redaction of the Markan traditional story best critiques any suggestion that the controversy story was primary. His eliminations illustrate the awkward fit of the apophthegm into the context of the earlier miracle story.[7]

Some scholars, such as William Lane and Robert Gundry, deny the signs of any division in the account on the basis that the supposed disjuncture at vv. 5b, 10 are insufficient evidence to support "this radical expedient" of an edited miracle story.[8] Gundry proposes that the controversy was meant to "heighten the tension" of the account.[9] However, the issue of the forgiveness of sins and the argument that follows divert attention from the open ceiling and the four petitioners looking down on the friend whom they just lowered to Jesus. They are forgotten, as now the subject turns to whether it is legitimate or blasphemous for

---

[7] See Ernst Haenchen, *Der Weg Jesu: Eine Erklärung des Markus-Evangeliums und der kanonischen Parallelen* (2d ed.; Berlin: de Gruyter, 1968), 99.

[8] William L. Lane, *The Gospel according to Mark: The English Text with Introduction, Exposition, and Notes* (NICNT: Grand Rapids: Eerdmans, 1974), 97.

[9] Gundry, *Mark*, 121.

Jesus to forgive sins. The form bumps from one point to another, and even Taylor, who holds that the controversy was primary, has to acknowledge a "peculiar" construction.[10]

Besides the awkwardness and interruptive character of the "pronouncement story," as Taylor identified Bultmann's apophthegm form, there is also the oddity of the presence of scribes in this house crammed full with ordinary people. Since Jesus was not known to socialize in their circles, it is a surprise to discover them in this house observing him. Thus, the accumulated evidence suggests that it is much more probable that the miracle anecdote was pried opened to insert the controversy story to turn the miracle to the service of Jesus' authority to forgive sins than that this particular miracle story was built around the controversy.

Once the controversy story was inserted, it effectively took command of the focus of the earlier miracle story, pulling attention away from the friends and their faith, to concentrate the argument on Jesus' authority to forgive sins on earth. In this chapter, however, I want to discuss Mark 2:1–5, 11–12, the early story that Taylor and Bultmann agree shows itself to have been unitary before the Markan insertion.

III. THE PRESENTATION OF THE PETITIONERS

[3]καὶ ἔρχονται φέροντες πρὸς αὐτὸν παραλυτικὸν αἰρόμενον ὑπὸ τεσσάρων.

[3]Then some people came, bringing to him a paralyzed man, carried by four of them.

The Seriousness of the Malady: Paralysis

The man's condition of paralysis has raised some scholarly debate. Hendrik van der Loos, relying on the distinction made by Ezra P. Gould, holds that the use of παραλυτικός in v. 3 could suggest a number of ailments. The word παραλυτικός as used in biblical Greek covered several ailments, while παραλελυμένος is the term used in Hellenistic sources

---

[10] "None the less the peculiar construction is there, and the incident is related in much greater detail than is usual, or necessary, in a Pronouncement-Story" (Taylor, *Gospel Tradition*, 66).

only for paralysis.[11] This distinction is supported by Alfred Plummer's commentary on Luke, where he notes that Luke alters Mark's description of the man's ailment in Mark 2:3 from το παραλυτικός to ὃς ἦν παραλελυμένος (Luke 5:18). Plummer quotes the 1882 monograph by W. K. Hobart, *The Medical Language in St. Luke*:

> Here and wherever St. Luke mentions this disease, he employs the verb παραλύεσθαι, and never παραλυτικός. The other N.T. writers use the popular form παραλυτικός and never use the verb, the apparent exception to this, Heb. xii. 12, being a quotation from the LXX, Is. xxxv 3.[12] St. Luke's use is in strict agreement with that of the medical writers.[13]

It needs to be observed, however, that Hobart's theory still relied on the presupposition that the writer of Luke used medical language. This would be challenged by Henry J. Cadbury, whose research indicated, first, that medical terms were far from overly specific or without synonyms, and, second, that the vocabulary of Luke that does coincide with medical terms is also the vocabulary found in the writings of the literati of the period, who certainly were not doctors. Thus, the presence of certain specific terms in Luke is not so much a sign that he supplies the more precise medical vocabulary as it is an indicator that his vocabulary reflects usage in more sophisticated circles.[14]

In fact, note that in Isa 35:3 LXX, Luke's supposedly exact verb for "paralysis," παραλύω, describes "feeble knees" ("Strengthen the weak hands, and make firm the feeble [παραλελυμένα] knees"). Celsus, a first-century man of medicine, notes that by his own day, the specific condition of paralysis, which was expressed as παράλυσις, had come to include ἀποπληξία, apoplexy. As we see below, Celsus includes only

---

[11] Hendrik van der Loos, *The Miracles of Jesus* (NovTSup 9; Leiden: Brill, 1965), 448 n. 1, quoting, Ezra P. Gould, *The Gospel according to St. Mark* (New York: Charles Scribner's Sons, 1896), 36 n. 3.

[12] Isa 35:3 LXX: ἰσχύσατε χεῖρες ἀνειμέναι καὶ γόνατα παραλελυμένα.

[13] W. K. Hobart, *The Medical Language of St. Luke* (Dublin: Hodges, Figgis, 1882), 6, quoted in Alfred Plummer, *A Critical and Exegetical Commentary on the Gospel according to S. Luke* (ICC; Edinburgh: T &T Clark, 1896), 152.

[14] Henry J. Cadbury, *The Diction of Luke and Acts* (vol. 1 of *The Style and Literary Method of Luke*; Cambridge, Mass.: Harvard University Press; London: Humphrey Milford, 1919), 39–72. See also Henry J. Cadbury, "Lexical Notes on Luke-Acts: II. Recent Arguments for Medical Language," *JBL* 45 (1926): 190–209.

these two conditions and does not suggest that παράλυσις covers a wide range of conditions.

> Relaxing of the sinews . . . is a frequent disease everywhere. It attacks at times the whole body, at times part of it.[15] Ancient writers named the former apoplexy [ἀποπληξίαν], the latter paralysis: I see that now *both* are called paralysis [παράλυσιν]. (Celsus, *Med.* 3.27)[16]

Apoplexy was brought on an attack like a stroke that left the person incapacitated to various degrees. "Medical writers, following Hippocrates (*Breaths*, 13), ascribed all forms of paralysis to collections of flatus and phlegm in the head, until Wepfer in 1658 discovered cerebral haemorrhage to be a cause."[17] From the account in Mark 2:1–12, one gathers that the man is totally paralyzed, for he is carried on a mat and remains unable to help as the friends dig through the roof and then lower him on the mat to Jesus. About such conditions Celsus states,

> Those who are gravely paralyzed in all their limbs are as a rule quickly carried off, but if not so carried off, some may live a long while, yet rarely however regain health. Mostly they drag out a miserable existence, their memory lost also. (Celsus, *Med.* 3.27)[18]

Celsus gauges the seriousness of the condition upon whether the paralysis is partial or total. His only suggestion for treatment is bleeding the patient, which may possibly work. Anything else just "postpones death."

> If all the limbs are gravely paralyzed withdrawal of blood either kills or cures. Any other kind of treatment scarcely ever restores health, it often merely postpones death, and meanwhile makes life a burden. If after

---

[15] In the New Testament, partial paralysis is described with the word χωλός, "lame" (Matt 21:14; John 5:3; Acts 3:2).

[16] "At resolutio nervorum frequens ubique morbus est: interdum tota corpora, interdum partes infestat. Veteres auctores illud ἀποπληξίαν hoc παράλυσιν nominarunt: nunc utrumque παράλυσιν apellari video" (*De Medicina* [trans. W. G. Spencer; 3 vols.; LCL; Cambridge, Mass.: Harvard University Press, 1960], 1:345 [my italics]).

[17] W. G. Spencer offers this note on the passage (ibid., n. b).

[18] "Solent autem qui per omnia membra vehementer resoluti sunt, celeriter rapi; ac si correpti non sunt, diutius quidem vivunt, sed raro tamen ad sanitatem perveniunt; plerumque miserum spiritum trahunt, memoria quoque amissa" (ibid., 1:345).

blood-letting, neither movement nor the mind is recovered, there is no hope left; if they do return, health also is in prospect. (Celsus, *Med.* 3.27)[19]

The hopelessness of the paralyzed person and the inevitability of death seem to have been well known, as shown by Artemidorus Daldianus, a second-century C.E. collector of dream interpretations who reports these common dream associations: ". . . and a dream that one is ugly, paralyzed or feeble has a similar outcome; indeed, *all of this portends death for the ailing.*"[20] In fact, these three aspects describe the dead: hideousness, immobility, and powerlessness.

The Characterization of the Friends of the Paralytic

αἰρόμενον ὑπὸ τεσσάρων

carried by four of them

In this account, the petitioners are described as "some people," among them four men carrying the paralytic. This is already a desperate measure. A person this ill would be tended inside, not carried through the street, jostled and shaken with the transport. The decision also means that the people's determination to bring their friend to Jesus outweighs the shame of the public exposure of their paralyzed friend to the gawking and staring. The indignity of this exposure is brought out somewhat by Suetonius's report of Tiberius's efforts to visit the sick while he was exiled on Rhodes:

> It happened once that, in arranging the next day's programme, he had expressed a wish to visit the local sick. His staff misunderstood him. Orders went out that all the patients in town should be carried to a public colonnade and there arranged in groups according to their ailments. Tiberius was shocked; for a while he stood at a loss, but at last went to see the poor fellows, apologizing even to the humblest and least important for the inconvenience he had caused them. (*Tib.* 11)[21]

---

[19] "Si omnia membra vehementer resoluta sunt, sanguinis detractio vel occidit vel liberat. Aliud curationis genus vix umquam sanitatem restituit, saepe mortem tantum differt, vitam interim infestat. Post sanguinis missionem si non redit et motus et mens, nihil spei superest; si redit, sanitas quoque prospicitur" (ibid.).

[20] Artemidorus Daldianus, *Onir.* 1.50. Translation by Dr. Gregory W. Dobrov, Loyola University, Chicago, Illinois (Italics mine).

[21] Suetonius, *Tiberius*, in *The Twelve Caesars* (trans. Robert Graves; rev. ed.; London: Penguin, 2002), 115.

Tiberius's embarrassment and his insistence on apologizing to each person indicate the degree of offense that he thought the group of sick people had suffered on his account. The rather radical measures employed by the paralytic's friends in the Markan story indicate their determination and at the same time their absolute conviction that Jesus could and would heal their paralyzed friend. The difficulty for them was in achieving the encounter with Jesus.

Overcoming the Obstacle to Reaching Jesus

⁴καὶ μὴ δυνάμενοι προσενέγκαι αὐτῷ διὰ τὸν ὄχλον ἀπεστέγασαν τὴν στέγην ὅπου ἦν, καὶ ἐξορύξαντες χαλῶσι τὸν κράβαττον ὅπου ὁ παραλυτικὸς κατέκειτο.

⁴And when they could not bring him to Jesus because of the crowd, they removed the roof above him; and after having dug through it, they let down the mat on which the paralytic lay.

Obstacles to reaching Jesus feature in three pericopae of the Markan tradition: (2) the blind beggar Bartimaeus (Mark 10:46–52), whose blindness keeps him from knowing where Jesus is in the crowd leaving the city; (2) Jairus, whose daughter is at the point of death (Mark 5:22–43) when Jesus is stopped by the flow of energy that he feels going out to heal the woman who has a hemorrhage (Mark 5:23–35); and (3) the present account, in which a crowd fills the room so that there is no way for the paralyzed man's friends to carry him in on the mat on which he is lying. In all these accounts it will be the faith of the petitioner(s) that will be complimented by Jesus and result in the saving miracle.

This anecdote stands apart from the other two because not a single word is spoken by the four carriers of the paralyzed man. It is their actions that express the amazing and outrageous conviction they hold that Jesus can and will save their friend. According to a literal reading of the text, their solution is to "unroof the roof" (ἀπεστέγασαν τὴν στέγην) over Jesus, digging through it to create an aperture to lower their friend down to him.

Scholarly Debates on the Significance of the Petitioners' Actions

The history of scholarship indicates great difficulty with the literal meaning of the Greek, and the theories that have been presented all work to show that the petitioners did no real harm to the roof. Indeed, C. C. McCown is perhaps quite correct when he observes, "No passage in the New Testament better illustrates the interpreter's need for archaeological intelligence than the few words in Mark 2:4 which refer to the uncovering of the roof above Jesus in order to lower the paralytic into his presence."[22] A review of the main theories brings this out more clearly.

Mark Is Responsible for the Extreme Description

As recently as 1968, Ernst Haenchen reasserted the position of David Friedrich Strauss that such a scene was impossible to imagine and therefore should be recognized as Mark's insertion to present a strong example of faith.[23] Haenchen, however, seems unaware that Strauss's conclusions were based on the Griesbach Hypothesis, which holds that Mark had seen the Gospels of both Matthew and Luke. Matthew's Gospel is devoid of the house scene, but Luke's Gospel that maintains that context, and there the petitioners remove enough roof tiles to allow the passage of the man's "bed" (Luke 5:19). Therefore, when Strauss saw the Markan description, which says that they "unroofed the roof" and dug through, it was only logical that he would assign those extreme elements to Mark's redaction.[24]

Jesus Was on the Second Floor, and the Roof Had a Door to the Upper Room

Strauss, like many scholars of his day, depended on the 1684 commentary of John Lightfoot,[25] whose deductions about the construction of Palestinian houses were drawn solely from literary references in the

---

[22] C. C. McCown, "Luke's Translation of Semitic into Hellenistic Custom," *JBL* 58 (1939): 213.

[23] Haenchen, *Der Weg Jesu*, 99–102.

[24] David Friedrich Strauss, *The Life of Jesus* (trans. George Eliot; 4th ed.; London: Swann Sonnenschein, 1906; repr., 3 vols. [Portland, Ore.: Gloger Family Books, 2006], 2.456–57), 456–57.

[25] John Lightfoot, *Horæ Hebraicæ et Talmudicæ: Hebrew and Talmudic Exercitations upon the Gospels, the Acts, Some Chapters of St. Paul's Epistle to the Romans, and the First Epistle to the Corinthians* (ed. Robert Gandell; 4 vols. Oxford: Oxford University Press, 1859 [a translation of the 1684 Latin text]). Strauss refers to Lightfoot's theory, drawing on a German edition of Lightfoot's text, *Horæ hebraicæ et talmudicæ in quatuor evangelistas* (Leipzig: J. H. Richter,

Old Testament and Talmud. Since certain talmudic texts refer to elders meeting in an "upper room,"[26] he concluded that all houses had an upper story where teaching took place. Lightfoot understood that when certain owners allowed renters in the upper room, the renters would not pass through the family area on the first floor but rather would use outside stairs to reach their own quarters. The stairs took them up to the roof, where a door allowed them to enter and drop down into their room.[27] Thus, Lightfoot proposed that Jesus was teaching in an upper room when the petitioners used the stairs to bring their friend to his quarters. Relying on the Lukan version, he explains,

> By ladders set up, or perhaps fastened there before, they first draw up the paralytic ἐπὶ δῶμα, *upon the roof*, Luke [5:]19. Then seeing there was a door in every roof through which they went up from the lower parts of the house into the roof, and this being too narrow to let down the bed and the sick man in it, they widen the space by pulling off the tiles that lay about it. Well, having made a hole through the roof, the paralytic is let down εἰς τὸ ὑπερῷον, *into the upper chamber*. There Christ sits, and the Pharisees and the doctors of the law with him, and not in the lower parts of the house.[28]

Lightfoot's reconstruction means that very little damage would be done to the roof. Just the tiles around the door would be removed to allow the passage of the mat with the prostrate paralytic. This seemed a sensible conclusion because if one presumed a two-story house such as this, the roof would be of sturdy construction. Any burrowing through would present grave danger to those below. The falling cement and

---

1684), 601. That volume was unavailable to me, but the references in the 1859 Oxford edition cohere with Strauss's representations of Lightfoot's position.

[26] See Lightfoot, *Horæ Hebraicæ*, 2:399–400. Lightfoot quotes from *b. Šabb.* 11a: "The elders went up לעלית *into an upper chamber* in Jericho. They went up also into an upper chamber in Jabneh." He supports this with a quotation from *Sepher Juchasin*, fol. 23.2: "Rabh Jochanan and his disciples went up εἰς ὑπερῷον, *to an upper chamber*, and read and expounded."

[27] Ibid. The influential text is a story in the Talmud (*b. Mo'ed Qaṭ.* 25a) where the bier on which lay the body of Rabbi Huna was too large to pass through the door of the house. "Therefore *they thought good to draw it out and let it down through the roof,* or *through the way of the roof*" (ibid., 2:399). Lightfoot clearly presumes that within the house there was a passageway up to the second floor so that one could take the bier up to the second floor, remove the body from the upper room, and then lower it down to the outside.

[28] Ibid., 2:400.

bricks could cause serious injury to those in the upper room. This is why Mark's so-called "redaction" was considered so extreme. But Strauss criticized Lightfoot, who tried to explain away Luke's idea of actually opening the roof itself.[29]

The Petitioners Dug through a Projection of the Roof Over the Front Door

Heinrich Paulus addressed Mark's text, explaining that when it says that they "unroofed the roof," the important qualifier is the clause "where he was." He proposed that Jesus was seated at the front of the house, where the teacher would sit. Scholars believed that there was a small projection of the roof with a parapet on top. What Mark meant, then, was that the men climbed onto the roof, carried the mat over to the place where Jesus was teaching, just under that projection, and dug through at that spot. Thus, there was no real damage to the roof, and no one was in danger from the debris that would have fallen.[30] In critical response, Strauss points to all the confusing elements that result. The precise vocabulary of the texts conflict with Paulus's suggestion, and the supposition that there was already a door in the roof raises the question of why the petitioners dug through the roof anyway.

> But both the phrase, διὰ τῶν κεράμων, in Luke, and the expressions of Mark, render this conception of the thing impossible, since here, neither can στέγη ["roof"] mean parapet, nor ἀποστεγάζω ["to unroof"] the breaking of the parapet, while ἐξορύττω ["to dig through"] can only mean the breaking of a hole. Thus the disturbance of the roof subsists, but this is further rendered improbable on the ground that it was altogether superfluous, inasmuch as there was a door in every roof. Hence help has been sought in the supposition that the bearers indeed used the door previously there, but because this was too narrow for the bed of the patient,

---

[29] Strauss, *Life of Jesus*, 2.456. See also S. Kraus, "Das Abdecken des Daches Mc 2:4, Lc 5:19," *ZNW* 25 (1926): 307–10. Kraus (p. 308) imagines a two-story house with a cement floor that had to be broken through in order to lower items, but that there was already an aperture so that items could be raised and lowered easily.

[30] Heinrich Paulus, *Das Leben Jesu als Grundlage einer reinen Geschichte des Urchristentums* (2 vols.; Heidelburg: C. F. Winter, 1828), 1:238. Alfred Edersheim (*Life and Times of Jesus the Messiah* [2 vols.; New York: E. R. Herrick, 1886], 1:501–4) returns to this interpretation of Paulus despite archeological conclusions regarding first-century village dwellings in Palestine.

they widened it by the removal of the surrounding tiles.[31] Still, however, there remains the danger to those below, and the words imply an opening actually made, not merely widened.[32]

These arguments help to explain why in the end Strauss saw Mark's version as extreme and there being no need to "unroof the roof" or "dig through." Ernst Haenchen's reliance on Strauss to claim that the description belongs to Mark will not hold in the light of the Two-Source Hypothesis.

Opening the Roof Was Simple: Palestinian Roofs Were Like Those of Rustic Arab Houses

Cunningham Geikie's 1888 work *The Holy Land and the Bible* corrected the older conclusions by Lightfoot that were dependent solely on Jewish Scripture and the Talmud. The book was the result of expedition to what had been Palestine, where he viewed the Arab peasant homes.

> One of the principal houses consisted of a single square room, of good size, plastered with mud, and roofed with branches long since varnished black by smoke. These hung down roughly over half the room; the other half was hidden by a canvas ceiling. The door had no hinges, but was lifted to its place, or from it, and the windows were only square holes in the mud walls.[33]

Based on Geikie's description, the opening of the roof on such a dwelling would not constitute major damage to the home. In fact, it would be quite simple to break through the mud and push aside the branches. Likewise, the repair of such an aperture would pose no great problem.

The Greek Translator Misunderstood the Aramaic: The Men Only Mounted the Roof

Julius Wellhausen proposed that each part of the description "unroofing the roof" and "digging through" should be studied separately. He argued that the story of the paralytic had begun in Aramaic, and

---

[31] Here, in a footnote, Strauss cites, among others, Lightfoot, *Horæ Hebraicæ*, 2:399–400.

[32] Strauss, *Life of Jesus*, 2.456. Here we may also place 1728 critiques by Thomas Woolston, who for the same reasons concluded, "In my Opinion no Tale more monstrously romantick can be told" (*A Fourth Discourse on the Miracles of Our Saviour in View of the Present Controversy between Infidels and Apostates* [1728; repr., New York: Garland, 1979], 54).

[33] Cunningham Geikie, *The Holy Land and the Bible: A Book of Scripture Illustrations Gathered in Palestine* (2 vols.; New York: John B. Alden, 1888), 1:49.

the Greek translator who wrote "unroofed the roof" had misread the Aramaic, *schaqluhi* or *arîmuhi liggâra,* which actually would have meant "they *mounted* the roof,"[34] and thought that it meant "unroofing the roof." Since the translator would have presumed the Greek and Roman roofs of his own experience, this would mean no more than lifting off a few roof tiles. As for "digging through," Wellhausen claimed that this was a later addition, since the participle is missing from both Codex Bezae and some of the Latin manuscripts (i.e., Western texts). He bolsters his proposal with the observation that if "digging through" had belonged to the earliest story, it is curious that there is no mention of people moving back from the falling debris.[35] In this way, Wellhausen could affirm that all that the men had done was mount the roof, not remove it, and somehow lower the man to those in the room.

The problem with Wellhausen's idea that the Greek translator presumed the roofs of the Greek and Roman world is that such roofs would have been extremely difficult to mount while balancing a stretcher because, as McCown observes, they were always built on a slant to shed rainwater.[36]

The Low Height of the Palestinian House Allowed for Easy Lowering of the Man

McCown saw "digging through" as a clarification of the more general "unroofing the roof" and understood this as a detailed style of narration common to the Markan Gospel, yet at the same time, he

---

[34] Julius Wellhausen, *Das Evangelium Marci: Übersetzt und Erklärt* (2d ed.; Berlin: Georg Reimer, 1909), 15 (my italics). Dennis Nineham repeats this argument in *The Gospel of St. Mark* (PGC; London: A & C Black, 1963), 92.

[35] Walter Grundmann (*Das Evangelium nach Markus* [2d ed.; THKNT; Berlin: Evangelische Verlagsanstalt, 1965], 56) reasserts Wellhausen's position. Eduard Schweizer (*The Good News according to Mark* [trans. Donald H. Madvig; Richmond: John Knox Press, 1970], 61) states that it is questionable whether one could open up such a roof if the house were full of people. Van der Loos (*Miracles of Jesus,* 442) also sees the falling debris as a problem, but here is a case in which he has no method to decide among the roof descriptions of Lightfoot, Paulus, and Wellhausen; he concludes, "It is not possible to reconstruct the situation, but in any case there must have been enough room to avoid the falling materials at the point where Jesus was standing."

[36] "It is hard to believe that flat stones or terra cotta tiles would ever have been laid in the flat mud roof. They would serve no purpose but to interfere with the flat stone or the roller which is used in autumn to smooth out the cracks left in the mud by the heat of summer" (McCown, "Luke's Translation," 214).

concluded that given the nature of the typical roof on a Palestinian house, there would have been no harm to anyone below.[37]

> The outside stairway to the roof, still quite common in Palestine and implied in the Old Testament, the New Testament and the Talmud, was so well known that Mark's racy account did not need to refer to it. The small height of the ordinary hut of peasant or working man made it was easy to ascend and easy to let the man down on a pallet. It is quite unnecessary to manufacture trouble for the faithful four or for the modern interpreter by assuming κράβαττος ["cot, mat"] to have a framework or legs. If one sets the story into its proper background, the whole is quite natural and entirely credible.[38]

This opinion is echoed by Vincent Taylor, who explains, "The roof was probably formed by beams and rafters across which matting, branches and twigs covered by earth trodden hard were laid," so that "to make an aperture large enough for the sick bed would not be difficult."[39] William Barclay agrees that the aperture would be easily opened,[40] as does Morna Hooker, who states, "It would have been a fairly simple matter to break up the mixture of twigs, matting and earth which filled space between the beams of the roof, although a considerable amount of debris would have fallen on the crowd below in the process."[41]

Summation: All these various theories come to the conclusion that little real damage was done to the roof of the dwelling. The most recent theories rest on the idea that the roof was rather makeshift and therefore easy to open.

"They Unroofed the Roof, and Digging through . . .": The Roof as Substantial

The research by A. C. Dickie and J. P. Payne on the purpose of a house's roof results in the conclusion that its construction required the capability of supporting the weight of more than one person.

---

[37] Ibid., 215.

[38] Ibid.

[39] Vincent Taylor, *The Gospel according to St. Mark: The Greek Text with Introduction, Notes, and Indexes* (London: Macmillan; New York: St. Martin's Press, 1955), 194.

[40] William Barclay, *The Gospel of Mark* (3d ed.; Philadelphia: Westminster), 45.

[41] Morna D. Hooker, *A Commentary on the Gospel according to St. Mark* (BNTC; London: A & C Black, 1991), 85.

It [the roof] was used for worship (2 K. 23:12; Jer. 19:13; 32:29; Zeph. 1:5; Acts 10:9). Absalom spread his tent on the "top of the house" (2 S. 16:22). In the Feast of Tabernacles temporary booths (*sukkôt*) were erected on the housetops. The Mosaic law required a parapet or railing for protection (Dt. 22:8). The people, as is their habit today, gathered together on the roof on high days and holidays (Jgs. 16:27). The wild wrangling which can be heard in any modern native village, resulting in vile accusations and exposure of family secrets hurled from the housetops of the conflicting parties, illustrates the passage, "And what you have whispered in private rooms shall be proclaimed upon the housetops" (Lk. 12:3).[42]

This description is very much like that of Geikie, who proposed that the Arab peasant's home was very like that of first century Palestine. The real difference, however, is in the roof construction which had to be sturdy enough to allow for its many uses: "To get over the difficulty of the larger spans, a common practice was to introduce a main beam (*qôrâ*) carried on the walls and strengthened by one or more intermediate posts let into stone sockets laid on the floor. Smaller timbers as joists ('rafters,' *rāhît*) were spaced out and covered in turn with brushwood; the final covering, being of mud mixed with chopped straw, was beaten and rolled."[43]

Actually, McCown, in presenting a precedent for "unroofing a roof," illustrates the sturdiness expected of these structures. In Josephus's description of the war between Herod and Antigonus, he tells an episode where Antigonius's soldiers fled to the village of Isana, where they took refuge inside the houses and also on the roofs (*Ant.* 14.456–61). McCown translates, "The dwellings being full of hoplites and some fleeing over the roofs, he [Herod] seized the latter, and digging up (ἀνασκάπτων) the roofs of the houses, saw the parts below filled with soldiers who they killed by hurling stones on them" (Josephus, *Ant.* 14.459–60).[44]

---

[42] A. C. Dickie and J. P. Payne, "House," *ISBE* 2:772.

[43] Ibid., 2:271.

[44] McCown, "Luke's Translation," 215. It is interesting that Ralph Marcus translates καὶ τοὺς ὀρόφους τῶν οἴκων ἀνασκάπτων with "and on *pulling down* the roofs of the houses" (Flavius Josephus, *Josephus* [trans. H. St. J. Thackeray et al.; 10 vols.; LCL; London: Heinemann; New York: Putnam; Cambridge, Mass.: Harvard University Press, 1926–1981], 7:686–87 [my italics]). Is this because he did not know how "digging through" was possible? Also, the noun ὄροφος is a collective for "reeds," which, understandably, is used for "roof" because they cover the beams and rafters.

This story shows that the roofs were strong enough so that men could hide on top of them and run across them, all of which supports the research by Dickie and Payne. This type of sturdy roof also coheres with the scene presented in Mark 2:4, because even if one grants to each man only one hundred pounds, the four men who brought the mat with their friend to the top of the roof would have created a pressure of five hundred pounds concentrated on the area right above Jesus. If the structure was not substantial and sturdy, there would have been no need to dig through, for they would have fallen through.

The Four Petitioners Make an Aperture in a Substantial Roof

The efforts of scholars to minimize the effects of the petitioners' solution is understandable, since the latter are to receive no reprimand from anyone, but only Jesus' compliment for their "faith." The fact is that the first-time listener would have been appalled at their solution. It was ingenious, perhaps, but audacious, to say the very least. Douglas Hare captures this sense in his re-creation of the scene: "Suddenly he [Jesus] is interrupted. The roof above him is being demolished!"[45] While "demolished" is perhaps too strong here, Hare rightly represents what would have been the astonishment of the listener. William Lane calls the men's action their "bold expedient."[46]

The degree of boldness and the tension introduced into the story by their action are severely diminished if one imagines a flimsy structure easily opened and just as easily patched. In fact, as mentioned above, this is a structure able to handle substantial weight and still require un-roofing and digging through. The shock value of the action is diverted almost immediately with the insertion of the apologetic, which turns the attention to Jesus' controversy with the scribes over his authority to forgive sins. Suddenly, the four men are left at the top of the roof, forgotten, while the controversy story proceeds in front of the paralyzed man.

Once the miracle story is allowed its context, apart from that insertion, the earlier story is allowed to function as a revelation of Jesus' virtue, a model for the disciples. This story presents petitioners so determined to have their friend presented to Jesus that they are

---

[45] Douglas Hare, *Mark* (WestBC; Louisville: Westminster John Knox, 1996), 35.

[46] Lane, *Mark*, 93.

willing to dig through a roof that belongs to someone else. It is the action of persons desperate for their friend's wholeness and determined to obtain it.

In Roman civil law this action of the men would constitute *damnum injuria datum*, the willful destruction of someone's property; "Any negligence short of mere accident suffices to render the defendant liable."[47] The Mishnah holds exactly the same principle, and while there is no example of someone willfully opening a hole in another person's roof, the entry in *b. B. Qam.* 9:3 is close enough: "A builder who took upon himself to destroy a wall, and who smashed the rocks or did damage is liable to pay compensation. If he was tearing down a wall on one side, and it fell down on the other side, he is exempt. But if it is because of the blow [which he gave it] he is liable."[48]

In point of fact, the four men did deliberate damage of a substantial nature to a solid roof capable of holding over five hundred pounds in any one spot.

IV. THE CORE HEALING STORY: JESUS HEALS THE PARALYTIC (MARK 2:5a, 11–12)

⁵ᵃκαὶ ἰδὼν ὁ Ἰησοῦς τὴν πίστιν αὐτῶν λέγει τῷ παραλυτικῷ· . . . ¹¹σοὶ λέγω, ἔγειρε ἆρον τὸν κράβαττόν σου καὶ ὕπαγε εἰς τὸν οἶκόν σου. ¹²καὶ ἠγέρθη καὶ εὐθὺς ἄρας τὸν κράβαττον ἐξῆλθεν ἔμπροσθεν πάντων, ὥστε πάντας δοξάζειν τὸν θεὸν λέγοντας ὅτι οὕτως οὐδέποτε εἴδομεν.

⁵ᵃWhen Jesus saw their faith, he said to the paralytic, . . . ¹¹"I say, to you, stand up, take your mat and go to your home." ¹²And he stood up, and immediately took the mat and went out before all of them; so that . . . they all . . . glorified God, saying, "We have never seen anything like this!"

---

[47] See the exhaustive treatment of the Aquilian law in Patrick Mac Chombaich de Colquhoun, *A Summary of the Roman Civil Law: Illustrated by Commentaries on and Parallels from the Mosaic, Canon, Mohammedan, English and Foreign Law*, vol. 3 (London: Stevens, 1854), 235, no. 1933 (see pp. 222–35, nos. 1916–33).

[48] Jacob Neusner, trans., *The Mishnah: A New Translation* (New Haven: Yale University Press, 1988), 523.

The narrator informs us that Jesus saw the men's behavior as an expression of their faith, and immediately he healed their paralyzed friend. So, the only conclusion to be drawn from this comment is that the damage to the roof was of no importance to Jesus, but only the faith of the petitioners. The mutilation of property, in this case the opening up of another person's roof, ordinarily would be seen as offensive. The fact that Jesus sees only faith is a manifestation of his *philanthrōpia* and, as Christians would name it, his *agapē*. The would-be follower surely was meant to understand that a disciple places the focus on the most important elements of the encounter, not on possessions.

In this encounter, the petitioners do not even address Jesus or fashion a request that he help their friend. Rather, they simply open up the roof and lower him. Jesus' reception and admiration of these heavy-handed and silent petitioners is also a lesson to would-be followers. They see in this story a representation of the petitioners who will come to them and not know how to address their petition. Yet their very trouble in coming is a sufficient petition and is an unmistakable expression of faith.

This story does not appeal to any like account in the Jewish Scriptures, but the acclamation of the people, praising God, tells the listener that the Jesus' power is a gift from God.

CONCLUSION

This little anecdote concerns more than Jesus' singular power to cure paralysis. The introduction of the outrageous petitioners who open the roof prepared would-be disciples for situations where petitioners would even be destructive in their determination to have Jesus' followers treat their friends. The degree to which first-time listeners would be shocked at the recourse of the men is the degree to which they reveal their own expectations and behavioral demands. To that degree, then, they would be equally shocked at Jesus' singular gaze at their "faith" and make no mention of the roof. Rather, in the light of their faith, Jesus fulfills their belief and heals their friend.

This demonstration of Jesus' "soul," as Plutarch would call it, modeled for the listener a profound *epieikia,* an understanding of the desperation of those who love the needy that banished any other consideration.

EPILOGUE: WHAT ATTRACTED THE ISSUE OF JESUS' AUTHORITY TO FORGIVE SINS?

The controversy apophthegm (Mark 2:5b–10, 12), outlined above, was subsequently inserted into this miracle story, but the question arises as to why this miracle anecdote was chosen to house the controversy. Why not choose a story of restored sight, for example?

The answer may be found in the overlapping images of the four men lowering the paralytic through the aperture in the roof and the similar actions at a tomb when the bearers of a stretcher lower a stiff, inert form through an aperture into a chamber below. Erwin R. Goodenough's essay on tombs found in the Hellenistic and Roman period in Palestine illustrates these house-like subterranean tombs reached by a shaft opened from what would be, in relation to these tombs, a ceiling.[49] Thus, opening the "ceiling" of the tomb, the bearers would lower the deceased to those waiting below to receive the body, where it would be placed in its resting place in one of the *loculi* of the chamber.

Goodenough distinguishes between two types of such tombs: those influenced by Egyptian custom, where the number of small rooms spread out at the bottom of the shaft, and "older Semitic idea of a rock chamber with special niches for the dead."[50] Both types of tombs were called "houses." In fact, Goodenough comments that the frequent inscription on tombs, οὗτος οἶκος α[ἰ]ώνιος ("this is [the] house eternal"), "is an excellent translation of the biblical בית עלם (Eccl. xii.5), indeed the translation found in the Septuagint."[51]

This is not to argue for a Palestinian venue for the account with its insertion, but only to show that whether the listener was a Palestinian Jew or a Gentile, this image of lowering a stiff body through an aperture above to be received by those below paralleled the action of burial.

In my view, the overlap of these images allowed for a metaphorical interpretation of the story. The state caused by sin is that of the living dead. Thus, the paralyzed man, alive but inert like the dead, was

---

[49] Erwin R. Goodenough, *Illustrations* (vol. 3 of *Jewish Symbols in the Greco-Roman Period*; Bollingen Series 37; New York: Pantheon Books, 1953), sketches 20, a.b., c.d. See also the sketches and discussion of "Family Tombs" by Rachel Hachlili, *Jewish Funerary Customs, Practices and Rites in the Second Temple Period* (Leiden; Boston: Brill, 2005), 235–310, esp. 235–77.

[50] Ibid.

[51] Ibid, 75.

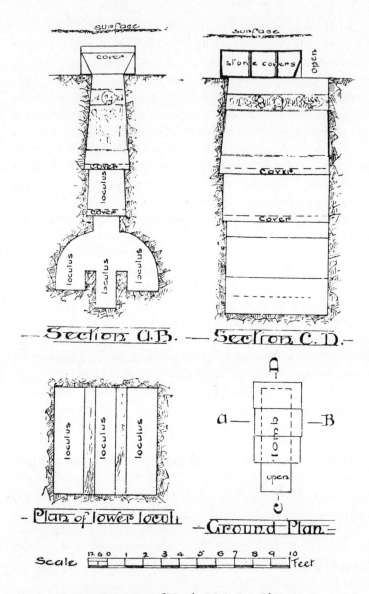

Drawings of Tombs Near Beit Jibrin[52]

---

[52] "The earliest graves of Palestine of the period after Alexander were taken by Watzinger to be those near Beit Jibrin, about twenty-five miles southwest of Jerusalem. They have been dated to the third and early second century B.C. In form the graves had a vertical entrance shaft leading down to a subterra-

a perfect symbol. As sin deadens the soul, so God's forgiveness returns the soul to its full life. If such an allegorical interpretation were used for this story, the petitioners would represent friends of a sinner who know that he no longer has the strength to go to God, and so they bring him to the Lord. And just as the dead received by Jesus are given new life, so this story suggested, in the lowering of a living man, the spiritual reality of the sinner being received and given new life, new freedom through the forgiveness of Jesus. The easy elision of images explains how perfect this healing story was for the insertion, at the moment of healing, of the words of Jesus to the paralyzed man just lowered down to him: "Son, your sins are forgiven."

The decision to insert the controversy story did not result in claiming that the man's physical paralysis was the punishment for his sinning. As mentioned above, the man does not become healed until Jesus pronounces that command in v. 12. Some scholars have logically concluded that the man's sins must have produced the physical paralysis. Rather, the inserted apophthegm is viewing the paralytic as a kind of metaphor about the soul, not a statement about the reason for the actual physical disease. Thus, the early healing story of the paralytic, which was contextualized to reveal Jesus' virtues of *philanthrōpia*, *praos*, and *epieikia* in his response to the petitioners, became an apologetic for Jesus' authority to forgive sins, "a salvation of the soul." The encounter between Jesus and the petitioners, with its paranetic message, moved to a secondary position.

---

nean chamber tomb from which open off individual graves in the form of *kokim*. . . . The type is familiar from earlier Phoenicia, but the objects found in these graves range in date from the hellenistic to the Roman period." Erwin R. Goodenough, "The Jewish Tombs of Palestine," in *The Archeological Evidence from Palestine* (vol. 1 of *Jewish Symbols in the Greco-Roman Period*; Bollingen Series 37; New York: Pantheon Books, 1953), 65.

4

Jesus and the Centurion (Q [Luke] 7:1, 3, 6b–9)

"Nothing is done without a word of command. At daybreak the rank and file report themselves to their respective centurions, the centurions go to salute the tribunes, the tribunes with all the officers then wait on the commander-in-chief, and he gives them, according to custom, the watchword and other orders to be communicated to the lower ranks." (Josephus, *J.W.* 3.87)[1]

The synoptic sayings source, usually called "Q," provides another stream of pre-Gospel traditions, and although this collection of roughly two hundred Jesus sayings belongs to the genre of wisdom collection, it holds two miracle accounts, the first being the centurion's petition for his servant boy (Matt 8:5a–b, 6–10 // Luke 7:3, 6b–9), and the second Jesus' exorcism of a demon that rendered the victim dumb (Matt 12:22 // Luke 11:14). In the latter case, the miracle is brief and leads to the Beelzebul controversy (Matt 12:23–28 // Luke 11:15–20). It could also be argued that the centurion's plea for his servant boy is not really in the form of a miracle story, because the evidence suggests that Q's account concluded with Jesus' word of praise, "I tell you, not even in Israel have I found such faith." Both Matthew and Luke have supplied their own confirmation of the healing: "And the servant was healed in that hour" (Mat 8:13); "When those who had been sent out returned to the house, they found the slave in good health" (Luke 7:10).

---

[1] Flavius Josephus, *Josephus* (trans. H. St. J. Thackeray et al.; 10 vols.; LCL; London: Heinemann; New York: Putnam; Cambridge, Mass.: Harvard University Press, 1926–1981), 2:31.

It may well have been that the story in the pre-Q state had some such statement of the healing, because otherwise this would be the only account where a petitioner's plea for a miracle was left without an affirmation that it had granted by Jesus. The purpose of the anecdote in Q, however, is not to attest Jesus' miracles but rather to shame the persons who belong to "this generation" with the extraordinary belief of this Gentile of Gentiles, which Jesus exclaims that he never saw in all of Israel.[2]

Traveling a different stream than Mark, it supplies another example of the interest in the portraiture of Jesus through encounter with a surprising petitioner.

I. Q RECONSTRUCTION:
MATTHEW 8:7–11 // LUKE 7:2–9

The reconstruction of the Q text has already been provided by the International Q Project in *The Critical Edition of Q*.[3] Where I argue with that reconstruction is in the elimination of κύριε ("sir") in the centurion's address in 3b, and in the translation of it as "master" in 7:6c. While it is quite true that Matthew's custom is to insert κύριε in the petitioner's opening address to Jesus, such as is found in v. 3b, redaction might be argued. The context of this story is special in that it features a Roman centurion whose world is the army, and the recognition of higher rank expected in every address to a superior officer. "Sir" is the best translation, since it is going to be made plain that the centurion thinks of Jesus as someone of lofty rank. For this reason, I present the Q Seminar's reconstruction, but I insert κύριε in the centurion's opening address, v. 3, as the proper address by a soldier seeking help from a person of higher rank and therefore more probably belonging to the story in Q. I translate it in v. 3 and v. 6 as "sir" for the same reason. I underline these modifications of mine.

---

[2] For further study of the forensic denunciations of "this generation" in Q, see John S. Kloppenborg Verbin, *Excavating Q: The History and Setting of the Sayings Gospel* (Minneapolis: Fortress, 2000), esp. 55–213.

[3] James M. Robinson, Paul Hoffmann, and John S. Kloppenborg, eds., *The Critical Edition of Q: Synopsis Including the Gospels of Matthew and Luke, Mark and Thomas with English, German, and French Translations of Q and Thomas* (Minneapolis: Fortress, 2000), 106–15.

Q (Matt 8:7) 7:3:[4] προσῆλθεν αὐτῷ ἑκατόνταρχος παρακαλῶν αὐτὸν [[καὶ λέγων·]]:[5] κύριε ὁ παῖς μου [κακῶς ἔχει].[6] καὶ λέγει αὐτῷ · ἐγὼ ἐλθὼν θεραπεύσω.

Q (Matt 8:8 // Luke 7:6bc–7) 7:6bc–7: καὶ ἀποκριθεὶς ὁ ἑκατόνταρχος ἔφη· κύριε, οὐκ εἰμὶ ἱκανὸς ἵνα μου ὑπὸ τὴν στέγην εἰσέλθῃς, ἀλλὰ εἰπὲ λόγῳ, καὶ ἰαθήτω ὁ παῖς μου.

Q (Matt 8:9 // Luke 7:8) 7:8: καὶ γὰρ ἐγὼ ἄνθρωπός εἰμι ὑπὸ ἐξουσίαν, ἔχων ὑπ᾽ ἐμαυτὸν στρατιώτας, καὶ λέγω τούτῳ· πορεύθητι, καὶ πορεύεται, καὶ ἄλλῳ· ἔρχου, καὶ ἔρχεται, καὶ τῷ δούλῳ μου· ποίησον τοῦτο, καὶ ποιεῖ.

Q (Matt 8:10 // Luke 7:9) 7:9: ἀκούσας δὲ ὁ Ἰησοῦς ἐθαύμασεν καὶ εἶπεν τοῖς ἀκολουθοῦσιν· λέγω ὑμῖν, οὐδὲ ἐν τῷ Ἰσραὴλ τοσαύτην πίστιν εὗρον.

Q (Matt 8:7) 7:3: There came to him a centurion exhorting him [[and saying:[7] (Sir)[8] My]] boy [[<is> doing badly."[9] And he said to him: "Am I]], by coming, to heal him?"

Q (Matt 8:8 // Luke 7:6bc–7) 7:6bc–7: And in reply the centurion said, "Sir, I am not equal[10] [in status/rank] for you to come under my roof; but say a word, and [[let]] my boy [[be]] healed."

---

[4] Since Luke's ordering of sources is conservative, Q units are identified in accord with their placement in Luke. In this case, as it happens, the Lukan introduction clearly shows his own redaction, and Matthew better represents the Q text. So as not to confuse the reader, the identification of the verse as Matt 8:5b is not inserted, and instead, no verse number is provided after the designation "Q 7:3".

[5] Double square brackets indicate a reconstruction that is probable but uncertain, with a rating of C.

[6] The Q Reconstruction committee chose Luke's more simple κακῶς ἔχων over Matthew's more extensive βέβληται ἐν τῇ οἰκίᾳ παραλυτικός, adjusting the participle ἔχων to the verb ἔχει as an accommodation.

[7] Double square brackets indicate a reconstruction which is probable but uncertain, with a rating of C.

[8] I have included "Sir" for the reasons stated above.

[9] The Q Reconstruction committee chose Luke's more simple κακῶς ἔχων over Matthew's more extensive βέβληται ἐν τῇ οἰκίᾳ παραλυτικός, adjusting the participle ἔχων to the verb ἔχει as an accommodation.

[10] The Greek word is ἱκανός (Matt 8:8 // Luke 7:6), not ἄξιος.

Q (Matt 8:9 // Luke 7:8) 7:8: "For I too am a person under authority, with soldiers under me, and I say to one, 'Go,' and he goes, and to another, 'Come,' and he comes, and to my slave, 'Do this,' and he does «it»."

Q (Matt 8:10 // Luke 7:9) 7:9: But Jesus, on hearing, was amazed, and said to those who followed, "I tell you, not even in Israel have I found such faith."

As noted above, the form of the Q pericope is such that it concludes with Jesus' amazed exclamation at the words of the centurion ("I tell you, not even in Israel have I found such faith") but does not relate the accomplishment of the miracle. Thus, the form is really that of an apophthegm.[11] The reconstruction of the Q account keeps favoring Matthew's version, with the exception of his conclusion. Thus, for this study, we will focus on the encounter between the centurion petitioner and Jesus and the way in which Jesus' response to him supplies the would-be follower with a revelation of Jesus' "soul" and thus a model of virtues for which to strive.

II. THE PRESENTATION OF THE PETITIONER

Q (Matt 8:7) 7:3: προσῆλθεν αὐτῷ ἑκατόνταρχος

There came to him a centurion.

Understanding the role, reputation, and religious obligations of centurions is basic to reconstructing the intended impact of the dialogue on the first time listener.

Is This Centurion Roman or Local?

Emil Schürer proposes that the centurion belongs to the auxiliary forces, not the Roman legions, because both Matthew and Luke agree that the location nearby is Capernaum (Matt 8:5 // Luke 7:1), and there was no Roman garrison situated there.[12] Second, Josephus (*J.W.* 2.52)

---

[11] Rudolf Bultmann, *The History of the Synoptic Tradition* (trans. John Marsh; Peabody, Mass.: Hendrickson, 1963), 38.

[12] Emil Schürer, *History of the Jewish People in the Age of Jesus Christ (175 B.C.–A.D. 135)* (rev. and ed. Geza Vermes and F. Millar; 3 vols.; Edinburgh:

reports that it was Herod the Great's soldiers who had controlled the region until he died in 4 B.C.E., after which about three thousand Sebastiani, both cavalry and infantry, were transferred to the Roman auxiliary forces.[13] Indeed, archeological investigations prove that these Sebastiani formed one cavalry *ala*, or wing (five hundred men), and also one cohort (five hundred men) of the five cohorts stationed in the area. Schürer assumes that the other four cohorts were also indigenous. That would complete the three thousand transferred Sebastiani, which matches Josephus's estimates. Finally, Josephus states that in 59 C.E. the troops on duty in Caesarea were largely Caesareans and Sebastiani (*Ant.* 19.363–366).[14]

For his part, Michael P. Speidel contests Schürer's conclusions with both historical and archeological evidence. First, since the Romans had taken charge of Palestine only in 6 C.E., because the province was judged to be politically unstable following the death of Herod the Great, it is unlikely that the Romans would have allowed all control to be given over to these newly transferred troops from Herod's army. It is much more likely that the Sebastiani were integrated among auxiliary units drawn from other provinces. Archeological findings support this conclusion because all inscriptions from the Sebastiani cohort carry the number "1," a number not found on the inscriptions of any other cohort among whom they are mixed. This helps to clarify Josephus's statement that only Caesarean and Sebastiani soldiers were in Caesarea because it points to the blend of the Sebastiani into the much larger auxiliary forces already stationed in the Caesarea garrison. Schürer had also argued that when Rome appointed King Agrippa over Palestine (41–44 C.E.), it would have been unlikely for him to be given any authority over Roman troops, but Speidel counters that Romans often allowed

---

T & T Clark, 1973), 1:363–64. See my article that discusses this matter in regard to Cornelius of Acts 10:1–18: Wendy Cotter, "Cornelius, the Roman Army and Religion," in *Religious Rivalries and the Struggle for Success in Caesarea Maritima* (ed. Terence L. Donaldson; SCJ 8; Waterloo, Ont.: Wilfrid Laurier University Press, 2000), 283.

[13] See Michael P. Speidel, "The Roman Army in Judea under the Procurators: The Italian and Augustan Cohort in the Acts of the Apostles," in vol. 2 of *Roman Army Studies* (Stuttgart: Franz Steiner, 1992), 233–34.

[14] Flavius Josephus, *Josephus* (trans. H. St. J. Thackeray et al.; 10 vols.; Cambridge, Mass.: Harvard University Press, 1965), 9:386–389. Schürer, *History of the Jewish People*, 363–64. For this reference I am indebted to Speidel, "The Roman Army in Judea," 233–34.

such arrangements as long as the local king had proved loyal to Rome. In fact, it was this very flexibility that accounts for the Roman army's successful victory over other peoples. This observation by Speidel is amply supported by Alan Keith Goldworthy, whose monograph *The Roman Army at War* offers multiple examples of the Roman capacity to send out cohorts on special assignment and to adapt themselves to any contingency.[15] Since, however, auxiliary forces were composed of soldiers who were not Roman citizens, does this mean that centurions on duty in Palestine were still not local, but not Roman either? Yann Le Bohec notes that Rome's ideal was that all centurions come from the legions and see to the proper discipline of troops, be they legionary, auxiliary forces, or cavalry.[16]

It is more likely, then, that the people were used to seeing Roman centurions even over the auxiliary forces, and so in this account it is most probable that a Roman would be imagined approaching Jesus, and this is the person I propose for this encounter with Jesus.

The Roman Centurion

The Rank of Centurion

Centurions commanded a "century," or ten *contubernia*, which, held eight legionaries (not ten). Thus in the first century, after the Marian reforms, the centurion governed eighty legionaries. These non-commissioned officers should not be confused with the officer class, as, for example, Lawrence Keppie was led to do[17] probably because in the American army a man who commands sixty to one hundred men holds the rank of captain, an officer. In Roman army organization, however, centurions were ranked as noncommissioned officers, which means that they had a more direct command of the men and imparted the rules of the officers to them. The allocation of the centurions' quarters underlines the difference. Whereas tribunes and other officers had quarters

---

[15] Alan Keith Goldworthy, *The Roman Army at War* (Oxford: Clarendon Press, 1996), esp. 12–38.

[16] Yann Le Bohec, *The Roman Imperial Army* (trans. Raphael Bate; London: Batsford, 1994), esp. 78.

[17] "They should not be thought of as sergeants, but as middle ranking officers, company commanders" (Lawrence Keppie, *The Making of the Roman Army: From Republic to Empire* [Norman: University of Oklahoma Press, 1984], 179).

close to the commander's house, the centurions were in the barracks with the men, their personal rooms located at the end of the building and twice the size of the room given to one *contubernium*.[18] This proximity to the men belongs to the disciplinarian role of the rank of centurion, as does the obligation to know the strengths and weaknesses of the men in the century. The discipline of the Roman army that resulted was their outstanding characteristic. Josephus expresses his amazement:

> Indeed as if they had been born fully armed they never take a holiday from training and do not wait for crises to appear. Their training maneuvers lack none of the vigor of genuine warfare and each soldier practices drill every day with great enthusiasm just as if he were in battle. Therefore, they sustain the shock of combat very easily. For their usual well ordered ranks are not disrupted by any confusion, or numbed by fear, or exhausted by toil; so, certain victory inevitably follows since the enemy cannot match

---

[18] See Birgitta Hoffman, "The Quarters of Legionary Centurions of the Principate," *Britannia* 26 (1995), 107–51, esp. 134, 139–40, where the conditions obtaining prior to the Flavian period are carefully distinguished. According to Hyginus Gromaticus, *De munitionibus castrorum* 127.1, it is stipulated that the centurion's quarters be twice the size of a *contubernium*, whether double tent size or double room size. The centurions lived in very close proximity to the men, with only a door separating their quarters from the cohort. See also Tony Henderson, "Roman Centurions—at Close Quarters," *The Newcastle Journal*, May 17, 2007, which announces the final completion of the restoration of the centurion's quarters at the Arbeia fort in South Shields, near Newcastle: "'In the barrack, eight soldiers had to fit into two rooms but the centurion had five rooms,' said Alex Croom, keeper of archeology at the fort. 'The centurion is the middle link between the spacious living conditions of the commanding officer and the soldiers in the barracks. While the commander's house had fine paintings and the squaddies had plain walls, the centurion's home has red lower walls and a whitewashed upper half.'" See also the drawing of the interior of such barracks illustrating the cramped quarters of the men in the *contubernium* as contrasted with the expansive quarters of the centurion, located at the end of the building, in Peter Connolly, *The Roman Fort* (Oxford: Oxford University Press, 1991), 13. Note the archeological discussion with a minute diagram illustrating the situation of barracks in relation to the house of the commander in I. A. Richmond et al., "The Agricolan Fort at Fendoch," *Proceedings of the Society of Antiquaries of Scotland* 73 (1938–39): 110–54, especially the diagram following p. 114 and also the reference to the barracks, pp. 134–36. In each discussion of the ten barracks mention is made of the condition of the centurion's rooms, which are always located at the end of the building, where the cohort is quartered. They live in the same building with the men. Also see John Ward, "Military Remains," in *Roman Era in Britain* (London: Methuen, 1911), 38–71, esp. 58.

this. Indeed one would not be wrong in saying that their training maneuvers are battles without bloodshed, and their battles maneuvers with bloodshed. (*J.W.* 3.72–76)[19]

The Centurion as Disciplinarian

Warren Carter interprets the presence of the Roman centurion in the Q story as "an agent and enforcer of the imperial status quo."[20] Certainly this is true, and in a vivid way, the rank of centurion embodies the roughness and ruthlessness of the unrelenting obedience to orders that characterized the Roman army and resulted in the subjugation of the people. One sign of the centurion rank is the *vitis*, a stick that was to be used to beat any legionary disobedient to orders. This *vitis* required the authorization of the senate because ordinarily the beating of a Roman citizen was not allowed. It was no mere symbol, but rather a daily tool for disciplining the men. Sometimes it was used savagely, as evidenced in Tacitus's well-known account of the centurion Lucilius. He was murdered, on account of his brutality, by the mutinying legionaries in Pannanoia: "The centurion Lucilius lost his life. In joking army talk his nickname was 'Another-Please,' because every time he broke a stick over a soldier's back he used to shout loudly for another and then another" (Tacitus, *Ann.* 1.23).[21] This does not allow the conclusion that all centurions were cruel, but only shows that beating the men to make them obey was a common practice. The centurions therefore represent the traditions of the army, instant obedience to orders.

The Ideals of the Men Chosen for the Rank of Centurion

Le Bohec's study of the backgrounds of most centurions results in his conclusion that they represent "the oldest and most deeply Romanized sections of the middle class."[22] Keppie states, "They provided

---

[19] Flavius Josephus, *Josephus* (trans. Thackeray et al.), 2:598–599.

[20] Warren Carter, *Matthew and the Margins: A Sociopolitical and Religious Reading* (Maryknoll, N.Y.: Orbis, 2000), 200.

[21] Tacitus, *Histories, Books 4–5; Annals, Books 1–3* (trans. C. H. Moore and J. Jackson; LCL; Cambridge, Mass.: Harvard University Press, 1925), 284–285.

[22] Le Bohec, *Roman Imperial Army*, 78. Here Le Bohec is not imposing our own stratification on ancient society but rather is making a distinction such that "elites" are upper class, and the indigent poor represent the lower class, whereas centurions usually came from families that were not among the nonelite poverty-stricken.

continuity of standards and traditions. Equally, however, they must have been bastions of conservatism, averse to innovation and change."[23] Most centurions had come up through the ranks,[24] which normally demanded fifteen to twenty years,[25] so they were experienced and proven soldiers. Even though it is true that sometimes certain influential families arranged for their sons to be given the centurion rank in order to gain the military service required to be eligible for public office,[26] Le Bohec's investigation of the sources leads him to conclude that on the whole, the appointed men upheld the centurions' reputation for great courage.

Vegetius's "history" of the imperial army is admittedly idealized, and even if his backward glance from the fifth century C.E. is rosier than the reality, it identifies those qualities most hoped for in a centurion:

> A centurion is chosen for great strength and tall stature, as a man who hurls spears and javelins skillfully and strongly, has expert knowledge how to fight with the sword and rotate the shield and has learned the whole art of armature, is alert, sober and agile, and *more ready to do the things ordered of him than speak*, keeps his soldiers in training, makes them practice their arms, and sees that they are well clothed and shod, and that the arms are burnished and bright. (*Epit. mil.* 2.14)[27]

The ideal of his disposition, "more ready to do the things ordered of him than speak," underlines the expectation of the centurion to display perfect obedience.[28]

---

[23] Keppie, *Making of the Roman Army*, 179.

[24] See the funereal inscription located near Cillium, Africa, that an eighty-year-old centurion and his sixty-five-year-old wife erected for their centurion son who died at thirty-five, which traces the long career of the older centurion in all the legions—a remarkable piece of evidence (Brian Campbell, *The Roman Army, 31 BC–337 AD: A Sourcebook* [London: Routledge, 1994], 48–49.)

[25] Keppie, *Making of the Roman Army*, 178.

[26] Le Bohec, *Roman Imperial Army*, 78. Yet, efforts to obtain rank by influence were not always successful, as Suetonius attests in his note that the nobleman Marcus Valerius Probus of Berytus finally gave up waiting altogether (Suetonius, *De Grammaticus et Rhetoribus*, 24). For this reference I am indebted to Campbell, *Roman Army*, 48.

[27] Vegetius, *Epitome of Military Science* (trans. N. P. Milner; TTH 16; Liverpool: Liverpool University Press, 1993), 46 (my italics).

[28] The bold statements of centurions usually are connected with valor. A typical if wrenching example, from Plutarch, is the loyal speech and courageous action of the centurion Gaius Crassinius: "As Caesar himself was about

Civilian Critique of the Centurion: Tough, Uncouth, and Readily Violent

Josephus communicates a complimentary view of Roman army discipline, but he does not represent the ordinary view of subjugated peoples, who mostly experienced the violent and bullying behavior of so many soldiers. Juvenal's *Satire* 16 on the army life illustrates how dangerous it was for a civilian to bring charges against soldiers. Presented with the extremes of satire, it nonetheless points to the truth of the power. Any soldier accused must be tried in the camp, "If he seek redress, he has appointed for him as judge a hob-nailed centurion with a row of jurors with brawny calves sitting before a big bench" (*Sat.* 16.13–15). The civilian reasons, "'Most right and proper it is,' you say, 'that a centurion should pass sentence on a soldier; nor shall I fail of satisfaction if I make good my case.'" Juvenal banishes this naivety: "But then the whole cohort will be your enemies; all the maniples will agree as one man in applying a cure to the redress you have received by giving you a thrashing which shall be worse than the first. So, as you possess a pair of legs, you must have a mulish brain worthy of the eloquent Vagellius to provoke so many jack-boots and all those thousands of hobnails" (*Sat.* 16.17–25). Thus, even "if thrashed himself, he [the civilian] must hold his tongue, and not venture to exhibit to the Praetor the teeth that have been knocked out, or the black and blue lumps upon his face, or the one eye left which the doctor holds out no hope of saving" (*Sat.* 16.9–12).[29]

Juvenal's "hob-nailed centurion" judge who will readily condemn the civilian out of loyalty to the army seems to be a kind of stock figure.

---

to move his lines of legionaries, and was already going forward into action, he saw first one of his centurions, a man experienced in war and faithful to him, encouraging his men and challenging them to vie with him in prowess. Him Caesar addressed by name and said: 'Gaius Crassinius, what are our hopes, and how does our confidence stand?' Then Crassinius, stretching forth his right hand, said with a loud voice: 'We shall win a glorious victory, O Caesar, and thou shalt praise me to-day, whether I am alive or dead.' So saying, he plunged foremost into the enemy at full speed, carrying along with him the one hundred and twenty soldiers under his command. But after cutting his way through the first rank, and while he was forging forward with great slaughter, he was beaten back by the thrust of a sword through his mouth, and the point of the sword actually came out at the back of his neck" (*Caes.* 49.5–6) (Plutarch, *Caesar*, in vol. 7 of *Plutarch's Lives* [trans. Bernadotte Perrin; LCL; Cambridge, Mass.: Harvard University Press, 1967], 549–51).

[29] Juvenal, *The Satires*, in *Juvenal and Persius* (trans. G. G. Ramsay; LCL; London: Heinemann; New York: Putnam, 1928), 303–5.

The poet Persius illustrates the coarseness of the centurions twice in his own satires. In his *Satire* 3, immediately after a philosopher completes his exhortation to the life of learning and virtue, Persius adds,

> Here one of the unsavoury tribe of Centurions may say, "What I know is enough for me; I have no mind to be an Arcesilas,[30] or one of your poor devils of Solons who go about with their heads bent down, pinning their eyes to the ground, champing and muttering to themselves like mad dogs, balancing their words on protruded lip, and pondering over the dreams of some sickly grey-beard that nothing can come out of nothing, and that nothing can into nothing return.[31] Is it over stuff like this that you grow pale? Is it worth while for this, to go without your dinner?" Such jests move the mob to mirth: peal after peal of laughter comes rippling forth from the curled nostrils of our brawny youth. (*Sat.* 3.77–87)[32]

Then, in *Satire* 5, Persius warns those who would want to discuss religious rituals and in particular the mystery cults, "If you talk in this fashion among your varicose Centurions, the hulking Pulfennius straightaway burst into a huge guffaw, and bids a clipped hundred-penny piece for a lot of a hundred Greeks" (*Sat.* 5.189–90).[33]

These comic satires agree on the image of the centurion as brawny, tough, outspoken, physical, and openly derisive of nuanced philosophical or religious thought. It would be unfair to claim that every soldier and every centurion was violent with the people, but Brian Campbell's research leads him to conclude that the most prevalent civilian experience of soldiers was one of abuse. The following quotation is extensive, but I hope the reader will agree that it helps in reconstructing what the immediate reaction of first-time listeners would be to the Gospel story where a centurion is the petitioner.

> Some communities did benefit from the proximity of army units or through the influence of fellow-citizens who were soldiers. But the dominating theme is the brutal oppression of civilians by soldiers, whom the

---

[30] "Arcesilas, or Arcesilaus, a Greek philosopher of the third century B.C., regarded as the founder of the Middle Academy" (Persius, *The Satires*, in *Juvenal and Persius* [trans. Ramsay], 351 n. 5).

[31] "The fundamental principle of Epicurean philosophy" (ibid., 352 n. 2).

[32] Ibid., 351–53.

[33] Persius, *The Satires*, in *Juvenal and Persius* (trans. Ramsay), 389. Here the centurion is presented as sweeping away all these "mysterious" cults as just more Greek foolishness.

emperors were apparently unable or unwilling to restrain. Soldiers were distinguished by special privileges and treatment in court; they were comrades of the emperor; they were armed; they were often in contact with local people, sometimes in a police capacity; in certain areas their officers were the only available source of legal jurisdiction. It is not surprising that in these circumstances soldiers exploited their status, prestige and physical might to oppress civilians, sometimes on their own initiative, sometimes on the orders of higher officials, since the system of provincial administration made demands (in the form of requisitions) on local communities, which were difficult to monitor and control. Inscriptions and papyri containing the complaints of provincial communities preserve an authentic record of serious, widespread and persistent abuse, and indicate that in any analysis of the failings of Roman provincial administration, soldiers appear as the most intransigent culprits.[34]

Religious Obligations in the Army[35]

Jesus' exclamation (Q 7:9) "I tell you, not even in Israel have I found such faith" invites the question as to what religious rituals or obligations would have helped form this man. The unspoken presupposition is that one could not expect a religious sentiment such as "faith" to belong to a centurion.

This invites a small review of the religious obligations of soldiers, and in this case, the centurions. First, the propaganda of the Romans was that they were outstanding among all nations for their attention to religion, as Cicero claims:

> However good an opinion we may have of ourselves, yet we do not excel the Spaniards in number, the Gauls in strength, the Carthaginians in cunning, the Greeks in art nor the Italians and Latins in the inborn sense of home and soil. *We do however excel all people in religiosity* and in that unique wisdom that has brought us to the realization that everything is subordinate to the rule and direction of the gods. (*Har. resp.* 19)[36]

---

[34] Campbell, *Roman Army*, 170.

[35] For a fuller treatment of this topic, see Cotter, "Cornelius," 285–300.

[36] Cicero, *Oratio de haruspicum responsis*, in *Speeches: Pro Archia Poeta; Post Reditum in Senatu; Post Reditum ad Quirites; De Domo Sua; De Haruspicum Responsis; Pro Plancio* (trans. N. H. Watts; LCL; London: Heinemann; New York: Putnam, 1923), 340–41 (my italics). For this reference I am indebted to John Helgeland, "Roman Army Religion," *ANRW* 16.2:1471–72.

In fact, a soldier's life began with his *sacramentum*, the oath that a soldier swore on his enrollment and renewed every year on January 3.[37] Every morning, a soldier made a holy promise to obey all customs and orders.[38] Devotions and signs of adoration and honor were multiple within the camp, notably the daily honoring of the military *genii*, the spirits that protected the camp: "Even though worshipped only by the army itself, they [the military *genii*] were so manifold and plentiful that one has rightly said that no other manifestation of Roman life left more remains of the cult of the Genii than the army."[39] Among these spirits, the most popular among the soldiers was each century's genius, the *genius centuriae*,[40] who received daily obeisance from each centurion and his men for protecting them. Next in order were the *genii legionis*, spirits guiding the legion: "dedications have been found inside and outside the camps; in the chapels of the *scholae* of the centurions or *mensores,* in the baths, on duty stations, in colonies where veterans had settled, and elsewhere, which again proves that the cult was spontaneous, not prescribed.[41]

Other foci of worship included the *numen* of the standards, such as the eagle belonging to each legion, and the totems representing the special animals whose spirit, it was believed, would be imparted to those who honored its power.[42] The deities of the camp walls and those of the parade ground were also rendered the soldiers' worship.[43]

---

[37] Michael Grant illustrates the oath taking on a commemorative coin with the image of the *imperator* and an army officer clasping hands over an altar (*The Army of the Caesars* [New York: Scribner, 1974], 79).

[38] Robert O. Fink, *Roman Military Records on Papyrus* (Philological Monographs of the American Philological Association 26; Cleveland: Press of Case Western Reserve University, 1971). See also G. R. Watson, "Documentation in the Roman Army," *ANRW* 16.1:493–507, esp. 502.

[39] Michael Speidel, "The Cult of the Genii in the Roman Army and a New Military Deity," *ANRW* 16.2:1543.

[40] "The Genii of military units are usually represented young, nude, and beardless, holding a horn of plenty and a bowl (patera) for the wine libation due them" (Ibid., 1547).

[41] Ibid., 1546.

[42] Bohec, *Roman Imperial Army*, 246–47.

[43] On January 3, Vow Day, a new altar was erected to replace the old one at the border of the parade grounds, the dividing line beyond which lay the open area around the camp. These altars were dedicated to the major gods of the Roman pantheon, in particular Jupiter Optimus Maximus, but also Military Mars, Eternal Rome, and Emperor's Victory (Graham Webster, *The Roman Imperial Army of the First and Second Centuries A.D.* [London: A. & C. Black, 1969], 269).

It is clear from this review that any religious devotions were connected to the army ethos itself and actually were quite simple. The
Roman military religious calendar unearthed in Dura Europus, although
dated 232 C.E.,[44] is good evidence of the character of army religion even
in first century, for traditions are sacred in the army. What is notable
there is that of the forty-two legible inscriptions, only eight feasts are directly related to gods of the army,[45] while the remaining thirty-six honor
imperial personages. This brings out the soldier's obligation of loyalty
to the emperor and his family as an intrinsic element of his life,[46] but it
also shows that army religion of itself was plain and focused on the task
of being an obedient soldier. Thus, the training, and the religious oaths
of the soldier and the centurion, prepared him for a life of orders and
obedience to orders, as had been sworn to the deities and powers.

III. A CENTURION COMES FORWARD
TO PETITION JESUS

Q 7:3:[47] προσῆλθεν αὐτῷ ἑκατόνταρχος παρακαλῶν αὐτὸν καὶ
λέγων· κύριε, ὁ παῖς μου κακῶς ἔχει.

A centurion approached him, exhorting him and saying, "Sir, my
boy is doing badly."

---

[44] See Helgeland, "Roman Army Religion," 1484–86.

[45] Of these eight army festivals, four honor gods of the Roman people
(March 19: the day of the Quinquatria, a festival to Minerva; April 21: the
birthday of Roma; June 9: Vesta Mater; August 5: Salus), and only four are
specific to the army (January 3: Vow Day; January 7: honor to soldiers being
discharged; May 9–11: honor to the standards of the army; May 12: circus races
in honor of Mars, protector of the army).

[46] As Allen Hoey concluded from his research "Official Policy Towards
Oriental Cults in the Roman Army" (*TAPA* 70 [1939]: 457–79), no matter
what cults the soldiers brought with them or adopted, none were ever incorporated into the official religious calendar of the legions.

[47] Since Luke's ordering of sources is conservative, Q units are identified
in accord with their placement in Luke. In this case, as it happens, the Lukan
introduction clearly shows his own redaction, and Matthew better represents
the Q text. So as not to confuse the reader, the identification of the verse as
Matt 8:5b is not inserted, and instead no verse number is provided after the
designation Q 7:3.

The Characterization of the Centurion

In light of Brian Campbell's assessment of the civilian experience of the army, the approach of a centurion would insert some tension into the account. From the Jewish side, and the side of nonelites, the fact that this centurion approaches Jesus to beg him[48] about any problem would be a surprise, since centurions usually are confident and authoritative. It must be noted, however, that the narrator has given him a very brief petition,[49] "Sir, my boy is doing badly," which may be an attempt to convey the plain speech of the soldier.

---

[48] This is the meaning of παρακαλῶν, "begging." It is curious that although the NRSV consistently translates the verb as "beg" for the Markan miracles stories (Mark 1:40; 5:10, 12, 17, 18, 23; 6:56; 7:32; 8:22), in the one Q usage here "appeal" is used, a cooler verb. It is chosen again for Matt 26:53, where Jesus informs his captors that he could "appeal" to his Father for angels to help him. Then it becomes "plead" in Matt 18:20–32 (the parable of the ungrateful steward). Where Luke shows that he does not wish to use Mark's παρακαλέω, however, and substitutes δέομαι, "pray" (Luke 5:12 vs. Mark 1:40; Luke 8:38 vs. Mark 5:18), the translators use "beg" just the same. The verb here, presented in a participial form, παρακαλῶν, conveys beseeching or begging. Perhaps "appeal" is used here under the influence of the petitioner's status as a centurion, a more elevated and distant figure than the characters who come to Jesus with a much lower status: the leper (Mark 1:40); the formerly demonized man who longs to follow Jesus (Mark 5:18); the friends of the deaf man with the speech impediment (Mark 7:32); and the friends of the blind man of Bethsaida (Mark 8:22). It is important to allow the same intensity for the centurion's request to Jesus that is easily afforded to these other figures, where παρακαλέω is rightly represented as "beg."

[49] Matthew's version of the petition, κύριε, ὁ παῖς μου βέβληται ἐν τῇ οἰκίᾳ παπαλυτικός, δεινῶς βασανιζόμενος ("Sir, my servant boy is lying in the house, suffering terribly, a paralytic"), shows signs of his redaction first in the address κύριε ("Sir" or "Lord") and in the precise identification of the illness as paralysis (Matt 8:6), which, if it had been in Q, would have been copied by Luke. As it is, Luke's text only holds that the servant boy "is doing badly" (κακῶς ἔχων [Luke 7:2:]). This must have been the general expression for "very sick" that stood in Q, and both evangelists, each in his own way, tried to increase the drama, Matthew by identifying it as a paralysis, while Luke adds that the boy is "close to death" (Luke 7:3). See the particular arguments in Steven R. Johnson, *Q 7:1–10: The Centurion's Faith in Jesus' Word* (Documenta Q; Leuven: Peeters, 2002; Robinson, Hoffmann, and Kloppenborg, eds., *Critical Edition of Q*, 104–7.

For Whom Is the Centurion Beseeching Jesus' Help?

A scholarly argument has been raised over for whom the centurion begs. Matthew's text reads παῖς ("boy," in the sense of either "servant boy" or "son"), whereas Luke's text reads δοῦλος ("slave").[50] Perhaps the most compelling evidence that Luke has redacted Q is that his version of the centurion's urging matches that of Matthew (Matt 8:8 // Luke 7:7), where παῖς is used: εἰπὲ λόγῳ, καὶ ἰαθήτω ὁ παῖς μου ("speak the word, and my boy will be healed").[51] Thus it is much more probable that παῖς stood in Q.

But does παῖς mean "servant" here or "son"? Some scholars, such as Amy-Jill Levine, conclude that it must mean "son" because ὁ υἱός is used in the similar story in John 4:46–54, where an official pleads for his own son. She also sees it as a parallel story to the Canaanite woman's petition for her daughter (Matt 15:21–28 [source, Mark 7:24–30]), and also to Matthew's substitution of an official for "Jairus" in the story of the father asking Jesus to raise his dead daughter (Matt 9:18–26 [source, Mark 5:21–43]).[52] First, it must be accepted that there is not just one stream of traditions, and the fact that similar stories can appear in Mark, Q, and John is not sufficient evidence to allow the claim that all belonged to one stream originally. Moreover, even if one had such grounds, evidence is lacking to point to which would be the most primitive. With respect to Matthew's parallels, it is curious why, if he thought that there was an intended parallel between 15:21–28 and 9:18–26, he did not balance the "daughter," θυγάτηρ, found in both accounts, with the particularity of υἱός. Matthew knows this particularity of identification, and he adopts Q 14:26's υἱός in Matt 10:37: ὁ φιλῶν πατέρα ἢ μητέρα ὑπὲρ ἐμὲ οὐκ ἔστιν μου ἄξιος, καὶ ὁ φιλῶν υἱὸν ἢ θυγατέρα ὑπὲρ ἐμὲ οὐκ ἔστιν μου ἄξιος ("Whoever loves father or mother more than me is

---

[50] See the extensive representation of scholarly argumentation in Johnson, *Q 7:1–10*, 167–84.

[51] Joseph A. Fitzmyer, *The Gospel of Luke* (2 vols.; AB 28, 28A; New York: Doubleday, 1981–1985), 1:649. Luke probably substituted δοῦλος ("slave") from the soldier's example of how his authority functions. Q (Matt 8:9 // Luke 7:8) 7:8: καὶ τῷ δούλῳ μου· ποίησον τοῦτο, καὶ ποιεῖ ("and to my slave, 'Do this,' and he does it").

[52] Amy-Jill Levine, *The Social and Ethnic Dimensions of Matthean Salvation History* (SBEC 14; Lewiston, N.Y.: Mellen Press, 1988), 108.

not worthy of me; and whoever loves *son or daughter* more than me is not worthy of me" [my italics]).[53]

In a recent article addressing the meaning of παῖς, Theodore Jennings Jr. and Tat-Siong Benny Liew observe that Matthew uses παῖς and παιδίον twenty-six times, ten of them with regard to Jesus' childhood, and bracketing the passage under consideration, "eleven of them are used generically to refer to a child or a group of children."[54] The problem here is that there is a distinct difference in the usage of παῖς and παιδίον because παιδίον is always used of children and never of servants. Of the eighteen usages of παιδίον in Matthew, the first nine belong to the pericope of the magi (Matt 2:8, 9, 11, 13 [bis], 14, 20 [bis], 21), while seven belong to Matthew's copying the Q 7:31 (Matt 11:16) and Markan texts, where the referents are children (Matt 18:2, 5; 19:13, 14), and finally to his own redaction, adding "women and children" to Mark's "men" in the conclusions of both accounts of the multiplication of the loaves and fishes (Matt 14:21 [Mark 6:44]; Matt 15:38 [Mark 8:9]). His own composition is found in Matt 18:3, 4 where παιδίον twice refers to children.

The word under examination, however, is παῖς, and Matthew's use of it beyond the one Q passage (Mark does not use the word) is found in only four texts: 12:18, the LXX of Isa 42:1, which refers to "my servant"; 14:2, a redactive insertion on Mark, where Herod tells his "boys" that Jesus is really John the Baptist, and here he cannot mean Herod's sons; 21:15, a reference to the "boys" crying out "Hosanna to the son of David"; 17:18, in the story of the boy who was demonized, the only one of the four where Matthew uses παῖς without it meaning "servant." At the same time, however, one wonders if "son" is the translation in 17:18:

---

[53] Theodore Jennings Jr. and Tat-Siong Benny Liew hold that Matthew's Gospel would give Levine good reason for her conclusions because "for servants and slaves, Matthew's overwhelming tendency is to use the word δοῦλος," listing the thirty-six occurrences of the word in his gospel ("Mistaken Identities but Model Faith: Rereading the Centurion, the Chap, and the Christ in Matthew 8:5–13," *JBL* 123 [2004]: 470). These conclusions are possible only if one ignores source theory, for of the thirty-six appearances of the word, all are derived from Mark or Q, and only two insertions are found, and these on the one Q text, Q 6:40, where the evangelist intensifies the relation of Q's student to teacher, so that it becomes slave to master (Matt 10:24–25). Matthew shows no "tendency" to use δοῦλος, except as it occurs in his sources.

[54] Ibid.

"the son was healed at that moment." Without υἱός stipulated, however, the more natural sense is: "the child/lad was healed at that moment."

As for Q, it would require special pleading to argue that παῖς means "son," because Q uses υἱός as seen in four Q pericopae (Q 11:11, 19; 12:53; 14:36), and this is the only appearance of the word παῖς in Q.[55]

Another factor that argues against παῖς meaning "son" is that Roman soldiers were not permitted to marry,[56] and although it is true that many had what we would understand as common-law wives, it seems unlikely that the centurion would be so blatant and boldly brief about a serious breach in army regulations like this in front of Jesus. Had that been intended, it seems more likely that the narrator would have made more of it instead of letting such a matter drop. The listeners, then, would be more likely to understand παῖς to indicate the servant boy. The Roman army traveled with myriads of servants, as Michael Speidel observes: "When Vitellius marched on Rome, he had sixty thousand soldiers with him, mainly legionaries. Yet the number of servants (*calones*) in that army, if we believe Tacitus, was even larger."[57]

If the Greek παῖς understood as a servant is translated into Latin, it becomes *puer* (even the Vulgate of Matt 8:6 presents *puer* as the translation of παῖς), and many Roman inscriptions refer to a man's personal servant, valet, so to speak, as a *puer*.[58] Jennings and Liew interpret the text

---

[55] The word υἱός occurs nineteen times in Q. Besides the four texts above, the other uses are in the construct of epithets, most frequently "Son of Man" (9x: Q 6:22; 7:34; 9:58; 11:30; 12:10, 40; 17:24, 26, 30), then "Son of God" (2x: Q 4:3, 9) and "Son of Peace" (1x: Q 10:6). Then there is the relation of the Father and the Son with regard to Jesus (3x: Q 10:22).

[56] Dio Cassius, *Hist.* 60.24.3. See Brian Campbell, "The Marriage of Soldiers under the Empire," *JRS* 68 (1978): 153–66. For this reference I am indebted to Keppie, *Making of the Roman Army*, 148, 252 n. This is not say that there were no common-law marriages, even if they were outlawed. It is just that in this case it would be unlikely for something unlawful to be spoken of so plainly by this officer. The more immediate reference would be to the houseboy/servant.

[57] Michael Speidel, "The Soldiers' Servants," in vol. 2 of *Roman Army Studies* (Stuttgart: Franz Steiner, 1992), 342. See Tacitus, *Hist.* 2.87.

[58] See, for example, the extensive entry for "Puer," in James Bailey, ed., *The Universal Latin Lexicon of Facciolatus and Forcellinus* (2 vols.; London: Baldwin & Craddock, 1828), 2:316, which stipulates as one of the meanings beyond "son," "Denique puer est servus, a boy, slave, lacquey, παῖς." See references in Cicero, *Rosc. Amer.* 21.59; 28.77, where the "boy" is called upon to arrange to bring the dinner; Plautus, *Mostelleria*, act 1, scene 3, line 150, where

in this way and reopen Donald Mader's proposal that these "boys" were the object of pederasty so that such a relationship could be presumed for this soldier and his "boy."[59] Mader presents two contrasting conclusions from his study. First, he claims that one must consider the possibility that "this passage in the New Testament does refer to homosexuality in its classical form of paederasty, *though there is no one fact that requires that it be seen that way*."[60] Then, astonishingly, he explains that since the existence of such accounts are not historical but rather reflect the early church: "the most that can be claimed is that a segment of the early church out of which the 'Q' document and Matthew arose, was not concerned, and *believed that Jesus was not concerned, when confronted by a responsible loving paederastic relationship, but rather held it subordinate to questions of faith*."[61] That is, in a circular reasoning, they argue that the silence over specifying pederasty is a sign that it was so common that no specificity was necessary, and this allows them to conclude that the Q community that reports the story does so because it accepted pederasty.

Together with Mader, Jennings and Liew provide copious references to pederasty in Greek texts of various genres from fourth century B.C.E. to imperial times and beyond. Their conclusion is that pederasty was practiced with impunity among Romans, as long as the *puer* was not freeborn.[62] The scholar of Greco-Roman antiquity can affirm that this is true, but the point is, as Mader admits, "there is no one fact that requires that it [the pericope] be seen that way."[63] Jennings and Liew, however, disagree on this matter and see evidence in the centurion's "reluctance to have Jesus come to his house."[64]

The problem with their research is that it does not present the Jewish abhorrence of sexual aberrations, which certainly included

---

the "boy" is called over to bring water for washing hands; Horace, *Sat.* 2.59, where the man pestered by unwanted company bends to give a message to his attending "boy."

[59] Jennings and Liew, "Mistaken Identities." See Donald Mader, "The *Entimos Pais* of Matthew 8:5–13 and Luke 7:1–10," in *Homosexuality and Religion and Philosophy* (ed. Wayne R. Dynes and Stephen Donaldson; New York: Garland, 1992), 223–35. (The *entimos* actually is derived from Luke 7:2, but through argument it is assigned to Matthew.)

[60] Mader, "*Entimos Pais*," 231 (my italics).

[61] Ibid. (my italics).

[62] Jennings and Liew, "Mistaken Identities," 473–78.

[63] Mader, "*Entimos Pais*," 231.

[64] Jennings and Liew, "Mistaken Identities," 478.

pederasty.[65] It is very unlikely that the mere presence of παῖς was understood as signaling a pederastic relationship, for Jesus' praise to the centurion for his "reluctance" in having Jesus come to his home, and praising him above everyone else in Israel for his astonishing "faith" in being content with a distance healing. That reluctance would constitute a shocking laxity for Jesus, a seemingly sinful condoning of evil. Moreover, it would be impossible to explain why Matthew would have preserved such a term in his story for this very Jewish Gospel and this very Jewish Jesus.

Michael Speidel, an expert on the Roman army, discusses the role of the "boys" who served the soldiers, and his treatment shows that παῖς/ *puer* generally is used for the servants without any pederastic meaning. In his remarks on the genuine affection that many Roman soldiers had for the boys who traveled with them and served them, he includes a poignant funereal tribute (which he and Silvio Panciera discovered) for two deceased servant boys. The boys' master, Aureliius Sanctinus, a cavalry officer (with a rank equal to that of a centurion) composed this memorial:

[D(is)] M(anibus).
"[—nat(ione) P]ontico ab[se]
[dilecto *puer*]o, Aur(elius) San[ctinus],
dec(urio), de se bene merito[o]
[Hic du]o sunt iuvenes positi, c[—]
[—]re in illo, diversisque lo[cis nati].
[Ille—] ibi, qui prior est posit[us, —]
[— Oceanique Marsa[c—],
[hunc P]ontus Achillea ge[nuit humus].
[Nunc] ac si fraternal sti[rpe orti]
[awq]uali Tiburti ponder[rpe tecti]
[Aure(elius] Sanctinus de s[ua V(ixit) a(nnos) —].

Two boys are buried here together in this grave, though born in different places. The one buried first is from the North Sea shore and the Marsacan

---

[65] See Sacha Stern, *Jewish Identity in Early Rabbinic Writings* (AGJU 23; Leiden: Brill, 1994), 23–26; Bryne Fone, *Homophobia: A History* (New York: Henry Holt, 2000), 86–101; Robin Scroggs, "Palestinian Judaism: Stern Opposition," and "Hellenistic Judaism: Pederasty Vilified," in *The New Testament and Homosexuality: Contextual Background for Contemporary Debate* (Philadelphia: Fortress, 1983), 66–84, and 85–98.

land; the other is born by the Black Sea, the land of Achilles. Now like brothers they lie under the same weight of Tiburtan stone.[66]

The scholars comment, "Revealing the love of an Emperor's horseman for those around him, even though they be of very different national origin, the epitaphs Sanctinus wrote for the two boys show forth a kindness Roman soldiers no doubt felt as much as other men of their time, but for which we too often lack documentation."[67]

This same spirit of kindness explains the centurion searching out Jesus to plead for his boy servant.

ὁ παῖς μου κακῶς ἔχει.

"My boy is doing badly."

The petition could not be briefer, as though the narrator were trying to convey the plainspoken, disciplined world of the centurion. The Roman army had its own medics,[68] so the centurion's appeal to Jesus suggests that the boy's condition is beyond ordinary medical treatment.

---

[66] See Michael P. Speidel and Silvio Panciera, "From the North and Black Sea Shores: Two New Gravestones for Boys of the 'Equites Singulares Augusti,'" in *Roman Army Studies* (2 vols.; Stuttgart: Franz Steiner, 1992), 2:353–60, esp. 354–55 (my italics).

[67] Ibid., 2:356. Luke's change of the παῖς to δοῦλος makes it more difficult for the exegete to capture the more tender concern suggested by the centurion's use of "boy" in Q/Matthew. Joel B. Green, representing the Lukan version, relies on the statements about the care of slaves in general from Xenophon (*Mem.* 2.10.1) and Columella (*Rust.* 12.3.6) and concludes that the centurion cannot be seen as especially caring, "since care for sick slaves was advised in Roman antiquity as a way to prolong their usefulness" (*Gospel of Luke* [NICNT; Grand Rapids: Eerdmans, 1997], 286). Such a cold and mercenary motivation, however, does not seem supported by the rest of Luke's version when the centurion sends a Jewish delegation to plead for the life of the slave. Such an elaborate decision and plan convey genuine concern for the slave himself, and indeed the Jewish delegation's endorsement of the centurion (Luke 7:4–5) confirms this impression.

[68] See R. W. Davies, "The *Medici* of the Roman Armed Forces," *Epigraphische Studien* 8 (1969): 83–99; "Some More Military *Medici*," *Epigraphische Studien* 9 (1972): 1–11; "The Roman Military Medical Service," *Saalburg Jahrbuch* 27 (1970): 84–104. For these references, and his own review, I am indebted to Campbell, *Roman Army*, 104. See also Juliane C. Wilmanns, "Der Arzt in der römischen Armee der frühen und hohen Kaiserzeit," in vol. 1 of *Ancient Medicine in Its Socio-Cultural Context: Papers Read at the Congress Held*

This may be the reason why Matthew provides an incurable illness, paralysis (Matt 8:6), whereas Luke stipulates that the boy is "near death" (Luke 7:2).

This begging by a centurion would humanize him for the listener. The situation shows a reversal, with the soldier, usually in a dominant position with the people, placing himself in a subservient position before Jesus, one of the dominated. This indicates the seriousness of the boy's condition, the centurion's degree of concern to save him, and the centurion's conviction that Jesus can do so. The idea of the centurion petitioning Jesus for a miracle is an enormous surprise for the listener.

IV. THE RESPONSE OF JESUS

Q 7:3b: καὶ λέγει αὐτῷ· ἐγὼ ἐλθὼν θεραπεύσω αὐτόν;

And he said to him, "Am I, by coming, to heal him?"

The Characterization of Jesus

The Greek supplied here to report Jesus' response requires special attention. If a straightforward assertion were intended, one would not expect the emphasis on "I," as occurs with the addition of the ἐγώ. It is for this reason that the Q Reconstruction team has translated the reply of Jesus as an inquiry. He is checking to confirm that the centurion indeed expects him to go to the bedside of the boy. Craig Blomberg suggests that Jesus' emphatic "I" is part of a reassuring statement of his readiness to help, "And, *I*, coming, will heal him!"[69] On the opposite side of this positive interpretation is Warren Carter's view that Jesus resists the centurion, who stands as a representative of the emperor and Roman oppression: "Hearing the report, Jesus answers with a resistant, rhetorical question which expresses doubt about helping a gentile, 'Will *I* come and heal him?"[70] David Cortés-Fuentes supports the idea that Jesus is resisting because in Matt 3:14 John's resistance to baptizing Jesus employs the emphatic "you": "And do *you* come to me?" (καὶ σὺ ἔρχῃ

---

at Leiden University, 13–15 April 1992 (ed. Ph. J. van der Eijk, H. F. J. Horstmanshoff, and P. H. Schrijvers; Clio medica 27; Amsterdam: Rodopi, 1995), 171–87.

[69] Craig Blomberg, *Matthew* (NAC; Nashville: Broadman, 1992), 141.

[70] Carter, *Matthew and the Margins*, 202 (my italics).

πρός μὲ).[71] The reason for this resistance, however, is different from the one that than Carter proposes. It is because the centurion is a Gentile that it is improper for Jesus to go to the home: "Jesus' reluctant answer to the centurion can be understood in the context of the purity traditions about entering into a Gentile house and touching a Gentile (cf. John 18:28; Acts 10:28–29, m. Oholoth 18.7)."[72] He sees a confirmation of this conclusion in three parallels between this account and the Markan account of Jesus and the Syrophoenician mother (Mark 7:24–30), another story where Jesus resists a Gentile: (1) both stories identify the petitioners in a generic way: "centurion," "Syrophoenician woman"; (2) both petition for a sufferer who is at a distance, not present; (3) both miracles are effective immediately although at a distance.[73]

These parallels, however, cannot lead to the conclusion that Jesus is resisting the centurion. Matthew 3:14 is the evangelist's own redaction, and one cannot secure the intent of the Q narrator through an appeal to another's style. The three simple content parallels that Cortés-Fuentes sees between this account and the story of Jesus and the Syrophoenician mother cannot allow for the claim that a match occurs between the indisputable insult that Jesus levels at the mother and the tentative response of Jesus to the centurion. There is nothing overtly insulting in his words, so one would have to make the case that anything strident such as a signal of insult or resistance is intended.

It is true that *m. 'Ohol.* 18:7 forbids entrance into Gentile dwellings,[74] but the soldier has not asked Jesus to accompany him. And as the story unfolds, it will become clear that he had no intention of ever doing so. It is Jesus who introduces the idea of going to his quarters, not the soldier. In fact, this distinguishes the centurion from all other petitioners, because he does not tell Jesus what he expects him to do about the servant boy. Although Q does not feature other stories of petitions for miracles, Mark's tradition illustrates the pattern that whenever a petitioner is said to be "begging" (παρακαλῶν), he or she always explains what it is that Jesus is being begged to do, as the following texts show.

---

[71] David Cortés-Fuentes, "Not Like the Gentiles: The Characterization of Gentiles in the Gospel According to Matthew," *JHT* 9 (2001): 17 n. 31.

[72] Ibid., 17.

[73] Ibid., 16.

[74] "Dwelling places of gentiles [in the land of Israel] are unclean" (Jacob Neusner, trans., *The Mishnah: A New Translation* [New Haven: Yale University Press, 1988], 980).

Mark 1:40–45: Jesus and the Leper

> [40]A leper came to him begging and said to him, "If you choose, you can make me clean."

> (*Pace* Cortés-Fuentes, Jesus does not demonstrate a pious Jew's reluctance to touch a leper, also unclean.)

Mark 5:1–20: Jesus and the Gerasene Demoniac

> *Demons begging Jesus:*

> [10]He begged him earnestly not to send them out of the country.

> [12]And the unclean spirits begged him, "Send us into the swine; let us enter them."

> *Witnesses to the miracle:*

> [17]Then they began to beg Jesus to leave their neighborhood.

> *The formerly demonized man:*

> [18]As he was getting into the boat, the man who had been possessed by the demons begged him that he might be with him.

Mark 5:22–24, 35–43: Jesus and Jairus

> [23]And he begged him repeatedly, "My little daughter is at the point of death. Come and lay your hands on her, so that she may be made well, and live."

Mark 6:53–56: Markan Summary[75]

> [56]And wherever he went, into villages or cities or farms, they laid the sick in the marketplaces, and begged him that they might touch even the fringe of his cloak; and all who touched it were healed.

Mark 7:24–30: Jesus and the Syrophoenician Mother

> [26]Now the woman was a Gentile, of Syrophoenician origin. She begged him to cast the demon out of her daughter.

---

[75]This summary belongs to Mark's own hand, but even here we see that begging is completed by the information about what people expected of Jesus.

Mark 8:22–26: Jesus and the Friends of the Blind Man of Bethsaida

> [22]They came to Bethsaida. Some people brought a blind man to him and begged him to touch him.

Compare those texts with the centurion in Q 7:3a: "There came to him a centurion begging[76] him and saying, 'My boy is doing badly.'"

Cortés-Fuentes, like many scholars, has overlooked that the centurion does not express what he wishes Jesus to do. With his tentative statement/question, Jesus is the one who is opening the topic of visiting the dwelling. Thus the listener to the story would hear Jesus check with the soldier, in Q 7:3b, "And *I*, coming, will heal him./?" (the punctuation indicates the option of statement or question).

Where the work of both Carter and Cortés-Fuentes has an important place is in proving the very real reasons for shock and protest at Jesus' compliance in the first-time listeners to this story. Jesus freely volunteers to enter a Gentile home, in this case a dwelling assuredly defiled, since it is army barracks. The fact that the centurion belongs to the harsh oppressor adds insult to the issue.

If one recalls that Jesus' final word in this story will be to claim that the centurion's demonstration of faith is above any that he had seen in Israel, there can be no doubt that the narrator deliberately intends this provocation for those confirmed in their hatred of the Romans or convinced of this centurion's very Gentile, irreligious life. Were that not so, Jesus' expansive compliment about the centurion's faith being greater than any Jewish example would not hold the obvious punch that it does. So Jesus' initial response to this man would constitute an astonishing betrayal of religious observance by Jesus and a betrayal of proper Jewish pride.

This action of Jesus models another attitude altogether. If Jesus treats this centurion with the same concern as any other Jewish petitioner, it means that he hears only the anguished concern of the soldier and the confidence he shows in appealing to Jesus for help. There are no barriers then. This *philanthrōpia* of Jesus and his *praos* in this situa-

---

[76]Although the Greek participle παρακαλῶν is exactly the same as in all the miracle stories of the Markan tradition, the NRSV translates the occurrences in the Markan material with "begging," but here in what is Q 7:3, that is, Matt 8:5, with "appealing," while the Q Reconstruction team, as noted earlier, chooses "exhorting."

tion would have been a hard lesson and a huge challenge for would-be followers who were non-Romans.

V. THE RESPONSE OF THE CENTURION

6bcκαὶ ἀποκριθεὶς ὁ ἑκατόνταρχος ἔφη· κύριε, οὐκ εἰμὶ ἱκανὸς ἵνα μου ὑπὸ τὴν στέγην εἰσέλθῃς, 7ἀλλὰ εἰπὲ λόγῳ, καὶ ἰαθήτω ὁ παῖς μου. 8καὶ γὰρ ἐγὼ ἄνθρωπός εἰμι ὑπὸ ἐξουσίαν, ἔχων ὑπ' ἐμαυτὸν στρατιώτας, καὶ λέγω τούτῳ· πορεύθητι, καὶ πορεύεται, καὶ ἄλλῳ· ἔρχου, καὶ ἔρχεται, καὶ τῷ δούλῳ μου· ποίησον τοῦτο, καὶ ποιεῖ.

6bcAnd in reply the centurion said, "Sir,[77] I am not equal[78] [in status/ rank] for you to come under my roof; 7but say a word, and [[let]] my boy [[be]] healed. 8For I too am a person under authority, with soldiers under me, and I say to one, 'Go,' and he goes, and to an- other, 'Come,' and he comes, and to my slave, 'Do this,' and he does [it]."

The Characterization of the Centurion Continues

Just as listeners would have been astonished at Jesus' suggestion of going to the bedside of the boy, the story illustrates the astonishment of the centurion. Commentators have supposed that he, like the listen- ers, recognized the inappropriateness of Jesus' visit to him, a Gentile, who was unworthy. This comes from mistranslating the soldier's state- ment οὐκ εἰμὶ ἱκανός as "I am not worthy." For example, Robert Gun- dry comments, "The centurion's unworthiness is the sole point—and it

---

[77] The Greek word is κύριος (Matt 8:8 // Luke 7:6), which can be trans- lated "master," but under the circumstances, I will argue, it is much more fit- ting to be translated as the usual respectful address of "sir," since the centurion belongs to the cosmos of the army, with its lines of authority. He does not act as though Jesus is his "master."

[78] The Greek word is ἱκανός (Matt 8:8 // Luke 7:6), not ἄξιος. Later in the discussion I will develop the better translation with the idea of the centurion indicating his lower rank, his "inequality" in status, rather than the issue of personal worthiness in the sense of his degree of holiness or the fact that he is a Gentile, which would be suggested had the narrator used ἄξιος.

contrasts with Jesus' authority."[79] Yet "unworthiness" is not the antonym of "authority"; rather, "worthiness" is. In any case, Gundry sees that the centurion recognizes that as a Gentile, his home would be "unclean." Moreover, Gundry adds that "the centurion's feeling unworthy may go beyond ceremonial defilement of his house, however, and extend to the recognition of his moral guilt."[80] It is possible that some Jewish listeners would conclude that if he lived among the Jewish people, he would know their religious sensibilities on this matter, but why would he feel *morally* guilty? In any case, the point is that the text does not hold the word for "worthy" (ἄξιος), but rather the word for "equal" (ἱκανός).

The differences between these two words matter. In fact, it is Luke who introduces ἄξιος into his version of the story, where he adds the element of Jewish elders telling Jesus that the centurion is "worthy": "He is worthy of having you do this for him, for he loves our people, and it is he who built our synagogue for us" (Luke 7:4–5). This indeed is the ordinary meaning of ἄξιος. The centurion is deserving because of his virtuous conduct, his love for the people, and his generosity in paying for the synagogue. But Luke must copy the soldier's words to Jesus from Q, where he tells Jesus that he is not ἱκανός. Clearly, Luke does not understand this word as "worthy." In lexicons, ἄξιος is defined as "weighing as much, worth as much," "worthy of, deserving of, meet for," "worthy, goodly,' of persons and things,"[81] while ἱκανός is translated as "becoming, befitting, sufficing," and when used of persons, "sufficient, competent," as in an example from Herodotus: "a man of sufficient prudence," while in comparisons with others, "a match for, equivalent to."[82] This idea of being "a match for, equivalent to" belongs to army life and to rank, which defines who is the superior, equal, and inferior, who gives the orders and who obeys. Thus, the soldier is referring to the exalted rank of Jesus and his own inferior rank, so that any visit of Jesus to his living quarters was unimaginable and certainly unnecessary. This is where the world of the centurion exhibits itself with the concepts fundamental to the centurion. Just as it would be unfitting for a tribune to accompany a centurion to observe the obedience to his orders among the men, how much more

---

[79] Robert H. Gundry, *Matthew: A Commentary on His Literary and Theological Art* (Grand Rapids: Eerdmans, 1982), 143.

[80] Ibid.

[81] LSJ, s.v. "ἄξιος."

[82] LSJ, s.v. "ἱκανός."

inappropriate it would be for Jesus, with his even greater rank, to lower himself to enter the living quarters of the centurion.

ἀλλὰ εἰπὲ λόγῳ, καὶ ἰαθήτω ὁ παῖς μου.

"But say a word, and let my boy be healed."

Again the army mentality exposes itself as the centurion now explains to Jesus what he presumed he knew to do: say the word, give the command. This is the way everything is done in the army, as obedience to orders. So Jesus has only to order it, and the forces at his command will instantly obey.

⁸καὶ γὰρ ἐγὼ ἄνθρωπός εἰμι ὑπὸ ἐξουσίαν, ἔχων ὑπ' ἐμαυτὸν στρατιώτας, καὶ λέγω τούτῳ· πορεύθητι, καὶ πορεύεται, καὶ ἄλλῳ· ἔρχου, καὶ ἔρχεται, καὶ τῷ δούλῳ μου· ποίησον τοῦτο, καὶ ποιεῖ.

⁸"For I too am a person under authority, with soldiers under me, and I say to one, 'Go,' and he goes, and to another, 'Come,' and he comes, and to my slave, 'Do this,' and he does it."

In this final piece of the speech, the centurion explains to Jesus that he can be sure that the centurion understands how authority functions, and as we have noted, there is no rank of soldiers in the Roman army more appropriate to explain this to Jesus than the centurions, renown for instilling obedience to commands and fulfilling them to perfection themselves.

VI. JESUS' FINAL RESPONSE

⁹ἀκούσας δὲ ὁ Ἰησοῦς ἐθαύμασεν καὶ εἶπεν τοῖς ἀκολουθοῦσιν· λέγω ὑμῖν, οὐδὲ ἐν τῷ Ἰσραὴλ τοσαύτην πίστιν εὗρον.

⁹But Jesus, on hearing, was amazed, and said to those who followed, "I tell you, not even in Israel have I found such faith."

The Characterization of Jesus Concludes

Now it is Jesus' turn to be astonished, and with him, the listeners too. From a man whose milieu was considered to be the most worldly and the least religiously deep comes the understanding of authority and confidence in Jesus' command that no one else has demonstrated.

The centurion is the only petitioner in the Gospels who not only does not require Jesus to come to the sick bed, but also declines Jesus' offer as unnecessary and unnecessarily demeaning to Jesus, since all that *is* necessary is his command. Thus, the very world that would have been considered most coarse and the greatest liability to religious understanding turns out to have imparted the best and purest insight into Jesus' authority.

Jesus awards this soldier's exercise of understanding and confidence with "faith," and he exclaims to those around him that it is greater than anything he has seen in Israel. And here, Jesus confirms his readiness to recognize faith wherever it is found and to give praise freely where others would be unwilling to do so because of prejudice.

CONCLUSION

This story told among Jewish listeners is intended to function beyond an attestation of Jesus' power to heal at a distance. The figure of the centurion coming onto the scene deliberately raises the issue of helping the enemy. Jesus' reception of the centurion from the very first, his readiness to listen to him, his willingness to forgo the visit to the bedside so as to comply with the man's sense of impropriety, his openness to being instructed by the man on the functioning of authority and command, and his free praise of the man's faith—all these are meant as models of the ideal behavior in the disciple.

The *epieikeia* of Jesus in this story, and in his praise of this centurion over anyone in the Jewish community, would have called for a difficult abandonment of what had been seen as justifiable resentment in this case and in parallel circumstances. The lesson here seems meant to illustrate in yet another way that the petitioner for a healing was to be received compassionately, without any prejudice condoned by society, or religious affiliation—a very great demand in that day.

Part III

Petitioners Who Ask on Behalf of Their Child

5

Jesus and the Syrophoenician Mother (Mark 7:24–30)

"The rest of the people . . . and all who have separated themselves from the peoples of the lands to adhere to the law of God . . . join with their kin, their nobles, and enter into a curse and an oath to walk in God's law which, was given to Moses the servant of God, and to observe and do all the commandments of the LORD our Lord and his ordinances and his statutes." (Neh 10:28–29)

Mark has situated the story of Jesus and the Syrophoenician mother in a section of his Gospel that addresses Jesus relationship with Gentiles (Mark 7:1–37) and the issue of what is "pure." The section is headed by a controversy between the Pharisees and Jesus over what constitutes true "purity" before God (Mark 7:1–23), and then Jesus moves to Gentile territory, where, against his wish for anonymity and privacy, a Syrophoenician mother beseeches him to exorcise an unclean spirit from her daughter. What is puzzling is why the Jesus who in Mark 7:6–23 claims that "purity" is far broader than what the Pharisees would allow is then shown to resist the mother's petition with the very insular, and indeed insulting, words "Let the children be fed first, for it is not fair to take the children's food and throw it to the dogs" (Mark 7:27). This position would seem to belong to the Pharisees! The story itself, however, features a change of mind in Jesus upon hearing her response to him. So, did Mark choose this story to show how Jesus was ready to accept a pagan correction, accept her greater wisdom?

What was the intent of this story before Mark employed it? To discuss the message of the account apart from Markan redaction, it is necessary to identify any obvious signs of his hand.

I. MARK 7:24–30: SIGNS OF MARKAN REDACTION

²⁴ἐκεῖθεν δὲ ἀναστὰς ἀπῆλθεν εἰς τὰ ὅρια Τύρου. καὶ εἰσελθὼν εἰς οἰκίαν οὐδένα ἤθελεν γνῶναι, καὶ οὐκ ἠδυνήθη λαθεῖν· ²⁵ἀλλ' εὐθὺς ἀκούσασα γυνὴ περὶ αὐτοῦ, ἧς εἶχεν τὸ θυγάτριον αὐτῆς πνεῦμα ἀκάθαρτον, ἐλθοῦσα προσέπεσεν πρὸς τοὺς πόδας αὐτοῦ· ²⁶ἡ δὲ γυνὴ ἦν Ἑλληνίς, Συροφοινίκισσα τῷ γένει· καὶ ἠρώτα αὐτὸν ἵνα τὸ δαιμόνιον ἐκβάλῃ ἐκ τῆς θυγατρὸς αὐτῆς. ²⁷καὶ ἔλεγεν αὐτῇ· ἄφες πρῶτον χορτασθῆναι τὰ τέκνα οὐ γάρ ἐστιν καλὸν λαβεῖν τὸν ἄρτον τῶν τέκνων καὶ τοῖς κυναρίοις βαλεῖν. ²⁸ἡ δὲ ἀπεκρίθη καὶ λέγει αὐτῷ· κύριε· καὶ τὰ κυνάρια ὑποκάτω τῆς τραπέζης ἐσθίουσιν ἀπὸ τῶν ψιχίων τῶν παιδίων. ²⁹καὶ εἶπεν αὐτῇ· διὰ τοῦτον τὸν λόγον ὕπαγε, ἐξελήλυθεν ἐκ τῆς θυγατρός σου τὸ δαιμόνιον. ³⁰καὶ ἀπελθοῦσα εἰς τὸν οἶκον αὐτῆς εὗρεν τὸ παιδίον βεβλημένον ἐπὶ τὴν κλίνην καὶ τὸ δαιμόνιον ἐξεληλυθός.

²⁴From there he set out and went away to the region of Tyre. He entered a house and did not want anyone to know he was there. Yet he could not escape notice, ²⁵but a woman whose little daughter had an unclean spirit immediately heard about him, and she came and bowed down at his feet. ²⁶Now the woman was a Gentile, of Syrophoenician origin. She begged him to cast the demon out of her daughter. ²⁷He said to her, "Let the children be fed first, for it is not fair to take the children's food and throw it to the dogs." ²⁸But she answered him, "Sir, even the dogs under the table eat the children's crumbs." ²⁹Then he said to her, "For saying that, you may go—the demon has left your daughter." ³⁰So she went home, found the child lying on the bed, and the demon gone.

Mark's redaction on this pericope is light.[1]

²⁴ἐκεῖθεν δὲ ἀναστὰς ἀπῆλθεν εἰς τὰ ὅρια Τύρου. Καὶ εἰσελθὼν εἰς οἰκίαν οὐδένα ἤθελεν γνῶναι, καὶ οὐκ ἠδυνήθη λαθεῖν·

²⁴From there he set out and went away to the region of Tyre. He entered a house and did not want anyone to know he was there. Yet he could not escape notice.

---

[1] See Camille Focant, "Mc 7,24–31 Par. Mat 15,21–29: Critique des Sources et/ou Études Narrative," in *The Synoptic Gospels: Source Criticism and the New Literary Criticism* (ed. Camille Focant; BETL 110; Leuven: Leuven University Press, 1993), 46 (esp. n 30), 47.

The introductory clause, v. 24a, certainly belongs to Markan redaction, as the explicit notice of Jesus' change of location would not make sense apart from the Gospel narrative. This account does not require Jesus to travel to Syrophoenicia, since Palestine, including the region of Galilee, had a mixed population.[2] But Mark creates a side trip for Jesus into Gentile territory,[3] following this account with the healing of the deaf mute of the Decapolis (Mark 7:31–37). Mark has Jesus go to Tyre, which is explained if one considers Strabo's report that Tyre vied with Sidon as the principal metropolis of Phoenicia. Although it was mentioned less by the ancients, it was the older and more prestigious of the two cities.[4]

Verse 24b also shows Markan redaction, since Jesus' entering into a house and unsuccessfully hiding there belongs assuredly to the Messianic Secret theme. To the degree that v. 24a and v. 24b both serve explicitly Markan interests and would otherwise invite question from pre-Gospel listeners, they can be identified as Markan.

To test for Markan redaction, vv. 25–26 should be discussed together.

[25]ἀλλ' εὐθὺς ἀκούσασα γυνὴ περὶ αὐτοῦ, ἧς εἶχεν τὸ θυγάτριον αὐτῆς πνεῦμα ἀκάθαρτον, ἐλθοῦσα προσέπεσεν πρὸς τοὺς πόδας αὐτοῦ· [26]ἡ δὲ γυνὴ ἦν Ἑλληνίς, Συροφοινίκισσα τῷ γένει· καὶ ἠρώτα αὐτὸν ἵνα τὸ δαιμόνιον ἐκβάλῃ ἐκ τῆς θυγατρὸς αὐτῆς.

---

[2] T. A. Burkill observes that Mark inferred from the mention of the woman being a Syrophoenician that Jesus should be described as having traveled to Tyre and Sidon, "disregarding the possibility that she was an *émigré*. Accordingly, the evangelist composed verses 24 and 31, introducing among the topographical details of verse 24 the characteristic motif that Jesus won widespread thaumaturgic fame despite his reticence and aversion to publicity" ("The Historical Development of the Story of the Syrophoenician Woman [Mark vii: 24–31]," *NovT* 9 [1967]: 173).

[3] Sharon Ringe maintains that "nothing in the narrative itself suggests that Mark viewed Jesus' 'going away' (ἀπέρχομαι) into this region as a foray into Gentile territory" ("A Gentile Woman's Story, Revisited: Rereading Mark 7:24–31," in *A Feminist Companion to Mark* [ed. Amy-Jill Levine and Marianne Blickenstaff; FCNTECW 2; Sheffield: Sheffield Academic Press, 2001], 85). She reasons that since Mark has not stipulated that Jesus entered a Gentile house, he must presume that the home was Jewish. Thus, she concludes that the woman has crossed over into Jesus' territory. But in the light of Mark's stipulation ἀναστὰς ἀπῆλθεν εἰς τὰ ὅρια Τύρου, the argument that Jesus went to the borderland but was still on Jewish soil seems to contradict Mark's intent, for to introduce Tyre is to invite the idea that Jesus was in Gentile territory.

[4] See Strabo, *Geogr.* 16.2.22.

²⁵But a woman whose little daughter had an unclean spirit imme-diately heard about him, and she came and bowed down at his feet. ²⁶Now the woman was a Gentile, of Syrophoenician origin. She begged him to cast the demon out of her daughter.

Verse 25a presumes the situation introduced by Mark in v. 24b, where it is said that Jesus wants no one to know that he is in the house. Other signs of Mark's introduction include his simple reference to "a woman" in v. 25, which lacks the more interesting and specific detail found in an introduction of the petitioner. Verse 26 supplies the par-ticularly pertinent detail that she is Syrophoenician—that is, a Gentile. Then there is the discrepancy in the vocabulary for the demon. It is called an "unclean spirit" in v. 25, but "demon" in v. 26, in v. 29, where Jesus announces the exorcism, and in v. 30, the confirmation of the ex-orcism as the woman enters the house. Less dramatic is the difference in the reference to the daughter, who is referred to in v. 25 with the diminutive θυγάτριον ("little daughter"), but in v. 26 and v. 29 with θυγάτηρ ("daughter"). In effect, Mark's introduction in v. 25 repeats the pre-Markan introduction in v. 26. Once it is recognized that v. 25 is an addition, then also the element of the woman's prostration before Jesus can be assigned to that later redaction. The evangelist may have been influenced by his knowledge of Mark 5:33, where the woman with the hemorrhage bows before Jesus. We see him use it in his summary state-ment of Mark 3:7–12, where he stipulates that the demons prostrate themselves to Jesus (Mark 3:11). In this case, he may have been con-cerned to use it because otherwise the woman's behavior would appear exceptionally bold.

Mark frequently provides an introduction to a story that already has one, and thus a duplication occurs that is common to this Gospel.[5]

Summary: This review shows that vv. 24–25, the added introduc-tion, belongs to Markan redaction. The remaining verses, vv. 26–30, hold the narrative elements necessary to a cogent account and belong to the pre-Markan, discrete story. This is not to say that Mark did not perhaps choose certain favored vocabulary as he used the account, but what narrative elements are represented here belong to the pre-Markan story.

---

[5] See Frans Neirynck, *Duality in Mark: Contributions to the Study of the Markan Redaction* (BETL 31; Leuven: Leuven University Press, 1972), 37–44.

II. THE PRE-MARKAN ANECDOTE: JESUS AND THE SYROPHOENICIAN MOTHER

As always, it must be stressed that simply removing the introductory verses does not allow one to claim that the remaining formulations are the exact vocabulary that Mark found in the pre-Markan composition. What I maintain, however, is that he presents the narrative elements that he found in vv. 26–30, and it is these that we examine for the signs of purpose they served.

²⁶ἡ δὲ γυνὴ ἦν Ἑλληνίς, Συροφοινίκισσα τῷ γένει· καὶ ἠρώτα αὐτὸν ἵνα τὸ δαιμόνιον ἐκβάλῃ ἐκ τῆς θυγατρὸς αὐτῆς. ²⁷καὶ ἔλεγεν αὐτῇ· ἄφες πρῶτον χορτασθῆναι τὰ τέκνα οὐ γάρ ἐστιν καλὸν λαβεῖν τὸν ἄρτον τῶν τέκνων καὶ τοῖς κυναρίοις βαλεῖν. ²⁸ἡ δὲ ἀπεκρίθη καὶ λέγει αὐτῷ· κύριε· καὶ τὰ κυνάρια ὑποκάτω τῆς τραπέζης ἐσθίουσιν ἀπὸ τῶν ψιχίων τῶν παιδίων. ²⁹καὶ εἶπεν αὐτῇ· διὰ τοῦτον τὸν λόγον ὕπαγε, ἐξελήλυθεν ἐκ τῆς θυγατρός σου τὸ δαιμόνιον. ³⁰καὶ ἀπελθοῦσα εἰς τὸν οἶκον αὐτῆς εὗρεν τὸ παιδίον βεβλημένον ἐπὶ τὴν κλίνην καὶ τὸ δαιμόνιον ἐξεληλυθός.

²⁶Now there was a woman, a Gentile, a Syrophoenician by origin, and she begged him that he might cast out the demon from her daughter. ²⁷And he said to her, "Let the children be satisfied first, for it is not good to take the children's bread and throw it to the dogs." ²⁸But she answered and said to him, "Sir, even the dogs under the table eat the children's crumbs." ²⁹Then he said to her, "Because of this saying, go, the demon has gone out of your daughter." ³⁰And going away to her house, she found the child, having been thrown down on the bed, and the demon having gone out [of her].⁶

Form-Critical Classification: A Mixed Apophthegm

Rudolf Bultmann classifies this account among the apophthegms of "mixed form"⁷ because "The miracle is not reported for its own sake, for the main point is the change in Jesus' behavior as the dialogue goes on. Indeed

---

⁶ My translation, albeit somewhat too literal, is meant to indicate elements that I will address in the discussion.

⁷ Rudolf Bultmann, *The History of the Synoptic Tradition* (trans. John Marsh; Peabody, Mass.: Hendrickson, 1963), 34.

this proves to be a controversy dialogue of sorts, though on this occasion Jesus proves not to be the victor, though this is in no way a denigration."[8]

For this reason, there is a similarity between this miracle story and the Q account of the centurion's plea for his "boy" (Q 7:3, 6bc–9) because there too the climax is found in the dialogue and not in the description of the bedside cure. One difference, however, is that the Q account probably left the focus on the pronouncement and did not have a report of the accomplished miracle as this story does.[9] A second similarity that they share, beyond the importance of their dialogue with Jesus, is the obvious one that both petitioners are Gentiles, and that both plead for sufferers who are not present. A similar form, however, does not allow one to assume a similar message in the story. This relies on the content of the dialogue. In this case, two important differences separate these two stories. First is the character of the miracle being requested, because whereas the centurion asks for a healing, the Syrophoenician mother asks for an exorcism, a much darker trouble than the physical sickness of the boy. Second, and very important, the degree of culpability is not the same at all. The illness of the servant boy could have been contracted in any number of ways, and none of them need place blame on the centurion, but the case is far different for child possession. What character of life in the home allows a demon to be attracted to the daughter and be able to enter her? The mother has to assume responsibility because the protection against evil spirits in her home, by her virtue and vigilance, is her duty. As we will see, the reaction of Jesus to each of these petitioners is distinct, and each carries its own final revelation about Jesus and his attitudes toward correction.

III. THE PRESENTATION OF THE PETITIONER: THE SYROPHOENICIAN MOTHER

[26]ἡ δὲ γυνὴ ἦν Ἑλληνίς, Συροφοινίκισσα τῷ γένει· καὶ ἠρώτα αὐτὸν ἵνα τὸ δαιμόνιον ἐκβάλῃ ἐκ τῆς θυγατρὸς αὐτῆς.

[26]Now there was a woman, a Gentile, a Syrophoenician by origin, and she begged him that he might cast out the demon from her daughter.

---

[8] Ibid., 38.
[9] See chapter 4, on Jesus and the Centurion (Q [Luke] 7:1, 3, 6b–9).

The Characterization of the Syrophoenician Mother

What is outstanding in this introduction is the detail that the narrator has identified the mother's background. Nowhere else in the Markan Gospel tradition does anyone receive this attention to Gentile background. It would have been sufficient to state that she was a "Greek" (Έλληνίς),[10] but there is an added modification, "Syrophoenician" (Συροφοινίκισσα). In the book of Acts, where "Greeks" is used as a general term for non-Jews,[11] no other specification is usual.

Lucian, a rhetorician and satirist, uses a Syrophoenician background in his work *The Parliament of the Gods*, where the god of satire, Momus, exposes the humble roots of Dionysus before Zeus:

> It is splendid, Zeus, that you actually urge me to frankness; this is truly royal, high-souled action. Therefore, I shall give the name. It is this peerless Dionysus, who is half human; in fact, on his mother's side he is not even Greek, but the grandson of a Syrophoenician trader named Cadmus. (*Deor. conc.* 4)[12]

In this case, Momus is refusing to allow "Greek" to stand as a generalization under which Dionysus can hide. Lucian's contrast between being Greek and being a "Syrophoenician trader" suggests that such a designation communicated a low-class foreigner.

In Juvenal's eighth satire it can also be noted that he uses a Syrophoenician for his oily tavern owner as he illustrates the depths to which the highborn fall. Here the aristocrat Lateranus, a one-time consul, has now become a muleteer,

> And when it pleases him [the noble] to go back to the all-night tavern, a Syro-Phoenician runs forth to meet him—a denizen of the Idumaean gate perpetually drenched in perfumes—and salutes him as lord and prince with all the airs of a host; and with him comes Cyane, her dress tucked up, carrying a flagon of wine for sale. (*Sat.* 8.158–62)[13]

---

[10] The word never occurs again in the Synoptic Gospels, and only thrice in John (John 7:35 [bis], 12:20).

[11] Acts 14:1; 16:1, 3; 17:4, 18:4; 19:10, 17; 20:21; 21:28.

[12] Lucian, *The Parliament of the Gods*, in vol. 5 of *Lucian* (trans. A. M. Harmon; LCL; Cambridge, Mass.: Harvard University Press, 1962), 423. Lucian plays with the name "Cadmus," the Phoenician prince in Greek mythology who reputedly gave the Greeks their alphabet.

[13] Juvenal, *The Satires*, in *Juvenal and Persius* (trans. G. G. Ramsay; LCL; London: Heinemann; New York: Putnam, 1928), 171.

This shameless Cyane has a Greek name, but would she be understood as a Syrophoenician as well? John DeFelice concludes that women who worked at these taverns often were the wives or common-law wives of the owners.[14]

How were Syrian women viewed? Natalie Kampen's study of the evidence of attitudes toward the working women of Ostia leads her to comment, "Syrian women seem to have been condemned as wild and lascivious, totally lacking in the moral standards of the ideal Roman matron."[15]

Does the narrator of this story take pains to identify the woman as Syrophoenician in order to prepare the audience for this mother, who will prove herself to be audacious?

IV. THE SYROPHOENICIAN MOTHER PETITIONS JESUS

[26b]καὶ ἠρώτα αὐτὸν ἵνα τὸ δαιμόνιον ἐκβάλῃ ἐκ τῆς θυγατρὸς αὐτῆς.

[26b]And she was asking him that he might expel the demon from her daughter.

This is the only miracle story in the Gospel where a woman initiates a petition to Jesus. The reason for this is found in societal expectations of the modest woman to be "invisible" in public, and certainly not to speak to men unknown to her and unconnected to her family. Sharon Ringe has challenged these ideas, claiming that they are undocumented and only presupposed.[16] Plutarch (46–120 C.E.), for example, expresses the ideals for the proper wife when her husband is away: "When the

---

[14]John DeFelice, *Roman Hospitality: The Professional Women of Pompeii* (Warren Center, Pa.: Shangri-La Publications, 2001), 142.

[15]Natalie Kampen, *Image and Status: Roman Working Women in Ostia* (Berlin: Mann, 1981), 112. This may be due to the simple fact that as foreigners, they had to find ways to make a living. John E. B. Mayor's commentary on Juvenal's *Satires* notes that employments associated with Syrians included their service as slaves (Juvenal, *Sat.* 6.351), as tavern keepers (Juvenal, *Sat.* 8.159), as we have seen, but also that the women were flute players (Horace, *Sat.* 1.2.1) (Juvenal, *Thirteen Satires of Juvenal* [trans. John E. B. Mayor; 2 vols.; Hildesheim: Georg Olms, 1966], 1:188).

[16]"What is curious is that such standards are assumed (without supporting evidence or documentation) in many scholarly studies and most Christian preaching about the passage" (Ringe, "Gentile Woman's Story Revisited," 88 n. 19).

moon is a long way from the sun, she looks large and bright to us; but when she comes near she fades away and hides. With a good wife it is just the opposite; she ought to be most conspicuous when she is with her husband, and to stay at home and hide herself when he is not there" (*Mor.* 139C).[17] We might also point to boasting by Cornelius Nepos (100–23 B.C.E.) about the superior customs of Romans over the Greeks with regard to women: "Many actions are seemly according to our code which the Greeks look upon as shameful. For instance, what Roman would blush to take his wife to a dinner-party? What matron does not frequent the front rooms of her dwelling and show herself in public? But it is very different in Greece; for there a woman is not admitted to a dinner-party, unless relatives only are present, and she keeps to the more retired part of the house called 'the woman's apartment,' to which no man has access who is not near of kin" (*Exc. duc.* praefatio 6–7).[18] But even in Rome, proper conduct in public for a woman demanded the utmost modestly and "invisibility." Valerius Maximus (14–30 C.E.), in his essay "On Severity," admiringly recalls Gaius Sulpicius's decision to divorce his wife "because he had caught her outdoors with her head uncovered: a stiff penalty but not without a certain logic. 'The law,' he said, 'prescribes for you my eyes alone to which you may prove your beauty. . . . If you, with needless provocation, invite the look of anyone else, you must be suspected of wrongdoing'" (*Fact. dict.* 6.3.9–10).[19] He supplies another example in the person of Publius Sempronius Sophus, "who disgraced his wife with divorce merely because she dared attend the games without his knowledge" (*Fact. dict.* 6.3.12).[20] In Valerius's opinion, these examples of strict punishments were wise: "And so, long ago, when the misdeeds of women were thus forestalled, their minds

---

[17] Plutarch, *Moralia* (trans. F. C. Babbitt; LCL; Cambridge, Mass.: Harvard University Press, 1936), 305–6. For this reference I am indebted to Mary R. Lefkowitz and Maureen B. Fant, *Women's Life in Greece and Rome: A Source Book in Translation* (3d ed.; Baltimore: Johns Hopkins University Press, 2005), 240.

[18] Cornelius Nepos, "Praefatio," Cornelius Nepos (trans. John C. Rolfe; LCL; Cambridge, Mass.: Harvard Univesity Press, 1984), 4–5. See also the article by Sheila K. Dickison, "Women in Rome," in vol. 3 of *Civilization of the Ancient Mediterranean: Greece and Rome* (ed. Michael Grant and Rachel Kitzinger; New York: Scribner, 1988), 1319–32.

[19] Valerius Maximus, "Of Severity," *Memorable Doings and Sayings* (trans. D. R. Shackleton Bailey; 2 vols.; LCL; Cambridge, Mass.; Harvard University Press, 2000), 2:38–43.

[20] Ibid., 40–41.

stayed far from wrongdoing" (*Fact. dict.* 6.3.12).[21] Thus, even in Rome these ideals of the modest woman were still considered correct by the men in Valerius Maximus's day.[22]

As for the Gospel evidence of proper behavior, the few stories where women do make contact with Jesus in public convey the notion that the cultural expectation is that they should not communicate with a strange man. In the story of the woman with the hemorrhage (Mark 5:25–34), her reluctance to make herself known when Jesus asks who touched him is one example. Thus, she came "in fear and trembling, fell down before him, and told him the whole truth" (Mark 5:33). In the Gospel of John, after Jesus converses with the Samaritan woman at the well, the narrator reports, "Just then his disciples came. They were astonished that he was speaking with a woman, but no one said, 'What do you want?' or, 'Why are you speaking with her?'" (John 4:27).

These texts support the idea that men and women unconnected to each other by blood or marriage or through family friendships were not to enter into conversation with each other. (Notice that in the healing of Peter's mother-in-law [Mark 1:29–31], it is the men who tell Jesus about her, and the lady herself never says a word to Jesus. Rising from her fever, she waits on them [Mark 1:31].)

Listeners to the story of the Syrophoenician mother would already recognize her breaches of modesty. A man from her family should have been the one to approach Jesus. If there was no such man on whom she could rely, then she should have had a female companion or a child, but not to come to Jesus by herself.

Besides the boldness of her personal approach, there is also the fact that she has asked the Jewish Jesus to exorcize a demon, while she herself shows no desire to convert, to turn to the saving God of the Jews, but only to have Jesus exorcize her daughter and return to her own devotions, those that left her daughter open to possession.

---

[21] Ibid.

[22] See the many sources in Bruce W. Winter, *Roman Wives, Roman Widows: The Appearance of New Women and the Pauline Communities* (Grand Rapids: Eerdmans, 2003). Winter, while using the sources to bring out the emergence of a "new woman," substantiates the contrast with proofs of the traditional expectations of men with respect to a woman's modesty, notably through recessive behavior, the degree of which depended on whether the culture was Romanized or resistant to its influence.

From another angle, her appeal to Jesus is also a disloyalty to the gods of her husband's religion: Plutarch writes, "A wife ought not to make friends of her own, but to enjoy her husband's friends together with him. And the first and best friends are the gods in whom her husband believes and to shut her door to all magic ceremonies and *foreign superstitions*" (*Mor.* 140D [my italics]).[23] Thus, this woman offends cultural ideals of modesty, the loyalty expected of a wife to her husband's deities, and she offends Jewish religious sensibility because she wants the exorcism but not the God who will effect the salvation.

καὶ ἠρώτα αὐτὸν

and she was asking him

The NRSV translates ἠρώτα as "begged," but that would require the verb παρακαλέω, the verb used in five miracle stories of the Markan tradition (Mark 1:40; 5:10, 12, 17, 18, 23; 6:56; 7:32; 8:22).[24] But the narrator has used ἠρώτα, which means "was asking,"[25] and in the light of the conventional use of παρακαλέω, the use of ἐρωτάω ("to ask") seems deliberate. The idea is that the mother is not groveling or imploring, but requesting. It may be due to this that Mark tried to insert some drama

---

[23] Cited in Lefkowitz and Fant, *Women's Life in Greece and Rome*, 240.

[24] It is curious that while the NRSV translators consistently translate the verb as "beg" for the Markan miracles stories (Mark 1:40; 5:10, 12, 17, 18, 23; 6:56; 7:32; 8:22), when translating the same verb in the centurion's begging for his servant boy (Matt 8:7) and for Jesus' pronouncement that he could beg his Father for angels (Matt 26:53), they use "appeal." Then, the same verb becomes "plead" in Matt 18:20–32 (the parable of the ungrateful steward). On the other hand, where Luke shows that he does not wish to use Mark's παρακαλέω and substitutes δέομαι, "pray" (Luke 8:5 vs. Mark 1:40; Luke 8:38 vs. Mark 5:18), the translators use "beg" just the same. Here too, the verb ἐρωτάω is being translated as "beg" when this time, unlike the five Markan miracle stories listed above, the description means "ask," nothing more.

[25] This verb occurs in Mark only twice more (Mark 4:10; 8:5), where it means "to ask." In Mark 4:10, the disciples ask Jesus for the meaning of the parable of the sower; and in Mark 8:5, in an interrogative context, Jesus, using the same imperfect form, ἠρώτα, as in Mark 7:26, asks his disciples how many loaves there are. Neither of these holds an urgency equal to "begging." (4x in Matthew [15:23; 16:13; 19:17; 21:24], all meaning "to ask"; and 15x in Luke [4:38; 5:3; 7:3, 36; 8:37; 9:45; 11:37; 14:18, 19, 32; 16:27; 19:31; 20:3, 22:68; 23:3], all redaction and meaning "to ask, inquire").

by having her bow at Jesus' feet. Without such signs of pleading and emotional appeal, the portrait of the mother as shameless is secured.

V. THE RESPONSE OF JESUS

[27]καὶ ἔλεγεν αὐτῇ· ἄφες πρῶτον χορτασθῆναι τὰ τέκνα οὐ γάρ ἐστιν καλὸν λαβεῖν τὸν ἄρτον τῶν τέκνων καὶ τοῖς κυναρίοις βαλεῖν.

[27]He said to her, "Let the children be fed first, for it is not fair to take the children's food and throw it to the dogs."

The Characterization of Jesus

Perhaps no other response of Jesus has given rise to such scholarly discussion, because not only does Jesus refuse her, but he does so in what appears to be a prejudicial and extremely insulting manner. The metaphor that Jesus uses, which identifies Jews as the children of God and Gentiles as dogs, stands out as uncharacteristically harsh. The flurry of scholarly reassurances that Jesus was neither prejudiced nor rude is proof itself that the evidence is sufficient for readers to conclude otherwise. For example, Vincent Taylor, who regards the response as a authentic remembrance of the historical Jesus, points out that Jesus uses κυνάριον ("puppy, house dog, little dog"), the diminutive of κύων ("dog"), suggesting a gentleness in his refusal. Although Taylor was a form critic and recognized the pre-Gospel form of the story, he appeals to Mark's placement of it on Jesus' journey to Tyre (Mark 7:24) for his explanation. Jesus was "preoccupied with the thought of his mission to the Jews; and it is to this tension that the apparent harshness of his words is due. . . . May we not dare to say that, when Jesus spoke to the woman, he was also speaking to himself?"[26] But even Taylor's argument that it may be intended as a rhetorical question does not remove the contrast that Jesus makes between Jews as children and Gentiles as animals, be they dogs or, as Taylor would have it, the gentler puppies. T. A. Burkill brushes aside

---

[26]Vincent Taylor, *The Life and Ministry of Jesus* (London: Macmillan; New York: St. Martin's Press, 1955), 137. See also Gerd Theissen's discussion of Johannes Weiss's similar interpretation according to Markan placement of the material: Gerd Theissen, *The Gospels in Context: Social and Political History in the Synoptic Tradition* (trans. Linda M. Maloney; Minneapolis: Fortress, 1991), 62.

these attempts to rescue the statement of Jesus from its direct meaning: "St. Mark nowhere affords any indication that Jesus goes to the region of Tyre because the Galilean mission failed, or that he is prone to talking to himself, or that he is uncertain about the nature and scope of his messianic task."[27] To those scholars who, like Taylor, focus on the tenderness of κυνάριον,[28] he counters, "We may safely assume that any intelligent Hellenistic woman, addressed in such terms by a barbarian, would have immediately reacted by slapping the man's face. And, as in English, so in other languages, to call a woman 'a little bitch' is no less abusive than to call her a 'bitch' without qualification."[29]

Another effort to prevent a judgment on Jesus as being harsh is found in the interpretation of scholars such as Alexander Jones, Jürgen Roloff, and Kenzo Tagawa, who hold that Jesus was only testing the mother's faith and/or humility, and Jerry Camery-Hoggatt,[30] who claims that Jesus was speaking "tongue in cheek," leveling a "verbal challenge intended to test the other's response."

---

[27] Burkill, "Syrophoenician Woman," 172.

[28] Ernst Lohmeyer, *Das Evangelium des Markus* (KEK 1/2; Göttingen: Vandenhoeck & Ruprecht, 1967), 147; Walter E. Bundy, *Jesus and the First Three Gospels: An Introduction to the Synoptic Tradition* (Cambridge, Mass.: Harvard University Press, 1955), 280–81; C. E. B. Cranfield, *The Gospel according to Saint Mark* (CGTC; Cambridge: Cambridge University Press, 1959), 248; Floyd V. Filson, *A Commentary on the Gospel according to St. Matthew* (BNTC; London: A & C Black, 1960), 178; Alexander Jones, *The Gospel according to St. Mark: A Text and Commentary for Students* (New York: Sheed & Ward, 1963), 127; Eduard Schweizer, *The Good News according to Mark* (trans. Donald H. Madvig; Richmond: John Knox Press, 1970). Schweizer writes, "The fact that Jesus called Gentiles 'dogs' has only indirect significance, if any, since the word chosen here indicates a household pet which was not greatly despised, and a dog is the only animal which would be suitable for the metaphor" (*Mark*, 152). Schweizer apparently does not recognize that another metaphor could have been chosen.

[29] Burkill, "Syrophoenician Woman," 172–73.

[30] Jones, *St. Mark*, 127 ("The woman survives the test of humility"); Jürgen Roloff, *Das Kerygma und der irdische Jesus: Historische Motive in den Jesus-Erzählungen der Evangelien* (Göttingen: Vandenhoeck & Ruprecht, 1970), 159–60; Kenzo Tagawa, *Miracles et évangile: La pensée personelle de l'évangéliste Marc* (EHPR 62; Paris: Presses Universitaires de France, 1966), 120; Jerry Camery-Hoggatt, *Irony in Mark's Gospel: Text and Subtext* (SNTSMS 72; Cambridge: Cambridge University Press, 1992), 151.

Everywhere else in this Gospel, however, where anyone is being tested, the narrator informs the listener (Mark 1:13; 8:11; 10:2; 12:15). Why in this situation, where the character of Jesus is at stake, would such crucial information be withheld? Perhaps these scholars are influenced by the Matthean version of the account, where the mother's response results in Jesus' immediate praise for her "faith,"[31] which could suggest that he was looking for the depth of her belief. In the Markan account, however, the element of the mother's response that moves Jesus to heal her daughter after all is left unspecified. So there is no signal that Jesus was looking for faith when he insulted her: "*For saying that*, you may go—the demon has left your daughter" (Mark 7:29 [my italics]). Without a signal from the narrator that some test was implied, this solution goes unsupported.

Petr Pokorný not only finds no difficulty in ascribing the harsh metaphor to Jesus but also offers a unique interpretation of it. Jesus bypasses the mother's request for an exorcism to point out to her instead that in the coming kingdom the Gentiles will follow the Jews into their eternal salvation. "Jesus' image of the 'coming' of the Kingdom of God most probably included the expectation of a progression of pagan nations to Mount Zion at the end of time, a theme well-known in some prophets."[32] Again he states, "Jesus did not confirm the woman's expectation that he would play the role of an exorcist, but confronted her with the comprehensive Israel-centered project of his ministry."[33] He does not explain how the listener would understand that Jesus had turned from the issue of exorcism to the end-time progression into the kingdom. Without allusions to Jewish Scripture, end-time allusions, or any hint of Mount Zion in Jesus' answer, Pokorný's proposal is unconvincing.

Summary: Most scholars seek to absolve Jesus' character of any harshness by focusing on the gentle use of κυνάριον in his contrast of child and

---

[31] For a detailed examination of the manner in which Matthew has developed the theme of faith in the miracle stories that he received from his tradition, see Heinz Joachim Held, "Matthew as Interpreter of the Miracle Stories," in *Tradition and Interpretation in Matthew*, by Günther Bornkamm, Gerhard Barth, and Heinz Joachim Held (trans. Percy Scott; NTL; Philadelphia: Westminster, 1963), 165–300, esp. 193, 195.

[32] Petr Pokorný, "From Puppy to Child: Problems of Contemporary Biblical Exegesis Demonstrated from Mark 7:24–30/Matt 15:21–28," *NTS* 41 (1995): 326.

[33] Ibid.

dog, or in the suggestion that Jesus was only provoking the woman as a test to see if her faith was strong. However, Burkill affirms the exclusionary and insulting intent of the saying, but he ascribes it to Christian *Sitz im Leben*, and Pokorný finds no problem in allowing the metaphor to stand as is, a teaching about the sequence of entering the kingdom.

Given the lack of supporting evidence for Pokorný's theory, it remains to discuss Burkill's explanation for the presence of such a rough response to the woman from Jesus. Burkill sees here, as noted above, a redactional addition relative to two movements in a Christian community, first to exclude Gentiles from membership, and then to accept them. But the woman does not ask Jesus to help her become a Jew or to receive her into any kind of discipleship, but only to heal her daughter. After this, as the story concludes, she goes back to her home, which suggests her usual pagan life. Second, if a Christian community did change its mind and see that it should accept Gentile converts, it is difficult to explain why it would decide to keep the original insulting response from Jesus. Third, even with the acceptance of the Gentiles, how willing would the Christian community be to retain the metaphorical image of dogs next to children, with the justification for their presence being their snapping up the children's crumbs?[34]

Where Burkill is right is in his identification of the answer that Jesus gives as belonging to the very conservative Jewish perspective. Thus, in this story the narrator intends to present a Jesus who is very much more like a righteous Jew focused on God's people. Mark 7:26 already shows her to give signs of immodesty in her aggression, her forward behavior in coming to Jesus herself instead of sending a man of her family, her arrival without a female companion, her boldness in initiating speech with Jesus, her lack of any awareness that she comes to Jesus the Jew with no intention of converting, but only to have the demon exorcised from her daughter, so she can go home and resume the very life that opened the daughter to possession in the first place.

The combination of these offenses is provocation enough to explain Jesus' initial refusal: he claims the need of those who are in distress but

---

[34] Just as Ben Witherington III observes, "The story of the Syrophoenician woman presents us with one of the hard sayings of Jesus, a saying it is nearly impossible to believe a largely Gentile church would invent" (*The Gospel of Mark: A Socio-Rhetorical Commentary* [Grand Rapids: Eerdmans, 2001], 231), may we also observe that it is nearly impossible to believe that they would find it acceptable even with the Gentile woman's reply?

know the true God, who belong to the family of God. Thus, a rather righteous Jesus puts her in her place, or tries to do so: "He said to her, 'Let the children be fed first, for it is not fair to take the children's food and throw it to the dogs.'" This presentation of Jesus in this very strict and censuring role is important to allow because, in my view, it deliberately connects with any listener who would share this same attitude and readiness to put this bold woman in her place.

Excursus: The Metaphor of the Gentile as Dog

Both Burkill and Theissen claim that Jesus' metaphor would not have been so stinging as we today imagine it to be, since it probably was commonly used,[35] yet neither of them can point to any known usage of a saying like this that does not take the form of a gross insult. Rather, the evidence shows that when a person is called "a dog" or paralleled to a dog, it is meant to degrade that person. In the Hebrew Scriptures, for example, people will use the question "Am I a dog?" (1 Sam 17:43; 2 Sam 3:8; 2 Kgs 8:13)[36] or, even worse, "Am I a dead dog?" (1 Sam 24:14; 2 Sam 9:8; 2 Sam 16:9) to measure their true worth against the most worthless.[37] Rabbinic references[38] use the "dog" metaphor for four types of persons: (1) the hateful,[39] (2) the ignorant,[40] (3) the godless,[41] and (4) the pagan.[42] Some of

---

[35] Burkill, "Syrophoenician Woman," 172–73; Theissen, *Gospels in Context*, 75.

[36] Goliath asks David, "Am I a dog, that you come to me with sticks?" (1 Sam 17:43); Abner is furious with Ishbosheth for suggesting that he had relations with Saul's concubine: "Am I a dog's head for Judah?" (2 Sam 3:8:); Hazael protests to the prophet Elisha when he hears of the devastation that he will bring to the Jews when he is made king: "What is your servant, who is a mere dog, that she should do this great thing?" (2 Kgs 8:13).

[37] Six texts use "dog" in an insulting reference to a person: 1 Sam 17:43; 1 Sam 24:14; 2 Sam 3:8; 2 Sam 9:8; 2 Sam 16:9; 2 Kgs 8:13. The other seven have separate contexts, unconnected to this.

[38] See P. Billerbeck and H. L. Strack, *Kommentar zum Neuen Testament aus Talmud und Midrasch* (4 vols; Munich: Beck, 1961), 1.722–26.

[39] *b. 'Abod. Zar.* 54b on Deut 4:24; *Tanḥ.* 100a on Mal 1:3.

[40] *Lev. Rab.* 9.110 d

[41] *Exod. Rab.* 9.73c on Ps 110:2; 59:7.

[42] *Midr. Ps.* 11.24a on Ps 4:8, and here the reference to Isa 56:11; *Gen Rab.* 81.52a; *y. Šabb.* 9.11d, 23; *b. Meg.* 7b on Exod 12:16; *Pirqe R. El.* 29 on Dan 3:16; *Num. Rab.* 15.179b; *Midr. Ps.* 2.115a on Ps 29.

these texts continue into the eighth and ninth centuries C.E., which indicates the prevailing sense of the dog being the lowest image. In this saying of Jesus the "dog" metaphor is used in its reference to a pagan.

Jesus tells the woman, "Let the children be fed first, for it is not fair to take the children's food and throw it to the dogs." In Hebrew Scripture, throwing something to dogs is an act used for food that is forbidden and base, as in Exod 22:31: "Therefore you shall not eat any meat that is mangled by beasts in the field; you shall throw it to the dogs." In the Mishnah, *m. Bek.* 5:6 gives an example where a cow pronounced unclean (*terefah*) for Jews to eat was accidentally sold. In the ruling that follows, note that the situation of selling the nonkosher meat to Gentiles is on a par with throwing it to the dogs: "[If] they sold it to gentiles or tossed it to the dogs, they return to him the value of the *terefah*."[43] There is reference to a "dog's dough" in *m. Ḥal.* 1:8, a bread made of the coarsest bran and usually inedible for humans. The ruling regards the situation if the shepherds are willing/able to eat it:

A. [As regards] dog's dough–

B. when shepherds [will] eat it,

C. (1) it is subject to dough offering; (2) [people] may make an *erub* with it; (3) [people] may make a partnership *erub* with it; (4) [people] say the blessing [for bread] over it [before eating it (M. Ber. 6:1)]; (5) [people] say a common grace over it [after eating it (M. Ber. 7:1)]; (6) it may be cooked on a festival [Exod 12:16]; and (7) a person fulfills his obligation [to eat unleavened bread] on Passover by means of [eating] it.

D. [But] if shepherds [will] not eat it,

E. (1) it is not subject to dough offering; (2) [people] may not make an *erub* with it; (3) [people] may not make a partnership *erub* with it; (4) [people] do not say the blessing [for bread] over it; (5) [people] do not say a common grace over it; (6) it may not be cooked on a festival; and (7) a person does not fulfill his obligation [to eat unleavened bread] on Passover by means of [eating] it.

---

[43]Jacob Neusner, trans., *The Mishnah: A New Translation* (New Haven: Yale University Press, 1988), 797.

F. *Whether or not [the shepherds will eat it], it is susceptible to unclean-*
ness as food [M. Toh. 8:6]. (*m. Ḥal.* 1:8)[44]

The contrast, then, not only is one of the order of feeding, but also
indicates the contrast in kind. What is thrown to the dogs is not
the children's bread, but dog's bread, a bread of the bran, suitable
for the iron jaws and stomach of the dog.

Burkill is quite right that "any intelligent Hellenistic woman, addressed in such terms by a barbarian, would have immediately reacted by slapping the man's face."[45] The blunt reply by Jesus allows
the listener to expect an angry retort from this woman.

VI. THE SYROPHOENICIAN MOTHER RESPONDS TO JESUS' REASONS FOR REFUSAL

[28]ἡ δὲ ἀπεκρίθη καὶ λέγει αὐτῷ· κύριε· καὶ τὰ κυνάρια ὑποκάτω τῆς
τραπέζης ἐσθίουσιν ἀπὸ τῶν ψιχίων τῶν παιδίων.

[28]But she answered and said to him, "Sir, even the dogs under the
table eat the children's crumbs."

The Further Characterization of the Syrophoenician Mother

J. D. M. Derrett understands the woman's reply as an answer to
Jesus' reference to Ps 17:14 (here given with the contextualizing v. 13):[46]

---

[44]*Mishnah* (trans. Neusner), 149–50 (my italics). Ben Witherington also
notes this reference and expresses doubt whether Jews even had domesticated dogs
at this time. The mother's reply to Jesus suggests that the listeners will presume domesticated dogs. Whether allowed in the house or used solely for work, no distinction is made in Mishnah. Sarcophagi of the Greco-Roman period, however, often
show little dogs as pets. Note, for example, a sarcophagus dated to 280 C.E. where
the deceased child is shown with his pet dog leaping toward him playfully (Beryl
Rawson, *Children and Childhood in Roman Italy* [Oxford: Oxford University Press,
2003], 79). It is a convention in representations of Endymion's myth to include a
pet dog. Note, for example, the Endymion sarcophagus in the Munich Glyptothek
Museum or the one on display in Metropolitan Museum of Art in New York.

[45]Burkill, "Syrophoenician Woman," 172–73.

[46]J. D. M. Derrett, "Law in the New Testament: The Syro-Phoenician
Woman and the Centurion of Capernaum," *NovT* 15 (1973): 171.

(¹³Rise up, O LORD, confront them, overthrow them!
By your sword deliver my life from the wicked,)
¹⁴from mortals—by your hand, O LORD—
from mortals whose portion in life is in this world.
May their bellies be filled with what you have stored up for them;
may their children have more than enough;
may they leave something over to their little ones.

For Derrett, the woman places special emphasis on the final hope of v. 14: "may they leave something over to their little ones." One could say that the woman was reaffirming the value of her child as a "little one" to Jesus and not a dog. The evidence on which Derrett relies is Jesus' first statement: "Let the children first have their fill." The difficulty is that the second part of Jesus' answer, "It is not right to take the children's bread and throw it to dogs," does not invite a search into Ps 17 for the spirit of his response to her. The narrator has not given the listener enough clues, and the final metaphor, which places the woman's child among the dogs, overpowers the first statement with its denigration of the pagan. Second, the attention given to the woman's identity as a Syrophoenician, and the reiteration of her pagan identity in Jesus' refusal to her on those grounds, do not lead the listener to imagine that this non-Jewish woman would hear the faint strands of Ps 17 in the first part of Jesus' answer.

F. Gerald Downing hears a completely different response from the woman as he focuses on the image of the dog, which her answer accepts and utilizes.⁴⁷ Downing argues that the woman's calm about this label is a sign of Cynic influence on her. He supplies a wealth of examples from Cynic chreia, especially at meals, to illustrate the context in which "dog" is a ready reference to a Cynic. So, for example, he points to Athenaeus's *Deipnosophists* where it reads, "He turned to his slave and said, 'Leucus, if you have any scraps of bread, give them to these Dogs' [δὸς τοῖς κυσίν)]" (*Deipn.* 6.270CD).⁴⁸ In fragment 469

---

⁴⁷ F. Gerald Downing, "The Woman from Syrophoenicia, and Her Doggedness: Mark 7:24–31 (Matt 15:21–28)," in *Women in Biblical Tradition* (ed. George J. Brooke; SWR 3; Lewiston, N.Y.: Mellen Press, 1992), 129–49, and esp. appendix 2.

⁴⁸ Athenaeus, *Deipnosophistae*, vol. 3 (trans. C. B. Gullick; LCL; Cambridge, Mass.: Harvard University Press, 1927), 214–215. For this reference (corrected here from 5.270CD). I am indebted to Downing, "Woman from Syrophoenicia," 149 n. 20.

of Euripides' *Cretan Women*, it reads, "It is the custom to throw the remnants to the dogs."[49]

If the narrator had given the listener some sign that the woman was a Cynic, then Jesus' answer would not have the ordinary sting, of course. But is the woman's lack of vituperative response sign enough that she is a Cynic. And even if she is, if Jesus did not know it, is not his answer just as harsh? What does the narrator achieve by arranging a story like this? In fact, the contrast presented by the narrator is between her being a Syrophoenician and Jesus being a Jew. His metaphor belongs to Jewish insults, where the classic reference to the lowest level of worth is a dog. This story deals not with philosophical contrasts, but religious ones.

The woman's answer is shaming in its evenness, its readiness to overlook the hostile rejection and accept the most denigrating metaphor if she can turn it to convince Jesus to save her daughter. So she does not leave, but instead she holds her position with the same boldness that brought her to plead by herself for her daughter.

She first agrees with Jesus' point: "Yes, sir." It is certain that the children should be filled before the nourishment is handed out freely to the dogs. But in her second response she shows Jesus where his division between child and dog does not require a strict sequence in feeding. Drawing on her mother's experience of feeding children, she points out to him that even as the children are served, their messy eating results in the crumbs of bread falling where the house dogs snap them up. So even though she does not serve the children's food to the dogs, they still manage to eat some of it simultaneously. Seen in a wider symbolism, her answer addresses the fact that Jews and pagans live together in God's world, and yet God nourishes the pagans as he does the Jews. She works with the metaphor and shows children and house dogs eating at the same time, the dogs catching the leftovers. She shows Jesus where his refusal is too categorical. If he is ministering to the Jews, is there not some crumb that can fall to her puppy from the abundance before them?

This answer may explain why the narrator stipulated that the pagan woman was a Syrophoenician, for they appear to have had a reputation

---

[49] Euripides, *Fragments: Aegeus–Meleager*, vol. 7 of *Euripides* (trans. Christopher Collard and Martin Cropp; LCL; Cambridge, Mass.: Harvard University Press, 2008), 526–27. See also Athenaeus, *Deipn.* 3.96F–97A. For both references I am indebted to Downing, "Woman from Syrophoenicia," 149 n. 19.

for sweetness and wit. Eunapius gives evidence about this reputation when writing the biography of Libanius, a Syrophoenician:

> His writings are full of charm and facetious wit, while a refined elegance pervades the whole and is at the service of his eloquence. *Moreover the peculiar charm and sweetness that all Syro-Phoenicians display in general intercourse one may safely look for in him, over and above his erudition.* I mean that quality of a keen scent or urbane wit. This he cultivated as the very crown of true culture; indeed he drew wholly on ancient comedy for his style of expression, and was master of all that shows a pleasing surface and enchants the ear. (*Vit. soph.* 496)[50]

The sweet wit that the woman displays to Jesus in order to overturn his readiness to refuse her seems in accord with this Syrophoenician reputation.

VII. JESUS CHANGES HIS MIND AND ANNOUNCES THE EXORCISM OF THE DAUGHTER

[29]καὶ εἶπεν αὐτῇ· διὰ τοῦτον τὸν λόγον ὕπαγε, ἐξελήλυθεν ἐκ τῆς θυγατρός σου τὸ δαιμόνιον.

[29]Then he said to her, "For saying that, you may go—the demon has left your daughter."

The Final Characterization of Jesus

It is clear from Jesus' response that the words of this mother changed his mind. In fact, this is the only exorcism story where the announcement of the exorcism is described in the perfect tense, ἐξελήλυθεν, rather than the aorist (Mark 1:25, 26; 5:13; 9:25, 26, 29), so that Jesus is announcing to the woman that the exorcism has been completed, as

---

[50] Eunapius, "Libanus," in *Lives of the Philosophers and Sophists* (trans. Wilmer C. Wright; LCL: Cambridge, Mass.: Harvard University Press, 1922), 523–25 (my italics). Greek text: καὶ ὃ πάντες οἱ Συροφοίνικες ἔχουσι κατὰ τὴν κοινὴν ἔντευξιν ἡδὺ καὶ κεχαρισμένον, τοῦτο παρ' ἐκείνου λαβεῖν μετὰ παιδείας ἔξεστιν· οἱ μὲν οὖν Ἀττικοὶ μυκτῆρα καὶ ἀστεϊσμὸν αὐτὸ καλοῦσιν· ὁ δὲ ὥσπερ κορυφὴν παιδείας τοῦτο ἐπετήδευσεν, ἐκ τῆς ἀρχαίας κωμῳδίας ὅλος εἰς τὸ ἀπαγγέλλειν εἰλκυσμένος, καὶ τοῦ κατὰ θύραν τερπνοῦ καὶ γοητεύοντος τὴν ἀκοὴν γενόμενος (ibid., 522–24).

though it was accomplished even while the woman was speaking, in the sense of "the demon has already gone out of your daughter."

But what is it about the saying that caused Jesus to exorcize the demon so immediately? Jesus says, "For this saying . . ." As noted earlier, Matthew identifies the character as "faith," ("Woman, great is your faith!" [Matt 15:28]). But how does her answer express faith? Surely, it is not the content of the answer on which Matthew comments, but her adamancy. Some scholars assign Matthew's "faith" to the Markan tradition even though it is not expressed,[51] while Robert Gundry and others hold that Jesus praises the woman's wit.[52] But does this conclusion address the dynamic that is represented here? Ben Witherington expresses it well when he observes, "Notice that in Jesus' final response to her it is *what* she says, not how she says it, or the cleverness of it, that he mentions as the reason she gains what she wants from him."[53] This is not a game of wit where the story aims to show Jesus outwitted. The context of the story shows an issue of division and serious resistance on what Jesus considers proper religious grounds.

"For this saying" indicates that Jesus sees that she is right, and that his division between the children and the dogs does not justify his dismissal of her, his refusal to exorcize the demon from her pagan daughter. But more, "for this saying" also conveys a shaming of Jesus at the readiness of the mother to sustain the blow of the insult if only she can show him how, retaining his attitudes toward her and her daughter, he will still save her. The Syrophoenician mother is the example of a love that endures even insult and maintains one's foothold if only help may be brought to the needy.

---

[51] Wilfrid Harrington, *Mark* (NTM 4; Wilmington, Del.: Michael Glazier, 1979), 105. Schweizer writes, "Although the word 'faith' does not occur in it, this story . . . portrays the humility and persistence of this woman who takes for granted that God will be merciful in Jesus, and who will not give up" (*Mark*, 153). So the content does not matter but only that she believe that God through Jesus would help her. But this takes away the point that Jesus makes: "for this saying," which points to what she said, not to the fact that she did not leave. See also Ezra P. Gould, *A Critical and Exegetical Commentary on the Gospel according to St. Mark* (ICC; Edinburgh: T & T Clark, 1926), 137; Cranfield, *Saint Mark*, 249.

[52] Robert Gundry, *Matthew: A Commentary on His Literary and Theological Art* (Grand Rapids: Eerdmans, 1982), 318; Burkill, "Syrophoenician Woman," 176.

[53] Witherington, *Mark*, 232.

But Jesus too provides an important example to listeners who may have agreed with his initial refusal of her request and with the reasons for his displeased dismissal. Here Jesus shows that virtue of *praos*, that meekness which recognizes the truth that a subordinate speaks; and also there is the virtue of *epieikeia*, that understanding which comes from listening to another, considered inferior, and recognizing the wisdom in that person's words.

Dio Cassius supplies two examples of this noble virtue in his praise of the emperor Hadrian. He begins by stating, "He led the Roman people by dignity rather than by flattery" (*Hist.* 69.6.1).[54] He continues,

> Once at a gladiatorial contest, when the crowd was demanding something very urgently, he not only would not grant it but further bade the herald proclaim Domitian's command, "Silence!" The word was not uttered, however, for the herald raised his hand and by that very gesture quieted the people, as heralds are accustomed to do (for crowds are never silenced by proclamation), and then, when they had become quiet, he [the herald] said, "This is what he [the emperor] wishes." *And Hadrian was not in the least angry with the herald, but actually honored him for not uttering the rude order. For he could bear such things, and was not displeased if he received aid either in an unexpected way or from ordinary men.* (*Hist.* 69.6.1–2)[55]

More pertinent to our story is the second example: "Once, when a woman made a request of him as he passed by on a journey, he at first said to her, 'I haven't time,' but afterwards, when she cried out, 'Cease, then, being emperor,' he turned about and granted her a hearing" (Dio Cassius, *Hist.* 69.6.3).[56]

This miracle story, in my view, was written to address religious prejudice against the Gentiles through the initial harsh response of Jesus, which articulated the reaction of many Jewish listeners or would-be followers of Jesus. The woman's response and her correction of Jesus' conclusion were bold but done sweetly and out of motherly love. The woman's answer also presented the attitude of the community, which a would-be follower would have to be willing to accept. The story does not address Gentile converts entering community, as Burkill suggests,

---

[54] Dio Cassius, *Roman History* (trans. Earnest Cary; 9 vols.; LCL; Cambridge, Mass.: Harvard University Press, 1914–1927), 8:434–435.

[55] Ibid. (my italics).

[56] Ibid., 8:434–437.

because, as we see, the woman goes home. Rather, this story set down the early Christian reason why no pagan petitioner could be turned away.

The Verification of the Miracle

³⁰καὶ ἀπελθοῦσα εἰς τὸν οἶκον αὐτῆς εὗρεν τὸ παιδίον βεβλημένον ἐπὶ τὴν κλίνην καὶ τὸ δαιμόνιον ἐξεληλυθός.

³⁰So she went home, found the child lying on the bed, and the demon gone.

The verification of the miracle emphasizes the power of Jesus, since the hold of the demon appears to have been grave indeed. The position in which the mother finds her daughter is described using the perfect of the passive participle, "having been thrown down" (βεβλημένον), while the perfect verb "gone out" (ἐξεληλυθός), in affirming the departure of the demon, echoes Jesus' announcement to the mother (ἐξελήλυθεν). The daughter having been flung down on the bed suggests a violent departure, and the girl's exhausted body resting indicates that she has been freed from a terrible tyranny, thanks to the power of Jesus and the adamancy of her mother.

CONCLUSION

The focus of this story clearly is on the way this mother overcomes Jesus' resistance to performing an exorcism for her daughter, not on the exorcism at a distance. It is not a battle of wits won by the mother. Something far deeper is shown in the story. It is Jesus' willingness to listen to the woman and change his mind in recognition, not of an explicit "faith," but because he recognizes that she is right. The story seems to present an example of the *ēpios* of Jesus, his readiness to listen. Jesus' announcement of the completed exorcism of the demon from her daughter lets the woman know that he accepts her insight. His action would represent community teaching and policy that non-Jews should be welcomed and assisted just as Jewish petitioners are, a very difficult teaching for those members represented by Jesus' initial response in Mark 7:27.

6

Jesus and the Father of a Demonized Boy (Mark 9:14–29)

"Above all, we pride ourselves on the education of our children, and regard as the most essential task in life the observance of our laws and of the pious practices based there upon, which we have inherited." (Josephus, *Ag. Ap.* 1.60)[1]

"For all men guard their own customs, but this is especially true of the Jewish nation. Holding that the laws are oracles vouchsafed by God and having been trained in this doctrine from their earliest years, they carry the likeness of the commandments enshrined in their souls." (Philo, *Embassy* 210)[2]

Mark has situated this story of the encounter between Jesus and the father of a demonized boy in the crucial middle section of his Gospel (Mark 8:22–10:52). This section might well be entitled "The Blindness of Jesus' Disciples." Straddled by stories about two blind men, an unnamed man in Bethsaida (Mark 8:22–26) and Bartimaeus (Mark 10:46–52),[3] this section features all the most difficult teachings concerning discipleship, as it also features the three passion predictions meant to prepare the disciples for the coming sufferings, death, and resurrection of Jesus (Mark 8:31; 9:31; 10:33–34). The entire section has been organized in such a way that the disciples demonstrate over and over again their desire for personal glory and their resistance to serving

---

[1] Flavius Josephus, *Josephus* (trans. H. St. J. Thackeray et al.; 10 vols.; LCL; London: Heinemann; New York: Putnam; Cambridge, Mass.: Harvard University Press, 1926–1981), 1:186–189.

[2] Philo of Alexandria, *On the Embassy to Gaius*, vol. 10 of *Philo* (trans. F. H. Colson; LCL; Cambridge, Mass.: Harvard University Press, 1939), 10.108–109.

[3] See chapter 2, on Jesus and Bartimaeus.

others, despite Jesus' patient reiteration of his teachings.[4] The account here occurs in the first third of this teaching block, immediately following Jesus' transfiguration (Mark 9:2–13). In that context, it is as Jesus and Peter, James, and John descend the mountain that they encounter the remaining disciples locked in dispute with the scribes. But what constitutes the narrative is the encounter between Jesus and the father and Jesus' ultimate concession to exorcize the spirit from the boy and then miraculously heal him. Mark's introduction allows him to attach a conclusion in which the disciples ask why they were unsuccessful, to which Jesus will offer the astonishing reply that situations this serious require prayer. This blatant evidence of the disciples' arrogance and spiritual obtuseness belongs to Mark's theme of the unknowing disciples. To discuss the pre-Markan story, it is necessary to examine the text for the most obvious Markan additions.

I. MARK 9:14–29: SIGNS OF MARKAN REDACTION

[14]καὶ ἐλθόντες πρὸς τοὺς μαθητὰς εἶδον ὄχλον πολὺν περὶ αὐτοὺς καὶ γραμματεῖς συζητοῦντας πρὸς αὐτούς. [15]καὶ εὐθὺς πᾶς ὁ ὄχλος ἰδόντες αὐτὸν ἐξεθαμβήθησαν καὶ προστρέχοντες ἠσπάζοντο αὐτόν. [16]καὶ ἐπηρώτησεν αὐτούς· τί συζητεῖτε πρὸς αὐτούς; [17]καὶ ἀπεκρίθη αὐτῷ εἷς ἐκ τοῦ ὄχλου· διδάσκαλε, ἤνεγκα τὸν υἱόν μου πρὸς σέ, ἔχοντα πνεῦμα ἄλαλον· [18]καὶ ὅπου ἐὰν αὐτὸν καταλάβῃ ῥήσσει αὐτόν, καὶ ἀφρίζει καὶ τρίζει τοὺς ὀδόντας καὶ ξηραίνεται· καὶ εἶπα τοῖς μαθηταῖς σου ἵνα αὐτὸ ἐκβάλωσιν, καὶ οὐκ ἴσχυσαν. [19]ὁ δὲ ἀποκριθεὶς αὐτοῖς λέγει· ὦ γενεὰ ἄπιστος, ἕως πότε πρὸς ὑμᾶς ἔσομαι; ἕως πότε ἀνέξομαι ὑμῶν; φέρετε αὐτὸν πρός με. [20]καὶ ἤνεγκαν αὐτὸν πρὸς αὐτόν. καὶ ἰδὼν αὐτὸν τὸ πνεῦμα εὐθὺς συνεσπάραξεν αὐτόν, καὶ πεσὼν ἐπὶ τῆς γῆς ἐκυλίετο ἀφρίζων. [21]καὶ ἐπηρώτησεν τὸν πατέρα αὐτοῦ· πόσος χρόνος ἐστὶν ὡς τοῦτο γέγονεν αὐτῷ; ὁ δὲ εἶπεν· ἐκ παιδιόθεν· [22]καὶ πολλάκις καὶ εἰς πῦρ αὐτὸν ἔβαλεν καὶ εἰς ὕδατα ἵνα ἀπολέσῃ αὐτόν· ἀλλ' εἴ τι δύνῃ, βοήθησον ἡμῖν σπλαγχνισθεὶς ἐφ' ἡμᾶς. [23]ὁ δὲ Ἰησοῦς εἶπεν αὐτῷ· τὸ εἰ δύνῃ, πάντα δυνατὰ τῷ πιστεύοντι. [24]εὐθὺς κράξας ὁ πατὴρ τοῦ παιδίου ἔλεγεν· πιστεύω· βοήθει μου τῇ ἀπιστίᾳ. [25]ἰδὼν δὲ ὁ Ἰησοῦς ὅτι ἐπισυντρέχει ὄχλος, ἐπετίμησεν τῷ πνεύματι τῷ ἀκαθάρτῳ

---

[4] See Robert C. Tannehill, "The Disciples in Mark: The Function of a Narrative Role," *JR* 57 (1977): 386–405; Philip Sellew, "Composition of Didactic Scenes in Mark's Gospel," *JBL* 108 (1989): 613–34.

λέγων αὐτῷ· τὸ ἄλαλον καὶ κωφὸν πνεῦμα, ἐγὼ ἐπιτάσσω σοι, ἔξελθε ἐξ αὐτοῦ καὶ μηκέτι εἰσέλθῃς εἰς αὐτόν. ²⁶καὶ κράξας καὶ πολλὰ σπαράξας ἐξῆλθεν· καὶ ἐγένετο ὡσεὶ νεκρός, ὥστε τοὺς πολλοὺς λέγειν ὅτι ἀπέθανεν. ²⁷ὁ δὲ Ἰησους κρατήσας τῆς χειρὸς αὐτοῦ ἤγειρεν αὐτόν, καὶ ἀνέστη. ²⁸καὶ εἰσελθόντος αὐτοῦ εἰς οἶκον οἱ μαθηταὶ αὐτοῦ κατ᾽ ἰδίαν ἐπηρώτων αὐτόν· ὅτι ἡμεῖς οὐκ ἐδυνήθημεν ἐκβαλεῖν αὐτό; ²⁹καὶ εἶπεν αὐτοῖς· τοῦτο τὸ γένος ἐν οὐδενὶ δύναται ἐξελθεῖν εἰ μὴ ἐν προσευχῇ.

¹⁴When they came to the disciples, they saw a great crowd around them, and some scribes arguing with them. ¹⁵When the whole crowd saw him, they were immediately overcome with awe, and they ran forward to greet him. ¹⁶He asked them, "What are you arguing about with them?" ¹⁷Someone from the crowd answered him, "Teacher, I brought you my son; he has a spirit that makes him unable to speak; ¹⁸and whenever it seizes him, it dashes him down; and he foams and grinds his teeth and becomes rigid; and I asked your disciples to cast it out but they could not do so." ¹⁹He answered them, "You faithless generation, how much longer must I be among you? How much longer must I put up with you? Bring him to me." ²⁰And they brought the boy to him. When the spirit saw him, immediately it convulsed the boy, and he fell to the ground and rolled about, foaming at the mouth. ²¹Jesus asked the father, "How long has this been happening to him?" And he said, "From childhood. ²²It has often cast him into the fire and into the water, to destroy him; but if you are able to do anything, have pity on us and help us." ²³Jesus said to him, "If you are able! — All things can be done for the one who believes." ²⁴Immediately the father of the child cried out, "I believe; help my unbelief!" ²⁵When Jesus saw that a crowd came running together, he rebuked the unclean spirit, saying to it, "You spirit that keeps this boy from speaking and hearing, I command you, come out of him, and never enter him again!" ²⁶After crying out and convulsing him terribly, it came out, and the boy was like a corpse, so that most of them said, "He is dead." ²⁷But Jesus took him by the hand and lifted him up, and he was able to stand. ²⁸When he had entered the house, his disciples asked him privately, "Why could we not cast it out?" ²⁹He said to them, "This kind can come out only through prayer."

164 THE CHRIST OF THE MIRACLE STORIES

¹⁴καὶ ἐλθόντες πρὸς τοὺς μαθητὰς εἶδον ὄχλον πολὺν περὶ αὐτοὺς καὶ γραμματεῖς συζητοῦντας πρὸς αὐτούς.

¹⁴When they came to the disciples, they saw a great crowd around them, and some scribes arguing with them.

Verse 14a⁵ is meant to connect the transfiguration pericope (Mark 9:2–13) to this account, which marks it as the evangelist's Gospel organization. The mention of the "great crowd" is suspiciously Markan, for not only does this evangelist show a tendency to include the crowds throughout the Gospel, but also in this case they serve to shame the unsuccessful disciples.⁶ The mention of the crowd here also creates a problem when Mark states that the approach of a crowd motivates Jesus to hurriedly exorcize the spirit from the boy (v. 25a). This second crowd serves the Markan theme of the Messianic Secret, but what happened to the first crowd of v. 14? The arguing scribes have no actual function in the story,⁷ and when Jesus asks about the substance of the argument between his disciples and them, these disciples do not answer. Instead, the father expresses his complaint over the ineptitude of the disciples.⁸ The presence of scribes in what appears to be open countryside is artificial and can only be explained as interfering enemies intent on sending Jesus to the cross. The presence of the disciples is unnecessary to the heart of the story. They never speak until the Markan conclusion in v. 28 when they ask why they could not heal the boy. For the most part, they are understood to be onlookers.

---

⁵Vincent Taylor notes the Markan vocabulary: μαθητής (2:16), ὄχλος (2:4), οἱ γραμματεῖς (1:22), συζητέω (1:27), εὐθύς (1:10), ἐκθαμβέομαι (14:33; 16:5, 6). "It is clear that for the most part Mark has himself supplied this introductory passage" (*The Gospel according to St. Mark: The Greek Text with Introduction, Notes, and Indexes* [London: Macmillan; New York: St. Martin's Press], 1955), 396.

⁶Paul Achtemeier points to Mark's characteristic of "public teaching to the masses (including the disciples) and private explanation to the disciples. That occurs in 4:1–12; 7:14–23; 9:14–29; 10:1–10; and 13:1–8" (*Mark* [PC; Philadelphia: Fortress], 33).

⁷See Rudolf Bultmann, *The History of the Synoptic Tradition* (trans. John Marsh; Peabody, Mass.: Hendrickson, 1963), 52.

⁸See Joachim Gnilka, *Das Evangelium nach Markus* (2 vols.; EKKNT 2; Zürich: Benziger; Neukirchen-Vlyun: Neukirchener Verlag, 1978–1979), 2:45.

¹⁵καὶ εὐθὺς πᾶς ὁ ὄχλος ἰδόντες αὐτὸν ἐξεθαμβήθησαν καὶ προστρέχοντες ἠσπάζοντο αὐτόν.

¹⁵When the whole crowd saw him, they were immediately overcome with awe, and they ran forward to greet him.

The response of the crowd belongs to the situation created by Mark (v. 14). Their reaction of being "overcome with awe" is typical of Markan vocabulary. James P. Edwards rightly notes that "Mark 9:14–15 describes a scene without focus,"⁹ another observation that adds to the broad scholarly consensus that vv. 14–15 belong to Mark.¹⁰

¹⁶καὶ ἐπηρώτησεν αὐτούς· τί συζητεῖτε πρὸς αὐτούς;

¹⁶He asked them, "What are you arguing about with them?"

Again, this question serves the conflictual setting introduced by Mark's introduction, vv. 14–15, and in particular it echoes v. 14: συζητοῦντας πρὸς αὐτούς.¹¹ The ordinary referent of αὐτούς ("them") would be the scribes. Robert Gundry observes that the correct translation of the Greek should be "*Why* are you arguing with them?" and not "*What* are you arguing about with them?" since the necessary περί ("about") is not there.¹² But either way, Jesus' question receives no answer from them. As noted above, they do not speak at all until the conclusion of the account, in vv. 28–29, already identified as redactional. Thus, Jesus' question to the disciples in v. 16 belongs to the Markan

---

⁹James P. Edwards, *The Gospel according to Mark* (PNTC; Grand Rapids: Eerdmans, 2002), 277.

¹⁰Bultmann, *Synoptic Tradition*, 211; Taylor, *St. Mark*, 396; Dietrich-Alex Koch, *Die Bedeutung der Wundererzählungen für die Christologie des Markusevangeliums* (BZNW 42; Berlin: de Gruyter, 1975), 120; Paul Achtemeier, "Miracles and the Historical Jesus: A Study of Mark 9:14–29," *CBQ* 37 (1975): 475; Wolfgang Schenk, "Tradition und Redaktion in der Epileptiker-Periocope Mk 9:14–29)," *ZNW* 63 (1972): 82; Ernst Haenchen, *Der Weg Jesu: Eine Erklärung des Markus-Evangeliums und der kanonischen Parallelen* (2d ed.; Berlin: de Gruyter, 1968), 318–19; Gnilka, *Markus*, 2:45.

¹¹Bultmann, *Synoptic Tradition*, 211; Taylor, *St. Mark*, 397; Koch, *Die Bedeutung der Wundererzählungen*, 120; Achtemeier, "Miracles," 476; Schenk, "Tradition und Redaktion," 82; Haenchen, *Der Weg Jesu*, 318–19; Gnilka, *Markus*, 2:45.

¹²Robert H. Gundry, *Mark: A Commentary on His Apology for the Cross* (Grand Rapids: Eerdmans, 1993), 488.

contextualization of the story. Meantime, the issue of dispute with the scribes is never explained.

¹⁷καὶ ἀπεκρίθη αὐτῷ εἷς ἐκ τοῦ ὄχλου· διδάσκαλε, ἤνεγκα τὸν υἱόν μου πρὸς σέ, ἔχοντα πνεῦμα ἄλαλον· ¹⁸καὶ ὅπου ἐὰν αὐτὸν καταλάβῃ ῥήσσει αὐτόν, καὶ ἀφρίζει καὶ τρίζει τοὺς ὀδόντας καὶ ξηραίνεται· καὶ εἶπα τοῖς μαθηταῖς σου ἵνα αὐτὸ ἐκβάλωσιν, καὶ οὐκ ἴσχυσαν.

¹⁷Someone from the crowd answered him, "Teacher, I brought you my son; he has a spirit that makes him unable to speak; ¹⁸and whenever it seizes him, it dashes him down; and he foams and grinds his teeth and becomes rigid; and I asked your disciples to cast it out, but they could not do so."

The crowd of v. 17 also belongs to Mark's introduction in v. 14. More redaction is present in the man's address to Jesus, "Teacher," a typical Markan insertion.¹³ If some other title for Jesus had stood in the pre-Markan tradition, it is most probable that Mark would have employed it here, since he shows himself disposed to do this elsewhere—for example, Mark 10:47 ("Son of David"). It is more probable that in the pre-Markan account the man did not address Jesus with any title at all.

Verse 18 is the description of the boy's problem and is therefore necessary to the miracle account. The final clauses, however, "and I asked your disciples to cast it out, but they could not do so," are Mark's addition preparing the way for v. 28 and the astonishing revelation that his disciples had not thought to pray (v. 29). In the Markan introduction, the man has interrupted Jesus' question to his disciples about their dispute with the scribes to explain his son's trouble and the ineptitude of the disciples, while the scribal dispute is dropped altogether. Vocabulary too signals Markan redaction in the father's last clause, because the verb used to express being "strong enough" is ἰσχύω (literally, "to be strong"), so that he says that the disciples "were not strong enough" (οὐκ ἴσχυσαν). Yet in the very heart of the story, when the man pleads with Jesus about his accomplishing of the exorcism (v. 22), he uses δύναμαι ("to be able"):

---

¹³Mark shows Jesus being addressed in this manner by the disciples in Mark 4:38; 9:38; 10:35; 13:1; the rich man in Mark 10:17, 20; the sincere scribe in Mark 12:32 (who later would be complimented by Jesus); and, in a sarcastic sense, by the Pharisees and Herodians in Mark 12:14; and the Sadducees in Mark 12:19. See the erudite treatment of Mark's theme in Vernon Robbins, *Jesus the Teacher: A Socio-Rhetorical Interpretation of Mark* (Philadelphia: Fortress, 1984).

"If you are able" (εἴ τι δύνῃ). This is the verb that Jesus throws back at the father in v. 23, "If you are able!" (τὸ εἰ δύνῃ), and that he uses to correct the father when he makes the pronouncement "All things are possible for the one who believes!"[14] (πάντα δυνατὰ τῷ πιστεύοντι). If the inability of the disciples in contrast to Jesus were unitary, the verb to complain about their failure would be δύναμαι, not ἰσχύω.

Once these Markan insertions are recognized and removed, the material in vv 17–18 fits the usual pattern whereby a petitioner approaches to ask Jesus for a miracle.

[19]ὁ δὲ ἀποκριθεὶς αὐτοῖς λέγει· ὦ γενεὰ ἄπιστος, ἕως πότε πρὸς ὑμᾶς ἔσομαι; ἕως πότε ἀνέξομαι ὑμῶν; φέρετε αὐτὸν πρός με.

[19]He answered them, "You faithless generation, how much longer must I be among you? How much longer must I put up with you? Bring him to me."

Mark has inserted the plural audience, "He answered them," due to the additions that he made with the crowd, disciples, and scribes. "Bring him to me" had been singular, but now it would be awkward if it included the whole crowd, when the father is speaking about his boy. Then, in v. 25, the text reads that Jesus saw a crowd forming. So was it a second crowd? Or did Mark forget that by using the plural, he had already brought the man and the crowd over to where Jesus would see the boy?

To whom does Jesus speak then when he cries out, ὦ γενεὰ ἄπιστος, ἕως πότε πρὸς ὑμᾶς ἔσομαι; ἕως πότε ἀνέξομαι ὑμῶν; φέρετε αὐτὸν πρός με? Does Jesus speak to his disciples who were unable to cast out the demon? Karl Kertelge claims that it is Mark who chose the ἄπιστος as the adjective describing this generation in v. 19 (and for the man's cry to Jesus in v. 24) because he wants to emphasize the importance of faith.[15] Gundry too understands that the disciples were meant to be those who lack faith, because the man already showed faith in bringing his son.[16] First of all, it must be noted that there is no Gospel tradition where Jesus uses "this generation" in a rebuke referring to his disciples. "This

---

[14] My translation.

[15] Karl Kertelge, *Die Wunder Jesu im Markusevangelium: Eine redaktionsgeschichtliche Untersuchung* (SANT 33; Munich: Kösel-Verlag, 1970), 176.

[16] Gundry, *Mark*, 488.

generation" is used either in a general way[17] or, when used specifically, to refer to someone well outside discipleship.[18] In this broad complaint of Jesus, Mark was ready to include the disciples, but he is not the one who intended them as the target for those lacking in faith, because if that had been his view of the reason for their failure, he would have underlined it as the reason for their failure when they ask him in the Markan redactional conclusion (v. 28). Rather, Jesus tells them that it is because they did not think to pray. Notice that Matthew's redaction of Mark's conclusion (Matt 17:20) does make lack of faith the reason. The disjuncture in the Markan version indicates that the idea of lack of faith belonged to the pre-Markan story. Indeed, the subject of ἄπιστος ("faithless") really controls the frictional encounter between Jesus and the father, finding its climax in the father's desperate shout to Jesus in v. 24. The evidence rules against Mark being the one to insert ἄπιστος to describe the disciples and in favor of it being integral to the story itself.

> [20]καὶ ἤνεγκαν αὐτὸν πρὸς αὐτόν. καὶ ἰδὼν αὐτὸν τὸ πνεῦμα εὐθὺς συνεσπάραξεν αὐτόν, καὶ πεσὼν ἐπὶ τῆς γῆς ἐκυλίετο ἀφρίζων.

> [20]And they brought the boy to him. When the spirit saw him, immediately it convulsed the boy, and he fell to the ground and rolled about, foaming at the mouth.

The elements of this verse verify the father's description in v. 18 and are part of the main narrative. Only the plural ἤνεγκαν ("they brought him") belongs to the crowd context supplied by Mark. Other than this, no other features address Markan themes or emphases. A number of verbs are particular to this pre-Markan account in relation to the New Testament canon: ἀφρίζω, the foaming of the mouth (vv. 18–20); τρίζω, the grinding of the teeth (v. 18); συσπαράσσω, the convulsion of the boy (v. 20 [paralleled in Luke 9:42]); κυλίομαι, the boy's rolling around (v. 20). With respect to the use here of ξηραίνω, "dried up" (v. 18), it metaphorically expresses rigidity (in its *literal* sense of something being without moisture, it occurs in four Markan pericope in pre-Markan

---

[17] Mark 8:38 // Matt 16:4; Matt 24:34 //Mark 13:30 //Luke 21:32; Q (Luke) 7:31; 11:29, 30, 31, 32; Matt 12:45; Luke 16:8; 17:25.
[18] Q (Luke) 11:50–51.

descriptions).[19] The boy's falling on the ground is a basic element of this story, thus the description shows no signs of Markan redaction.

[21]καὶ ἐπηρώτησεν τὸν πατέρα αὐτοῦ· πόσος χρόνος ἐστὶν ὡς τοῦτο γέγονεν αὐτῷ; ὁ δὲ εἶπεν· ἐκ παιδιόθεν· [22]καὶ πολλάκις καὶ εἰς πῦρ αὐτὸν ἔβαλεν καὶ εἰς ὕδατα ἵνα ἀπολέσῃ αὐτόν· ἀλλ' εἴ τι δύνῃ, βοήθησον ἡμῖν σπλαγχνισθεὶς ἐφ' ἡμᾶς. [23]ὁ δὲ Ἰησοῦς εἶπεν αὐτῷ· τὸ εἰ δύνῃ, πάντα δυνατὰ τῷ πιστεύοντι. [24]εὐθὺς κράξας ὁ πατὴρ τοῦ παιδίου ἔλεγεν· πιστεύω· βοήθει μου τῇ ἀπιστίᾳ.

[21]Jesus asked the father, "How long has this been happening to him?" And he said, "From childhood. [22]It has often cast him into the fire and into the water, to destroy him; but if you are able to do anything, have pity on us and help us." [23]Jesus said to him, "If you are able! — All things can be done for the one who believes." [24]Immediately the father of the child cried out, "I believe; help my unbelief!"

Verses 21–24 flow from vv. 18–20 and hold no elements that could be identified as a Markan. Jesus' question to the father about his son (v. 21) receives an answer that concludes with an indication of doubt (v. 22), which draws Jesus' protest (v. 23) and the father's impassioned response (v. 24). Christopher Marshall has proposed that the father's reply to Jesus should be recognized as Markan, since it brings out the importance of faith in Jesus:

> The formula [v. 24 bc] also reveals that while Mark considers faith to be a free volitional decision (πιστεύω), it is not simply a human aptitude or achievement. It is finally a gift, not only because it emerges from encounter with Jesus, but also because it remains forever contingent upon the sustaining power of the one in whom it is placed (βοήθει μου τῇ ἀπιστίᾳ).[20]

Marshall surely is right about the message, but it is not Mark's hand that has inserted it, because, as noted previously, where Mark's hand is

---

[19] Mark 3:1: the man's dried-up hand (condition to be healed); Mark 4:6: a plant dried up (feature of a parable); Mark 5:29: the woman's former flow of blood dried up (efficacy of a miracle); Mark 11:20–21: a fig tree's roots dried up (efficacy of a miracle).

[20] Christopher D. Marshall, *Faith as a Theme in Mark's Narrative* (SNTSMS 84; Cambridge: Cambridge University Press, 1988), 121.

indisputably in view, vv. 28–29, Jesus offers his disciples a counsel to pray with no mention of faith.[21]

²⁵ἰδὼν δὲ ὁ Ἰησοῦς ὅτι ἐπισυντρέχει ὄχλος, ἐπετίμησεν τῷ πνεύματι τῷ ἀκαθάρτῳ λέγων αὐτῷ· τὸ ἄλαλον καὶ κωφὸν πνεῦμα, ἐγὼ ἐπιτάσσω σοι, ἔξελθε ἐξ αὐτοῦ καὶ μηκέτι εἰσέλθῃς εἰς αὐτόν.

²⁵When Jesus saw that a crowd came running together, he rebuked the unclean spirit, saying to it, "You spirit that keeps this boy from speaking and hearing, I command you, come out of him, and never enter him again!"

The reappearance of a crowd "running together" (v. 25a) is a point of disjuncture, since the initial crowd of v. 14 presumably is still there,[22] assumed to be among the "they" whom Jesus orders to bring him the boy (vv. 19e–20a) and in whose presence Jesus questions the father. Mark's report of Jesus' discussion with the father seems to have allowed him to forget the context of a crowd that he himself created. So this disjuncture, along with the idea that Jesus must avoid public viewing of his miracles, shows that this belongs to Mark's secrecy theme.[23] The remainder of v. 25 is the command of exorcism itself and is indispensable to the story. The vocabulary recalls the pre-Markan formulation of exorcism in Mark 1:21–28: (1) the description of the demon, πνεῦμα ἀκάθαρτον (Mark 1:23; 9:25); (2) Jesus' command to the demon ἐπιτάσσω (Mark 1:17; 9:25).[24] There is nothing distinctively Markan about these formulations.

---

[21]Marshall perhaps is influenced by Matt 17:20–21. Notice, however, that Matthew has also removed any sign of ambivalence in the father, Jesus' objection and correction, and the man's impassioned reply. The father is a model of total faith.

[22]Bultmann (*Synoptic Tradition*, 211) interprets this confusing reintroduction as a sign that two similar miracle stories have been joined, one featuring the inability of the disciples to perform the miracle, and the other being more like an apophthegm between the father and Jesus.

[23]Étienne Trocmé (*The Formation of the Gospel according to Mark* [trans. Pamela Gaughan; Philadelphia: Westminster, 1975], 153 n. 2) notes the tendency in Mark to have Jesus avoid crowds, plainly articulated in a Markan summary, Mark 3:7–12 (in particular vv. 9–10), and to perform miracles in private, or to silence demons in private, and to move to places of privacy, as in Mark 1:33–34, 38.

[24]Certain vocabulary also finds similarity with the pre-Markan account of the healing of the deaf and dumb man in Mark 7:31–37: (1) κωφός ("deaf") in the description of the deaf person and the crowd's acclamation (7:32, 37)

²⁶καὶ κράξας καὶ πολλὰ σπαράξας ἐξῆλθεν· καὶ ἐγένετο ὡσεὶ νεκρός, ὥστε τοὺς πολλοὺς λέγειν ὅτι ἀπέθανεν. ²⁷ὁ δὲ Ἰησους κρατήσας τῆς χειρὸς αὐτοῦ ἤγειρεν αὐτόν, καὶ ἀνέστη.

²⁶After crying out and convulsing him terribly, it came out, and the boy was like a corpse, so that most of them said, "He is dead." ²⁷But Jesus took him by the hand and lifted him up, and he was able to stand.

Gregory Sterling argues on grammatical grounds it is Mark who composed vv. 26–27.²⁵ A double participle precedes the verb ἐξῆλθεν ("it came out"), so that the text reads κράξας . . . σπαράξας ἐξῆλθεν ("screaming . . . convulsing, it came out"), and he sees this as the same pattern found in six other texts in this Gospel: Mark 3:12; 5:10, 23, 38, 43; 6:20. What Sterling has not noted is that only two of the six belong to Mark's hand, while the remaining four are pre-Markan. That is, 3:12 is a Markan seam (3:7–12) where Jesus enjoins his disciples not to make him known, and 5:43 is the Markan conclusion to the pre-Markan miracle of the raising of Jairus's daughter (5:22b–24, 35–43), where Jesus forbids anyone to tell about the miracle and orders the parents to give her something to eat. These are plainly Markan due to the "Messianic Secret" theme. The four remaining are not Markan redaction but are integral to the pre-Markan account: (1) 5:10 (the Gerasene demoniac [5:1–20]), where the legion begs Jesus not to send them out of the country; (2) 5:23 (the raising of Jairus's daughter [5:22b–24, 35–43]), where Jairus asks Jesus to come and lay his hand on his daughter, who is near death; (3) 5:38, of that same narrative, where Jesus arrives at the house and sees the flute players and the whole crowd; (4) 6:20 (the death of John the Baptist [6:14–29]), which tells of Herod's ambivalence, both fearing John and liking to listen to him.

All four instances are necessary to the narrative itself. In the same way, Mark 9:26 is necessary to the account because Jesus orders the mute spirit to leave, and its vindictive screams of protest belong to the spirit taking its final vengeance on the boy and leaving him looking like he is dead. It is this situation that Jesus will remedy with a second miracle in

---

and in Jesus' address to the spirit (9:25); (2) ἄλαλος ("mute") in the crowd's acclamation (7:37) and in Jesus' address to the spirit (9:25).

²⁵Gregory Sterling, "Jesus as Exorcist: An Analysis of Matthew 17:14–20; Mark 9:14–29; Luke 9:37–43A," *CBQ* 55 (1993): 464.

the healing of the boy (v. 27). Thus, v. 26 is the result of Jesus' command in v. 25 and in turn leads to Jesus' rescue in v. 27. The integral role of vv. 26–27 shows that they belong to the pre-Markan material.

Where we can see the hand of Mark is in the reference to the crowd that he has inserted beginning with vv. 14–15, 17 and again in v. 25a. In v. 26c Mark has the crowd repeat what is reported in v. 26b, καὶ ἐγένετο ὡσεὶ νεκρός ("and he was as [a] dead [person]"), with ὥστε τοὺς πολλοὺς λέγειν ὅτι ἀπέθανεν ("so that most of them said, 'He is dead'"). He affirms again the presence of the witnessing crowd.

Markan insertions usually are identifiable by the manner in which they serve the theme of the Messianic Secret or the uncomprehending disciples, and literarily they often exhibit disjuncture, as we have already seen above, where in the account Jesus bemoans the lack of faith but Mark's addition assigns the failure of the disciples to be lack of prayer. That disjuncture is not found in v. 26. Mark 9:26 also shows great similarity to Mark 1:26, where a shouting demon comes out of the victim:

καὶ κράξας καὶ πολλὰ σπαράξας ἐξῆλθεν. (Mark 9:26)

After crying out and convulsing him terribly, it came out.

καὶ σπαράξαν αὐτὸν τὸ πνεῦμα τὸ ἀκάθαρτον καὶ φωνῆσαν φωνῇ μεγάλῃ ἐξῆλθεν ἐξ αὐτοῦ. (Mark 1:26)

And the unclean spirit, convulsing him and crying with a loud voice, came out of him.

While the use of ἐξέρχομαι ("to come out") in both stories is unremarkable, it is worth noting that in the New Testament canon the verb σπαράσσω ("to convulse") occurs only here in these two verses, and in Luke 9:39, a text dependent on Mark 9:14–29. The demon expressing its anger as it leaves also occurs in Mark 1:26, but whereas Mark 1:26 uses a Hebraic form, "calling with a great call," Mark 9:26 uses the vivid verb of screaming. This brings out the fury of the demon, which has been hiding as "mute" but now has been identified by Jesus: τὸ ἄλαλον καὶ κωφὸν πνεῦμα, "you mute and deaf spirit" (v. 25). Now it screams out its protest; no longer mute or keeping the boy forever mute, but overpowered by the authority of Jesus, it must leave immediately and forever. Both descriptions of the expulsion of a demon in these two

Markan exorcisms belong to the pre-Markan accounts. They cannot be considered insertions on the story.

²⁶ᵇκαὶ ἐγένετο ὡσεὶ νεκρός, ὥστε τοὺς πολλοὺς λέγειν ὅτι ἀπέθανεν.

²⁶ᵇ*And he was as if dead, so that many said that he had died.*

There is an artificiality in the appearance of "many" since the conversation with the father gives the impression of being private, but it is necessary for others to note the grievous state of the boy.

²⁷ὁ δὲ Ἰησους κρατήσας τῆς χειρὸς αὐτοῦ ἤγειρεν αὐτόν, καὶ ἀνέστη.

²⁷*But Jesus took him by the hand and lifted him up, and he was able to stand.*

No Markan vocabulary is in view. Conventional expressions for other Jesus' healings and raisings from the dead are in evidence as found in the healing of Peter's mother-in-law (Mark 1:29–31) and raising of Jairus's daughter (Mark 5:22–24, 35–43).

ὁ δὲ Ἰησοῦς *κρατήσας τῆς χειρὸς αὐτοῦ ἤγειρεν αὐτόν*, καὶ ἀνέστη. (Mark 9:27)

But Jesus, *grabbing his hand*, raised him, and he stood up.

καὶ προσελθὼν ἤγειρεν αὐτὴν *κρατήσας τῆς χειρός*. (Mark 1:31a)

And approaching, he raised her, *grabbing her hand*.

καὶ *κρατήσας τῆς χειρὸς τοῦ παιδίου* λέγει αὐτῇ· ταλιθα κουμ, ὅ ἐστιν μεθερμηνευόμενον· τὸ κοράσιον, σοὶ λέγω, ἔγειρε. καὶ εὐθὺς ἀνέστη τὸ κοράσιον καὶ περιεπάτει. (Mark 5:41–42)

And *grabbing the child's hand*, he said to her, "Talitha cum," which means, "Little girl, I say to you, arise!" And immediately, the little girl stood up and began to walk.

All these narrative elements belong to the curing of the patient and cannot be assigned to an intervention by Mark.

²⁸καὶ εἰσελθόντος αὐτοῦ εἰς οἶκον οἱ μαθηταὶ αὐτοῦ κατ' ἰδίαν ἐπηρώτων αὐτὸν· ὅτι ἡμεῖς οὐκ ἐδυνήθημεν ἐκβαλεῖν αὐτό; ²⁹καὶ

εἶπεν αὐτοῖς· τοῦτο τὸ γένος ἐν οὐδενὶ δύναται ἐξελθεῖν εἰ μὴ ἐν προσευχῇ.

²⁸When he had entered the house, his disciples asked him privately, "Why could we not cast it out?" ²⁹He said to them, "This kind can come out only through prayer."

Vincent Taylor notes that we do not find the expected acclamation of the exorcism, but only this concluding conference between the disciples and Jesus about their inability to successfully expel the demon.[26] This shows that the "crowd" does not belong to the pre-Markan text but was inserted only when it served Mark's themes. The pre-Markan story could conclude without any attesting acclamation because, in a way, the healing miracle is that attestation. It was a rescue needed due to the success of the exorcism. And more will be said about this later.

Verse 29 begins with Jesus entering "the house," typical of Markan additions, where the disciples will be counseled.[27] It has already been noted several times that Mark does not show that being ἄπιστος ("faithless") is the disciples' problem, but rather it is their lack of prayer. Graham Twelftree notes, "For though it is possible that this inconsistency existed in Mark's tradition, inconsistencies would have been omitted or ironed out in the transmission of tradition."[28] Paul Achtemeier reasons that the best explanation for Mark's deliberate choice of prayer for the final emphasis "appears to be that such an emphasis met a particular need in the community for which Mark was writing."[29] Actually, once one recognizes where Mark situates this account, in the middle section (Mark 8:22–10:52) where the disciples are shown to maintain a hardened pursuit of ambition, this revelation of their spiritual superficiality in Jesus' counsel to them to pray fits very well into the Markan purpose.

Summary: Study of the passage reveals that Markan redaction is present in vv. 14–16, the context of the crowd in v. 17, and the address

---

[26] Taylor, *St. Mark*, 400.

[27] Mark 4:10–12, 33–34; 7:17; 10:10–12. See Bultmann, *Synoptic Tradition*, 67, 330; Taylor, *St. Mark*, 400; Gnilka, *Markus*, 2:44; Ernest Best, *Following Jesus: Discipleship in Mark* (JSNTSup 14; Sheffield: JSOT Press, 1981), 68; Edwards, *Mark*, 281; Achtemeier, "Miracles," 477; Graham Twelftree, *Jesus the Exorcist: A Contribution to the Study of the Historical Jesus* (WUNT 2/54; Tübingen: Mohr Siebeck, 1993), 97.

[28] Twelftree, *Jesus the Exorcist*, 97.

[29] Achtemeier, "Miracles," 476.

to Jesus as "Teacher." Mark has also inserted the father's complaint that the disciples were unable to exorcise the demon (v. 18c) so that it can be addressed in the redactional conclusion, vv. 28–29. There the disciples will be told that they should pray. Mark's redaction is also seen in the approaching crowd (v. 25), which causes Jesus to hurry with the exorcism.

II. THE PRE-MARKAN ANECDOTE: JESUS AND THE FATHER OF A DEMONIZED BOY

With the understanding that the pre-Markan vocabulary cannot be proven with certainty, but rather that the narrative elements are represented by the text below, we now consider the story without the Markan insertions.

¹⁷καὶ ἀπεκρίθη αὐτῷ εἷς . . . ἤνεγκα τὸν υἱόν μου πρὸς σέ, ἔχοντα πνεῦμα ἄλαλον· ¹⁸καὶ ὅπου ἐὰν αὐτὸν καταλάβῃ ῥήσσει αὐτόν, καὶ ἀφρίζει καὶ τρίζει τοὺς ὀδόντας καὶ ξηραίνεται· . . . ¹⁹ὁ δὲ ἀποκριθεὶς . . . λέγει· ὦ γενεὰ ἄπιστος, ἕως πότε πρὸς ὑμᾶς ἔσομαι; ἕως πότε ἀνέξομαι ὑμῶν; [φέρε] αὐτὸν πρός με. ²⁰καὶ [ἤνεγκεν] αὐτὸν πρὸς αὐτόν. καὶ ἰδὼν αὐτὸν τὸ πνεῦμα εὐθὺς συνεσπάραξεν αὐτόν, καὶ πεσὼν ἐπὶ τῆς γῆς ἐκυλίετο ἀφρίζων. ²¹καὶ ἐπηρώτησεν τὸν πατέρα αὐτοῦ· πόσος χρόνος ἐστὶν ὡς τοῦτο γέγονεν αὐτῷ; ὁ δὲ εἶπεν· ἐκ παιδιόθεν· ²²καὶ πολλάκις καὶ εἰς πῦρ αὐτὸν ἔβαλεν καὶ εἰς ὕδατα ἵνα ἀπολέσῃ αὐτόν· ἀλλ' εἴ τι δύνῃ, βοήθησον ἡμῖν σπλαγχνισθεὶς ἐφ' ἡμᾶς. ²³ὁ δὲ Ἰησοῦς εἶπεν αὐτῷ· τὸ εἰ δύνῃ, πάντα δυνατὰ τῷ πιστεύοντι. ²⁴εὐθὺς κράξας ὁ πατὴρ τοῦ παιδίου ἔλεγεν· πιστεύω· βοήθει μου τῇ ἀπιστίᾳ. ²⁵ὁ [δὲ] Ἰησοῦς . . . ἐπετίμησεν τῷ πνεύματι τῷ ἀκαθάρτῳ λέγων αὐτῷ· τὸ ἄλαλον καὶ κωφὸν πνεῦμα, ἐγὼ ἐπιτάσσω σοι, ἔξελθε ἐξ αὐτοῦ καὶ μηκέτι εἰσέλθῃς εἰς αὐτόν. ²⁶καὶ κράξας καὶ πολλὰ σπαράξας ἐξῆλθεν· καὶ ἐγένετο ὡσεὶ νεκρός, ὥστε τοὺς πολλοὺς λέγειν ὅτι ἀπέθανεν. ²⁷ὁ δὲ Ἰησοῦς κρατήσας τῆς χειρὸς αὐτοῦ ἤγειρεν αὐτόν, καὶ ἀνέστη.

¹⁷Someone [said to] him, ". . . I brought you my son; he has a spirit that makes him unable to speak; ¹⁸and whenever it seizes him, it dashes him down; and he foams and grinds his teeth and becomes rigid. . . ." ¹⁹He answered . . . , "You faithless generation, how much longer must I be among you? How much longer must I put up with you? Bring him to me." ²⁰And [he] brought the boy to him. When

the spirit saw him, immediately it convulsed the boy, and he fell to the ground and rolled about, foaming at the mouth. ²¹Jesus asked the father, "How long has this been happening to him?" And he said, "From childhood. ²²It has often cast him into the fire and into the water, to destroy him; but if you are able to do anything, have pity on us and help us." ²³Jesus said to him, "If you are able! — All things can be done for the one who believes." ²⁴Immediately the father of the child shouted, "I believe; help my unbelief!" ²⁵Then Jesus . . . rebuked the unclean spirit, saying to it, "You spirit that keeps this boy from speaking and hearing, I command you, come out of him, and never enter him again!" ²⁶After crying out and convulsing him terribly, it came out, and the boy was like a corpse so that many said that he had died. ²⁷But Jesus took him by the hand and lifted him up, and he was able to stand.

The presence of so much Markan editing in the story helps to explain why Bultmann proposed that this account represented two forms joined together, one a story about the lack of power in a magician's disciples (vv. 14–20), and the other "more of an apophthegm" about "the paradox of unbelieving faith" (vv. 20–27).[30] However, once vv. 14–16 are recognized as Markan redaction, together with the father's complaint about the disciples' failure to exorcize the demon (v. 18c) and Jesus' counsel to the disciples to pray in vv. 28–29 (which Bultmann himself agrees are Markan),[31] the first story proposed by him dissolves away as redactional. It is significant that Bultmann identified the second remaining form as an "apophthegm," because he recognized the importance of the dialogue between the father of the boy and Jesus.

The basic elements of an exorcism story can still be seen in vv. 17–18 (the explanation of the problem), v. 25 (Jesus' command that the demon depart), and in the partial conclusion, v. 26a: "after convulsing him terribly, it came out."[32] And exorcism usually concludes with an acclamation of some kind. But in this story, the one miracle connects to another; the departure of the demon leaves the boy looking like a corpse (v. 26c). Since the healing of the boy is necessitated by the

---

[30] Bultmann, *Synoptic Tradition*, 211.
[31] Ibid., 67, 330.
[32] Ibid., 211.

departure of the demon, that healing miracle is the acclamation of the exorcism's success, as it is also Jesus' further generous answer to the father's frustrated shout that Jesus should help his lack of faith and not see it as an impediment to helping the boy. Thus, the story stands apart from all others as one where a double miracle is granted to one person.

III. THE FATHER OF A DEMONIZED BOY PETITIONS JESUS

¹⁷καὶ ἀπεκρίθη αὐτῷ εἷς . . . ἤνεγκα τὸν υἱόν μου πρὸς σέ, ἔχοντα πνεῦμα ἄλαλον· ¹⁸καὶ ὅπου ἐὰν αὐτὸν καταλάβῃ ῥήσσει αὐτόν, καὶ ἀφρίζει καὶ τρίζει τοὺς ὀδόντας καὶ ξηραίνεται· . . .

¹⁷Someone [said to] him, ". . . I brought you my son; he has a spirit that makes him unable to speak; ¹⁸and whenever it seizes him, it dashes him down; and he foams and grinds his teeth and becomes rigid. . . ."

The Characterization of the Petitioning Father

The character of the father in his approach and speech to Jesus can be ascertained for the listener by noting the redaction of it by Matthew and Luke. Matthew writes, "A man came to him, knelt before him, and said, 'Lord, have mercy on my son. . . .'" (Matt 17:14b–15a). He wants the man to express his deference to Jesus by kneeling and by addressing Jesus as "Lord" or "Sir." Moreover, the plain announcement of the man that he has brought his son is transformed into a plea: "Have mercy on my son." Luke's version works with the Markan setting of a man in the crowd but injects more emotion, having the man "shout" as though afraid that Jesus might not hear him, and he too supplies an opening plea: "I beg you to look at my son" (Luke 9:38). The two evangelists' changes attest to the inadequacies that they perceived in the way the man presented himself and told Jesus about his son. His manner is too brusque.

IV. JESUS RESPONDS TO THE FATHER
OF THE DEMONIZED BOY

¹⁹ὁ δὲ ἀποκριθεὶς . . . λέγει· ὦ γενεὰ ἄπιστος, ἕως πότε πρὸς ὑμᾶς ἔσομαι; ἕως πότε ἀνέξομαι ὑμῶν; [φέρε] αὐτὸν πρός με.

He answered . . . , "You faithless generation, how much longer must I be among you? How much longer must I put up with you? Bring him to me."

The Characterization of Jesus

Jesus' response brings to mind the cry of the prophets, as Christopher Marshall has illustrated in eight passages of the Hebrew Scriptures.[33] Note that in the list below, "people" is translating γενεά ("generation"):

1. Num 14:27: (Moses): "How long shall this wicked congregation complain against me?"

2. Deut 32:5: (Moses): "A perverse and crooked generation!"

3. Deut 32:20 (the Lord): "They are a perverse generation!"

4. 1 Kgs 18:21 (Elijah): "How long will you go limping with two different opinions?"

5. Isa 6:11 (Isaiah): "Then I said, 'How long, O LORD?'"

6. Isa 65:2 (the Lord): "A rebellious people!"

7. Jer 5:21 (the Lord): "O foolish and senseless people, who have eyes, but do not see, who have ears, but do not hear."

8. Ezek 12:2–3 (the Lord): "You are living in the midst of a rebellious house, who have eyes to see but do not see, who have ears to hear but do not hear; for they are a rebellious house."

Nevertheless, Jesus, in his protest, does not use the overtly condemning adjectives found in those texts: "wicked," "perverse and crooked," "rebellious," "foolish and senseless." The issue here is their being ἄπιστος ("faithless").

As for Jesus' lament, "How much longer must I be among you? How much longer must I put up with you?" Martin Dibelius proposes the

---

[33] Christopher Marshall, *Faith as a Theme*, 117 n 1.

innocuous interpretation that Jesus is longing for his heavenly home.[34] The cry, attached to the protest, however, is meant to express his frustration at his apparently futile efforts to move the hearts of these people to faith, a feeling in keeping with the LXX examples of rebuke above, without a confusion of reasons. Once the Markan insertion of the disciples removes them from among those being rebuked, and the pre-Markan story is then considered without them, Jesus is responding to the father alone. This response is not because the disciples could not cast out the demon, then, but rather stands as a rebuke to what the father has just told Jesus about his son. This situation of a demon being able to possess this man's son is, according to Jesus' protest, the result of a life without faith. Jesus' cry of protest is made to echo the prophets.[35] Here he takes on that role, and his great sweeping lament makes it clear that he holds the father responsible for this terrible situation. Dennis Nineham, commenting on the account in relation to its purpose in Mark's community, remarks, "No doubt in the Church of St. Mark's day, it was commonly held that children of a believing household were in some sense included in the faith of their parents and could hope to enjoy the benefits of it."[36] He certainly is right about the attitude conveyed by Jesus' protest and frustrated cry, although this predates Mark. In an essay, John M. G. Barclay clarifies the explicit obligations that Jewish parents were to impart all aspects of Jewish religious practice to their children.[37] Barclay notes, "Josephus claims that the Jewish tradition is distinguished by the care it devotes to the instruction of children (*paidotrophia;* cf Paul, Rom 2:20), and he makes that claim in a context where he emphasizes the special character of the Jewish life-style and the commitment of Jews to preserve their inherited piety as 'the most important duty in life' (*Contra Apionem* 1.60–61)."[38] The example of a parent's expected vigilance over

---

[34] Martin Dibelius, *From Tradition to Gospel* (trans. Bertram Lee Woolf; 1934; repr., Cambridge: J. Clarke, 1971), 298.

[35] Gundry, *Mark*, 497.

[36] Dennis E. Nineham, *The Gospel of St. Mark* (PGC; London: A & C Black, 1963), 244.

[37] See John M. G. Barclay, "The Family as the Bearer of Religion in Judaism and Early Christianity," in *Constructing Early Christian Families: Family as Social Reality and Metaphor* (ed. Halvor Moxnes; London: Routledge, 1997), 66–80.

[38] Ibid., 69. I am indebted to Barclay for the Josephus quotation at the start of this chapter.

a child is demonstrated in *Jub.* 10:1–6.[39] When Noah learns that his grandchildren are in danger from demons, he prays,

> Do not let them [the demons] cause corruption among the sons of your servant, O my God, because they are cruel and were created to destroy. And let them not rule over the spirits of the living because you alone know their judgment, and do not let them have power over the children of the righteous henceforth and forever. (*Jub.* 10:5–6)[40]

The situation of a child being possessed raises the question of how this could happen if the parent was vigilant and faithful.

Jesus' blunt order, "Bring him to me!" continues to communicate his agitation. In the case of the Syrophoenician mother asking for an exorcism for her daughter (Mark 7:24–30), Jesus exhibits this same blunt disapproval. In her case, however, her pagan background has been made plain, and she has been, not unfaithful, but rather without faith to start, so that her child would have been open to demons constantly. There is no guarantee that even after an exorcism the daughter would be forever free of demonic possession, a futile situation. This case presumes a Jewish father because he is not singled out as a Gentile, and because the narrator's phrasing of Jesus' lament seems to presume familiarity with the prophets—"You faithless generation!"—which makes sense only if the expectation presumes Jewish faith. So the characterization of Jesus at this point in the story is that of the denouncing prophet.

V. THE SERIOUS STATE OF THE DEMONIZED BOY IS UNDERLINED

²⁰καὶ [ἤνεγκεν] αὐτὸν πρὸς αὐτόν. καὶ ἰδὼν αὐτὸν τὸ πνεῦμα εὐθὺς συνεσπάραξεν αὐτόν, καὶ πεσὼν ἐπὶ τῆς γῆς ἐκυλίετο ἀφρίζων. ²¹καὶ ἐπηρώτησεν τὸν πατέρα αὐτοῦ· πόσος χρόνος ἐστὶν ὡς τοῦτο γέγονεν αὐτῷ; ὁ δὲ εἶπεν· ἐκ παιδιόθεν· ²²καὶ πολλάκις καὶ εἰς πῦρ αὐτὸν ἔβαλεν καὶ εἰς ὕδατα ἵνα ἀπολέσῃ αὐτόν.

---

[39] See chapter 5, on Jesus and the Syrophoenician mother.

[40] O. S. Wintermute, "Jubilees," in vol. 2 of *The Old Testament Pseudepigrapha* (ed. James H. Charlesworth; New York: Doubleday, 1985), 76.

²⁰And [he] brought the boy to him. When the spirit saw him, immediately it convulsed the boy, and he fell to the ground and rolled about, foaming at the mouth. ²¹Jesus asked the father, "How long has this been happening to him?" And he said, "From childhood. ²²It has often cast him into the fire and into the water, to destroy him."

The Characterization of the Demon

The demon's reaction to Jesus upholds the father's description of its behavior, without repeating the man's vocabulary, so that it acts as an attestation.

1. The Convulsion That Results in the Boy Thrown Down

καὶ ὅπου ἐὰν αὐτὸν καταλάβῃ ῥήσσει αὐτόν (v. 18a)

"Whenever it seizes him, it dashes him down."

εὐθὺς συνεσπάραξεν αὐτόν, καὶ πεσὼν ἐπὶ τῆς γῆς (v. 20b)

When the spirit saw him, immediately it convulsed the boy, and he fell to the ground.

2. The Boy's Foaming at the Mouth and Rigid Body

καὶ ἀφρίζει καὶ τρίζει τοὺς ὀδόντας καὶ ξηραίνεται (v. 18b)

"And he foams and grinds his teeth and becomes rigid."

ἐκυλίετο ἀφρίζων (v. 20c)

He rolled about, foaming at the mouth.

In other exorcism stories from Markan tradition, demons cry out to Jesus from the start (Mark 1:24; 3:11; 5:7), but in this case the demon has been ἄλαλος ("mute"), so that the demon manifests its presence by its murderous actions. Thus, the cruelty of the demon is shown in its freedom to brutalize the boy, who cannot even cry out for help.

Jesus asks the father how long the boy has suffered this possession (v. 21). William Lane suggests, "It is evident that the Lord was deeply moved. His question concerning the length of time the boy had been subject to such attacks shows his deep humanity and concern, for the source of the question is compassion."[41] The problem here is that Jesus has just been shown to be outraged by the man's "faithlessness," which has resulted in this possession of the boy. The narrator would need more to show that Jesus' question indicated that he was suddenly moved with compassion. Wilfrid Harrington's suggestion that Jesus' question emphasizes the gravity of the possession fits better with the preceding frustrated lament of Jesus.[42] Certainly, when the listener learns from the father that the demon has had possession of his son "since childhood" (ἐκ παιδιόθεν), it signals that the exorcism will be very difficult because the demon has owned the boy for most of his life, and to surrender him means that the demon will be without a subject to inhabit and will no longer be able to torture the boy. Thus, these verses signal that the exorcism will be dangerous because the viciousness of this demon will be manifest when it is ordered to leave. In this way, the narrator prepares the listener for the results of the successful exorcism, when the demon, upon leaving, takes its last chance to murder the boy and almost succeeds.

VI. THE FATHER PETITIONS JESUS

[22b]ἀλλ' εἴ τι δύνῃ, βοήθησον ἡμῖν σπλαγχνισθεὶς ἐφ' ἡμᾶς.

[22b]"But if you are able to do anything, have pity on us and help us."

The Further Characterization of the Father

In the conclusion to his plea, the father begins by saying, "But if you are able to do anything," and this shows the listener that Jesus was right to target lack of faith in this man. But the conclusion of his appeal, "have pity on us and help us," makes him the only petitioner who includes himself with the needy one for whom he pleads.[43] Then the

---

[41] William L. Lane, *The Gospel according to Mark: The English Text with Introduction, Exposition, and Notes* (NICNT: Grand Rapids: Eerdmans, 1974), 332.

[42] Wilfrid Harrington, *Mark* (NTM 4; Wilmington, Del.: Michael Glazier, 1979), 142.

[43] Contrast, for example, the Syrophoenician mother (Mark 7:24–30).

father calls on Jesus' virtue: "have pity on *us*." Here, we should note that while the verb βοηθέω ("to help") is common in written petitions and prayers,[44] the verb σπλαγχίνζομαι ("to have pity, compassion, sympathy") is not, and it suggests familiarity of the narrator with LXX.[45] Here the position of the participle σπλαγχνισθείς is unusual because ordinarily the adverbial participle would precede the main verb, not follow it. Placed here, it claims special attention.

VII. JESUS RESPONDS TO THE FATHER'S PETITION

[23]ὁ δὲ Ἰησοῦς εἶπεν αὐτῷ· τὸ εἰ δύνῃ, πάντα δυνατὰ τῷ πιστεύοντι.

[23]Jesus said to him, "If you are able! — All things can be done for the one who believes."

The Further Characterization of Jesus

In this second response, Jesus pounces on the man's doubt, using "if you can" and throwing it back to him (τό before εἰ δύνῃ allows a translation such as "What's this 'If you are able'?"). Following objection, Jesus teaches him the importance of complete faith: "All things can be done for the one who believes." Scholarly interpretation here seems to be unaware of the tone of objection that colors it. Lane says that Jesus is urging the man to have faith in God: "Faith must always free itself from the disastrous presumptions of doubt, in the certainty that with God nothing is impossible."[46] But is it "urging"? Or is it a pronouncement of correction to this man whose lack of faith is on display, the very lack of faith that Jesus holds responsible for the boy being an available target for the demon? Gundry wants to clarify that Jesus is asking not just for "faith," but faith in him: "To see in these verses a lesson in faith is to stop midstream. This lesson teaches Jesus' worthiness to be the object of faith."[47] Günther Bornkamm agrees and, referring to Mark 6:6, comments, "Where Jesus does not find this faith,

---

[44] MM 113.
[45] MM 584. See also BAGD 762–63.
[46] Lane, *Mark*, 333.
[47] Gundry, *Mark*, 498.

he cannot work a miracle."[48] Then James Edwards links both: "True faith is unconditional openness to God, a decision in the face of all to the contrary, that Jesus *is* able."[49] In my view, aside from the modern concept "unconditional openness" that Edwards has projected onto the first-century writer, Jesus is saying that with perfect faith anything is possible. But in the context, following the protest of Jesus, this ideal of faith is telling the man that his doubt is an impediment, and his very situation is the result of his doubt.

Ernst Lohmeyer seems to be the most on target, catching the tone of disapproval that colors this response by Jesus when he holds that Jesus' pronouncement stipulates his expectation of the father.[50] This interpretation connects with the whole topic of lack of faith, which was introduced by Jesus' cry of lament and protest in v. 19. With the father now openly showing that he is a man who has doubt about Jesus' ability to expel the demon, Jesus is demanding that he summon that faith.

VIII. THE FATHER REPLIES

²⁴εὐθὺς κράξας ὁ πατὴρ τοῦ παιδίου ἔλεγεν· πιστεύω· βοήθει μου τῇ ἀπιστίᾳ.

²⁴Immediately the father of the child cried out, "I believe; help my unbelief!"

The Final Characterization of the Father

For Hans Dieter Betz[51] and Dennis Nineham,[52] the father's response in v. 24, "memorable and haunting,"[53] is the climax of the story. It breaks the impasse between the father's exposed doubt and Jesus' insistence

---

[48] Günther Bornkamm, *Jesus of Nazareth* (trans. Irene and Fraser McLuskey; New York: Harper, 1960), 131.

[49] Edwards, *Mark*, 280.

[50] Ernst Lohmeyer, *Das Evangelium des Markus* (KEK 1/2; Göttingen: Vandenhoeck & Ruprecht, 1967), 188.

[51] Hans Dieter Betz, "The Early Christian Miracle Story: Some Observations on the Form Critical Problem," *Semeia* 11 (1978): 79.

[52] Nineham, *St. Mark*, 244.

[53] Ibid.

on full faith. The father's answer results in Jesus exorcizing the demon from the boy. To account for this, scholars presume that the father must have complied with Jesus' demands for full faith. Vincent Taylor states, "The man's cry is his giving birth to faith."[54] Betz sees a conversion in "his paradoxical confession of faith" and explains, "V. 24 'flips over' into a 'conversion story,' another literary genre. The dialogue between the father and Jesus in verses 22–23 not only leads to the conversion of the father climaxing in his paradoxical confession of faith (v. 24). . . . Despite the length of the exorcism scene, the main focus is not upon the boy's healing but upon the father and his conversion."[55]

Christopher Marshall seems to waver, stating, "The belief he [the father] confesses is an unreserved trust in that power,"[56] but then observing, "Elsewhere, faith and unbelief appear to be mutually exclusive categories (e.g., 4:40; 6:6; 15:32) whereas here they seem to be contemporaneous experiences. How is this to be understood?"[57] Marshall finds his answer in "process": "The father pleads for deliverance from his ἀπιστία [lack of faith], and it is this that proves and constitutes his faith."[58] Bornkamm also appeals to process, arguing that the man is "becoming" true:

> I believe!—here the petitioner has indeed exceeded his own ability, and confesses a faith greater than he really has. Help my unbelief!—here he who falls short of faith has thrown himself on the power and help of Jesus. In this paradox of faith and unfaith, . . . faith *becomes* true and capable of receiving the miracle of God.[59]

The problem with these appeals to "process" is that such a concept was unavailable in the Greco-Roman world, unavailable to the narrator. It is Marshall's observation that ἀπιστία and πίστις are "mutually exclusive categories,"[60] which clarifies the statement of the father as presented by the narrator. The very word ἀπιστία intends the opposite of belief,

---

[54] Taylor, *St. Mark*, 399.

[55] Betz, "Early Christian Miracle Story," 79.

[56] Marshall, *Faith as a Theme*, 120.

[57] Ibid., 120–21.

[58] Ibid., 121.

[59] Bornkamm, *Jesus of Nazareth*, 131 (my italics). See also, relying on Bornkamm, Reginald H. Fuller, *Interpreting the Miracles* (Philadelphia: Westminster, 1963), 62.

[60] Marshall, *Faith as a Theme*, 120–21.

so that when the listener hears the father use ἀπιστία in v. 24, it is plain that the man is asking for relief from the doubt that he does have. By identifying that doubt, the father would not communicate to a first-century listener that the plea itself was faith. R. T. France understands the father to be identifying his ambivalence, but that his statement is still a sign of his faith, *"His belief, however uncertain, was all that was needed,* and from this point he plays no further part in the narrative, so that all the attention falls where it should, on the power of Jesus."[61] But why would the man's acknowledgment of his doubt be "all that was needed" if Jesus had protested that it was the reason for the possession of the boy? "All things can be done for the one who believes" is a statement that is sweeping and does not allow for doubt. This is Jesus' demand, not the accommodation of doubt. How does the father's reply result in Jesus' exorcism of his son?

These philosophical analyses leave out the prominent displeasure of Jesus and his two replies to this man, both of which hold up his doubt as culpable, first for the boy's vulnerability to the demon and the demon's years of possession, and now for the inadequacy of the faith that Jesus could "do anything" here, not even naming exorcism. The narrator has already presented Jesus somewhat in the prophetic righteousness of one of Israel's prophets. This is the tone that would be heard by any listener. The man's reply must be seen as a reply to Jesus' statement, which sounds very much like an ultimatum. Now, in v. 24, the narrator reports that the father shouted at Jesus. The NRSV translation hides the roughness of the verb κράζω by the use of "crying out" to describe the father's response rather than by using the most frequent rendering of the verb as "shouting."[62] The use of "crying out" in English, in my view, seems to allow more a sense of grief than frustration. Perhaps the translators were influenced to use "crying out" due to the influence of Codices Ephraemi and Alexandrinus, as well as of the Byzantine lectionaries that soften the verb κράξας by the addition of the adverbial phrase μετὰ δακρύων (with tears). The Greek, however, permits the listener to imagine frustration

---

[61] R. T. France, *The Gospel of Mark: A Commentary on the Greek Text* (NIGTC; Grand Rapids: Eerdmans; Carlisle: Paternoster, 2002), 368 (my italics).

[62] Of the eight uses of κράζω outside this pericope, "shout" is used in six. "Howl" appears in Mark 5:5 for the demon's shouts, which will be described as such in Mark 5:7. "Cry out" is used once outside the Mark 9:14–26 pericope, in Mark 10:52 to describe the repeated "shouting" of Bartimaeus described in Mark 10:47.

and fear that his son will not receive help in the face of what appears to be Jesus' expectation of a perfect faith he does not have to give him.

First, he corrects Jesus' judgment that he is ἄπιστος ("faithless") by exclaiming, "I do believe!" With this, it must be agreed that the father has brought his son to Jesus, and this is faith. But Jesus' expectation of perfect faith is one that the father cannot meet, for he does not have it. Frustrated that his weakness will prove to be the impediment to his son's receiving some kind of help from Jesus, he asks Jesus to accept this sign of his imperfect faith and to regard his doubt in another way: not as an impediment to helping his son in whatever way he can, but rather as a weakness of his own that requires Jesus' help.

Earlier, in v. 22, in pleading for his son, the father had asked, "Help us." Now he becomes a petitioner for himself as he asks Jesus, "Help my unbelief."

IX. JESUS RESPONDS WITH TWO MIRACLES

²⁵ὁ [δὲ] Ἰησοῦς . . . ἐπετίμησεν τῷ πνεύματι τῷ ἀκαθάρτῳ λέγων αὐτῷ· τὸ ἄλαλον καὶ κωφὸν πνεῦμα, ἐγὼ ἐπιτάσσω σοι, ἔξελθε ἐξ αὐτοῦ καὶ μηκέτι εἰσέλθῃς εἰς αὐτόν. ²⁶καὶ κράξας καὶ πολλὰ σπαράξας ἐξῆλθεν· καὶ ἐγένετο ὡσεὶ νεκρός . . . ²⁷ὁ δὲ Ἰησοῦς κρατήσας τῆς χειρὸς αὐτοῦ ἤγειρεν αὐτόν, καὶ ἀνέστη.

²⁵Then Jesus . . . rebuked the unclean spirit, saying to it, "You spirit that keeps this boy from speaking and hearing, I command you, come out of him, and never enter him again!" ²⁶After crying out and convulsing him terribly, it came out, and the boy was like a corpse. . . . ²⁷But Jesus took him by the hand and lifted him up, and he was able to stand.

The Final Characterization of Jesus

When R. T. France asserts that the father plays no further part after his response to Jesus "so that all the attention falls where it should, on the power of Jesus,"⁶³ he misses the way in which the father's correction is accepted by Jesus so that the miracles that follow indicate that change of perspective in Jesus. First, without saying another word, Jesus

---

⁶³ France, *Mark*, 368.

pronounces the command of exorcism with detail, length, and formality not found in the other two exorcism stories of the Markan Gospel:

1. Exorcism of the man in the synagogue (Mark 1:25): "Be silent, and come out of him!"

2. Exorcism of the Gerasene demoniac (Mark 5:8) "For he had said to him, 'Come out of the man, you unclean spirit!'"

3. Exorcism of the father's demonized boy (Mark 9:25): "You spirit that keeps this boy from speaking and hearing, I command you, come out of him, and never enter him again!"

In Jesus' command in Mark 9:25, there is first the address to the spirit, then the actual command, and, finally, as if to extend the command, the order "never enter him again."

Betz claims that "Despite the length of the exorcism scene, the main focus is not upon the boy's healing but rather upon the father and his conversion."[64] He is right that the focus is on the encounter between the father and Jesus, but it is Jesus who is shown to have neglected the father's efforts in even bringing his son, and Jesus was corrected from his platitude in recognizing that rather than trying to force complete faith, he needed to provide support for what faith was there. So, it is Jesus who is seen to have changed, not the father.

The departure of the demon is the most vicious of the three exorcisms in this Gospel. The listener was prepared for this when the father told Jesus that the demon had possessed the boy since he was a child (v. 21). With Jesus' command, the demon takes this last opportunity to torture the boy, throwing him into a convulsion while shouting in fury.

> [26]καὶ κράξας καὶ πολλὰ σπαράξας ἐξῆλθεν· καὶ ἐγένετο ὡσεὶ νεκρός . . . [27]ὁ δὲ Ἰησους κρατήσας τῆς χειρὸς αὐτοῦ ἤγειρεν αὐτόν, καὶ ἀνέστη.

> [26]After crying out and convulsing him terribly, it came out, and the boy was like a corpse.... [27]But Jesus took him by the hand and lifted him up, and he was able to stand.

As noted earlier, in place of an acclamation, the success of Jesus' exorcism is attested by the corpse-like state of the boy, now freed from the demon that has injured him in its departure. This situation is a bridge

---

[64] Betz, "The Early Christian Miracle Story," 80.

to connect a second miracle. "But Jesus took him by the hand and lifted him up, and he was able to stand" (ὁ δὲ Ἰησους κρατήσας τῆς χειρὸς αὐτοῦ ἤγειρεν αὐτόν, καὶ ἀνέστη). More literally it reads, "But Jesus, grasping his hand, lifted him [up], and he rose." Jesus' taking the hand of someone and lifting that person up occurs in both the healing of Peter's mother-in-law, καὶ προσελθὼν ἤγειρεν αὐτὴν κρατήσας τῆς χειρός ("And approaching, he lifted her up, grasping [her] hand" [Mark 1:31]), and the raising of Jairus's daughter, καὶ κρατήσας τῆς χειρὸς τοῦ παιδίου λέγει αὐτῇ· ταλιθα κουμ, ὅ ἐστιν μεθερμηνευόμενον· τὸ κοράσιον, σοὶ λέγω, ἔγειρε. καὶ εὐθὺς ἀνέστη τὸ κοράσιον καὶ περιεπάτει ("And grasping the child's hand, he said to her, 'Talitha cum,' which means, 'Little girl, I say to you, get up!' And immediately, the little girl rose and began to walk" [Mark 5:41–42a])

In comparison to Mark 9:27, ὁ δὲ Ἰησους κρατήσας τῆς χειρὸς αὐτοῦ ἤγειρεν αὐτόν, καὶ ἀνέστη ("But Jesus, grasping his hand, lifted him [up], and he rose"), with its three elements of "grasping the hand," "lifting/ getting up," and "rising," it is the raising of Jairus's daughter that has all three. When the narrator writes that the boy appeared as if "dead," it seems that he wanted to convey that Jesus' miracle had healed the boy just in time.

It was noted above that this is the only miracle story in which the victim receives two miracles. The reason for this is found in the father's final upset and frustrated answer to Jesus: "Help my unbelief." In response to that, Jesus not only performs the most solemn pronouncement of exorcism and immediately dislodges this insidious demon, but also grants the boy an immediate healing. In this way, Jesus not only attends to the complete restoration of the boy to his father, which answers the father's petition for his son, but with these two miracles, Jesus also answers the father's petition for himself. In witnessing these two great miracles of Jesus, the father has been helped to a full faith.

CONCLUSION

Both Bultmann and Betz want to note the importance of an apophthegm in this story: the encounter of Jesus with the father of this boy takes center stage, not the miracle. Significantly, in this story the pronouncement that provides the climax is the father's shouted reply to Jesus. It is the father who brings to Jesus another way to see his partial doubt. Jesus' initial presentation as somewhat of the righteous prophet undergoes a change with the father's response. His shouting certainly is offensive, but the narrator shows by Jesus' response that this was bypassed as Jesus heard the man's truth. This is the modeling of Jesus' *philanthrōpia* and his *epieikia*, his understanding. The formal and full pronouncement of exorcism demonstrates the "meekness" of Jesus, for not only does he command the exorcism, but also, emphasizing his change of heart, he immediately heals the boy, showing the compassion for which the father had hoped. In this way, Jesus fulfills not only the father's plea for his son, but also his petition for help to dispel his doubt.

If the purpose of this miracle story were only to show that Jesus could dislodge a demon, then the father would simply petition conventionally, and Jesus would perform the miracle. That is very much the way Matthew redacts the account (Matt 17:14–21). He works with the Markan context of the father complaining that the disciples could not cast the demon out of his son. Then Jesus laments over the faithlessness of this generation (v. 17) and later explains the disciples' failure to them as their lack of faith (v. 20). No other word is heard from the father. Jesus casts out the demon, and the boy is cured instantly. Thus, Matthew focuses on a lesson on faith from Jesus to his disciples and jettisons the encounter with the conflictual climax between Jesus and the father. Matthew's emphasis is more represented by Jesus' expectation of complete faith than by Jesus' acceptance of the father's ambivalence, his doubt being seen as a situation also in need of help. Luke follows Mark a little more closely (Luke 9:37–43a), but he too removes the abrasive encounter between Jesus and the father and has the demon exorcized and the boy completely "healed." These redactions indicate the change in the purpose of the miracle stories for these two communities. In this case, the elevated Christologies would have made the encounter with the father's shouting of his answer at Jesus entirely inappropriate.

Mark's preservation of the earlier story shows us the manner in which stories of Jesus' miracles allowed for these encounters where Jesus would model the virtues expected of the would-be follower. Dio Cassius's praise of Hadrian's readiness to accept a correction from a commoner[65] fits well here: "For he could bear such things and was not

---

[65] See chapter 5, on Jesus and the Syrophoenician mother.

displeased if he received aid either in an unexpected way or from ordinary men" (*Hist.* 69.6.2).[66]

Moreover, the response of Jesus to the father would have demonstrated to the listener that the disciple must recognize in the very presence of the petitioner a sign of faith. Perfect faith is not to be demanded, and doubts are not an impediment but only another weakness to be strengthened by the effective ministry of the disciple(s).

---

[66] Dio Cassius, *Roman History* (trans. Earnest Cary; 9 vols.; LCL; Cambridge, Mass.: Harvard University Press, 1914–1927), 8:434–435.

Part IV

*Petitioners Who Are
Jesus' Disciples*

7

Jesus and His Storm-Tossed Disciples (Mark 4:35–41)[1]

"You rule the raging of the sea; when its waves rise, you still them." (Ps 89:9)

"The voice of the LORD is over the waters; the God of glory thunders, the LORD, over mighty waters." (Ps 29:3)

""Blustering and violent winds signify men who are annoying and heedless. Hurricanes and fierce winds bring danger and great disturbances in their wake." (Artemidorus Daldianus, *Onir.* 2.36)[2]

In the Markan Gospel, the miracle story usually called "the stilling of the storm" links Jesus' preaching of the parables (Mark 4:1–34) to the set of anecdotes of his astonishing power over natural and supernatural forces: the stilling of the storm (Mark 4:35–42); the exorcism for the Gerasene demoniac (Mark 5:1–20); the healing of the woman with the hemorrhage (Mark 5:25–34); the raising of Jairus's daughter (Mark 5:22–24, 35–43). But each also offers it own example of Jesus' *philanthrōpia* and *epieikia*.

---

[1] Much of the research in this chapter draws on my doctoral dissertation, "The Markan Sea Miracles: Their History, Formation, and Function in the Literary Context of Greco-Roman Antiquity" (PhD diss., University of St. Michael's College, 1991). In that work I focused on the context of the power that Jesus demonstrates over the sea, setting it against a backdrop of well-known attributions to gods and heroes known to the populace of the Greco-Roman world. Here my interest is in the context of the miracle, the manner in which Jesus encounters his own disciples. In other words, in this chapter and the next I seek to discover how the encounter functions to show Jesus' great personal virtue, what Plutarch would call "his soul," and how that carries its own message to the listener.

[2] Translation by Dr. Gregory W. Dobrov, Loyola University, Chicago, Illinois.

Paul Achtemeier's interpretation of the "sea miracles" (Mark 4:35–6:44; 6:45–8:26) belongs to his theory of the service that the two pre-Markan catenae supplied to that earlier community.[3] For him, both the sea miracles and the feeding miracles function to show that "he is the Lord of creation as shown in his mastery of the sea, and the wondrous provider of food."[4] With respect to the perspective of Jesus, the catenae reveal, he suggests, "There is reason to believe then, that the communities from which the catenae came saw in Jesus a kind of θεῖος ἀνήρ sharing the power of God which he made visible in his acts, and perhaps serving as a kind of 'model' for the activity of those who followed him and, in some measure, shared in the epiphany that characterized him."[5]

Achtemeier surely is right that these miracle stories provide a model to the followers, but not necessarily as a promise for similar powers available to them. Rather, as we have seen in the previous chapters, Jesus demonstrates the "soul" that should be their ideal, the virtues that he shows toward all manner of petitioners and those who need him.

In this last section, the two sea miracles present a special function because those in need are Jesus' own disciples. Here the virtue displayed by Jesus does not serve as a model of how to treat other petitioners so much as it does to act as a constant reassurance to the community of the commitment of Jesus despite his followers' fragile faith and fearfulness.

I. MARK 4:35–41: SIGNS OF MARKAN REDACTION

[35]καὶ λέγει αὐτοῖς ἐν ἐκείνῃ τῇ ἡμέρᾳ ὀψίας γενομένης· διέλθωμεν εἰς τὸ πέραν. [36]καὶ ἀφέντες τὸν ὄχλον παραλαμβάνουσιν αὐτὸν ὡς ἦν ἐν τῷ πλοίῳ, καὶ ἄλλα πλοῖα ἦν μετ' αὐτοῦ. [37]καὶ γίνεται λαῖλαψ μεγάλη ἀνέμου καὶ τὰ κύματα ἐπέβαλλεν εἰς τὸ πλοῖον, ὥστε ἤδη γεμίζεσθαι τὸ πλοῖον. [38]καὶ αὐτὸς ἦν ἐν τῇ πρύμνῃ ἐπὶ τὸ προσκεφάλαιον καθεύδων. καὶ ἐγείρουσιν αὐτὸν καὶ λέγουσιν αὐτῷ· διδάσκαλε, οὐ μέλει σοι ὅτι ἀπολλύμεθα; [39]καὶ διεγερθεὶς ἐπετίμησεν τῷ ἀνέμῳ καὶ εἶπεν τῇ θαλάσσῃ· σιώπα, πεφίμωσο. καὶ ἐκόπασεν ὁ ἄνεμος καὶ ἐγένετο γαλήνη μεγάλη. [40]καὶ εἶπεν αὐτοῖς· τί δειλοί

---

[3] Paul J. Achtemeier, "Toward the Isolation of Pre-Markan Miracle Catenae," *JBL* 89 (1970): 266–74.

[4] Paul J. Achtemeier, "The Origin and Function of the Pre-Markan Miracle Catenae," *JBL* 91 (1972): 206.

[5] Ibid., 210.

ἐστε; οὔπω ἔχετε πίστιν; ⁴¹καὶ ἐφοβήθησαν φόβον μέγαν καὶ ἔλεγον πρὸς ἀλλήλους· τίς ἄρα οὗτός ἐστιν ὅτι καὶ ὁ ἄνεμος καὶ ἡ θάλασσα ὑπακούει αὐτῷ;

³⁵On that day, when evening had come, he said to them, "Let us go across to the other side." ³⁶And leaving the crowd behind, they took him with them in the boat, just as he was. Other boats were with him. ³⁷A great windstorm arose, and the waves beat into the boat, so that the boat was already being swamped. ³⁸But he was in the stern, asleep on the cushion; and they woke him up and said to him, "Teacher, do you not care that we are perishing?" ³⁹He woke up and rebuked the wind, and said to the sea, "Peace! Be still!" Then the wind ceased, and there was a dead calm. ⁴⁰He said to them, "Why are you afraid? Have you still no faith?" ⁴¹And they were filled with great awe and said to one another, "Who then is this, that even the wind and the sea obey him?"

³⁵καὶ λέγει αὐτοῖς ἐν ἐκείνῃ τῇ ἡμέρᾳ ὀψίας γενομένης· διέλθωμεν εἰς τὸ πέραν.

³⁵On that day, when evening had come, he said to them, "Let us go across to the other side."

Both καὶ λέγει αὐτοῖς ("and he said to them") and διέλθωμεν εἰς τὸ πέραν ("let us go across to the other side") are necessary to the account and may not be considered later insertions by Mark.⁶ Other features, however, show the Markan hand. The notification of time, ἐν ἐκείνῃ τῇ ἡμέρᾳ ὀψίας γενομένης ("on that day, when evening had come"), is an example of the duality that occurs throughout the Markan Gospel. A similar example occurs in Mark 1:32, where ὀψίας γενομένης is followed by ὅτε ἔδυ ὁ ἥλιος. Frans Neirynck uses this verse to make the observation that Mark's addition is usually the one that is more precise—that is, ὅτε ἔδυ ὁ ἥλιος.⁷ Applying that to Mark 4:35, the more precise

---

⁶Herman Hendrickx has argued that εἰς τὸ πέραν ("to the other side") may be Markan because it is picked up again in Mark 5:1 (*The Miracle Stories of the Synoptic Gospels* [SSG; San Francisco: Harper & Row, 1987], 174). But in this case it completes the invitation of Jesus (διέλθωμεν), which acts as the introduction to alert the listener that Jesus and the disciples will be in the boat together.

⁷Frans Neirynck, *Duality in Mark: Contributions to the Study of the Markan Redaction* (BETL 31; Leuven: Leuven University Press, 1988), 45. Erich

stipulation of ἐν ἐκείνῃ τῇ ἡμέρᾳ ("on that day") would be seen as the Markan addition. But another reason also shows that it belongs to the evangelist: "that day" refers to Mark's Gospel organization. It is Mark who has Jesus preaching the parables from the boat earlier in the day.[8] Finally, the usage of the phrase here differs from the meaning when it occurs in pre-Markan material, be it in the singular ἐν ἐκείνῃ τῇ ἡμέρᾳ or the plural ἐν ἐκείναις ταῖς ἡμέραις, where it refers to judgment day,[9] which plainly not the intention here.

The reason Bultmann assigned ὀψίας γενομένης to pre-Markan material was because Jesus falls asleep (v. 38)[10] However, this does not require nighttime, as shown by Luke's redaction, where the story occurs in the daytime, and Jesus is asleep as they sail (Luke 8:23). Rather, Eduard Schweizer supplies the better argument when he observes that if the situation of the story at night was a deliberate decision and insertion of Mark, he would also have wanted the story of the Gerasene demoniac (Mark 5:1–20) to happen at night.[11] It seems most probable that the pre-Markan story of the stilling of the storm was situated to occur at night, and only by the linkage of the Gerasene demoniac did the insertion of both into the Gospel create a chronological attachment so that Mark 5:1–20 would seem to have occurred at night. The pre-Markan story, then, situated the story as evening came, ὀψίας γενομένης, which was then followed by Jesus' suggestion to those in his company that they go to the other side, λέγει αὐτοῖς· διέλθωμεν εἰς τὸ πέραν.

[36]καὶ ἀφέντες τὸν ὄχλον παραλαμβάνουσιν αὐτὸν ὡς ἦν ἐν τῷ πλοίῳ, καὶ ἄλλα πλοῖα ἦν μετ᾽ αὐτοῦ.

Klostermann holds that both time designations belong to Mark, but the phenomenon of "duality" had not yet been recognized and explored in his day (*Das Markusevangelium* [3d ed.; HNT 3; Tübingen: Mohr Siebeck, 1936], 46).

[8] See Joachim Gnilka, *Das Evangelium nach Markus* (2 vols.; EKKNT 2; Zürich: Benziger; Neukirchen-Vlyun: Neukirchener Verlag, 1978–1979), 1:193; Karl Kertelge, *Die Wunder Jesu im Markusevangelium: Eine redaktionsgeschichtliche Untersuchung* (SANT 33; Munich: Kösel-Verlag, 1970), 91.

[9] Mark 2:20: ἐν ἐκείνῃ τῇ ἡμέρᾳ; Mark 13:24: ἐν ἐκείναις ταῖς ἡμέραις; Mark 13:32: περὶ δὲ τῆς ἡμέρας ἐκείνης. For the scholarly consensus, see E. J. Pryke, *Redactional Style in the Marcan Gospel* (SNTSMS 33; Cambridge: Cambridge University Press, 1978), 10–23.

[10] Rudolf Bultmann, *The History of the Synoptic Tradition* (trans. John Marsh; Peabody, Mass.: Hendrickson, 1963), 215.

[11] Eduard Schweizer, *The Good News according to Mark* (trans. Donald H. Madvig; Richmond: John Knox Press, 1970), 109.

³⁶And leaving the crowd behind, they took him with them in the boat, just as he was. Other boats were with him.

Καὶ ἀφέντες τὸν ὄχλον ("and leaving the crowd behind") presumes the crowd established by Mark in the scene that he created for Jesus' teaching the parables from the boat (Mark 4:1–32).[12] But παραλαμβάνουσιν[13] αὐτὸν ὡς ἦν ἐν τῷ πλοίῳ cannot be assigned to Mark, for it is the necessary response to Jesus' invitation to the disciples in v. 35. The most persuasive argument is that it provides the explicit mention of the boat. The phrase ὡς ἦν ("as he was") however, shows a Markan recognition that Jesus has already been in the boat teaching from it.[14] Hendrickx concludes that when Mark added ὡς ἦν, he had to change what had been the pre-Markan formulation, εἰς τὸ πλοῖον, to ἐν τῷ πλοίῳ because once Mark had Jesus in the boat, he could not be said to enter into it again.[15] The sheer awkwardness of the clause καὶ ἄλλα πλοῖα ἦν μετ᾽ αὐτοῦ ("and other boats were with him") apparently signals an effort by Mark to supply some kind of realism.[16] Since these

---

[12] Note that the verb ἀφίημι ("to take one's leave") occurs only in Markan redaction (Mark 1:18, 20; 7:8; 8:13). For the scholarly consensus, see Pryke, *Redactional Style*, 107, 109, 111, 112. Markan redaction where Jesus and the disciples separate themselves from crowds is found in Mark 1:35–38; 3:7–10, 13–14; 4:10–12; , 36; 5:40; 6:30–33; 45–46; 7:17; 8:10, 13; 9:30–32; 10:10, 23–31; 11:19.

[13] For the acceptance of the phrase παραλαμβάνουσιν αὐτόν as pre-Markan, see Dietrich-Alex Koch, *Die Bedeutung der Wundererzählungen für die Christologie des Markusevangeliums* (BZNW 42; Berlin: de Gruyter, 1975), 95; Hendrickx, *Miracles Stories*, 175.

[14] Bultmann, *Synoptic Tradition*, 215.

[15] Hendrickx, *Miracle Stories*, 175–76.

[16] It has already been observed with respect to Mark's γάρ clauses that he inserts descriptive clauses in interruptive places. C. H. Bird first brought attention to Mark's use of the γάρ clause ("Some γάρ Clauses in St. Mark's Gospel," *JTS* 4 [1953]: 171–87). In my own research related to Mark 11:12–14 ("For It Was Not the Season for Figs," *CBQ* 48 [1986]: 62–66), it became clear that sometimes the comment was meant to have been inserted one clause before it had been added. In Mark 16:4b, the explanation that the stone was very large belongs at the end of the preceding verse (v. 3), providing the reason why the women were asking who would roll the stone away. As it is, it comes after the statement that the stone had been rolled away, "for it was very large," a confusing reason! In the same way, Mark's comment "for it was not the season for figs" (11:13e) is placed after "he found nothing but leaves" (11:13d), making Jesus' subsequent cursing of the tree sound illogical. But if the explanation

boats have no other role in the rest of the account, it seems unlikely that such a detail would have traveled with the pre-Markan story.

[37]καὶ γίνεται λαῖλαψ μεγάλη ἀνέμου καὶ τὰ κύματα ἐπέβαλλεν εἰς τὸ πλοῖον, ὥστε ἤδη γεμίζεσθαι τὸ πλοῖον.

[37]A great windstorm arose, and the waves beat into the boat, so that the boat was already being swamped.

This verse generally is assigned in its entirety to the pre-Markan tradition.[17] Joachim Gnilka, E. J. Pryke, and Frans Neirynck argue that ὥστε ἤδη γεμίζεσθαι τὸ πλοῖον (literally, "so that the boat was already filled") is, on grounds of vocabulary and style, Markan. The reasons add up to four: (1) seven of the thirteen occurrences of ὥστε followed by an infinitive are Markan redaction;[18] (2) the adverb ἤδη is common in Markan compositions;[19] (3) the repetition of πλοῖον suggests redac-

---

"for it was not the season for figs" is placed so that it follows "And seeing a fig tree in leaf [and here we recall that fig trees put out their leaves after their fruit buds], he went over to see if *perhaps* there *might be* something to eat" (11:13ab), then the subsequent cursing makes sense. In the account of the stilling of the storm, Mark's description of the other boats around might simply be an added description meant to be colorful, but in the end it is confusing.

[17] See Ernst Lohmeyer, *Das Evangelium des Markus* (KEK 1/2; Göttingen: Vandenhoeck & Ruprecht, 1967), 90; Schweizer, *Mark*, 109; Kertelge, *Die Wunder Jesu*, 92; Ernst Haenchen, *Der Weg Jesu: Eine Erklärung des Markus-Evangeliums und der kanonischen Parallelen* (2d ed.; Berlin: de Gruyter, 1968), 186–87; Hendrickx, *Miracle Stories*, 176; Koch, *Die Bedeutung der Wundererzählungen*, 95; Étienne Trocmé, *La formation de l'Évangile selon Marc* (EHPR 57; Paris: Presses Universitaires de France, 1963), 47; Dieter Lührmann, *Das Markusevangelium* (HNT 3; Tübingen: Mohr Siebeck, 1987), 96–97; Johannes Schreiber, *Theologie des Vertrauens: Eine redaktionsgeschichtliche Untersuchung des Markusevangeliums* (Hamburg: Furche-Verlag, 1967), 95–96, 122; Vincent Taylor, *The Gospel according to St. Mark: The Greek Text with Introduction, Notes, and Indexes* (London: Macmillan; New York: St. Martin's Press, 1955), 274.

[18] Mark 1:27, 45; 2:2, 12; 3:10, 20; 4:1. The remaining six belong to the pre-Markan tradition: Mark 2:28; 4:32, 37; 9:26; 10:8; 15:5. See Pryke, *Redactional Style*, 118. There appears to have been an unwitting error, since, as will be noticed, the example under discussion, Mark 4:37, is actually listed in the pre-Markan set. Thus, Pryke's number of occurrences assigned to Mark would be eight out of thirteen.

[19] Pryke (ibid., 136, 139–48) notes that five out of eight occurrences of ἤδη belong to Mark: Mark 4:37; 6:35; 11:11; 13:28; 15:42. Gnilka (*Markus*, vol. 1

tion; (4) the entire phrase is a repetition of the previous clause καὶ τὰ κύματα ἐπέβαλλεν εἰς τὸ πλοῖον ("and the waves beat into the boat").[20] Pryke explains that Mark's addition was meant to "build up a primitive section into a livelier narrative."[21] The reason most other scholars have decided that it is pre-Markan is that it explains the disciples' statement to Jesus, "We are perishing" (v. 38). The signs of redaction, however, prove stronger than these latter surmises. Furthermore, as will be noted in the discussion of the storm, telling a first-century person that the waves were beating into the boat is, on its own, sufficient to signal an impending doom. So, the vocabulary and linguistic evidence shows that this last clause was added by Mark, indeed to heighten the drama.

> [38]καὶ αὐτὸς ἦν ἐν τῇ πρύμνῃ ἐπὶ τὸ προσκεφάλαιον καθεύδων. καὶ ἐγείρουσιν αὐτὸν καὶ λέγουσιν αὐτῷ· διδάσκαλε, οὐ μέλει σοι ὅτι ἀπολλύμεθα;

> [38]But he was in the stern, asleep on the cushion; and they woke him up and said to him, "Teacher, do you not care that we are perishing?"

Verse 38 generally is assigned to the pre-Markan account.[22] Only the title of Jesus, "Teacher," appears to have been inserted by Mark, a singularly Markan title for Jesus in the pre-Markan material.[23]

> [39]καὶ διεγερθεὶς ἐπετίμησεν τῷ ἀνέμῳ καὶ εἶπεν τῇ θαλάσσῃ· σιώπα, πεφίμωσο. καὶ ἐκόπασεν ὁ ἄνεμος καὶ ἐγένετο γαλήνη μεγάλη.

> [39]He woke up and rebuked the wind, and said to the sea, "Peace! Be still!" Then the wind ceased, and there was a dead calm.

---

passim) also identifies five as Markan, the only difference being that he does not accept Mark 13:28 as redaction, and unlike Pryke, he does accept Mark 15:44. In agreement is Frans Neirynck, "The Redactional Text of Mark," *ETL* 57 (1981): 154.

[20] Frans Neirynck, "Les expressions double chez Marc et le problème synoptique," *ETL* 59 (1983): 312.

[21] Pryke, *Redactional Style*, 118.

[22] Lohmeyer, *Markus*, 91; Schweizer, *Mark*, 109; Gnilka, *Markus*, 1:196–97; Kertelge, *Die Wunder Jesu*, 95; Lührmann, *Markusevangelium*, 97.

[23] Mark 4:38; 9:17, 38; 10:17, 20, 35; 12:14, 19, 32; 13:1. See Vernon Robbins, *Jesus the Teacher: A Socio-Rhetorical Interpretation of Mark* (Philadelphia: Fortress, 1984), esp. 198.

Scholars are generally agreed that this verse belongs to the pre-Markan tradition[24] It has often been observed that the composition of Mark 4:39a is similar to Mark 1:25, another pre-Markan text:

καὶ ἐπετίμησεν αὐτῷ ὁ Ἰησοῦς λέγων· φιμώθητι καὶ ἔξελθε ἐξ αὐτοῦ. (Mark 1:25)

καὶ ... ἐπετίμησεν τῷ ἀνέμῳ καὶ εἶπεν τῇ θαλάσσῃ· σιώπα, πεφίμωσο. (Mark 4:39a)

The comparison indicates that the imperative form of φιμόω ("to muzzle") belonged to at least one other pre-Markan story in which Jesus takes charge over a superhuman force. Since that verb only appears twice in the entire Markan Gospel, there is little sign that it was a favorite of Mark.[25]

[40]καὶ εἶπεν αὐτοῖς· τί δειλοί ἐστε; οὔπω ἔχετε πίστιν;

[40]He said to them, "Why are you afraid? Have you still no faith?"

The question of the authorship of v. 40 is by no means an easy one to answer, and a prestigious set of scholars stands on each side of the issue. Those who assign it to Mark[26] cite three major reasons. (1) Jesus' reproach serves two Markan motifs: (a) the disciples' timidity, such as can be seen elsewhere (Mark 9:32; 10:32; 16:8); (b) the disciples' inability to understand who Jesus is (Mark 4:13; 6:52; 7:18; 8:17, 21). (2.) Linguistically, the adverb οὔπω is a favorite of Mark, and when it occurs in reprimands, as it does in Mark 8:17, 21, it is always Markan redaction.

---

[24]Bultmann, *Synoptic Tradition*, 216; Lohmeyer, *Markus*, 91; Schweizer, *Mark*, 109; Gnilka, *Markus*, 1:195; Kertelge, *Die Wunder Jesu*, 92; Ernest Best, *The Temptation and the Passion: The Markan Soteriology* (SNTSMS 2; Cambridge: Cambridge University Press, 1965), 73; Hendrickx, *Miracle Stories*, 177–78; Koch, *Die Bedeutung der Wundererzählungen*, 97; Schreiber, *Theologie des Vertrauens*, 96 n. 29; Taylor, *St. Mark*, 275–76.

[25]Lohmeyer, *Markus*, 97; Schweizer, *Mark*, 109; Gnilka, *Markus*, 1:196–97; Kertelge, *Die Wunder Jesu*, 90; Klostermann, *Markusevangelium*, 46; Trocmé, *Mark*, 150 n. 3; Lührmann, *Markusevangelium*, 97; Taylor, *St. Mark*, 297.

[26]Ernest Best, *Disciples and Discipleship: Studies in the Gospel according to Mark* (Edinburgh: T & T Clark, 1986), 92; Ludger Schenke, *Das Markusevangelium* (KUT 405; Stuttgart: Kohlhammer, 1988), 79; Rudolf Pesch, *Das Markusevangelium* (3d ed.; 2 vols.; HTKNT; Freiberg: Herder, 1984), 1:274–77; Koch, *Die Bedeutung der Wundererzählungen*, 97; Hendrickx, *Miracle Stories*, 177–78.

(3) The placement of v. 40 in the overall structure of the story is inter-ruptive to the smooth flow that otherwise exists between Jesus' miracle and the disciples' response. That is, Jesus stills the storm and then asks them about their faith, so that their amazement at the miracle does not seem to be connected as an answer to Jesus. Matthew illustrates what must be done to remove that disjuncture by having Jesus challenge the disciples about their faith first and then still the storm. In that way, their amazement comments on the miracle and does not bypass Jesus' ques-tion, as the disciples in the Markan version seem to do.

On the other side of the argument are scholars who support the challenge to faith as pre-Markan.[27] They base their decision on two main arguments. (1) Themes of fear and faith occur together in Mark 5:36, a pre-Markan tradition, where Jesus tells Jairus, μὴ φοβοῦ, μόνον πίστευε ("Do not be afraid, only believe"). (2) A link occurs between the petitioner's faith and the miracle in five pre-Markan healing stories: the paralytic (Mark 2:1–12); the woman with the hemorrhage (Mark 5:25–34; the raising of Jairus's daughter (Mark 5:35–43); the demon-ized boy (Mark 9:14–29); the healing of Bartimaeus (Mark 10:46–52). Étienne Trocmé notes that even the noun πίστις ("faith") is rare in Mark, and of the five times it occurs (Mark 2:5; 4:40; 5:34; 10:52; 11:22), only Mark 11:22 is not part of a miracle story, but is also a pre-Markan say-ing.[28] It must also be noted that in Mark, the problem of the disciples is not that they do not have faith, although his insertion of them in the pre-Markan story of the demonized boy (Mark 9:14–29) results in their inclusion in Jesus' general frustrated cry about "this faithless generation" (Mark 9:19) along with the father of the boy. But note that in the con-clusion to the story, an addition by Mark, when the disciples wonder why they could not cast out the demon, the problem was not their lack of faith, as Matthew will have it, but rather their arrogance and obtuse spiritual sight, in that none of them thought to pray (Mark 9:28–29).

---

[27] Lohmeyer, *Markus*, 97; Gnilka, *Markus*, 1:196–97; Kertelge, *Die Wunder Jesu*, 90; Klostermann, *Markusevangelium*, 46; Schweizer, *Mark*, 109; Trocmé, *Mark*, 150 n. 3; Lührmann, *Markusevangelium*, 97; Taylor, *St. Mark*, 297.

[28] In Mark 2:5, the faith of the paralytic friends is the motivation for Jesus' pronouncement of the forgiveness of the man's sins; in Mark 5:34, Jesus tells the woman that she is healed due to her faith; in Mark 10:52, Jesus tells Bartimaeus that it was his faith that saved him. All of these uses are clearly indispensable to the pre-Markan account and cannot be assigned to redaction. See Trocmé, *Mark*, 150 n. 3.

Markan reproaches use verbs of knowing (γινώσκω) and understanding (οἶδα), such as in Mark 4:13: "And he said to them, 'Do you not understand this parable? Then how will you understand all the parables?'"[29]

Thus, the appearance of πίστις belongs to pre-Markan stories. With regard to the function of v. 40, is it as artificial and obstructive as the scholars who identify it as Markan claim it to be? Jesus' question to his disciples actually explains why he could sleep and why the disciples could remain calm. But the question presumes that they would understand that the forces of nature knew that they could not sink a boat in which Jesus sailed. This is the only meaning possible for Jesus' question, and it acts as an astonishing revelation of the scope of his divine status. He has revealed an identity and power about which they had no idea. It is also the revelation to the listener of the supreme cosmic authority of Jesus as recognized by the elements. This is of another class than healings and exorcisms or even raisings from the dead, since the prophets Elijah and Elisha both had such miracles attributed to them. But only God has power over the sea, and the fact that Jesus takes this control signifies that he has been endowed with this singular authority, and the elements know it. So the question of Jesus about faith also indicates a new content of that faith, the revelation of his status and empowerment. Thus, it belongs to the pre-Markan text. The possible addition of the evangelist would be οὔπω ("yet"), since according to the Gospel placement, the disciples have been with Jesus to see his many miracles.

> [41]καὶ ἐφοβήθησαν φόβον μέγαν καὶ ἔλεγον πρὸς ἀλλήλους· τίς ἄρα οὗτός ἐστιν ὅτι καὶ ὁ ἄνεμος καὶ ἡ θάλασσα ὑπακούει αὐτῷ;

> [41]And they were filled with great awe and said to one another, "Who then is this, that even the wind and the sea obey him?"

Scholars assign this acclamation to the pre-Markan stratum of the story. The amazement of witnesses is a familiar feature of the anecdotes that climax in a miracle. The expression of fear in v. 41a (καὶ ἐφοβήθησαν φόβον μέγαν) is an imitation of the LXX, and the best parallel is found in the first chapter of the book of Jonah, where the sailors, following Jonah's orders, throw him into the storm-tossed sea,

---

[29] The verb συνίημι occurs in Mark 4:12; 7:14; 8:17, 21, all redactional, while the verb νοέω also occurs in two of the three passages: Mark 7:18; 8:17. All these constitute passages of Jesus' direct rebuke to disciples. Mark 6:52 is Markan redaction as well, and uses συνίημι, but as indirect narrative.

but first ask the God of Jonah for forgiveness and deliverance from the tempest. They then witness the sea become calm, and they experience this holy fear.

καὶ ἔλαβον τὸν Ιωναν καὶ ἐξέβαλον αὐτὸν εἰς τὴν θάλασσαν καὶ ἔστη ἡ θάλασσα ἐκ τοῦ σάλου αὐτῆς. καὶ ἐφοβήθησαν οἱ ἄνδρες φόβῳ μεγάλῳ τὸν κύριον καὶ ἔθυσαν θυσίαν τῷ κυρίῳ καὶ εὔξαντο εὐχάς. (Jonah 1:15–16)

So they picked Jonah up and threw him into the sea; and the sea ceased from its raging. Then the men *feared* the LORD *with a great fear* and sacrificed a sacrifice to the LORD and vowed vows.

The second part of the acclamation of Mark 4:41 bears a close re-semblance to Mark 1:27b:

ὥστε συζητεῖν πρὸς ἑαυτοὺς λέγοντας·

τί ἐστιν τοῦτο; διδαχὴ καινὴ κατ᾽ ἐξουσίαν· καὶ τοῖς πνεύμασι τοῖς ἀκαθάρτοις ἐπιτάσσει, καὶ ὑπακούουσιν αὐτῷ. (Mark 1:27)

καὶ ἔλεγον πρὸς ἀλλήλους·

τίς ἄρα οὗτός ἐστιν ὅτι καὶ ὁ ἄνεμος καὶ ἡ θάλασσα ὑπακούει αὐτῷ; (Mark 4:41bc)

In both of these acclamations the witnesses wonder who Jesus is that he demonstrates such authority over superhuman forces.

Verse 41 functions as an acclamation integral to the pre-Markan stratum.

Summary: The redactional analysis of Mark 4:35–41 has shown that the evangelist did not alter this account in any substantial way. It is prob-able that he moved καὶ λέγει αὐτοῖς from its position just before Jesus' invitation διέλθωμεν εἰς τὸ πέραν and made it an introductory clause of the story (v. 35). In this way, he was able to maintain the connection with the preaching mode that he had established in the preaching from the boat in Mark 4:1–34. He then added ἐν ἐκείνῃ τῇ ἡμέρᾳ to the pre-Markan statement that evening had come in order to link the activities of the day. In v. 36, he added a reference to the crowds (καὶ ἀφέντες τὸν ὄχλον) to maintain the context that he had established in Mark 4:1–34. Then, because Jesus was already in the boat due to the previous account (Mark 4:1–2), he inserted ὡς ἦν just after παραλαμβάνουσιν αὐτόν and possibly altered what might have been εἰς τὸ πλοῖον to ἐν τῷ πλοίῳ because Jesus was already seated in the boat. He added the descriptive καὶ ἄλλα πλοῖα ἦν μετ' αὐτοῦ. In v. 37, he increased the drama about the water coming into the boat with ὥστε ἤδη γεμίζεσθαι τὸ πλοῖον. The vocative address διδάσκαλε was inserted into the disciples' cry to Jesus in v. 38, as is his custom elsewhere in the Gospel. Finally, he added οὔπω to Jesus' reprimand to his disciples to match the context of the Gospel, as the disciples have been with Jesus constantly.

II. THE PRE-MARKAN ANECDOTE: JESUS AND HIS STORM-TOSSED DISCIPLES

[35]καὶ λέγει αὐτοῖς . . . ὀψίας γενομένης· διέλθωμεν εἰς τὸ πέραν. [36]καὶ . . . παραλαμβάνουσιν αὐτὸν . . . ἐν τῷ πλοίῳ . . . [37]καὶ γίνεται λαῖλαψ μεγάλη ἀνέμου καὶ τὰ κύματα ἐπέβαλλεν εἰς τὸ πλοῖον . . . [38]καὶ αὐτὸς ἦν ἐν τῇ πρύμνῃ ἐπὶ τὸ προσκεφάλαιον καθεύδων· καὶ ἐγείρουσιν αὐτὸν καὶ λέγουσιν αὐτῷ· . . . οὐ μέλει σοι ὅτι ἀπολλύμεθα; [39]καὶ διεγερθεὶς ἐπετίμησεν τῷ ἀνέμῳ καὶ εἶπεν τῇ θαλάσσῃ· σιώπα, πεφίμωσο. καὶ ἐκόπασεν ὁ ἄνεμος καὶ ἐγένετο γαλήνη μεγάλη. [40]καὶ εἶπεν αὐτοῖς· τί δειλοί ἐστε; οὐ[. . .] ἔχετε πίστιν; [41]καὶ ἐφοβήθησαν φόβον μέγαν καὶ ἔλεγον πρὸς ἀλλήλους· τίς ἄρα οὗτός ἐστιν ὅτι καὶ ὁ ἄνεμος καὶ ἡ θάλασσα ὑπακούει αὐτῷ;

[35]When evening had come . . . , he said to them, "Let us go across to the other side." [36]And . . . they took him . . . with them in the boat. . . . [37]A great windstorm arose, and the waves beat into the boat. . . . [38]But he was in the stern, asleep on the cushion; and they woke him up and said to him, ". . . Do you not care that we are perishing?" [39]He woke up and rebuked the wind, and said to the sea, "Peace! Be still!" Then the wind ceased, and there was a dead calm. [40]He said to them, "Why are you afraid? Have you . . . no faith?" [41]And they were filled with great awe and said to one another, "Who then is this, that even the wind and the sea obey him?"

This miracle story features an astonishing revelation of Jesus' cosmic authority and power over nature, but it has been placed in a context where that power is revealed only to calm his frightened and unknowing disciples.

The Characterization of Jesus and His Disciples

³⁵καὶ λέγει αὐτοῖς . . . ὀψίας γενομένης· διέλθωμεν εἰς τὸ πέραν. ³⁶καὶ . . . παραλαμβάνουσιν αὐτὸν . . . ἐν τῷ πλοίῳ . . .

³⁵When evening had come . . . , he said to them, "Let us go across to the other side." ³⁶And . . . they took him . . . with them in the boat. . . .

These first two verses convey the closer relationship of Jesus to his disciples, since Jesus spontaneously chooses to cross the Sea of Galilee and his "Let us go to the other side" creates a sense of familiarity not found elsewhere. "They took him into the boat" communicates the instant compliance with Jesus' wishes by these companions who are already in the boat. A second feature of closeness is the fact that it is the end of the day, the time when one goes back to family and home—work is done.

What Is the Nature of the Storm?

³⁷καὶ γίνεται λαῖλαψ μεγάλη ἀνέμου καὶ τὰ κύματα ἐπέβαλλεν εἰς τὸ πλοῖον . . .

³⁷A great windstorm arose, and the waves beat into the boat. . . .

καὶ γίνεται λαῖλαψ μεγάλη ἀνέμου

a great windstorm arose

The interpretation of this miracle story is greatly affected by the decision whether this storm is natural or sent by some supernatural power. Stories about sea storms were plentiful and popular in the ordinary Mediterranean world in the Greco-Roman period,³⁰ and H. H. Huxley

---

³⁰ See, for example, Herodotus, *Hist.* 7.34; Horace, *Carm.* 1.3, 5, 14; Ovid, *Metam.* 11.475–574; Diodorus Siculus, *Hist.* 4.48, 5–6; Dio Chrysostom, *Ven.* 1–2; Plutarch, *Caes.* 38.3–4; Josephus, *Life* 13–16; also Apuleius, *Metamorphoses*; Achilles Tatius, *Leucippe and Cleitophon*; Xenophon, *An Ephesian Tale*; Heliodorus, *An Ethiopian Romance*. Stories of sea storms are featured in the "novels": *Ninus and Semiramis*; *Chaereas and Callirhoe*; *Metiochus and Parthenope*. See H. H. Huxley, "Storm and Shipwreck in Roman Literature," *GR* 21 (1952): 117–24; Lionel Casson, *Ships and Seamanship in the Ancient World* (Princeton,

notes that the usual pattern is for the travelers to begin their voyage on a sea that appears tranquil, only to meet with a life-threatening storm. In this Markan account, the fact that it is night adds an even more frightening aspect to the λαῖλαψ, that gale of wind that whips up the storm on the sea. Such a beginning is to be seen in, for example, Theocritus's "Hymn to the Dioscuri": "Night comes, and with it a great storm from the sky, and the broad sea rattles and splashes with the battery of the blast and of the irresistible hail." Then he praises the sea-rescuing deities: "But for all that, ye, even ye, do draw both ship and despairing shipmen from out of hell; *the winds abate, the sea puts on a shining calm*, the clouds run asunder this way and that way" (*Id.* 22.14–20).[31]

Something of that brevity is found in Mark 4:37: καὶ γίνεται λαῖλαψ μεγάλη ἀνέμου καὶ τὰ κύματα ἐπέβαλλεν εἰς τὸ πλοῖον ("a great windstorm arose, and the waves beat into the boat"). While Pamela Thimmes has claimed that this brevity separates the "Biblical Sea-Storm Type-Scene" from Greco-Roman sea storm stories, the answer is found in the difference between the well-known adventure tale that she cites from the non-Jewish world and any anecdote from that same world. For the miracle story is an anecdote and therefore brief. The adventure story, in contrast, is designed as an entertainment, and in the popular sea storm stories the listener is provided the frightening details[32] designed to prolong the suspense as long as possible until at last, the final scene concludes with a sudden calm, or rescue, or a tragic drowning.[33]

N.J.: Princeton University Press, 1971); also, a masterly article that supplies abundant examples meticulously organized chronologically, Vernon K. Robbins, "By Land and by Sea: The We-Passages and Ancient Sea Voyages," in *Perspectives on Luke-Acts* (ed. C. H. Talbert; PRSt 5; Danville, Va.: Association of Baptist Professors of Religion, 1978), 215–42.

[31] Theocritus, "The Hymn to the Dioscuri," in *The Greek Bucolic Poets* (trans. J. M. Edmonds; LCL; London: Heinemann; New York: Putnam, 1919), 257 (my italics).

[32] Pamela Thimmes, *Studies in the Biblical Sea-Storm Type-Scene: Convention and Invention* (San Francisco: Mellen Press, 1992), esp. 107, 110.

[33] In a satirical essay, Lucian warns a young philosopher of these long-winded accounts: "'Where shall I make a beginning,' my friend, 'and where make an end of relating' all that must be done and suffered by those who take salaried posts and are put on trial in the friendship of our wealthy men . . . ? I listened to them while they spun their yarns about their shipwreck and unlooked-for deliverance, just like the men with shaven heads who gather in

But anecdotes, like thanksgiving prayers, Jewish or Gentile, by genre are briefer, moving quickly to the hero's virtue and some special feature of the hero's rescue. A good example of a rescue miracle is attributed to Rabbi Tanhuma:

> Rabbi Tanhuma said: It happened that a pagan ship made a voyage on the Great Sea [the Mediterranean], and on it was one Jewish child. While they were at sea, a great storm on the sea arose against them, and then each one stood and began to raise his hands and call out to his god. But the boy did nothing. Seeing that he did nothing, they said to the Jewish boy, "My son stand up! Call on your god! For we have heard that he answers you if you cry out to him, and he is strong." Thereupon the child stood up and with his whole heart he cried out [to God], and the sea was silent. (*y. Ber.* 9)[34]

In the same way, the beginning of this little story with the gale arising on the sea belongs with the regular stories of the Greco-Roman world, though not the novelistic type.

καὶ τὰ κύματα ἐπέβαλλεν εἰς τὸ πλοῖον

and the waves beat into the boat

The water rushing into the boat is the sign that the end is not far away. The description is found in a thanksgiving prayer of Aelius Aristides: "O Universal Light for all humankind, you who recently manifested to us when, at the time that *the vast sea arose from all sides and rushed in upon us* and nothing was visible except *the destruction which was approaching and had well-nigh arrived,* you stretched out your hand, revealed the hidden heavens, and granted us to behold the earth and to make port, *so much beyond our expectation that we were unconvinced*

---

crowds at the temples and tell of third waves, tempests, headlands, strandings, masts carried away, rudders broken, and to cap it all, how the Twin Brethren [the Dioscuri] appeared (they are peculiar to this sort of rhodomontade), or how some other *deus ex machina* sat on the masthead or stood at the helm and steered the ship to a soft beach where she might break up gradually and slowly and they themselves get ashore by the grace and favour of the god" (*Merc. cond.* 3.1) (*Lucian,* vol. 3 [trans. A. M. Harmon; LCL; London: Heinemann; New York: Putnam, 1921], 413–15).

[34] Cited in Paul Fiebig, *Rabbinische Wundergeschichten des neutestamentlichen Zeitalters: In vokalisiertem Text mit sprachlichen und sachlichen Bemerkungen* (2d ed.; KTVÜ 78; Berlin: de Gruyter, 1933), 23–24 (my translation).

when we set foot ashore" (*Serap.* 45.33).[35] For the listener to the Jesus story, then, the fact that the waves are falling in the boat spells everyone's imminent destruction.

The Further Characterization of Jesus

[38a]καὶ αὐτὸς ἦν ἐν τῇ πρύμνῃ ἐπὶ τὸ προσκεφάλαιον καθεύδων·

[38a]But he was in the stern, asleep on the cushion;

In v. 38a, the detail of Jesus sleeping on the cushion in the stern recalls Odysseus similarly sleeping as a storm raged (Homer, *Od.* 13.73–75).[36] Dennis MacDonald notes another adventure in which Odysseus sleeps during a storm while the sailors are terrified (Homer, *Od.* 10.1–69).[37] Yet a parallel from Jewish tradition is also invited because Jonah is said to sleep while a storm threatens the life of those on board. The impression that would be given in both cases is that of a callous person. The peaceful calm of sleeping on a cushion contrasts most dramatically with the terrifying sounds that the listener imagines, the howling wind and heaving boat as the huge swells spill over onto the deck. The refined mention of the pillow seems to convey the idea of distance and uncaring in Jesus to join his disciples and share those last minutes with them.

The Further Characterization of the Disciples

[38b]καὶ ἐγείρουσιν αὐτὸν καὶ λέγουσιν αὐτῷ· . . . οὐ μέλει σοι ὅτι ἀπολλύμεθα;

[38b]and they woke him up and said to him, ". . . Do you not care that we are perishing?"

---

[35] Aelius Aristides, *Regarding Serapis*, in *Aelius Aristides and the Sacred Tales* (trans. C. A. Behr; Amsterdam: Hakkert; Chicago: Argonaut, 1968), 268 (my italics).

[36] "Then for Odysseus they spread a rug and a linen sheet on the deck of the hollow ship at the stern [πρύμνῃ], that he might sleep soundly" (Homer, *Odyssey* [trans. A. T. Murray; 2 vols., LCL; London: Heinemann, 1931], 2:6–9).

[37] See Dennis R. MacDonald, "Sleeping Sailors," in *The Homeric Epics and the Gospel of Mark* (New Haven: Yale University Press, 2000), 55–62.

This is the element that recalls the Jonah account. There, it is the captain who reproaches Jonah for sleeping instead of joining everyone and praying for a cessation of the storm.

In this account, however, the question is more personal: "Do you not care that we are perishing?" It is a hurt and panic-stricken question that doubts Jesus' love and commitment to them. This is distinct from the Matthean Gospel, where the disciples know that Jesus can command the wind and sea, so that they reverently go to him with the plea "Lord, save us! We are perishing!" (Matt 8:25).[38] In Mark, there is no sign at all that the disciples understand that Jesus can control the elements of the wind and the sea. When they go to ask Jesus, "Do you not care that we are perishing?" they mean to include him in that "we." The point is that Jesus seems unconcerned at the very moment when death is upon them, and their being together at the end means most.

The Further Characterization of Jesus

[39]καὶ διεγερθεὶς ἐπετίμησεν τῷ ἀνέμῳ καὶ εἶπεν τῇ θαλάσσῃ· σιώπα, πεφίμωσο. καὶ ἐκόπασεν ὁ ἄνεμος καὶ ἐγένετο γαλήνη μεγάλη.

And rising up, he rebuked the wind, and he said to the sea, "Be silent! Be shut up!" And the wind fell, and there was a great calm.[39]

Jesus' answer to the disciples' panic-stricken reproach is the point of surprise in the story. Now awakened, he realizes that the disciples do not understand. He immediately rebukes the elements as though they have taken things too far, terrifying the disciples, who believe that they are about to drown.

[40]καὶ εἶπεν αὐτοῖς· τί δειλοί ἐστε; οὐ[. . .] ἔχετε πίστιν;

[40]And he said to them, "Why are you afraid? Have you . . . no faith?"

---

[38]Although Luke's disciples do not indicate that they imagine that Jesus could stop the storm, notice that they only cry out to inform Jesus of what is happening: "Master, Master, we are perishing!" (Luke 8:24) so that Luke also eliminates the reproach. With that elimination, goes the more vigorous relationship of disciples and master that obtains in the pre-Markan material.

[39]Here I have provided a rather literal rendering of the Greek to capture some of its force.

Jesus now counters the reproachful question of the disciples with questions that explain why they had no need to be afraid at all. Jesus' questions reveal that he did not realize that they were so unaware of his empowerment. They also explain how it was that Jesus could sleep while the elements raged. Clearly, the wind and sea know that Jesus has been given a divine authorization on earth, and they are subject to him. The storm, then, was a show of power and might, but in no way was it free to sink the ship that held the sleeping Jesus. Had the disciples understood this power of Jesus, they too could have remained calm.[40] Therefore, Jesus proves that it was not hard-heartedness toward them, but he had rested under the mistaken impression that the disciples understood that no sea storm could harm them because he was in the boat there with them.

[41]καὶ ἐφοβήθησαν φόβον μέγαν καὶ ἔλεγον πρὸς ἀλλήλους· τίς ἄρα οὗτός ἐστιν ὅτι καὶ ὁ ἄνεμος καὶ ἡ θάλασσα ὑπακούει αὐτῷ;

[41]And they feared [with] a great fear and said to each other, "Who then is this, that both the wind and the sea obey him?"[41]

---

[40] Ian G. Wallis (*The Faith of Jesus Christ in Early Christian Traditions* [SNTMS 84; Cambridge; New York: Cambridge University, 1995], 36–39) holds that Jesus' previous saying that faith could cause a mountain to fall (Mark 11:22–23) means that here he was scolding the disciples about their lack of faith. Had their faith been strong enough, they could have stopped the storm themselves. This theory rests on the idea that the storm actually could have drowned them all. In this case, Jesus' sleep would be seen to be very callous. Furthermore, Wallis seems unaware that having power over the sea was a potent symbol in the imperial world. It proved a heavenly authorized hero whom nature was not free to impede. In this story, Jesus, by silencing the storm because it was frightening the disciples, shows that nature recognizes his authority. Actually, there would have been no need to stop the storm, then, because it could never have actually taken the boat down. The questions of Jesus and the acclamation in v. 41 make this a story about the revelation of Jesus' divine sovereignty. Adela Yarbro Collins (*Mark: A Commentary* [Hermeneia; Minneapolis: Fortress, 2007], 260–61) supports Wallis's interpretation, although she cites the references in Jewish Scriptures and intertestamental literature as well as the Roman propaganda connected to the meaning of Julius Caesar's sea trip. All of these demonstrate the idea that special, divinely empowered heroes have power over the sea; it cannot overpower them or their plans.

[41] Here my literal translation brings out the word "fear," which is prominent here and not captured by "they were filled with great awe" (NRSV), which misses the intended allusion to the Jewish Scriptures regarding what happens when one meets God.

The question that the disciples direct to each other serves as the answer to Jesus' question. They had no idea of the true scope of Jesus' power. The narrator's use of "fearing with great fear" signals their awareness that they are in the presence of the divine. The question of the disciples invites the listener to answer, even as the narrator shows what that answer must be.

The Power of Jesus and His Revealed Identity: Jewish and Gentile Sources

Who Is This Whom Even the Winds and the Sea Obey?

There are three interpretations of Jesus' identity based on this exercise of his authority that flow from a singular focus on Old Testament and singularly Jewish sources. The most common is founded on the allusions between the Jesus miracle story and references to LXX texts. Since these texts ascribe command of the sea to God alone, Jesus is shown to be standing in God's place. Alan Richardson notes texts such as Ps 29:3 ("The voice of the LORD is over the waters; the God of glory thunders"), Ps 89:9 ("You rule the raging of the sea; when its waves rise, you still them"), Nah 1:4 ("He rebukes the sea and makes it dry, and he dries up all the rivers"), and Hab 3:15 ("You trampled the sea with your horses, churning the mighty waters").[42] Dennis Nineham adds Ps 93:3–4 ("The floods have lifted up, O LORD, the floods have lifted up their voice; the floods lift up their roaring. More majestic than the thunders of mighty waters of the sea, more majestic than the waves of the sea, majestic on high is the LORD!") and Ps 104:6–7 ("You cover it with the deep as with a garment; the waters stood above the mountains. At your rebuke they flee; at the sound of your thunder they take to flight").[43] C. F. D. Moule concludes that the miracle story provides "a vigorous picture-language to describe Jesus as Master of the storms of life; of God it is said in Ps 107:29, 'He maketh the storm a calm, so that the waves thereof are still.'"[44]

---

[42] Alan Richardson, *The Miracle Stories of the Gospels* (1941; repr., London: SCM Press, 1963), 91.

[43] Dennis E. Nineham, *The Gospel of St. Mark* (PGC; London: A & C Black, 1963), 146.

[44] C. F. D. Moule, *The Gospel according to Mark* (CBC; Cambridge: Cambridge University Press, 1965), 42.

Others turn to sources that suggest an apocalyptic message of Jesus as master of the end time in the similarity that they see between the miracle story and various accounts of God's initial power over the primordial chaos of creation.[45] Paul Achtemeier takes the allusion back to the more ancient Canaanite, Akkadian, and Babylonian creation myths where Marduk is victorious over Tiamat, goddess of the sea. For him, this "semitic mentality" is the allusion in this story and plainly links Jesus to God.[46] Rudolf Pesch sees in the Jesus miracle story an eschatological reading of Ps 107.[47] John Paul Heil turns to the documents of Qumran and comments, "The New Testament took shape in the apocalyptic-eschatological milieu similar to that of Qumran. Those who formed the gospel stories were similarly inspirited by and thoroughly at home in the Old Testament."[48] For Heil, the sea storm story in the *T. Naph.* 6:1–10[49] and the symbols provided in 1QH^a, the *Book of Hymns*, function as the interpretational tools. The *Testament of Naph-*

---

[45] C. H. Dodd, "The Appearances of the Risen Christ: An Essay in Form-Criticism of the Gospels," in *Studies in the Gospels: Essays in Memory of R. H. Lightfoot* (ed. D. E. Nineham; Oxford: Blackwell, 1955), 26. See also Reginald Fuller, *Interpreting the Miracles* (Philadelphia: Westminster, 1963), 41.

[46] Paul J. Achtemeier, "Person and Deed: Jesus and the Storm-Tossed Sea," *Int* 16 (1962):170. See also Howard Clark Kee, *Miracle in the Early Christian World: A Study in Sociohistorical Method* (New Haven: Yale University Press, 1983), 163.

[47] "Die Christologie der undergeschichten ist vom alt.-jüdischen Horizont her entworfen, von der Erwartung des eschatologischen Propheten her" (Pesch, *Markusevangelium*, 1:279).

[48] John Paul Heil, *Jesus Walking on the Sea: Meaning and Gospel Functions of Matt. 14:22–33, Mark 6:45–52, and John 6:15b–21* (AnBib 87; Rome: Biblical Institute Press, 1981), 30.

[49] Heil's translation of *T. Naph.* 6:1–10 is as follows: "And again after seven days I saw our father Jacob standing at the sea of Jamnia and we, his sons, with him. And behold, a ship came sailing by without sailors and pilot, and the ship was inscribed, 'Jacob.' And our father said to us, 'Let us climb into our ship'!' As we entered, there came a violent storm, and a tempest of strong wind. And our father, who was holding the helm, was taken from us. And overtaken by the storm we were driven over the sea. And the ship was filled with water, beaten here and there by the waves, so that it was also shattered. And Joseph fled upon a little boat. And we also were divided upon ten planks. And Levi and Juda were together. We were all scattered then to the ends of the earth. But Levi, girt about with sackcloth, prayed for us all to the Lord. And as the storm ceased, the ship came upon the land as in peace. And behold, our father came, and we all rejoiced with one accord" (ibid., 19).

tali assures the faithful Jews that the Lord will intervene in any future disaster, while Mark 4:35–41 (and Mark 6:45–52 as well) promises that Jesus will save the Christians from the impending apocalyptic crisis.[50] 1QH[a] 11[3]:6, 13 hold the key images necessary to understand the full meaning of the Christian story.[51]

> 1QH[a] 11[3]:6: "They have made [my] life like a ship in the [de]pths of the sea."

> 1QH[a] 11[3]:13: "And the foundations to the wall break in pieces like a ship on the face of the sea, and clouds roar with a roaring voice."

"The image of the ship beset by the destructive power of the chaotic sea heightens the expression of the extreme instability of this eschatological crisis. The security of the enemies is shattered like a ship in the storm of this apocalyptic upheaval."[52] Heil adds that the disciples' fear shows the futility of human efforts to stop the impending "eschatological cataclysm"; only the power of God, shown in the power of Jesus, can overcome the chaos.[53]

All of these various suggestions for a hugely cosmic message concerning the end time require some special sign from the Markan narrator, who has provided only the message that a gale arose. Jesus' command to the wind and the sea cannot bear the weight of these conclusions, for, as we will see, addressing the sea and wind as rational entities is common in the Greco-Roman world and its compositions.

It may be that these scholars have been influenced by the Matthean redaction of Mark's story, where Mark's simple λαῖλαψ, the natural word for a gale, is replaced with σεισμός ("earthquake"), which is indeed

---

[50] Ibid., 30.

[51] Translation of Hodayoth is by Heil, *Jesus Walking on the Sea,* 23–28.

[52] Ibid., 25. Heil also cites 1QH[a] 11[3]:13b–14a and in particular 1QH[a] 14[6]:22b–25, which he underlines as having undeniable relevance to the Christian sea miracles: "And I was like a sailor on a ship in the storming seas, their waves and all their breakers raged against me, a whirlwind so that there was no pause to revive the soul, and there was no path to straighten a way on the surface of the waters, and the abyss roared at my anguish, and I approached the gates of death. And I was as one who comes into a fortified city and strengthened by a high wall unto deliverance. And I rejoiced in your truth, O my God, for you set a foundation on rock" (ibid., 27–28).

[53] Ibid., 30, 127–30.

a very unusual element in a sea storm story and suggests a convulsion of the earth itself.

The third main interpretation of the story is as an exorcism of a demon that has taken possession of the wind and sea, or an exorcism of these elements as demonic. For example, Lamar Williamson proposes that "just as God had authority over the primeval chaos at creation (Job 38:8–11; Ps 74:13–14), so Jesus has authority over the demonic forces of nature."[54] James Kallas describes the exorcism in dramatic terms: "Jesus comes to strangle this man-opposing, God-opposing force [the storm]. He comes to still the storms, to drive out the demons of the deep, to advance the kingdom of God."[55] These scholars are following the observations of C. J. Cadoux, who notes the verbal similarities between the exorcism in the synagogue (Mark 1:23–28) and Mark 4:35–41, in particular with the use of the same, odd verb φιμόω to command silence from the demon in Mark 1:25 (φιμώθητι) and of the storm in Mark 4:39 (πεφίμωσο).[56] Second, the acclamations of both accounts are also close:

ἐπετίμησεν αὐτῷ ὁ Ἰησοῦς λέγων· φιμώθητι καὶ ἔξελθε ἐξ αὐτοῦ. (Mark 1:25)

Jesus *rebuked* it, saying, "*Be shut up* and come out of him!" (my translation)

ἐπετίμησεν τῷ ἀνέμῳ καὶ εἶπεν τῇ θαλάσσῃ· σιώπα, πεφίμωσο.(Mark 4:39)

He *rebuked* the wind and said to the sea, "Silence! *Be completely shut up!*" (my translation)

καὶ ἐθαμβήθησαν ἅπαντες ὥστε συζητεῖν πρὸς ἑαυτοὺς λέγοντας· τί ἐστιν τοῦτο; . . . τοῖς πνεύμασι τοῖς ἀκαθάρτοις ἐπιτάσσει, καὶ ὑπακούουσιν αὐτῷ. (Mark 1:27)

---

[54] Lamar Williamson, *Mark* (IBC; Atlanta: John Knox Press, 1983), 101–2.

[55] James Kallas, *The Significance of the Synoptic Miracles* (London: SPCK, 1961).

[56] C. J. Cadoux, *The Historic Mission of Jesus: A Constructive Re-examination of the Eschatological Teaching in the Synoptic Gospels* (London: Lutterworth, 1941), 61.

They were all amazed, and they kept on asking one another, "What is this? . . . He commands even the unclean spirits, and they obey him."

καὶ ἐφοβήθησαν φόβον μέγαν, καὶ ἔλεγον πρὸς ἀλλήλους· τίς ἄρα οὗτος ἐστιν ὅτι καὶ ὁ ἄνεμος καὶ θάλασσα ὑπακούει αὐτῷ; (Mark 4:41)

And they feared with a great fear and said to one another, "Who then is this, that even the wind and the sea obey him?" (my translation)

These similarities cause T. A. Burkill to conclude, "The wind is rebuked as though it were a storm-demon which has taken possession of the sea for a time."[57] Likewise, Pamela Thimmes casts this "biblical sea-storm type-scene" as an exorcism, commenting, "Exorcisms are a common way of displaying this [Jesus'] power (1:21–28; 5:1–20; 8:33; 9:14–29), so the fact that Jesus performs an exorcism is not unusual." Nevertheless, she adds, "What is unusual is the subject: the sea."[58] Moreover, she rightly observes, Jesus' rebuke to his disciples "is not a conventional exorcistic display of Jesus' authority."[59]

The difficulty with using Mark 1:23–27 to interpret Mark 4:35–41 as an exorcism is that in Mark 4:35–41, Jesus does not order out any force of any kind, but only orders silence. So if one even conjectures that a demon was hidden in the storm somehow, this would be the first time that Jesus allowed it to stay and just remain muzzled. Thus, this would not be an exorcism at all, since in an exorcism the demon must depart, not just remain silent.

The Wind and the Sea as Rational Entities

Jesus' address to the wind and sea is probably a chief factor in convincing scholars that a demon must be present. Key here is the recognition that by the first century C.E., the four components of creation—wind, water, earth, fire—were considered to be intelligent

---

[57] T. A. Burkill, "The Notion of Miracle with Special Reference to St. Mark's Gospel," *ZNW* 50 (1959): 38. See also Kertelge, *Die Wunder Jesu*, 95–96.

[58] Thimmes, *Biblical Sea-Storm*, 141.

[59] Ibid.

entities[60] and were attributed with an untrammeled knowledge of the truth.[61] The first study of what would become the "new" cosmology is attributed to Pythagoras (580–500 B.C.E.), and his intimacy with nature's components resulted in his being freely addressed by them. Among the legends that remark on this relationship is this story of the mutual greeting of Pythagoras and the river Caucasus reported by Porphyry: "It is said that the river Caucasus, while he [Pythagoras], with many of his associates, was passing over it, said to him very clearly, 'Hail, Pythagoras!'" (*Vit. Pyth.* 27).[62]

This growing recognition of the elements as rational entities is evinced in the address of them in various historical accounts and adventure novels. Regarding historical reports, Herodotus describes Xerxes' fury when a sea storm destroyed a bridge that he had been building across the Hellespont, so that he ordered the sea to be given three hundred lashes. Those scourging the sea were ordered to upbraid it while doing so: "You bitter water, our master punishes you, because you did him wrong although he had done no wrong to you" (*Hist.* 7.35).[63] As for the "novels," the address to the sea is common, as in Chariton's second-century C.E. *Chaereas and Callirhoe.* There the hero, searching for his wife, boards a ship and calls out, "Sea! Take me over the same route as you took Callirhoe!" (*Chaer.* 3.5),[64] and later cries, "Kindly sea! Why have you pre-

---

[60] For a discussion of the "new cosmology" that typifies the Hellenistic and Greco-Roman period with its implications for the wind and sea, see Cotter, "Markan Sea Miracles," 152–80.

[61] On the manner in which this concept was integral to the many rituals of divination, see John Pollard, "Divination and Oracles: Greece," in vol. 2 of *Civilization of the Ancient Mediterranean: Greece and Rome* (ed. Michael Grant and Rachel Kitzinger; New York: Scribner, 1988), 941–50; John Ferguson, "Divination and Oracles: Rome," in vol. 2 of *Civilization of the Ancient Mediterranean* (ed. Grant and Kitzinger), 951–58; Fritz Graf, *Magic in the Ancient World* (trans. Franklin Philip; RA 10; Cambridge, Mass.: Harvard University Press, 1997); Tamsyn Barton, "Greece and Rome," in *Ancient Astrology* (London: Routledge, 1994), 32–63.

[62] Porphyry, *The Life of Pythagoras*, in *The Pythagorean Sourcebook and Library: An Anthology of Ancient Writings Which Relate to Pythagoras and Pythagorean Philosophy* (trans. Kenneth Sylvan Guthrie et al.; Grand Rapids: Phanes Press, 1987), 128.

[63] Herodotus, *The Persian Wars* (trans. A. D. Godley; 4 vols.; LCL; Cambridge, Mass.: Harvard University Press, 1922), 3:334.

[64] Chariton, *Chaereas and Callirhoe*, in *Collected Ancient Greek Novels* (ed. B. P. Reardon; Berkeley: University of California Press, 1989), 59.

served me so far?" (*Chaer.* 3.6)[65] And in Achilles Tatius's *Leucippe and Cleitophon*, the hero, Cleitophon, pleads with the sea for his life: "O Sea! You spared my life when I was sailing across you, but after saving me you destroyed me by sending two corpses to haunt me" (*Leuc. Clit.* 5.26).[66]

Such addresses to the sea illustrate that Jesus' command to the wind and the sea would not have invited ideas of demon possession, or of the primordial myths of Marduk and Tiamat, if such myths were even available in the first century. This is not to say that the obedience of the sea to Jesus does not carry a cosmic message of his divine authorization and his significance to the world, something recognized by the elements, which know all. But it does show that exorcism would not have occurred to the listener. The sea was famous for its mercurial character, as Heliodorus shows in his description of the sea storm in *An Ethiopian Story*: "The sea suddenly started to turn rough. This alteration may have been the spontaneous product of the moment, or perhaps the change was due to the whim of some fate" (*Aeth.* 5.27).[67] That uncertainty of the sea is well expressed by Melite in *Leucippe and Cleitophon*: "The moods of the sea are fickle; the winds cannot be trusted" (*Leuc. Clit.* 5.15).[68] When she speaks of the sea and the winds in a personified manner, she represents the perception of the times. These elements have a character and are not regarded in the objective manner of our own times.

Perhaps the strongest evidence that this is not an exorcism is the acclamation the Markan narrator gives to the disciples: "Who then is this, that even the wind and the sea obey him?" (Mark 4:41). Here the wind and the sea are treated in the usual manner of the Greco-Roman world, as knowing powerful constituent elements of the earth, not at all as demonized forces.

Conclusion: Of the three interpretations that rely on Jewish sources, the clear allusions to the Hebrew Scriptures identify Jesus as empowered by God. But even for a Gentile, the command of the forces of the wind and the sea attests to Jesus' divinity.[69]

---

[65] Ibid.

[66] Achilles Tatius, *Leucippe and Cleitophon*, in *Collected Ancient Greek Novels* (ed. Reardon), 248.

[67] Heliodorus, *An Ethiopian Story*, in *Collected Ancient Greek Novels* (ed. Reardon), 465. Fate is usually the reason for a storm, as we see also in Petronius.

[68] Achilles Tatius, *Leucippe and Cleitophon*, 240.

[69] It must be emphasized that in non-Jewish texts, Poseidon/Neptune, Zeus/Jupiter's brother, claims the realm of the sea as his own, and control of

Jesus and the Jonah Allusions

Although, as we have seen, certain similarities in vocabulary exist between Mark 4:37–41 (the calming of the sea) and Mark 1:23–27 (the exorcism in the synagogue), a far less examined similarity is the one between the miracle of Jesus calming the sea and the story of Jonah. O. Lamar Cope's study led him to conclude that the Jesus story "was already shaped in accord with the Jonah story in the oral tradition."[70] He lists six narrative elements shared by the two accounts: (1) a departure by boat; (2) a violent sea storm; (3) the sleeping hero; (4) the badly frightened sailors; (5) the hero's act that causes the storm to cease; (6) a marveling response by the sailors.[71] Mark 4:41 and Jonah 1:16 LXX even share an idiom, "fearing with great fear":

Jonah 1:16 LXX: ἐφοβήθησαν φόβῳ μεγάλῳ

Mark 4:41: ἐφοβήθησαν φόβον μέγαν

At the same time, Cope recognizes three important differences: (1) Jesus is not running away from God's command as Jonah is, and the sea storm is not a result of disobedience; (2) Jonah must be cast into the sea for the storm to cease; (3) geographically, the Jonah story takes place on the Great Sea, whereas the Jesus story occurs on the Sea of Galilee. Yet, the many parallels between the stories leave Cope puzzled, as when

---

the sea ultimately is his. In the lore of the imperial period, among the Olympians, both Athena of the Winds (Pausanias, *Descr.* 4.32.2) and Apollo Seafaring (Pausanias, *Descr.* 2.32.2) calm a sea storm for Diomedes, and Aphrodite does so in response to the prayers of Herostratus of Naucratis, who has brought her statue on board (Athenaeus, *Deipn.* 7.15.676a–b). Among the non-Olympians, the Samothrace deities (Diodorus Siculus, *Hist.* 4.43.1–2) and the Dioscuri (*The Homeric Hymns* 33.4–16; Diodorus Siculus, *Hist.* 4.48.7) are famous for being saviors on the sea. Foreign deities include Isis (*The Four Hymns of Isidorus* 1.1–2m 25–34, 39, 43, 49, 50; Apuleius, *Metam.* 11.5) and Serapis (Aelius Aristides, *Serap.* 45.33). For a discussion of the non-Jewish gods who intervene in a storm, see Wendy Cotter, *Miracles in Greco-Roman Antiquity: A Sourcebook* (London: Routledge, 1999), 132–37; "Markan Sea Miracles," 182–90.

[70] O. Lamar Cope, *Matthew: A Scribe Trained for the Kingdom of Heaven* (CBQMS 5; Washington. D.C.: Catholic Biblical Association of America, 1976), 97. Cope is to be credited with the close comparison of Jesus' stilling of the storm with the sea storm section of the book of Jonah, although he used the Matthean version of the Jesus story.

[71] Ibid., 96.

he says, "It is difficult to ascertain just what this evidence [similarity between Jonah 1:16 and Mark 4:41] means."[72]

I hope to show how the Markan narrator's leading the listener to think of Jonah serves the Christian teaching here. First, to clarify the number of points where the Jesus story in Mark 4:37–41 and that of Jonah exhibit parallels, over against the more popular parallel of Mark 1:23–27, the chart below compares all three.

MARK 1:23–27; MARK 4:37–41; JONAH 1:4–6, 15–16

I. The Situation to Be Addressed

A. A demonized man in the synagogue challenges Jesus

²³[...] ἦν [...] ἄνθρωπος ἐν πνεύματι ἀκαθάρτῳ, καὶ ἀνέκραξεν ²⁴λέγων, τί ἡμῖν καὶ σοί, Ἰησοῦ Ναζαρηνέ; ἦλθες ἀπολέσαι ἡμᾶς; οἶδά σε τίς εἶ, ὁ ἅγιος τοῦ θεοῦ. (Mark 1)

B. A storm arises and threatens the lives of those on board

*1. Wind and waves crash into the boat *(asterisks mark narrative elements that are the same)*

³⁷καὶ γίνεται λαῖ-λαψ μεγάλη ἀνέμου καὶ τὰ κύματα ἐπέβαλλεν εἰς τὸ πλοῖον. (Mark 4)	⁴καὶ κύριος ἐξήγειρεν πνεῦμα εἰς τὴν θάλασσαν, καὶ ἐγένετο κλύδων μέγας ἐν τῇ θαλάσσῃ, καὶ τὸ πλοῖον ἐκινδύνευεν συντριβῆναι. (Jonah 1)

2. The sailors are afraid and each calls on his god

⁵καὶ ἐφοβήθησαν οἱ ναυτικοὶ καὶ ἀνεβόων ἕκαστος πρὸς τὸν θεὸν αὐτῶν καὶ ἐκβολὴν ἐποιήσαντο τῶν σκευῶν τῶν ἐν τῷ πλοίῳ εἰς τὴν θάλασσαν τοῦ κουφισθῆναι ἀπ' αὐτῶν· (Jonah 1)

*3. The protagonist of the story sleeps while the storm rages

³⁸καὶ αὐτὸς ἦν ἐν τῇ πρύμνῃ ἐπὶ τὸ προσκεφάλαιον καθεύδων. (Mark 4)	⁵Ἰωνας δὲ κατέβη εἰς τὴν κοίλην τοῦ πλοίου καὶ ἐκάθευδεν καὶ ἔρρεγχεν. (Jonah 1)

---

[72] Ibid., 97.

*4. The protagonist is wakened and rebuked for his lack of care

³⁸καὶ ἐγείρουσιν αὐτὸν
καὶ λέγουσιν αὐτῷ·
[. . .] οὐ μέλει σοι

ὅτι *ἀπολλύμεθα;*
(Mark 4)

⁶καὶ προσῆλθεν πρὸς αὐτὸν ὁ
πρωρεὺς καὶ εἶπεν αὐτῷ Τί σὺ
ῥέγχεις; ἀνάστα καὶ ἐπικαλοῦ τὸν
θεόν σου, ὅπως διασώσῃ ὁ θεὸς
ἡμᾶς καὶ μη *ἀπολώμεθα.* (Jonah
1)

II. The Manner in Which the Situation Is Remedied

*A. The protagonist rebukes the superhuman force/s

²⁵καὶ
ἐπετίμησεν αὐτῷ
ὁ Ἰησοῦς λέγων·
φιμώθητι καὶ ἔξελθε
ἐξ αὐτοῦ. (Mark 1)

³⁹καὶ διεγερθεὶς
ἐπετίμησεν τῷ ἀνέμῳ
καὶ εἶπεν τῇ θαλάσσῃ· σιώπα,
πεφίμωσο. (Mark 4)

B. At his urging, the sailors throw the protagonist into the sea

¹⁵καὶ ἔλαβον τὸν Ιωναν καὶ ἐξέβαλον αὐτὸν εἰς τὴν θάλασσαν,
(Jonah 1)

III. The Results

A. The demon convulses the man and, crying out, leaves him

²⁶καὶ σπαράξαν αὐτὸν τὸ πνεῦμα τὸ ἀκάθαρτον καὶ φωνῆσαν φωνῇ
μεγάλῃ ἐξῆλθεν ἐξ αὐτοῦ. (Mark 1)

*B. The storm subsides and the sea becomes calm

³⁹καὶ ἐκόπασεν ὁ ἄνεμος καὶ
ἐγένετο γαλήνη μεγάλη. ⁴⁰καὶ
εἶπεν αὐτοῖς· τί δειλοί ἐστε; οὐ
[. . .] ἔχετε πίστιν; (Mark 4)

¹⁵καὶ ἔστη ἡ θάλασσα
ἐκ τοῦ σάλου αὐτῆς. (Jonah 1)

IV. The Response of the Witnesses

*A. The witnesses of the stilling of the storm are filled with a great
fear

⁴¹καὶ ἐφοβήθησαν
φόβον μέγαν (Mark 4)

¹⁶καὶ ἐφοβήθησαν οἱ
ἄνδρες *φόβῳ μεγάλῳ*
τὸν κύριον (Jonah 1)

*B. The witnesses ask each other who is this who can command such obedience of these superhuman forces

²⁷καὶ ἐθαμβήθησαν ἅπαντες ὥστε συζητεῖν πρὸς ἑαυτοὺς λέγοντας· τί ἐστιν τοῦτο; . . . καὶ τοῖς πνεύμασι τοῖς ἀκαθάρτοις ἐπιτάσσει, καὶ ὑπακούουσιν αὐτῷ. (Mark 1)	⁴¹καὶ ἔλεγον πρὸς ἀλλήλους· τίς ἄρα οὗτός ἐστιν ὅτι καὶ ὁ ἄνεμος καὶ ἡ θάλασσα ὑπακούει αὐτῷ; (Mark 4)

C. The witnesses offer sacrifice and make vows

¹⁶καὶ ἔθυσαν θυσίαν τῷ κυρίῳ καὶ εὔξαντο εὐχάς. (Jonah 1)

Conclusion: With respect to the elements of similarity between Mark 4:37–41 and Mark 1:23–27, only the two elements mentioned previously can be tallied.

First, there is the command by Jesus, "rebuke" and "muzzle."

²⁵καὶ ἐπετίμησεν αὐτῷ ὁ Ἰησοῦς λέγων· φιμώθητι καὶ ἔξελθε ἐξ αὐτοῦ. (Mark 1)	³⁹καὶ διεγερθεὶς ἐπετίμησεν τῷ ἀνέμῳ καὶ εἶπεν τῇ θαλάσσῃ· σιώπα, πεφίμωσο. (Mark 4)

Second, there is the response of the witnesses, "Who is this?" followed by the acclamation that the forces "obey him."

²⁷καὶ ἐθαμβήθησαν ἅπαντες ὥστε συζητεῖν πρὸς ἑαυτοὺς λέγοντας· τί ἐστιν τοῦτο; . . . καὶ τοῖς πνεύμασι τοῖς ἀκαθάρτοις ἐπιτάσσει, καὶ ὑπακούουσιν αὐτῷ. (Mark 1)	⁴¹καὶ ἔλεγον πρὸς ἀλλήλους· τίς ἄρα οὗτός ἐστιν ὅτι καὶ ὁ ἄνεμος καὶ ἡ θάλασσα ὑπακούει αὐτῷ; (Mark 4)

Since an exorcism features the expulsion of a demon, and not simply its muzzling, and since the disciples affirm that it is the wind and sea that obey, and no mention of a demonized force is mentioned, listeners would understand that this story concerns Jesus' authority over wind and sea.

The parallels between the story lines of Mark 3:37–41 and Jonah are remarkably similar. It is precisely in the climax of both stories that one finds the significant difference. Whereas Jonah must urge the sailors to throw him overboard into the sea in order to appease God so that he will stop the storm, Jesus rises from his sleep and orders the elements to cease their behavior. But this very action brings out another difference. In the Jonah story, the storm was sent by God and would have continued until Jonah was cast into the sea one way or the other. Jesus' order to the elements shows that the storm could never have taken down the boat. Thus, the sleep of Jesus is of a different kind. It is not the belligerent and defiant determination of the prophet to resist God and ignore the storm; rather, it is the confident sleep of the tired Jesus, who knows that no storm can sink the ship. His question to his disciples shows that he thought that they were aware of this and would also remain unshaken by the posturing of the elements.

This being so, the order given by Jesus to the elements is in fact totally unnecessary, except out of a love for the panic-stricken disciples. For he immediately rebukes the wind and sea in a kind of protective anger in regard to the panic that they have caused these men who were unaware of the impotence of the elements to drown them if Jesus is on board.

Thus, the story outshines Jonah not only with Jesus' power over the elements, but also in that the revelation of that power was only on account of the disciples' panic. It is only Jesus' love for them that causes him to manifest his authority in this way and sternly rebuke the wind and sea, calling for a restoration of calm, for the sake of the unknowing disciples.

What could the narrator count on being understood about his story, built on Jonah only to surpass it, by a non-Jewish listener?

The Greco-Roman World and the Hero Who Commands Wind and Sea

There are two classes of persons who were thought to have power over nature's forces: (1) the Pythagorean philosophers, such as Pythagoras, Empedocles, and Apollonius of Tyana; (2) military/political leaders, especially Julius Caesar and Augustus, whose followers longed to say that their divine empowerment resulted in nature recognizing their plans and knowing that these could not be obstructed.[73] Each of these concepts has its own positive significance to bring to the meaning of Jesus and his control of wind and sea.

Pythagoras, that holy philosopher who respectfully probed nature on a sacred quest to be allowed to know its secret principles and patterns, was in turn known by nature's elements, as we noted earlier in the chapter. Concerning his reputation for power over these elements that respected him, Iamblichus writes, "Many other more admirable and divine particulars are likewise unanimously and uniformly related of the man, such as infallible predictions of earthquakes, rapid expulsions of pestilences, and hurricanes, instantaneous cessations of hail, *and tranquilizations of the waves of rivers and seas, in order that his disciples might the more easily pass over them*" (*Vit. Pyth.* 28).[74]

The authority of Pythagoras over the elements is for the service of others. Iamblichus records public response to him in this way:

> Such was their [the people's] reverence for Pythagoras that they ranked him with the Gods, as a genial and beneficent divinity. While some celebrated him as the Pythian, others called him Hyperborean Apollo. Others considered him Paeon [Apollo as the physician of the gods], others, one of the divinities that inhabit the moon; yet others considered that he was one of the Olympian Gods, who, in order to correct and improve terrestrial existence, appeared to their contemporaries in human form, to extend to them the salutary light of philosophy and felicity. (*Vit. Pyth.* 6)[75]

It is notable that in these efforts to assign an identity to Pythagoras, the people sought out various roles of Apollo, as god of wisdom and

---

[73] These texts are part of the presentation of sources in my essay "Miracle Stories: The God Asclepius, the Pythagorean Philosophers, and the Roman Rulers," in *The Historical Jesus in Context* (ed. Amy-Jill Levine, Dale C. Allison Jr., and John Dominic Crossan; Princeton, N.J.: Princeton University Press, 2006), 166–79.

[74] Iamblichus, *The Life of Pythagoras*, in *The Pythagorean Sourcebook and Library: An Anthology of Ancient Writings Which Relate to Pythagoras and Pythagorean Philosophy* (trans. Kenneth Sylvan Guthrie et al.; Grand Rapids: Phanes Press, 1987), 91 (my italics).

[75] Ibid., 63.

healer. The popular idea that sprang to mind, as expressed by Iamblichus, "that he was one of the Olympian Gods, who, in order to correct and improve terrestrial existence, appeared to their contemporaries in human form, to extend to them the salutary light of philosophy and felicity," seems to express what many listeners might gather about the identity of Jesus due to his benevolent use of his power.

But Pythagoreans owed their authority over nature not to Apollo or any other god but rather to their philosophical focus on the secret patterns of nature, carried on with attention to purity and freedom from vice. The response of the people shows that they could only see this as connected to the Olympians, not to the quest for knowledge.

The disciples of Pythagoras, due to their continuation of the philosophical quest for knowledge of nature, also enjoy nature's acquiescence to their desires. Diogenes Laertius, dependent on the biographer Satyrus (ca. third century C.E.), quotes Empedocles:

> And thou shalt learn all the drugs that are a defence to ward off ills and old age, since for thee alone shall I accomplish all this. *Thou shalt arrest the violence of the unwearied winds that arise and sweep the earth, laying waste the cornfields with their blast; and again, if thou so wilt, thou shalt call back the winds in requital.* Thou shalt make after the dark rain a seasonable drought for men, and again after the summer drought thou shalt cause tree-nourishing streams to pour from the sky. (*Vit. phil.* 8.59)[76]

Again, these disciples use their authority over nature to help others.

Iamblichus records others who were reputed to enjoy this easy relationship with nature's forces:

> The power of effecting miracles of this kind [predictions of earthquakes, expulsion of diseases and hurricanes, instantaneous cessations of hail, and tranquilizations of seas and rivers] was achieved by Empedocles of Agrigentum, Epimenides the Cretan, and Abaris the Hyperborean, and these they performed in many places. Their deeds were so manifest that Empedocles was named a *wind-stiller*, Epimenides an *expiator*, and Abaris an *air-walker*. (*Vit. Pyth.* 28)[77]

---

[76] Diogenes Laertius, *Lives of Eminent Philosophers* (trans. R. D. Hicks; 2 vols.; LCL; London: Heinemann; New York: Putnam, 1925), 2:375 (my italics).

[77] Iamblichus, *Life of Pythagoras* (trans. Guthrie), 91.

Apollonius of Tyana, a holy man of the first century,[78] claimed to be a Pythagorean, and like the founder, he was honored by nature's forces so that he could control them, and always for a beneficent reason. Philostratus relates a story that indicates public recognition of his powers over the sea:

> It was already autumn and the sea was not much to be trusted. They [the people sailing for Aeolia] all then regarded Apollonius as *one who was master of the tempest and of fire and of perils of all sorts*, and so wished to go on board with him, and begged him to allow them to share the voyage with him. But as the company was many times too great for the ship, spying a larger ship, . . . he said: "Let us go on board this, for it is a good thing to get home safely with as many as may be." (*Vit. Apoll.* 4.13)[79]

This story shows that the people simply know that the forces of the sea will not rise up against this philosopher, but the reason that he is "master of the tempest" is not due to his authorization by a god. Here, it is just the understanding that Apollonius is recognized by nature due to his own holy life, not through a deity's empowerment.

These two ideas prove to have been available to the populace in the Greco-Roman period. The first is articulated by Iamblichus, where the people presume that the reason for Pythagoras's miracles is that he is a deity come to teach wisdom and happiness to those on earth; the second is simply that nature's forces hold Pythagoras in respect and obey his wishes.

---

[78] Scholars have identified such men as θεῖος ἄνδρες. For a treatment of the understanding of the "divine man," see Hans Dieter Betz, "Gottmensch II," in vol. 12 of *Reallexikon für Antike und Christentum: Sachwörterbuch zur Auseinandersetzung des Christentums mit der antiken Welt* (ed. Theodor Kluser et al.; Stuttgart: Hiersemann, 1983), 234–312; Morton Smith, "Prolegomena to a Discussion of Aretalogies, Divine Men, the Gospels and Jesus," *JBL* 90 (1971): 174–99; Moses Hadas and Morton Smith, *Heroes and Gods: Spiritual Biographies in Antiquity* (New York: Harper & Row, 1965); David L. Tiede, *The Charismatic Figure as Miracle Worker* (SBLDS 1; Missoula: Society of Biblical Literature, 1972); Paul J. Achtemeier, "Gospel Traditions and the Divine Man," *Int* 26 (1972): 174–97; Howard C. Kee, "Aretalogy and Gospel," *JBL* 92 (1973): 402–22; Jonathan Z. Smith, "Good News Is No News: Aretalogy and Gospel," in vol. 1 of *Christianity, Judaism and Other Graeco-Roman Cults: Studies for Morton Smith at Sixty* (ed. Jacob Neusner; SJLA 12; Leiden: Brill, 1975), 21–38.

[79] Philostratus, *The Life of Apollonius of Tyana* (trans. F. C. Conybeare; 2 vols.; LCL; London: Heinemann; New York: Macmillan, 1912), 1:371.

The other major source of ideas about those who have power over the sea come from the propaganda around military/political leaders, and these always hold that such power is a sign of divinization, empowerment from God as his select leader. A classic example is the famous story of Julius Caesar facing a raging sea storm and remaining confident that it could not drown him.[80] During his war with Pompeii (48 B.C.E.), Caesar crossed from Brundisium to Dyrrachium and waited for Marc Antony to cross there with troops. At nightfall, with no sign of Antony and fearing a mutiny, Caesar decided to return to Brundisium. Disguised as a messenger, he convinced the owner of a boat to take him across despite the sky that promised a storm. But Caesar was confident: "*Believing that Heaven was more true to him that he to Heaven, he ventured in the dangerous darkness to defy the sea.* . . . He knew that rashness succeeds when Heaven favours" (Lucan, *Bell. civ.* 5.500–503).[81] When the storm descended, the owner of the boat pleaded with his passenger to return. Then Caesar cast off his disguise to reveal his true identity to the man:

> But Caesar was *confident that all dangers would make way for him.* "Despise the angry sea," he cried, "and spread your sail to the raging wind. *If you refuse to make for Italy when Heaven forbids, then make for it when I command. One cause alone justifies your fear—that you know not whom you carry. He is a man whom the gods never desert,* whom Fortune treats scurvily when she comes merely in answer to his prayer. Burst through the heart of the storm, *relying on my protection.* Yonder trouble concerns the sky and the sea but not our bark; *for Caesar treads the deck, and her freight shall insure her against the waves. No long duration shall be permitted to the fierce fury of the winds: this bark shall be the salvation of the sea.* . . . You know not the meaning of this wild confusion: *by this hurly-burly of sea and sky Fortune is seeking a boon to confer on me.*" (Lucan, *Bell. civ.* 5.577–88, 591–93)[82]

Just as Caesar completed his speech, the wind tore the sails and broke apart the boat. The fact that Caesar did not drown was proof to

---

[80] Lucan, *Bell. civ.* 5.500–503; Appian, *Hist. rom.* 2.57, 150 (where Appian compares Caesar to Alexander the Great); Plutarch, *Caes.* 38.1–6; *Mor.* 319D; Suetonius, *Jul.* 58; Florus, *Hist. rom.* 2.35–38; Dio Cassius, *Hist.* 4.41.46.

[81] Lucan, *The Civil War* (trans. J. D. Duff; LCL; Cambridge, Mass.: Harvard University Press, 1962), 277 (my italics).

[82] Ibid., 283 (my italics).

him that heaven forbade it (Lucan, *Bell. civ.* 5.672–77). Plutarch comments, "Thus firmly was he convinced that Fortune accompanied him on his voyages, his travels, his campaigns, his commands; Fortune's task was to *enjoin calm upon the sea,* summer weather upon the winter-time, speed upon the slowest of men, courage upon the most dispirited, and (more unbelievable than these) to enjoin flight upon Pompey" (*Mor.* 319D [my italics]). With the combination of heaven's help and fortune's favor, Caesar considered himself a man set apart for greatness.

Caesar struck a coin upon which the Roman goddess Fortuna was modified to also communicate the goddess Tyche, so that besides the cornucopia that she carried in her left arm, her right hand touched the rudder of a ship.[83] This message was clear: with Fortuna on Caesar's side, all those aboard his ship had nothing to fear. Was it this story which introduced the modification to the Roman goddess Fortuna, so that her usual image of a woman holding a cornucopia became that of a woman with the cornucopia in the left hand while her right hand was on a tiller/rudder of a ship? With Fortuna on Caesar's side, all those on board his ship had nothing about which to worry. Upon his death, Caesar was officially declared divine.[84]

The easy elision from nature being subservient to someone empowered by the gods is shown in Calpurnius's sycophantic *Ecologue IV* in praise of Nero. There, the shepherd Amytas asks his brother Corydon, "Do you see how the green woods are hushed at the sound of Caesar's [Nero] name? I remember how, despite the swoop of a storm, the grove, even as now, sank suddenly into peace with boughs at rest. And I said, 'A god, surely a god has driven the east winds hence'" (*Ecologue IV,* 97–100).[85]

---

[83] Stefan Weinstock, *Divus Julius* (Oxford: Clarendon Press, 1971), 124–25.

[84] In 45 B.C.E. a statue of Julius Caesar was erected in the temple of Quirinius (the deified founder of Rome, Romulus), carrying the inscription "To the unconquered god" (Dio Cassius, *Hist.* 43.45.3). One year later, the senate declared Caesar a god (Dio Cassius, *Hist.* 44.6.4). Cicero, commenting on the honors given to Caesar even before his death, calls Antony *flamen divo Iulio* (Cicero, *Phil.* 2.110). See Weinstock, *Divus Julius,* 287–317. Until 45 B.C.E., Roman coins had always carried an image of a god. Julius Caesar's image was the first to appear on the money. See Weinstock, *Divus Julius,* 90–132.

[85] Calpurnius Siculus, "Ecologue IV," *Bucolica in Minor Latin Poets* (trans. John Wight Duff; LCL; London: Heinemann, 1961), 252–53.

Even Philo, a Jewish man of letters, in his metaphorical description of Augustus's political miracles for the Mediterranean world, draws on the notion that nature is commanded by an emperor divinely empowered:

> The whole human race exhausted by mutual slaughter was on the very verge of utter destruction, had it not been for one man and leader, Augustus whom men fitly call the averter of evil. *This is the Caesar who calmed the torrential storms on every side,* who healed pestilences common to Greeks and barbarians, pestilences which descending from the south and east coursed to the west and north sowing the seed of calamity over the places and waters which lay between. (*Embassy* 144–45)[86]

This use of the metaphor would have been very well understood, as Artemidorus Daldianus, a second-century C.E. collector of dream interpretations, attests the connections between storms and situations in life when he reports what it means to even dream of a storm: "Blustering and violent winds signify men who are annoying and heedless. Hurricanes and fierce winds bring danger and great disturbances in their wake." (*Onir.* 2.36).[87] Philo's use of metaphor for miracle indicates how stilling a storm, in the political sense, indicates a kind of world power that removes the dangers and restores peace. This is not to deny the brutality of the legions that maintained that "peace" or the other forms of robbery and extortion that characterized so much of the administration. But Philo used this language in an effort to present to Gaius the ideals of soul and the virtuous use of his authorization from above to overcome the chaotic forces of the world with a command for the cessation of these storms so that peace might reign.

Summary: These two types of heroes and the propaganda about them show that the idea of a man controlling wind and sea was not foreign or new to the world of Greco-Roman antiquity. The main significance that it held was that of a god come to earth, like Pythagoras, or that God had empowered a special man to do his will on earth. This latter meaning was the one that the Romans longed to claim for Julius Caesar and most certainly for Augustus, for it sanctified imperial decisions.

---

[86] Philo of Alexandria, *On the Embassy to Gaius*, vol. 10 of *Philo* (trans. F. H. Colson; LCL; Cambridge, Mass.: Harvard University Press, 1939), 72–75 (my italics).

[87] Artemidorus Daldianus, *Onir.* 2.36. Translation by Dr. Gregory W. Dobrov, Loyola University, Chicago, Illinois.

The Final Characterization of Jesus

The listener to his story would understand that Jesus' presence on earth was that of a god or that Jesus shows himself to be divinely empowered by God to bring about his will on earth. The context of the story shows the character of Jesus' use of that divine authorization. Only in the face of the disciples' alarm did he command the elements to be silent. His startling and surprising response to the disciples' reproach "Do you not care that we are perishing?" shows that giving them reassurance is paramount. Here is a major difference between Jesus' use of power and the story about Caesar's claim to it. Jesus, unlike Caesar, does not exhort his disciples to be courageous and unconcerned because with him aboard they cannot drown. Instead, he rebukes the elements that have frightened them, and only after the calm is restored does he reply with his own questions about their lack of understanding.

More than an example of *philanthrōpia* such as Jesus shows to petitioners unknown to him, this story demonstrates Jesus' love for his disciples and his desire that they be sure of his care. Jesus uses his cosmic power for establishing peace of heart.

The Final Characterization of the Disciples

⁴¹καὶ ἐφοβήθησαν φόβον μέγαν καὶ ἔλεγον πρὸς ἀλλήλους· τίς ἄρα οὗτός ἐστιν ὅτι καὶ ὁ ἄνεμος καὶ ἡ θάλασσα ὑπακούει αὐτῷ;

⁴¹And they feared with a great fear and said to one another, "Who then is this, that even the wind and the sea obey him?"

The disciples fear and their awe-struck question illustrate their realization that they have not known Jesus. Their reproach to Jesus belongs to their ignorance of his truly divine stature. The stunned question that they asked of one another surely was meant to be answered by the listener.

CONCLUSION

In this story, the context of the frightened disciples and their question "Do you not care that we are perishing?" followed by Jesus' silencing of the storm holds a teaching greater than the fact that Jesus has power over wind and sea, that Jesus acts with God's power to effect his will on earth. The context addresses Jesus' love for vulnerable, weak disciples who may doubt his care. In the other miracles where petitioners unknown to Jesus display rough or rude behavior, his kindness acts as a lesson of the attitudes of acceptance and compassion, understanding and "meekness." The purpose of this story, I suggest, is to engender confidence in the community about the life-threatening circumstances that surround them. The associations are those articulated by Artemidorus: "Winds that are boisterous and violent signify men who are unpleasant and brutal. Tempests and whirlwinds portend dangers and great disturbances" (*Onir.* 2.26). The Jesus story promises that no sociopolitical life-threatening force should shake them, for Jesus' commitment to them will prevent their destruction by any seemingly murderous "storm."

8

The Sea-Walking Jesus and His Disciples (Mark 6:45–52)[1]

"Thy way was through the sea, thy path through the great waters; yet thy footsteps were unseen" (Ps 77:19 RSV)

"[The sea] portends uncommon profit and great celebrity for all those who, like government officials and popular leaders, depend on the masses for their livelihood; for the sea, like the masses, is chaotic." (Artemidorus Daldianus, *Onir.* 3.16)[2]

The story of Jesus walking on the water is situated in the Markan Gospel so that it follows his feeding of the five thousand, another "nature miracle." There, Jesus uses his authority over nature to feed a multitude of hungry people. The connection of these two explains Mark's reference to the disciples' continued confusion over the "loaves" at the conclusion of this sea miracle story (Mark 6:52). The walking

---

[1] Much of this chapter is dependent on my doctoral dissertation, "The Markan Sea Miracles: Their History, Formation, and Function in the Literary Context of Greco-Roman Antiquity" (PhD diss., University of St. Michael's College, 1991). Since then, other scholars have drawn on that work and continued the research, such as Adela Yarbro Collins, "Rulers, Divine Men, and Walking on the Water Mark (6:45–52)," in *Religious Propaganda and Missionary Competition in the New Testament World: Essays Honoring Dieter Georgi* (NovTSup 74; Leiden: Brill, 1994), 207–28. While the meaning of the image of walking on water was rich and varied, as will be shown, the way in which the narrator juxtaposed the grandeur of the miraculous power shown by Jesus with his surrender of that power to comfort the weak and fragile disciples shows that more study is required on the portrait of Jesus' person as revealed in this anecdote.

[2] Translation by Dr. Gregory W. Dobrov, Loyola University, Chicago, Illinois.

on the water is a discrete account, however, and does not require any attachment to the feeding of the five thousand. The issue being explored here is what function the story of Jesus walking on the water served apart from the Gospel and prior to its attachment to any other miracle story. What message does the narrator communicate through this anecdote?

I. MARK 6:45–52: SIGNS OF MARKAN REDACTION

[45]καὶ εὐθὺς ἠνάγκασεν τοὺς μαθητὰς αὐτοῦ ἐμβῆναι εἰς τὸ πλοῖον καὶ προάγειν εἰς τὸ πέραν πρὸς Βηθσαϊδάν, ἕως αὐτὸς ἀπολύει τὸν ὄχλον. [46]καὶ ἀποταξάμενος αὐτοῖς ἀπῆλθεν εἰς τὸ ὄρος προσεύξασθαι. [47]καὶ ὀψίας γενομένης ἦν τὸ πλοῖον ἐν μέσῳ τῆς θαλάσσης, καὶ αὐτὸς μόνος ἐπὶ τῆς γῆς. [48]καὶ ἰδὼν αὐτοὺς βασανιζομένους ἐν τῷ ἐλαύνειν, ἦν γὰρ ὁ ἄνεμος ἐναντίος αὐτοῖς, περὶ τετάρτην φυλακὴν τῆς νυκτὸς ἔρχεται πρὸς αὐτοὺς περιπατῶν ἐπὶ τῆς θαλάσσης καὶ ἤθελεν παρελθεῖν αὐτούς. [49]οἱ δὲ ἰδόντες αὐτὸν ἐπὶ τῆς θαλάσσης περιπατοῦντα ἔδοξαν ὅτι φάντασμά ἐστιν, καὶ ἀνέκραξαν· [50]πάντες γὰρ αὐτὸν εἶδον καὶ ἐταράχθησαν. ὁ δὲ εὐθὺς ἐλάλησεν μετ᾽ αὐτῶν, καὶ λέγει αὐτοῖς· θαρσεῖτε, ἐγώ εἰμι· μὴ φοβεῖσθε. [51]καὶ ἀνέβη πρὸς αὐτοὺς εἰς τὸ πλοῖον καὶ ἐκόπασεν ὁ ἄνεμος, καὶ λίαν ἐκ περισσοῦ ἐν ἑαυτοῖς ἐξίσταντο. [52]οὐ γὰρ συνῆκαν ἐπὶ τοῖς ἄρτοις, ἀλλ᾽ ἦν αὐτῶν ἡ καρδία πεπωρωμένη.

[45]Immediately he made his disciples get into the boat and go on ahead to the other side, to Bethsaida, while he dismissed the crowd. [46]After saying farewell to them, he went up on the mountain to pray. [47]When evening came, the boat was out on the sea, and he was alone on the land. [48]When he saw that they were straining at the oars against an adverse wind, he came towards them early in the morning, walking on the sea. He intended to pass them by. [49]But when they saw him walking on the sea, they thought it was a ghost and cried out; [50]for they all saw him and were terrified. But immediately he spoke to them and said, "Take heart, it is I; do not be afraid." [51]Then he got in to the boat with them and the wind ceased. And they were utterly astounded, [52]for they did not understand about the loaves, but their hearts were hardened.

⁴⁵καὶ εὐθὺς ἠνάγκασεν τοὺς μαθητὰς αὐτοῦ ἐμβῆναι εἰς τὸ πλοῖον καὶ προάγειν εἰς τὸ πέραν πρὸς Βηθσαϊδάν, ἕως αὐτὸς ἀπολύει τὸν ὄχλον.

⁴⁵Immediately he made his disciples get into the boat and go on ahead to the other side, to Bethsaida, while he dismissed the crowd.

The introductory εὐθύς ("immediately") is typical of Markan style (e.g., Mark 1:21, 29; 8:10). The verb ἀναγκάζω ("to force") appears only this once in Mark's Gospel. Henry Cadbury includes it among the strong emotional verbs of Mark's Gospel that Luke usually eliminates,[3] but there is no reason to deny strong emotional verbs to the pre-Markan tradition. The phrase ἐμβαίνω τὸ πλοῖον ("to get into the boat") occurs in the introduction to four other Markan compositions: Mark 4:1; 5:18; 8:10, 13.[4] These phrases serve Mark's sea-crossing motif to link pre-Markan material into a series of events. In this case, however, the narrative itself requires that Jesus separate himself from his disciples, who will sail away without him. It has been recognized that a disjunction occurs between the stipulated destination of Bethsaida and the actual destination of Gennesaret in the Markan summary statement that follows (Mark 6:53–56). Since Bethsaida and Gennesaret are on different sides of the Sea of Galilee, to say that the boat landed at Gennesaret, although headed for Bethsaida, would mean that somehow the boat turned around and headed back in the direction from which it came. Since Mark is the one who wrote the summary,[5] it is unlikely that he

---

[3] Cadbury further says of the entire section, "The section [Mark 6:45–8:26] is greatly at variance with Luke's tastes, which is only another way of saying that it is very typical of Mark" (*The Diction of Luke and Acts* [vol. 1 of *The Style and Literary Method of Luke*; Cambridge, Mass.: Harvard University Press; London: Humphrey Milford, 1919], 96).

[4] See E. J. Pryke, *Redactional Style in the Marcan Gospel* (SNTSMS 33; Cambridge: Cambridge University Press, 1978), 13, 14, 16.

[5] Scholars who recognize Markan composition in v. 45 as well as v. 53 include Rudolf Bultmann, *The History of the Synoptic Tradition* (trans. John Marsh; Peabody, Mass.: Hendrickson, 1963), 341; Martin Dibelius, *From Tradition to Gospel* (trans. Bertram Lee Woolf; 1934; repr., Cambridge: J. Clarke, 1971), 224; Ernest Best, *The Temptation and the Passion: The Markan Soteriology* (SNTSMS 2; Cambridge: Cambridge University Press, 1965), 79; T. A. Burkill, *Mysterious Revelation: An Examination of the Philosophy of St. Mark's Gospel* (Ithaca, N.Y.: Cornell University Press, 1963), 64; Karl Kertelge, *Die Wunder Jesu im Markusevangelium: Eine redaktionsgeschichtliche Untersuchung*

also inserted Bethsaida.⁶ It appears that Bethsaida belongs to the pre-Markan stratum. The reference to the crowd, ἕως αὐτὸς ἀπολύει τὸν ὄχλον, belongs to the present attachment of this miracle to the feeding of the five thousand, and it is an unnecessary addition to the discrete account. Thus, the story began with Jesus sending his disciples into the boat to go to the other side, to Bethsaida (καὶ ἠνάγκασεν τοὺς μαθητὰς αὐτοῦ ἐμβῆναι εἰς τὸ πλοῖον καὶ προάγειν εἰς τὸ πέραν πρὸς Βηθσαϊδάν).

⁴⁶καὶ ἀποταξάμενος αὐτοῖς ἀπῆλθεν εἰς τὸ ὄρος προσεύξασθαι.

⁴⁶After saying farewell to them, he went up on the mountain to pray.

Since any confusion over whether Jesus is taking his leave of the crowds or the disciples is due only to the attachment of this account to the feeding of the five thousand, the removal of that context makes it plain and understandable that Jesus is shown to say goodbye to his disciples. The element of Jesus going up on the mountain to pray necessarily belongs to the story itself and is not redactional.

⁴⁷καὶ ὀψίας γενομένης ἦν τὸ πλοῖον ἐν μέσῳ τῆς θαλάσσης, καὶ αὐτὸς μόνος ἐπὶ τῆς γῆς.

⁴⁷When evening came, the boat was out on the sea, and he was alone on the land.

(SANT 33; Munich: Kösel-Verlag, 1970), 35–39; Heinz-Wolfgang Kuhn, *Ältere Sammlungen im Markusevangelium* (SUNT 8; Göttingen: Vandenhoeck & Ruprecht, 1971), 217–18; Frans Neirynck, *Duality in Mark: Contributions to the Study of the Markan Redaction* (BETL 31; Leuven: Leuven University Press, 1988), 75, 78, 122; Rudolf Pesch, *Das Markusevangelium* (3d ed.; 2 vols.; HTKNT; Freiberg: Herder, 1984), 1:58 n. 58; Pryke, *Redactional Style*, 15, 24, 142; Johannes Schreiber, *Theologie des Vertrauens: Eine redaktionsgeschichtliche Untersuchung des Markusevangeliums* (Hamburg: Furche-Verlag, 1967), 102; Eduard Schweizer, *The Good News according to Mark* (trans. Donald H. Madvig; Richmond: John Knox Press, 1970), 143; Vincent Taylor, *The Gospel according to St. Mark: The Greek Text with Introduction, Notes, and Indexes* (London: Macmillan; New York: St. Martin's Press, 1955), 331.

⁶Paul Achtemeier explains the discrepancy very effectively in his reconstruction of a pre-Markan "catena," where this account would have been followed by the account of Jesus' healing of the blind man of Bethsaida. Achtemeier posits that Mark disturbed this arrangement when he created his section on the spiritual blindness of the disciples. He moved the story of the blind man story out of position to what is now Mark 8:22–26 ("Toward the Isolation of Pre-Markan Miracle Catenae," *JBL* 89 [1970]: 265–91, esp. 285–87).

Some scholars have argued that ὀψίας γενομένης may be Mark's addition,[7] but it is not exclusive to his hand, and here it performs the function of alerting the reader that even as night approached, the disciples were about midway. This clarifies that when Jesus goes out to the disciples in the third watch of the night, there will be a great distance to cover. The boat is not still close to shore. Thus, this verse clarifies that Jesus' walk on the sea will involve some distance.

Again, this verse belongs to the plot of the anecdote, to bring out the separation of the two parties. The advance of evening prepares for Jesus' going out on the sea at the third watch.

48a–cκαὶ ἰδὼν αὐτοὺς βασανιζομένους ἐν τῷ ἐλαύνειν, ἦν γὰρ ὁ ἄνεμος ἐναντίος αὐτοῖς, περὶ τετάρτην φυλακὴν τῆς νυκτὸς ἔρχεται πρὸς αὐτοὺς περιπατῶν ἐπὶ τῆς θαλάσσης

48a–cAnd seeing them struggling in the rowing, for the wind was against them, about the fourth watch of the night he came to them, walking upon the sea.[8]

This action constitutes the miracle, which frightens the disciples, and it belongs to the heart of the story.

48dκαὶ ἤθελεν παρελθεῖν αὐτούς.

48dHe wanted to pass by them.

The LXX allusions here, as will be discussed later, show that this is not a Markan intervention but rather is a careful identification of Jesus' power with that of the Lord.

49οἱ δὲ ἰδόντες αὐτὸν ἐπὶ τῆς θαλάσσης περιπατοῦντα ἔδοξαν ὅτι φάντασμά ἐστιν, καὶ ἀνέκραξαν· 50aπάντες γὰρ αὐτὸν εἶδον καὶ ἐταράχθησαν.

49But when they saw him walking on the sea, they thought it was a ghost and cried out; 50afor they all saw him and were terrified.

---

[7] The expression ὀψίας γενομένης (or something quite similar) is used six times in the Markan Gospel (Mark 1:32; 4:35; 6:47; 11:11; 14:17; 15:42), but Mark 14:17; 15:42 seem to belong to pre-Markan narratives. For a summary of scholarly judgments, see Pryke, *Redactional Style*, 11, 13, 15, 19, 22, 23. See also Alex Koch, *Die Bedeutung der Wundererzählungen für die Christologie des Markusevangeliums* (BZNW 42; Berlin: de Gruyter, 1975), 95 n. 18.

[8] This translation is somewhat literal.

Verse 49 belongs to the dynamic of the core story. Verse 50a, however, is a Markan γάρ clause, "for they all saw him and were terrified," which states the obvious but is meant to increase the drama of the moment.[9] This element is necessary to the account because it creates the encounter between Jesus and his disciples. It belongs to the main narrative.

[50b]ὁ δὲ εὐθὺς ἐλάλησεν μετ' αὐτῶν, καὶ λέγει αὐτοῖς· θαρσεῖτε, ἐγώ εἰμι· μὴ φοβεῖσθε.

[50b]But immediately he spoke to them and said, "Take heart, it is I; do not be afraid."

This response by Jesus belongs to the core of the story and holds no redaction.

[51]καὶ ἀνέβη πρὸς αὐτοὺς εἰς τὸ πλοῖον καὶ ἐκόπασεν ὁ ἄνεμος, καὶ λίαν ἐκ περισσοῦ ἐν ἑαυτοῖς ἐξίσταντο.

[51]Then he got in to the boat with them and the wind ceased. And they were utterly astounded.

Jesus' entrance into the boat belongs to the main pre-Markan anecdote. The response of the disciples such as we have it here shows signs of Markan composition. The use of the verb ἐξίστημι ("to be astonished") in witnesses to Jesus' miracles occurs in other Markan conclusions (Mark 2:12; 3:21; 5:42). Did Mark substitute his own favorite response for the previous pre-Markan conclusion? It is usual for the witnesses to make some acclamation, but it is not possible to argue from the absence of the evidence here. What can be said is that this response shows all the signs of the Markan hand.

[52]οὐ γὰρ συνῆκαν ἐπὶ τοῖς ἄρτοις ἀλλ' ἦν αὐτῶν ἡ καρδία πεπωρωμένη.

[52]For they did not understand about the loaves, but their hearts were hardened.

---

[9] See C. H. Bird, "Some γάρ Clauses in St. Mark's Gospel," *JTS* 4 (1953): 171–87. The majority of Markan scholars recognize Mark's hand: Bultmann, *Synoptic Tradition*, 216; Taylor, *St. Mark*, 330; Best, *The Temptation and the Passion*, 78; Kertelge, *Die Wunder Jesu*, 146; Kuhn, *Ältere Sammlungen im Markusevangelium*, 203 n. 1; Pesch, *Markusevangelium*, 1:60; Pryke, *Redactional Style*, 15, 24, 75, 91, 93, 94, 126, 129, 134; Schreiber, *Theologie des Vertrauens*, 98; Schweizer, *Mark*, 137, 142; Étienne Trocmé, *La formation de l'Évangile selon Marc* (EHPR 57; Paris: Presses Universitaires de France, 1963), 155.

This γάρ clause, besides showing signs of a Markan explanation, is surely redactional on other grounds as well, for it appeals to the confusion of the disciples over the miracle to which this account is now attached, the feeding of the five thousand, and it serves to underline the Markan theme of the spiritually obtuse disciples. Notice the use of the verb πωρόω, which recalls Mark 8:17, a Markan composition where Jesus rebukes his disciples for their hardness of heart as they worry over having no bread. The entirety of v. 52 belongs to Mark.

Summary: The discussion of the pre-Markan account then, will address the anecdote apart from the most obvious Markan additions, and with the possibility that Mark's portrayal of the response of the astonished disciples quite possibly replaced an earlier ending.

II. THE PRE-MARKAN ANECDOTE: THE SEA-WALKING JESUS AND HIS DISCIPLES

⁴⁵καὶ . . . ἠνάγκασεν τοὺς μαθητὰς αὐτοῦ ἐμβῆναι εἰς τὸ πλοῖον καὶ προάγειν εἰς τὸ πέραν πρὸς Βηθσαϊδάν . . . ⁴⁶καὶ ἀποταξάμενος αὐτοῖς ἀπῆλθεν εἰς τὸ ὄρος προσεύξασθαι. ⁴⁷καὶ ὀψίας γενομένης ἦν τὸ πλοῖον ἐν μέσῳ τῆς θαλάσσης, καὶ αὐτὸς μόνος ἐπὶ τῆς γῆς. ⁴⁸καὶ ἰδὼν αὐτοὺς βασανιζομένους ἐν τῷ ἐλαύνειν, ἦν γὰρ ὁ ἄνεμος ἐναντίος αὐτοῖς, περὶ τετάρτην φυλακὴν τῆς νυκτὸς ἔρχεται πρὸς αὐτοὺς περιπατῶν ἐπὶ τῆς θαλάσσης· καὶ ἤθελεν παρελθεῖν αὐτούς. ⁴⁹οἱ δὲ ἰδόντες αὐτὸν ἐπὶ τῆς θαλάσσης περιπατοῦντα ἔδοξαν ὅτι φάντασμά ἐστιν, καὶ ἀνέκραξαν· ⁵⁰ . . . ὁ δὲ εὐθὺς ἐλάλησεν μετ᾽ αὐτῶν, καὶ λέγει αὐτοῖς· θαρσεῖτε, ἐγώ εἰμι· μὴ φοβεῖσθε. ⁵¹καὶ ἀνέβη πρὸς αὐτοὺς εἰς τὸ πλοῖον καὶ ἐκόπασεν ὁ ἄνεμος . . .

⁴⁵And . . . he made his disciples get into the boat and go on ahead to the other side, to Bethsaida. . . . ⁴⁶After saying farewell to them, he went up on the mountain to pray. ⁴⁷When evening came, the boat was out on the sea, and he was alone on the land. ⁴⁸And seeing them struggling with the rowing, for the wind was against them, about the fourth watch of the night he came towards them, walking on the sea, and he intended to pass them by. ⁴⁹But when they saw him walking on the sea, they thought it was a ghost and cried out. ⁵⁰ . . . But immediately he spoke to them and said, "Take heart, it is I; do not be afraid." ⁵¹Then he got in to the boat with them and the wind ceased. . . .

The Characterization of Jesus

⁴⁶καὶ ἀποταξάμενος αὐτοῖς ἀπῆλθεν εἰς τὸ ὄρος προσεύξασθαι.

⁴⁶After saying farewell to them, he went up on the mountain to pray.

This is one of the three times in the Markan Gospel where Jesus is said to leave his disciples to pray (also Mark 1:35; 14:32), so that this reason belongs to the tradition and presents Jesus as a man of prayer. When Jesus goes up a mountain (εἰς τὸ ὄρος), it is usually followed by a manifestation of his heavenly empowerment. For example, he goes up a mountain to call his disciples (Mark 3:13), and when he is transfigured before Peter, James, and John (Mark 9:), and when he seats himself to prophesy the end of the world (Mark 13:3), and when he prays before being arrested (Mark 14:26). In the present story the location of the mountain explains how Jesus could see the boat out on the "sea," but his ascension of the mountain to pray also prepares the listener for a manifestation of his divine power/authority.

⁴⁷καὶ ὀψίας γενομένης ἦν τὸ πλοῖον ἐν μέσῳ τῆς θαλάσσης, καὶ αὐτὸς μόνος ἐπὶ τῆς γῆς. ⁴⁸καὶ ἰδὼν αὐτοὺς βασανιζομένους ἐν τῷ ἐλαύνειν, ἦν γὰρ ὁ ἄνεμος ἐναντίος αὐτοῖς, περὶ τετάρτην φυλακὴν τῆς νυκτὸς ἔρχεται πρὸς αὐτοὺς περιπατῶν ἐπὶ τῆς θαλάσσης· καὶ ἤθελεν παρελθεῖν αὐτούς.

⁴⁷When evening came, the boat was in the middle of the sea and he was alone on the land. ⁴⁸And seeing them suffering in the rowing, for the wind was against them, about the fourth watch of the night he came to them walking upon the sea, and he intended to pass them by.

What Does It Mean for a Man to Walk on the Sea?

Martin Dibelius concludes that this story betrays "deterioration" and "spoiling" of pure paradigms through the introduction of "foreign" (i.e., Hellenistic) material. In his understanding, a pure paradigm that had featured Jesus' assistance to his disciples during a sea storm was transitioned into a fantastic epiphany designed to reveal Jesus' nature.[10] From there it was attached to a sea story by means of Mark 6:48, "He meant to pass them by," which for Dibelius showed a typical "secular"

---

[10] Dibelius, *From Tradition to Gospel*, 95.

interest in the hero's intention that belongs to "tales."[11] As a result, the Gentile world was all too present in this story, which "could be applied in a Christian sense, but which on account of its air, quite unlike that of the Gospels, must be traced back to non-Christian influence"[12] and was representative of the efforts of the "Hellenistic church" in its outreach to pagans.[13] Dibelius's erudition is on display here, as he shows himself to be well aware not only of the popularity of sea storm stories but also of the miraculous deeds often afforded gods and heroes as part of these "tales." Rudolf Bultmann saw the element of Jesus' walking on the water not as an addition to some original paradigm but rather as the central motif of the account. The mention of the wind was simply a borrowing from Mark 4:39.[14] Bultmann was aware of Greco-Roman texts that made allusion to certain men crossing water dry-shod as a sign of divine favor, and in some cases, divine empowerment. The key figure here was Xerxes, whom the gods had allowed to build a bridge of boats to cross the Hellespont. As artificial as this is, it is instructive to note that even this achievement was seen to parallel in a human way the divine power of Neptune and suggest a man to whom nature's forces must bow. Something of this is captured in Dio Chrysostom's *Third Discourse on Kingship* when an imagined interrogator presents the idea to the imagined Socrates:

> "Socrates," said he, "you know perfectly well that of all men under the sun that man [Xerxes] is most powerful and in might no whit inferior to the gods themselves who is able *to accomplish the seemingly impossible*—if it should be his will, *to have men walk dryshod over the sea*, to sail over mountains, to drain rivers by drinking—or have you not heard that Xerxes, the king of the Persians, made of the dry land a sea by cutting through the loftiest of mountains and separating Athos from the mainland, and that *he led his infantry through the sea, riding upon a chariot just like Poseidon in Homer's description?*" (*3 Regn.* 30–31)[15]

This ability to conquer the powers of the sea is shown to hold as a powerful signal of divine favor. Why else would legends of Alexander

---

[11] Ibid., 77.
[12] Ibid., 100.
[13] Ibid., 92.
[14] Bultmann, *Synoptic Tradition*, 216.
[15] Dio Chrysostom, *The Third Discourse, On Kingship*, in *Discourses 1–11* (trans. J. W. Cohoon; LCL; London: Heinemann, 1932), 119 (my italics).

take care to claim, for example, that the Pamphylian Sea moved back to allow his crossing, the curling waves being interpreted as obeisance? The particular "miracle" is found in commentary by Eustathius (1110–1198 C.E.) on the *Iliad*, where the sea "did not fail to know its lord." When Callisthenes speaks about Alexander's crossing the Pamphylian sea, "even though he [Callisthenes] does not make the sea part before him [Alexander] in delight, as in making way before Poseidon, nevertheless [he] says that it withdrew from before his march as though recognizing him, and that it too did not fail to know its lord, so that in arching itself and bowing it may seem to do obeisance" (Eustathius, *On the Iliad* 29).[16] What does this attribution mean except that the crossing is interpreted as the sea recognizing the divine empowerment of Alexander, which makes him its lord, so that nothing natural is allowed to impede this hero's destiny?

Even Josephus draws on the accepted interpretation of such power over the sea to argue for the veracity of the account of Moses' walking dry-shod on the seabed itself, waters pulled back before him, and the conclusion to be drawn, that Moses was divinely authorized by heaven, and the seas knew it:

> Nor let anyone marvel at the astonishing nature of the narrative or doubt that it was given to men of old, innocent of crime, to find a road of salvation through the sea itself, whether by the will of God or maybe by accident, seeing that the hosts of Alexander, king of Macedon, men born the other day, beheld the Pamphylian Sea retire before them and when there was none, offer passage through itself, what time it pleased God to overthrow the Persian Empire; and on that all are agreed who have recorded Alexander's exploits. (*Ant.* 2.347–48)[17]

This kind of argument proves to be ubiquitous. See, for example, Plutarch's comparison of the Greek general Cimon (ca. 469 B.C.E.) and the Roman statesman and soldier Lucius Licinius Lucullus (ca. 88 B.C.E.),

[16] Lionel Pearson, *The Lost Histories of Alexander the Great* (Philological Monographs 20; New York: American Philological Association, 1960), 37. Callisthenes of Olynthus, Aristotle's nephew, was the first to compose a work on Alexander's exploits, which must now be recovered through quotations from later scholars.

[17] Flavius Josephus, *Josephus* (trans. H. St. J. Thackeray et al.; 10 vols.; LCL; London: Heinemann; New York: Putnam; Cambridge, Mass.: Harvard University Press, 1926–1981), 4:316–317.

because both had "noble and god-like natures."[18] Plutarch's proof for Lucius features a story of the Euphrates conforming to his plans. He had arrived at the banks of the Euphrates with the intention of creating a bridge of boats that would allow the men to cross dry-shod, but the turbulent river made those plans impossible. During the night, however, the Euphrates calmed so that the general could effect those plans.

> Here he found the stream [Euphrates] swollen and turbid from the winter storms, and was vexed to think of the delay and trouble which it would cost him to collect boats and build rafts. But at evening the stream began to subside, went on diminishing through the night, and at daybreak the river was running between lofty banks. The natives, observing that sundry small islands in the channel had become visible, and that the current near them was quiet, made obeisance to Lucullus, saying that this had seldom happened before, and that the river had voluntarily made itself tame and gentle for Lucullus, and offered him an easy and speedy passage. (*Luc.* 24.4–5)[19]

---

[18] "Heaven seems to have been kindly disposed to both, directing the one as to what he must perform, and the other as to what he must avoid. Both, therefore, may be said to have received the vote of the gods as noble and god-like natures" (*Comp. Cim. Luc.* 3.6) (Plutarch, *Cimon and Lucullus*, in vol. 2 of *Plutarch's Lives* [trans. Bernadotte Perrin; LCL; Cambridge, Mass.: Harvard University Press, 1967], 621).

[19] Ibid., 547. See also the example of the effort to attribute special portents in the Euphrates for the political success of the consul Lucius Vitellius (ca. 20 B.C.E.–51 C.E.]. Tacitus reports of Vitellius and the Persian king Tiridates meeting at the Euphrates to offer preliminary sacrifices before crossing the river to wage war against the Parthian king Artabanus: "During the sacrifice, while the Roman was paying the national offering to Mars and the Persian had prepared a horse to placate the river, word was brought by the people of the neighborhood that, without any downpour of rain, the Euphrates was rising spontaneously and to a remarkable height: at the same time, the whitening foam was wreathing itself into circles after the fashion of a diadem [the white band around the head of an Eastern monarch]—an omen of a happy crossing" (*Ann.* 6.37) (Tacitus, *Annals, Books 4–6, 11–12* [trans. J. Jackson; LCL; Cambridge, Mass.: Harvard University Press, 1931], 218–219). Tacitus, however, presents the other way in which this portent could be read, one that would cohere with actual history: "Others gave a more skilled interpretation: the first results of the venture would be favorable, but fleeting; for the presages given by the earth or the sky had a surer warranty, but rivers, unstable by nature, exhibited an omen, and in the same instant, swept it away" (*Ann.* 6.37) (ibid.). In fact, Vitellius did build a bridge of boats and made a successful crossing, and Tiridates was made king in Cresiphon in 35 C.E. However, his reign was short-lived, for King Artabanus regained his power in three years. The fact that this story and its interpretation

Perhaps the strongest evidence of the powerful significance that could be applied to someone crossing the sea with ease, without falling in, is the ride of Caligula (Gaius Caesar) across the Bay of Baiae in 39 C.E. on a bridge of boats. Suetonius calls it "a novel and unheard of kind of pageant" (*Cal.* 19).[20] Merchant ships were lashed together to span the distance between Baiae and the mole at Puteoli (a distance of three and a half Roman miles). The ships were anchored in double file, and the road over them had to be constructed in the same involved manner as the Appian Way. The description of his ride suggests that Gaius was trying to imitate Alexander:

> Over this bridge he rode back and forth for two successive days, the first day on a caparisoned horse, himself resplendent in a crown of oak leaves, a buckler, a sword, and a cloak of cloth of gold; on the second, in the dress of a charioteer in a car driven by a pair of famous horses, carrying before him a boy named Dareus, one of the hostages from Parthia, and attended by the entire praetorian guard and a company of his friends in Gallic chariots. (*Cal.* 19)[21]

Importantly, Suetonius offers the two most common interpretations of his behavior by the people, and then reports a third told to him by his grandfather.

> I know that many have supposed that Gaius devised this kind of bridge in rivalry of Xerxes, who excited no little admiration by bridging the much narrower Hellespont; others, that it was to inspire fear in Germany and Britain, on which he had designs, by the fame of some stupendous work. But when I was a boy, I used to hear my grandfather say that the reason for the work, as revealed by the emperor's confidential courtiers, was that Thrasyllus the astrologer had declared to Tiberius, when he was worried about his successor and inclined towards his natural grandson [Tiberius Gemellus], that *Gaius had no more chance of becoming emperor than of riding about over the gulf of Baiae on horseback.* (*Cal.* 19)[22]

This review underlines once again the power of Xerxes' feat for everyone, Gaius as well as the people, for Xerxes had overcome Posei-

---

survived indicates that people were ready to see in the obedience of free waters a divine acknowledgement of a legitimate, heavenly guided ruler.

[20] Suetonius, *Gaius Caligula*, in *Lives of the Caesars* (trans. J. C. Rolfe; 2 vols.; LCL; Cambridge, Mass.: Harvard University Press, 1959), 1:431.

[21] Ibid., 1:431–33.

[22] Ibid., 1:433 (my italics).

don and crossed the sea without being subject to his power. Second, Thrasyllus's use of a man riding over the water is clearly the example of what is impossible to a human being, but Poseidon's right. Interestingly, it is this element of power over Poseidon that comes out in Dio Cassius's report of Gaius's ride. The emperor had first offered sacrifice to Neptune (Poseidon), to other gods, and to Envy, "in order that no jealously should attend him" (*Hist.* 59.17.4)[23] The water had remained calm enough to allow the bridge of boats to hold. "This, too [the calm sea], caused the emperor some elation, and he declared that even Neptune was afraid of him" (*Hist.* 59.17.11).[24]

Most pertinently, Josephus comments, "He considered it his privilege as *lord of the sea* to require the same service from the sea as he received from the land. So the thirty furlongs from headland to headland were connected by pontoons, which cut off the whole bay, and over this bridge he drove in his chariot. That way of travelling, he said, *befitted his godhead*" (*Ant.* 19.6).[25]

These examples show how the image of traveling over the sea without falling in was considered a feat possible only for the divine, or those empowered by the divine. Poseidon/Neptune dare not create opposition to the destiny of such a person.

Artemidorus and the Meaning of a Dream in Which One Walks on the Sea

Before turning from the associations that were common for one who could travel on top of the sea, it is interesting to review the collection of associations that dream interpreters around the Mediterranean made with someone actually walking on water.[26] The point here, of

---

[23] Dio Cassius, *Roman History* (trans. Earnest Cary; 9 vols.; LCL; Cambridge, Mass.: Harvard University Press, 1914–1927), 7:313.

[24] Ibid., 7:315.

[25] Flavius Josephus, *Josephus* (trans. Thackeray et al.), 9:216–217 (my italics).

[26] Artemidorus Daldianus was a second-century C.E. man of letters who traveled around the Mediterranean gathering the dream interpretations that he found in various ports. "There is no book on dream-interpretation that I have missed in my zeal to acquire everything on the subject. Moreover, I have kept company for many years with the greatly-reviled marketplace soothsayers, ignoring the disparagement of pompous and supercilious critics who dismiss them as beggars, illusionists, and fools. I spent time at sacred festivals throughout the cities of Greece as well as in Asia, Italy and the most populous islands,

course, is not whether the associations are correct or not, but only that they provide evidence that such associations were common. In this way, we can see the way that Jesus' actual walking on water could also arouse these associations in the listener as portents. Artemidorus reports,

> "[The sea] portends uncommon profit and great celebrity for all those who, like government officials and popular leaders, depend on the masses for their livelihood; for the sea, like the masses, is chaotic." (*Onir.* 3.16)[27]

Since the listener would understand Jesus' role as a leader, the association with his walk on the sea, coupled with the divine association usually awarded such power, would suggest that Jesus was destined to bring great calm to the people and, if one thinks of it in its imperial context, to the world.

The Particular, Jewish Interpretation of One Who Walks on the Sea

Within the Jewish religious literature and tradition, two main "worlds" have been proposed to supply the interpretation of Jesus' walk on the sea. The first is the apocalyptic lens through which Jesus is seen to be controlling the chaos of the end time.[28] Reginald Fuller, however, interprets all of Jesus' miracles as a "sign of the dawn of the age of salvation, the end-time Reign of God."[29] "The theological point of this story," he claims, "is that in Jesus, God is asserting his sovereignty over the uncanny realm of Satan."[30]

The problem here is that the narrator has not supplied enough evidence of a satanic world, in contrast to the impression that one receives simply of rough water. It is notable that scholars who propose an eschatological or apocalyptic worldview for the interpretation of Jesus' still-

---

patiently recording old dreams and their outcomes. It was not otherwise possible to gain practice in this matter. I am able therefore to bring a wealth of examples [more than might be expected] to bear on each individual topic in order to speak truthfully without nonsense, adducing clear proofs in terms that are simple and accessible to all" (*Onir.* 1.1). (Translation by Dr. Gregory W. Dobrov, Loyola University, Chicago, Illinois.)

[27] Ibid.

[28] See Dibelius, *From Tradition to Gospel*, 95.

[29] Reginald H. Fuller, *Interpreting the Miracles* (Philadelphia: Westminster, 1963), 41.

[30] Ibid., 59.

ing of the storm, such as C. J. Cadoux,[31] C. H. Dodd,[32] Karl Kertelge,[33] and Lamar Williamson,[34] find no warrants for making the same claim for the story of his walking on the sea.

By far, the most common interpretation calls on the LXX[35] references to God's unique power to walk on the sea. For example, A.-M. Denis associates Jesus' walking on the sea with a similar miracle in Moses parting the Red Sea (Exod 14), Elisha parting the Jordan (2 Kgs 2:14; cf. 6:4–7), and Jonah quieting the sea by having himself flung into it (Jonah 1:13–15).[36] The power exhibited in these miracles belong to God, as one finds in Job 9:8, where περιπατέω is the verb that describes God's passing over the sea, as it is in Job 38:16, where God challenges Job, "Have you gone to the source of the sea? Have you walked [περιεπάτησας] on the waves of the sea?"[37] This image also occurs in Ps 77:19: "Your way was through the sea, your path, through mighty waters; yet your footprints were unseen," and Isa 43:16, "Thus says the LORD, who makes a way in the sea, a path in the mighty waters."

Where scholars are particularly sure of this is in the seemingly awkward note in Mark 6:48: καὶ ἤθελεν παρελθεῖν αὐτούς ("And he

---

[31] Cadoux only comments that the historicity of the miracle is doubtful (*The Historic Mission of Jesus: A Constructive Re-examination of the Eschatological Teaching in the Synoptic Gospels* [London: Lutterworth, 1941], 64).

[32] Dodd suggests that the walking on the sea is a postresurrection account that may have been "transplanted, whether intentionally or not, into a different context" ("The Appearances of the Risen Christ: An Essay in Form-Criticism of the Gospels," in *Studies in The Gospels: Essays in Memory of R. H. Lightfoot* [ed. Dennis E. Nineham; Oxford: Blackwell, 1955], 26).

[33] Kertelge sees an epiphany influenced by θεῖος ἀνήρ ("divine man") traditions, the miracle revealing the δύναμις ("power") and ἐξουσία ("authority") of the earthly Jesus (*Die Wunder Jesu*, 147–49).

[34] According to Williamson, Jesus' walking on the sea "is tied more specifically to Old Testament pictures of God" (*Mark* [IBC; Atlanta: John Knox Press, 1983], 130).

[35] *Septuaginta* (ed. Alfred Rahlfs; 2 vols.; 9th ed.; Deutsche Bibelstiftung: Stuttgart, 1935).

[36] A.-M. Denis, "Jesus' Walking on the Waters: A Contribution to the History of the Pericope in the Gospel Tradition," *Louvain Studies* 1 (1967), 284–97. See also Dennis E. Nineham, *The Gospel of St. Mark* (PGC; London: A & C Black, 1963), 180.

[37] Denis, "Jesus' Walking on the Waters," 292. Denis also includes the use of the verb in Sir 24:5, where Wisdom claims sole power to walk on the bottom of the sea (but this is another image).

intended to pass them by"). The identification of Jesus' power with that of God seems especially clear here because the verb παρέρχομαι occurs in contexts where the holy presence of God comes near. Ernst Lohmeyer offers as examples Exod 33:19, 22; 34:6; 1 Kgs 19:11, which describe God's presence "passing by" Moses and Elijah.[38]

1. Moses

Exod 33:19, 22 LXX

> ἐγὼ *παρελεύσομαι* πρότερός σου τῇ δόξῃ μου
> καὶ καλέσω ἐπι τῷ ὀνόματί μου κύριος ἐναντίον
>   σου· . . .
> ἡνίκα δ' ἂν *παρέλθῃ* μου ἡ δόξα, καὶ θήσω σε εἰς
>   ὀπὴν τῆς πέτρας
> καὶ σκεπάσω τῇ χειρί μου ἐπὶ σέ, ἕως ἂν *παρέλθω·*

"I will *pass by* before you in my glory,
    and I will call by my name 'Lord' before you. . . .
Now, whenever my glory *passes by*, then I will put you in
    a hole of the rock,
and I will cover you with my hand until *I pass by*."
(NETS)

Exod 34:6 LXX

> καὶ *παρῆλθεν* κύριος πρὸ προσώπου αὐτοῦ
> καὶ ἐκάλεσεν κύριος ὁ θεὸς οἰκτίρμων καὶ ἐλεήμων,
> μακρόθυμος καὶ πολυέλεος καὶ ἀληθινός·

And the Lord *passed by* before his face,
and he called, "The Lord, the Lord God is
    compassionate and merciful,
    patient and very merciful and truthful." (NETS)

---

[38] Ernst Lohmeyer, "Und Jesus ging vorüber," *NThT* 23 (1934), 206–24, esp. 216–19. See also Ernst Lohmeyer, *Das Evangelium des Markus* (KEK 1/2; Göttingen: Vandenhoeck & Ruprecht, 1967), 133–34. Harry Fleddermann proposes that Amos 7:8; 8:2 form a closer verbal parallel ("'And He Wanted to Pass by Them' (Mark 6:48c)," *CBQ* 45 [1983]: 389–95), but the difficulty is the context of God's anger at his people, wherein he tells the prophet that he will never pass by them again. However, Fleddermann's parallel underlines the use of "passing by" as an expression of a holy visitation.

2. Elijah

1 Kgs 19:11 LXX

καὶ εἶπεν ἐξελεύσῃ αὔριον καὶ στήσῃ ἐνώπιον
κυρίου ἐν τῷ ὄρει·
ἰδοὺ *παρελεύσεται* κύριος.

And he said, "You shall go out tomorrow and shall stand
before the Lord on the mountain;
behold, the Lord *will pass by.*" (NETS)

These allusions take place in deserted places when the holy presence of God comes near his chosen leader. In the Jesus miracle story, the context of night and the great expanse of the sea all around re-create the solitary circumstances when the presence of God comes near. The fact that Jesus has just come from a mountain where he has been in prayer only serves to associate Jesus' power to walk on the water with the power of the Lord as he "passes by."

Denis also draws attention to Job 9:11b LXX: καὶ ἐὰν παρέλθῃ με, οὐδ' ὡς ἔγνων ("If he passed by me, I would not even know").[39] Hubert Ritt agrees with Denis's references but concludes that the intent here is to show Jesus as the manifestation of God[40] because when Jesus calls out to his disciples to calm them, saying ἐγώ εἰμι, "Der tiefe Sinn dieser Formel ἐγώ εἰμι ist die Übertragung der alt Offenbarung des lebendigen Bundesgottes auf Jesus."[41] Ritt calls attention to Exod 3:14 LXX, where God gives his name to Moses using ἐγώ εἰμι (καὶ εἶπεν ὁ θεὸς πρὸς Μωυσῆν Ἐγώ εἰμι ὁ ὤν).[42]

Ritt claims that the rest of the account is meant to suggest Isa 43:1–3, where God promises to protect his people from water (Isa 43:2 LXX: "And if you should pass through water, I am with you; and rivers shall not overwhelm you" [NETS]), while Isa 43:10–11 LXX explains the miracle's significance: "Be my witnesses; I too am a witness, says the Lord God, and the servant whom I have chosen so that you may know

---

[39] Denis, "Jesus' Walking on the Waters," 292 n. 46.

[40] Hubert Ritt, "Der 'Seewandel Jesu' (Mk 6,45–52 par): Literarische und theologische Aspekte," *BZ* 23 (1979): 71–84.

[41] "The profound sense of the formulation ἐγώ εἰμι is the application of the Old Testament of the living Sovereign God to Jesus" (ibid., 81 [my translation]).

[42] See also Williamson, *Mark*, 130–31.

and believe and understand that I am. Before me there was no other god, nor shall there be any after me. I am God, and besides me there is none who saves" (NETS).[43]

This would be exactly the claim that one could make to any non-Jewish listener. Here, then, is an image that holds rich meaning for anyone in the Mediterranean world, Jew or Gentile. Jesus is clearly being identified as one who has been endowed with a cosmic mandate for the world, and it is one of peace. Unlike the stories of the emperors, whose actions on the sea are always in the context of war, this story features Jesus, who is from God and of peace.

This only serves to highlight the artificiality of the narrative around the attestation of Jesus' power to walk on the sea. How could Jesus be attested with this power unless someone sees him? When Jesus tells his disciples to go to the other side while he goes to pray, do they not wonder how he will travel there himself, alone? Then the story tells us that Jesus saw the disciples struggling with their rowing and went out to them. Yet this addition of "he meant to pass them by," for all its identification of Jesus' power with that of God, creates confusion. What was Jesus' intent in coming so close? (Matthew solves the problem by removing the note completely.) The storyteller is not content to have Jesus simply be seen. The narrator is not content to tell a story about Jesus' great power over nature's forces. The continuance of the story holds its own important attestation and revelation.

The Characterization of the Disciples

> [49]οἱ δὲ ἰδόντες αὐτὸν ἐπὶ τῆς θαλάσσης περιπατοῦντα ἔδοξαν ὅτι φάντασμά ἐστιν, καὶ ἀνέκραξαν·

> [49]But when they saw him walking on the sea, they thought it was a ghost and cried out.

The disciples are shown here to be extremely fearful. The portrait is not one of the brave and "manly" sort people who stand with Jesus, but rather one of very vulnerable people who are completely unraveled at what they see as a vision on the sea. The Greek word φάντασμα can convey the idea of a "vision" or an "appearance" as well as "ghost," but

---

Ritt, "Der 'Seewandel Jesu,'" 81.

certainly the idea is that they do see a human figure but cannot allow that it is actually a living human being. The context of night makes the facial features impossible to see. Their crying out makes it clear that all of them are in a panic.

This whole scene is so contrived! Trying to have Jesus' power to walk on the sea seen by credible witnesses means that Jesus will have to be clearly identified.

The Further Characterization of Jesus

⁵⁰. . . ὁ δὲ εὐθὺς ἐλάλησεν μετ' αὐτῶν, καὶ λέγει αὐτοῖς· θαρσεῖτε, ἐγώ εἰμι· μὴ φοβεῖσθε. ⁵¹καὶ ἀνέβη πρὸς αὐτοὺς εἰς τὸ πλοῖον καὶ ἐκόπασεν ὁ ἄνεμος . . .

⁵⁰. . . But immediately he spoke to them and said, "Take heart, it is I; do not be afraid." ⁵¹Then he got in to the boat with them and the wind ceased. . . .

The narrator has chosen a situation where the identification of Jesus happens only because he is concerned for their state of panic and changes his mind about "passing them by" in order to enter the boat and reassure them. This response of Jesus holds the key to the efforts of the narrator in forming this awkward story. The listener to the story would already have recognized that Jesus' walking on the sea is a claim to his divine empowerment, for the sea's submission to Jesus is a sign of its recognition of his special status, his authorization over the earth. The second part of the account illustrates that Jesus' power is oriented to bring peace, calm, and reassurance, not fearful obedience. His cheerful call, "Take heart, it is I," breaks the spell of the mystery, and his climbing into the boat brings a practical, comforting element to the story. At the same time, the cessation of the wind alerts the listener to the story that nature is in tune with Jesus' desires to bring complete calm to the disciples. He is the master. The contrast between the otherworldly power of Jesus and the earnestness with which he decides to join his disciples to calm them reveals his κοινωνία,[44] that special virtue connected to

---

[44] This virtue is found in close association with *philanthrôpia*, and especially in Plutarch, "il ne faut pas oublier les mots significant l'association facile avec autrui, comme κοινός et κοινωνικός que Plutarch lie aisément à *philanthrôpos*, ou bien significant l'abord facile, comme εὐπροσήγορος qui peut, à

philanthrōpia and especially to *praos* which emphasizes the importance of sharing things in common with the group, being one with the others. The story attests to the listener that Jesus' love for his disciples as they are, weak and vulnerable, makes him vulnerable to their needs. He halts the grandest example of his divine empowerment because his disciples are too fragile to bear it.

CONCLUSION

Although scholars have identified this story as an "epiphany" of Jesus' divinity, and others have emphasized it as a "sea story," both categories miss the narrator's efforts to show the cosmic power of Jesus being vulnerable to the needs of his disciples. There is no haughty rebuke for their fear, but the story shows the "meekness" (*praos*) of Jesus in respecting their limitations and helping them. Earlier in this discussion, we noted the story of Dio Chrysostom's *Third Discourse on Kingship*, where the interlocutor presented to Socrates the example of Xerxes' feat of crossing the Hellespont as a sign of his divinity. Now the answer of Socrates seems to fit here: "If for example, he was temperate, brave, and just, if all his acts were marked by judgment, I think he was a powerful man and really had the greatest might" (*3 Regn.* 32).[45] These great Stoic virtues are demonstrated by Jesus in the story, and they serve especially his own love for his disciples. The virtues of Jesus here hold a special message to the church of followers. I believe that this story was fashioned to impress on the disciples the immanence of Jesus in the community, and that his power will direct them through a safe crossing in a world that he will eventually bring to peace.

---

l'occasion, qualifier la *philanthrōpia*. Ils surtout le synonyme de *praos*" (Jacqueline de Romilly, *La douceur dans la pensée grecque* [Paris: Société d'Édition, "Les Belles Lettres," 1979], 277).

[45] Dio Chrysostom, *The Third Discourse, On Kingship* (trans. Cohoon), 119.

Conclusion

The Christ of the Miracle Stories

Rudolf Bultmann rightly notes that the importance of the miracle story is the person of Jesus: "[The miracle stories] are not told just as remarkable occurrences, but as miracles of Jesus." At the same time, Bultmann warns against seeing the miracle stories as in any way biographical, saying, "... their purpose is hardly biographical in the strict sense. The miraculous deeds are not proofs of his character but of his messianic authority, or his divine power."[1] It is true that the climax of a miracle anecdote is the act of power, but what Bultmann does not weigh is the purpose of the encounter, the anecdote itself, which functions in the stories we have examined here, as "biographical," so to speak. As Plutarch noted, it is in the gesture and the word that the character, "the soul," is revealed. Thus there is no need to choose between "biographical interest" and a demonstration or proof of "authority and divine power." Both can and do exist in the same narrative, as we have seen in these chapters.

Since Bultmann focuses solely on the act of power and the authority he concludes that miracle stories served to impress converts:

> They [the miracle stories] played a special part in missionary preaching as Acts 2:22, 10:38 show. The more the proof from prophecy was developed, the more the need for stories of Jesus was felt in connection therewith, especially of the Passion narrative. For the rest it is that the sheer weight of the extant tradition availed for its propagation even though there was no longer any concrete need for many of its constituent sections.[2]

If, however, the story was fashioned only to display the power of Jesus, one would expect narratives where the petitioner is treated as only an

---

[1] Bultmann, *History of the Synoptic Tradition*, 219.
[2] Ibid., 370.

avenue to the miracle of Jesus, such as Matthew accomplishes in his redaction of the Markan narratives, where the removal of awkward, irreverent, or distractingly challenging petitioners allows the spotlight to fall quickly and singularly on Jesus' miracle and his teachings on faith.[3] The evidence in these chapters, however, indicates that their narrators were keenly interested in the encounter, so that the light falls on both Jesus and the outrageous or presumptuous petitioner(s) as the miracle is effected. The function of such stories seems to presume an audience keen on observing Jesus' manner of receiving these petitioners, who are imperfect, poor, rude, rough, and objectionable to polite society.

An irony of sorts exists between the set of anecdotes where the petitioners are strangers and those where the needy are Jesus' own followers. In the former, the petitioners amaze Jesus with their bold determination, which Jesus names their "faith," while in the stories of the disciples, it is precisely their lack of confidence, their lack of faith, about which Jesus comments. In the Stilling of the Storm, for instance, Jesus remarks, "Why are you afraid? Have you still no faith?" (Mark 4:40); and he seeks to calm their fear in the Walking on the Water ("Take heart, it is I; do not be afraid." [Mark 6:50]) This pattern of difference between the miracles with stranger-petitioners and those with disciples points to a different function for each.

In Jesus' encounters with petitioners who are strangers, as in chapters 1–4 of this study, the revelation of his virtues in receiving people who are on the fringes of society (Mark 1:40–45; 10:45–52), non-elites/working people (Mark 2:1–12), and foreigners who would ordinarily be deliberately avoided (Q [Luke] 7:5–12 [dependent however on Matt 8:5–10]) suggest that these people actually provide a model for the virtues to be sought by followers of Jesus. In these accounts Jesus shows

---

[3] See Heinz Joachim Held, "Matthew as Interpreter of the Miracle Stories," (*Tradition and Interpretation in Matthew* [Günther Bornkamm, Gerhard Barth, Heinz Joachim Held, eds; trans. Percy Scott; Philadelphia: SCM Press, 1963] 165–299) where he illustrates this redaction in detail, "If miracles are passed over because they do not admit of any devotional interpretation, this shows that the miracle stories for Matthew are the bearers of a message, of teaching or admonition. . . . Their handing on and interpretation take place for the sake of the material statement they contain. They are intended to show the Church by means of the picture of the eathly Jesus who is her Lord, and what provision she might expect from him. . . . 'What Jesus once did on earth he does still'" (Ibid., 299).

more than his *philanthrōpia* and *praotēs*; he also shows *epiekeia,* what de Romilly expresses as *douceur,* a "sweetness," a "gentleness" in his astonishment at the confidence these petitioners have in him—again, what Jesus calls their "faith." Certainly, Elizabeth Struthers Malbon and Joel F. Williams are quite correct, then, when they identify the petitioners in the miracle stories as models of faith.[4] But therein is the challenge, because it is Jesus who identifies them as such, which means that his followers must be ready to abandon a cautious cultivation of public honor by conformity to social strictures and obedience to social norms in their outreach to others and, by the same token, abandon demands of special deferential treatment by those who come to them for help. Anyone who wishes to emulate Jesus' virtues must aim for his *philanthrōpia, praotēs,* and *epiekeia.*

As has been seen with the vivid petitioners of chapters 1–4, whose characters are communicated with only a gesture and a word, the stories of these encounters with Jesus survived until the first gospels and sayings collections because the dynamics in each encounter enrich the meaning of Jesus' miracle, because the act of power is contextualized as a response to that amazing, if bold, confidence in him. Moreover, petitioners are received with the same equanimity, respect, and concern, no matter their background or status. This presents yet another ideal for followers trained in the conventional rubrics of social encounter according to status and class.

The miracle stories of chapters 5 and 6, where parents petition Jesus for their demonized children (Mark 7:31–35, the Syrophoenician Woman; and Mark 9:14–29, the Father of the Demonized Boy) hold a special dynamic. In no way is Jesus' initial response to these parents meek or gentle, but rather it is dismissive and disapproving, for it is clear that Jesus holds them responsible for permitting a climate devoid of faith to allow the demon access to the child. The Syrophoenician mother shows no intention of turning to the one God of the Jews and the father of the demonized boy, who for lack of identification as a Gentile is presumed to be Jewish, demonstrates his doubt to Jesus ("But if you are able to do anything . . ." [Mark 9:22]). Yet in each story, the response of the parent to Jesus is heard by him, recognized for its own truth, and results in Jesus exorcizing the daughter and the son immediately. Perhaps here

---

[4] Malbon, *In the Company of Jesus,* esp. 198–205; Williams, *Other Followers of Jesus,* esp. 163–71.

the narrator shows Jesus in the role of the righteous Jewish prophet, but only to overturn that stiffness with the demonstration of his *praotēs* and *epiekeia,* the humility which allows him to see things in another way and grant generously what had been withheld.

In the stories where the needy are Jesus' own followers, chapter 7 and 8 (Mark 4:35–41: The Stilling of the Storm and Mark 6:45–52, The Walking on the Water), each story takes place on the open water, where the followers are alone and have their safety threatened. It is very easy to see in these accounts a message concerning the church moving through the darkness of political threat. It is in that darkness that Jesus reveals to his followers the scope of his power and authority that is not shown to any other petitioners in the gospels. In the Stilling of the Storm, as Jesus orders the elements to silence, that very obedience of the elements shows that they did not have authority to sink a boat in which Jesus sailed. Jesus' question to his followers also makes that point: "Why are you afraid? Have you still no faith?" (Mark 4:40). This story not only testifies to the ultimate authority of Jesus over the world's course, but it clearly claims that Jesus recognizes the fears of his followers and that he will use that cosmic authority to care for them, despite their weakness. In the Walking on the Water, Jesus stops his miraculous walk because the disciples have seen him and are terrified. Calling out to them to assure them it is he, Jesus prosaically then climbs into the boat with them to finish the crossing together. The divine power of Jesus to walk on the sea is not primary to Jesus. He can also show his human face to his disciples and be one with them to share the journey and restore their calm. It is clear that the function of these discipleship miracle stories both reaffirm the immensity of Jesus' divine authority over the cosmos, but, in the very same account, indicate how this is placed at the service of his weak and needy followers.

The survival of these miracle anecdotes of encounter in the pre-Markan collections and the Centurion story in Q indicate how frequently they were told within the Christian circles. More than the miraculous act itself holds center stage. The petitioners remain spunky, noisy, pushy, and outrageous. Jesus meets them on their own ground and moves to their side, recognizing their need, their confidence, and the rightness of radical resolution when salvation from disease, demons, death, or danger is within reach. The miracles of Jesus are always the climax of these stories, but inside the picture with Jesus is the petitioner, whose meeting with Jesus results in this manifestation of power and portrait. For, as Plutarch notes, it is in an anecdote that one can see a glimpse of the soul. In Jesus' meeting with bold and brash petitioners or with his own fearful disciples, with a gesture, a word, or both, Jesus reveals something of his soul. Thus the miracles made present not only the power and divine authority of Jesus, but his person, his portrait, even as his followers celebrated his resurrected presence among them.

Bibliography

A. ANCIENT SOURCES

Achilles Tatius. *Leucippe and Clitophon*. Pages 170–284 in *Collected Ancient Greek Novels*. Edited by B. P. Reardon. Berkeley: University of California Press, 1989.

Aelius Aristides. *Regarding Serapis*. Pages 261–68 in *Aelius Aristides and the Sacred Tales*. Translated by C. A. Behr. Amsterdam: Hakkert; Chicago: Argonaut, 1968.

Artemidorus Daldianus. *Artemidori Daldiani Onirocriticon libri V*. Edited by Roger A. Pack. Leipzig: Teubner, 1963.

——. *The Interpretation of Dreams: Oneirocritica*. Translated by Robert J. White. Park Ridge, N.J.: Noyes Press, 1975. Repr., Torrance, Calif.: Original Books, 1990.

Athenaeus. *Deipnosophistae*. Vol. 3. Translated by C. B. Gullick. Loeb Classical Library. Cambridge, Mass.: Harvard University Press, 1927.

Calpurnius Siculus. "Ecologue IV." *Bucolica in Minor Latin Poets*. Translated by John Wight Duff. LCL. London: Heinemann, 1961.

Celsus. *De Medicina*. Translated by W. G. Spencer. 3 vols. Loeb Classical Library. Cambridge, Mass.: Harvard University Press, 1960–1961.

Chariton. *Chaereas and Callirhoe*. Pages 17–124 in *Collected Ancient Greek Novels*. Translated by B. P. Reardon. Berkeley: University of California Press, 1989.

Cicero. *De Haruspicum Responsis*. Pages 312–401 in *Speeches: Pro Archia Poeta; Post Reditum in Senatu; Post Reditum ad Quirites; De Domo Sua; De Haruspicum Responsis; Pro Plancio*. Translated by N. H. Watts. Loeb Classical Library. London: Heinemann; New York: Putnam, 1923.

Dio Cassius. *Roman History*. Translated by Earnest Cary. 9 vols. Loeb
    Classical Library. Cambridge, Mass.: Harvard University Press,
    1914–1927.

Dio Chrysostom. *Discourses 1–11*. Translated by J. W. Cohoon. Loeb
    Classical Library. London: Heinemann, 1932.

Diogenes Laertius. *Lives of Eminent Philosophers*. Translated by R. D.
    Hicks. 2 vols. Loeb Classical Library. London: Heinemann; New
    York: Putnam, 1925.

Epictetus. *The Discourses as Reported by Arrian, the Manual, and Frag-
    ments*. Translated by W. A. Oldfather. 2 vols. Loeb Classical Library.
    Cambridge, Mass.: Harvard University Press, 1959–1961.

Eunapius. "Libanus." Pages 519–27 in *Lives of the Philosophers and Soph-
    ists*. Translated by Wilmer C. Wright. Loeb Classical Library. Cam-
    bridge, Mass.: Harvard University Press, 1922.

Euripides. *Fragments: Aegeus–Meleager*. Vol. 7 of *Euripides*. Translated
    by Christopher Collard and Martin Cropp. Loeb Classical Library.
    Cambridge, Mass.: Harvard University Press, 2008.

———. *Helen; Phoenician Women; Orestes*. Vol. 5 of *Euripides*. Trans-
    lated by David Kovacs. Loeb Classical Library. Cambridge, Mass.:
    Harvard University Press, 2002.

Galen. *Opera Omnia*. Vol. 6. Translated by C. G. Kühn. Hildesheim:
    George Olms, 1965.

Heliodorus. *An Ethiopian Story*. Pages 349–588 in *Collected Ancient
    Greek Novels*. Edited by B. P. Reardon. Berkeley: University of Cali-
    fornia Press, 1989.

Herodotus, *The Persian Wars*. Translated by A. D. Godley. 4 vols. Loeb
    Classical Library. Cambridge, Mass.: Harvard University Press, 1922.

Hippocrates. *Affections; Diseases I; Diseases II*. Translated by Paul Pot-
    ter. Loeb Classical Library. Cambridge, Mass.: Harvard University
    Press, 1988.

Homer. *The Odyssey*. Translated by A. T. Murray. 2 vols. Loeb Classical
    Library. London: Heinemann, 1919.

Iamblichus. *The Life of Pythagoras*. Pages 57–122 in *The Pythagorean
    Sourcebook and Library: An Anthology of Ancient Writings Which
    Relate to Pythagoras and Pythagorean Philosophy*. Translated by
    Kenneth Sylvan Guthrie et al. Grand Rapids: Phanes Press, 1987.

Josephus, Flavius. *Josephus*. Translated by H. St. J. Thackeray et al. 10 vols.
    Loeb Classical Library. London: Heinemann; New York: Putnam;
    Cambridge, Mass.: Harvard University Press, 1926–1981.

Juvenal. *The Satires.* Pages 2–307 in *Juvenal and Persius.* Translated by G. G. Ramsay. Loeb Classical Library. London: Heinemann; New York: Putnam, 1928.

Lucan. *The Civil War.* Translated by J. D. Duff. Loeb Classical Library. Cambridge, Mass.: Harvard University Press, 1962.

Lucian. "On Salaried Posts in Great Houses." Pages 413–82 in vol. 3 of *Lucian.* Translated by A. M. Harmon. Loeb Classical Library. London: Heinemann; New York: Putnam, 1921.

———. *The Parliament of the Gods.* Pages 419–41 in vol. 5 of *Lucian.* Translated by A. M. Harmon. Loeb Classical Library. Cambridge, Mass.: Harvard University Press, 1962.

Martial. *Epigrams.* Edited by Walter C. A. Ker. 2 vols. Loeb Classical Library. London: Heinemann, 1919–1920.

Nepos, Cornelius. *Cornelius Nepos.* Translated by John C. Rolfe. LCL. Cambridge, Mass.: Harvard University Press; London: Heinemann, 1984.

Persius. *The Satires.* Pages 311–401 in *Juvenal and Persius.* Translated by G. G. Ramsay. Loeb Classical Library. London: Heinemann; New York: Putnam, 1928.

Philo of Alexandria. *On the Embassy to Gaius.* Vol. 10 of *Philo.* Translated by F. H. Colson. Loeb Classical Library. Cambridge, Mass.: Harvard University Press, 1939.

Philostratus. *The Life of Apollonius of Tyana.* Translated by F. C. Coneybeare. 2 vols. Loeb Classical Library. London: Heinemann: New York: Macmillan, 1912.

Plato. *Laws.* Translated by R. G. Bury. 2 vols. Loeb Classical Library. London: Heinemann, 1926.

Plautus. *Trinummus.* Pages 96–220 in vol. 5 of *Plautus.* Translated by Paul Nixon. Loeb Classical Library. Cambridge: Mass.: Harvard University Press, 1912.

Pliny the Elder. *Natural History.* Translated by H. Rackham et al. 10 vols. Loeb Classical Library. Cambridge, Mass.: Harvard University Press, 1947–1963.

Plutarch. *Alexander.* Pages 243–439 in vol. 7 of *Plutarch's Lives.* Translated by Bernadotte Perrin. Loeb Classical Library. Cambridge, Mass.: Harvard University Press, 1967.

———. *Caesar.* Pages 442–609 in vol. 7 of *Plutarch's Lives.* Translated by Bernadotte Perrin. Loeb Classical Library. Cambridge, Mass.: Harvard University Press, 1967.

————. *Cimon and Lucullus*. Pages 403–621 in vol. 2 of *Plutarch's Lives*. Translated by Bernadotte Perrin. Loeb Classical Library. Cambridge, Mass.: Harvard University Press, 1967.

————. *Moralia, IV*. Translated by F. C. Babbitt. Loeb Classical Library. Cambridge, Mass.: Harvard University Press, 1936.

Porphyry, *The Life of Pythagoras*. Pages 123–36 in *The Pythagorean Sourcebook and Library: An Anthology of Ancient Writings Which Relate to Pythagoras and Pythagorean Philosophy*. Translated by Kenneth Sylvan Guthrie et al. Grand Rapids: Phanes Press, 1987.

Sophocles. *Oedipus at Colonus*. Pages 141–307 in vol. 1 of *Sophocles*. Translated by F. Storr. Loeb Classical Library. Cambridge, Mass.: Harvard University Press, 1962.

————. *Oedipus the King*. Pages 1–139 in vol. 1 of *Sophocles*. Translated by F. Storr. Loeb Classical Library. Cambridge, Mass.: Harvard University Press, 1962.

————. *Philoctetes*. Pages 361–493 in vol. 2 of *Sophocles*. Translated by F. Storr. Loeb Classical Library. London: Heinemann; New York: Macmillan, 1913.

Suetonius. *De Grammaticus et Rhetoribus*. Translated and edited by Robert A. Kaster. Oxford: Clarendon Press, 1995.

————. *Lives of the Caesars*. Translated by J. C. Rolfe. 2 vols. Loeb Classical Library. Cambridge, Mass.: Harvard University Press, 1959.

————. *Tiberius*. Pages 108–49 in *The Twelve Caesars*. Translated by Robert Graves. Rev. ed. London: Penguin, 2002.

Tacitus. *Annals, Books 4–6, 11–12*. Translated by J. Jackson. Loeb Classical Library. Cambridge, Mass.: Harvard University Press, 1931.

————. *Histories, Books 4–5; Annals, Books 1–3*. Translated by C. H. Moore and J. Jackson. Loeb Classical Library. Cambridge, Mass.: Harvard University Press, 1925.

Theocritus. "The Hymn to the Dioscuri." Pages 255–75 in *The Greek Bucolic Poets*. Translated by J. M. Edmonds. Loeb Classical Library. London: Heinemann; New York: Putnam, 1919.

Theophrastus. *Characters*. Translated by Jeffrey Rusten. Loeb Classical Library. Cambridge, Mass.: Harvard University Press, 1993.

Valerius Maximus. "Of Severity." Pages 38–43 in vol. 2 of *Memorable Doings and Sayings*. Translated by D. R. Shackleton Bailey. Loeb Classical Library. Cambridge, Mass.: Harvard University Press, 2000.

Vegetius. *Epitome of Military Science*. Translated by N. P. Milner. Translated Texts for Historians 16. Liverpool: Liverpool University Press, 1993.

B. TOOLS AND REFERENCE TEXTS

Bailey, James, ed. *The Universal Latin Lexicon of Facciolatus and Forcellinus*. Vol. 2. London: Baldwin & Craddock, 1828.

Billerbeck, P. and H. Strack, *Kommentar zum Neuen Testament aus Talmud und Midrasch*. 4 Vols. Munich: Beck, 1961.

Campbell, Brian. *The Roman Army, 31 BC–337 AD: A Sourcebook*. London: Routledge, 1994.

Cotter, Wendy. *Miracles in Greco-Roman Antiquity: A Sourcebook*. London: Routledge, 1999.

Dickie, A. C., and J. P. Payne. "House." Pages 770–72 in vol. 2 of *International Standard Bible Encyclopedia*. Edited by G. W. Bromiley. 4 vols. Grand Rapids: Eerdmans, 1979–1988.

Edelstein, Emma J., and Ludwig Edelstein. *Asclepius: Collection and Interpretation of the Testimonies*. 2 vols. in 1. Baltimore: John Hopkins University Press, 1998.

Fink, Robert O. *Roman Military Records on Papyrus*. Philological Monographs of the American Philological Association 26. Cleveland: Press of Case Western Reserve University, 1971.

Geikie, Cunningham. *The Holy Land and the Bible: A Book of Scripture Illustrations Gathered in Palestine*. 2 vols. New York: John B. Alden, 1888.

Goodenough, Erwin R. *The Archeological Evidence from Palestine*. Vol. 1 of *Jewish Symbols in the Greco-Roman Period*. Bollingen Series 37. New York: Pantheon Books, 1953.

———. *Illustrations*. Vol. 3 of *Jewish Symbols in the Greco-Roman Period*. Bollingen Series 37. New York: Pantheon Books, 1953.

Kloppenborg, John S. *Q Parallels*. Sonoma, Calif.: Polebridge Press, 1988.

Lefkowitz, Mary R., and Maureen B. Fant. *Women's Life in Greece and Rome: A Source Book in Translation*. 3d ed. Baltimore: John Hopkins University Press, 2005.

Mac Chombaich de Colquhoun, Patrick. *A Summary of the Roman Civil Law: Illustrated by Commentaries on and Parallels from the Mosaic, Canon, Mohammedan, English and Foreign Law*. Vol. 3. London: Stevens, 1854.

Mayor, John E. B. *Thirteen Satires of Juvenal*. 2 vols. Hildesheim: Georg Olms, 1966.

Metzger, Bruce M. *The Text of the New Testament: Its Transmission, Corruption, and Restoration*. 3d ed. New York: Oxford University Press, 1992.

Neusner, Jacob, trans. *The Mishnah: A New Translation.* New Haven: Yale University Press, 1988.

Pearson, Lionel. *The Lost Histories of Alexander the Great.* Philological Monographs 20. New York: American Philological Association, 1960.

Robbins, Vernon. *Ancient Quotes and Anecdotes: From Crib to Crypt.* Sonoma, Calif.: Polebridge Press, 1989.

Robinson, James M., Paul Hoffmann, and John S. Kloppenborg, eds. *The Critical Edition of Q: Synopsis Including the Gospels of Matthew and Luke, Mark and Thomas with English, German, and French Translations of Q and Thomas.* Minneapolis: Fortress, 2000.

Roussin, Lucille. "Costume in Roman Palestine: Archeological Remains and the Evidence from Mishnah." Pages 182–90 in *The World of Roman Costume.* Edited by Judith Lynn Sebesta and Larissa Bonfante. Madison: University of Wisconsin Press, 1994.

Rubens, Alfred. "Biblical and Talmudic Periods." Pages 5–28 in *A History of Jewish Costume.* New York: Funk & Wagnalls, 1967.

Smith, William. "Nudus/γυμνός." Page 409 in *Dictionary of Greek and Roman Antiquities.* Boston: Little, Brown, 1859.

Speidel, Michael P., and Silvio Panciera. "From the North and Black Sea Shores: Two New Gravestones for Boys of the 'Equites Singulares Augusti.'" Pages 353–60 in vol. 2 of *Roman Army Studies.* Stuttgart: Franz Steiner, 1992.

Symons, David J. *Costume of Ancient Greece.* London: Batsford, 1987.

Watson, G. R. "Documentation in the Roman Army." *ANRW* 16.1:493–507. Part 2, *Principat,* 16.1. Edited by H. Temperini and W. Haase. Berlin: de Gruyter, 1974.

Wettstein, Jacob. *Novum Testamentum Graecum.* 2 vols. Amsterdam: Ex officina Dommeriana, 1752. Repr., Graz: Akademische Druck, 1962.

Wintermute, O. S., trans. "Jubilees." Pages 35–142 in vol. 2 of *The Old Testament Pseudepigrapha.* Edited by James H. Charlesworth. New York: Doubleday, 1985.

C. SECONDARY SOURCES

Achtemeier, Paul. "'And He Followed Him': Miracles and Discipleship in Mark." *Semeia* 11 (1978): 115–45.

———. "Gospel Traditions and the Divine Man." *Interpretation* 26 (1972): 174–97.

———. *Mark*. Proclamation Commentaries. Philadelphia: Fortress, 1975.

———. "Miracles and the Historical Jesus: A Study of Mark 9:14–29." *Catholic Biblical Quarterly* 37 (1975): 471–91.

———. "The Origin And Function of The Pre-Marcan Miracle Catenae." *Journal of Biblical Literature* 91 (1972): 198–221.

———. "Person and Deed: Jesus and the Storm-Tossed Sea." *Interpretation* 16 (1962): 169–76.

———. "Toward the Isolation of Pre-Markan Miracle Catenae." *Journal of Biblical Literature* 89 (1970): 265–91.

Albertz, Martin. *Die Synoptischen Streitgespräche: Ein Beitrag zur Formengeschichte des Urchristentums*. Berlin: Trowitzsch, 1921.

Anderson, J. G. "Studies in Medical Diagnosis of Leprosy in Denmark." *Danish Medical Bulletin* 16, supplement 9 (1969): 6–142.

Barclay, John M. G. "The Family as the Bearer of Religion in Judaism and Early Christianity." Pages 66–80 in *Constructing Early Christian Families: Family as Social Reality and Metaphor*. Edited by Halvor Moxnes. London: Routledge, 1997.

Barclay, William. *The Gospel of Mark*. 3d ed. Philadelphia: Westminster, 1975.

Barton, Tamsyn. "Greece and Rome." Pages 32–63 in *Ancient Astrology*. London: Routledge, 1994.

Bernidaki-Aldous, Eleftheria. "Blindness as Ignorance: Seeing as Light, Truth, Moral Goodness." Pages 49–56 in *Blindness in a Culture of Light: Especially the Case of "Oedipus at Colonus" of Sophocles*. American University Studies 17/8. New York: Peter Lang, 1990.

Best, Ernest. *Disciples and Discipleship: Studies in the Gospel according to Mark*. Edinburgh: T & T Clark, 1986.

———. *Following Jesus: Discipleship in the Gospel of Mark*. Journal for the Study of the New Testament: Supplement Series 4. Sheffield: JSOT Press, 1981.

———. *The Temptation and the Passion: The Markan Soteriology*. Society for New Testament Studies Monograph Series 2. Cambridge: Cambridge University Press, 1965.

Betz, Hans Dieter. "The Early Christian Miracle Story: Some Observations on the Form Critical Problem." *Semeia* 11 (1978): 69–81.

———. "Gottmensch II." Pages 234–312 in vol. 12 of *Reallexikon für Antike und Christentum: Sachwörterbuch zur Auseinandersetzung des Christentums mit der antiken Welt.* Edited by Theodor Kluser et al. Stuttgart: Hiersemann, 1983.

Bird, C. H. "Some γάρ Clauses in St. Mark's Gospel." *Journal of Theological Studies* 4 (1953): 171–87.

Blomberg, Craig. *Matthew. The New American Commentary.* Nashville: Broadman, 1992.

Bornkamm, Günther. *Jesus of Nazareth.* Translated by Irene and Fraser McLuskey. New York: Harper, 1960.

Bultmann, Rudolf. *The History of the Synoptic Tradition.* Translated by John Marsh. Peabody, Mass.: Hendrickson, 1963.

Bundy, Walter E. *Jesus and the First Three Gospels: An Introduction to the Synoptic Tradition.* Cambridge, Mass.: Harvard University Press, 1955.

Burger, Christoph. *Jesus als Davidssohn: Eine traditionsgeschichtliche Untersuchung.* Forschungen zur Religion und Literatur des Alten und Neuen Testaments 98. Göttingen: Vandenhoeck & Ruprecht, 1970.

Burkill, T. A. "The Historical Development of the Story of the Syrophoenician Woman (Mark vii: 7:24–31)." *Novum Testamentum* 9 (1967): 161–77.

———. *Mysterious Revelation: An Examination of the Philosophy of St. Mark's Gospel.* Ithaca, N.Y.: Cornell University Press, 1963.

———. "The Notion of Miracle with Special Reference to St. Mark's Gospel." *Zeitschrift für die neutestamentliche Wissenschaft* 50 (1959): 33–73.

Cadbury, Henry J. *The Diction of Luke and Acts.* Vol. 1 of *The Style and Literary Method of Luke.* Cambridge, Mass.: Harvard University Press; London: Humphrey Milford, 1919.

———. "Lexical Notes on Luke-Acts: II. Recent Arguments for Medical Language." *Journal of Biblical Literature* 45 (1926): 190–209.

Cadoux, C. J. *The Historic Mission of Jesus: A Constructive Re-examination of the Eschatological Teaching in the Synoptic Gospels.* London: Lutterworth, 1941.

Camery-Hoggatt, Jerry. *Irony in Mark's Gospel: Text and Subtext.* Society for New Testament Studies Monograph Series 72. Cambridge: Cambridge University Press, 1992.

Campbell, Brian. "The Marriage of Soldiers under the Empire." *Journal of Roman Studies* 68 (1978): 153–66.

Carter, Warren. *Matthew and the Margins: A Sociopolitical and Religious Reading.* Maryknoll, N.Y.: Orbis, 2002.

Casson, Lionel. *Ships and Seamanship in the Ancient World*. Princeton, N.J.: Princeton University Press, 1971.

Cave, C. H. "The Leper: Mark 1:40–45." *New Testament Studies* 25 (1978–1979): 245–50.

Chilton, Bruce. "Jesus ben David: Reflections on the Davidssohnfrage." *Journal for the Study of the New Testament* 14 (1982): 88–112.

Collins, Adela Yarbro. *Mark: A Commentary*. Hermeneia. Minneapolis: Fortress, 2007.

———. "Rulers, Divine Men, and Walking on the Water (Mark 6:45–52)." Pages 207–28 in *Religious Propaganda and Missionary Competition in the New Testament World: Essays Honoring Dieter Georgi*. Supplements to Novum Testamentum 74. Leiden: Brill.

Connolly, Peter. *The Roman Fort*. Oxford: Oxford University Press, 1991.

Cope, O. Lamar. *Matthew: A Scribe Trained for the Kingdom of Heaven*. Catholic Biblical Quarterly Monograph Series 5. Washington, D.C.: Catholic Biblical Association of America, 1976.

Cortés-Fuentes, David. "Not Like the Gentiles: The Characterization of Gentiles in the Gospel According to Matthew." *Journal of Hispanic Theology* 9 (2001): 6–26.

Cotter, Wendy J. "Cornelius, the Roman Army and Religion." Pages 279–302 in *Religious Rivalries and the Struggle for Success in Caesarea Maritima*. Edited by Terrence L. Donaldson. Studies in Christianity and Judaism 8. Waterloo, Ont.: Wilfrid Laurier University Press, 2000.

———. "For It Was Not the Season for Figs." *Catholic Biblical Quarterly* 48 (1996): 62–66.

———. "The Markan Sea Miracles: Their History, Formation, and Function in the Literary Context of Greco-Roman Antiquity." PhD dissertation. University of St. Michael's College, Toronto, 1991.

———. "Miracle Stories: The God Asclepius, the Pythagorean Philosophers, and the Roman Rulers." Pages 166–79 in *The Historical Jesus in Context*. Edited by Amy-Jill Levine, Dale C. Allison Jr., and John Dominic Crossan. Princeton, N.J.: Princeton University Press, 2006.

Cranfield, C. E. B. *The Gospel according to Saint Mark*. Cambridge Greek Testament Commentary. Cambridge: Cambridge University Press, 1959.

Davies, R. W. "The *Medici* of the Roman Armed Forces." *Epigraphische Studien* 8 (1969): 83–99.

————. "The Roman Military Medical Service." *Saalburg Jahrbuch* 27 (1970): 84–104.

————. "Some More Military *Medici*." *Epigraphische Studien* 9 (1972): 1–11.

DeFelice, John. *Roman Hospitality: The Professional Women of Pompeii.* Warren Center, Pa.: Shangri-La Publications, 2001.

Denis, A.-M. "Jesus' Walking on the Waters: A Contribution to the History of the Pericope in the Gospel Tradition." *Louvain Studies* 1 (1967): 284–97.

de Romilly, Jacqueline. *La douceur dans la pensée grecque.* Paris: Société d'Édition, "Les Belles Lettres," 1979.

Derrett, J. D. M. "Law in the New Testament: The Syro-Phoenician Woman and the Centurion of Capernaum." *Novum Testamentum* 15 (1973): 161–86.

Dibelius, Martin. *From Tradition to Gospel.* Translated by Bertram Lee Woolf. 1934. Repr., Cambridge: J. Clarke, 1971.

Dickison, Sheila K. "Women in Rome." Pages 1319–32 in vol. 3 of *Civilization of the Ancient Mediterranean: Greece and Rome.* Edited by Michael Grant and Rachel Kitzinger. New York: Scribner, 1988.

Dodd, C. H. "The Appearances of the Risen Christ: An Essay in Form-Criticism of the Gospels." Pages 9–35 in *Studies in The Gospels: Essays in Memory of R. H. Lightfoot.* Edited by Dennis E. Nineham. Oxford: Blackwell, 1955.

Downing, F. Gerald. "The Woman from Syrophoenicia, and Her Doggedness: Mark 7:24–31 (Matt 15:21–28)." Pages 129–49 in *Women in Biblical Tradition.* Edited by George J. Brooke. Studies in Women and Religion 3. Lewiston, N.Y.: Mellen Press, 1992.

Duff, Tim. *Plutarch's Lives: Exploring Virtue and Vice.* Oxford: Clarendon Press, 1999.

Duling, Dennis. "Solomon, Exorcism and the Son of David." *Harvard Theological Review* 68 (1975): 235–52.

Dupont, J. "L'aveugle de Jericho recouvre la vue et suit Jesus (Marc 10,46–52)." *Revue Africaine de théologie* 8, no. 16 (1984): 165–81.

Edersheim, Alfred. *The Life and Times of Jesus the Messiah.* 2 vols. New York: E. R. Herrick, 1886.

Edwards, James P. *The Gospel according to Mark.* Pillar New Testament Commentary. Grand Rapids: Eerdmans, 2002.

Ernst, Josef. *Das Evangelium nach Markus.* Regensburger Neues Testament. Regensburg: Pustet, 1981.

Ferguson, John. "Divination and Oracles: Rome." Pages 951–58 in vol. 2 of *Civilization of the Ancient Mediterranean: Greece and Rome*. Edited by Michael Grant and Rachel Kitzinger. New York: Scribner, 1988.

Fiebig, Paul. *Rabbinische Wundergeschichten des neutestamentlichen Zeitalters: In vokalisiertem Text mit sprachlichen und sachlichen Bemerkungen*. 2d ed. Kleine texte für Vorlesungen und Übungen 78. Berlin: de Gruyter, 1933.

Filson, Floyd V. *A Commentary on the Gospel according to St. Matthew*. Black's New Testament Commentaries. London: A & C Black, 1960.

Fitzmyer, Joseph A. *The Gospel of Luke*. 2 vols. Anchor Bible 28, 28A. New York: Doubleday, 1981–1985.

Fleddermann, Harry. "'And He Wanted to Pass by Them' (Mark 6:48c)." *Catholic Biblical Quarterly* 45 (1983): 389–95.

Focant, Camille. "Mc 7,24–31 Par. Mat 15,21–29: Critique des Sources et/ou Études Narrative." Pages 39–76 in *The Synoptic Gospels: Source Criticism and the New Literary Criticism*. Bibliotheca ephemeridum theologicarum lovaniensium 110. Leuven: Leuven University Press, 1993.

Fone, Bryne. *Homophobia: A History*. New York: Henry Holt, 2000.

France, R. T. *The Gospel of Mark: A Commentary on the Greek Text*. New International Greek Testament Commentary. Grand Rapids: Eerdmans; Carlisle: Paternoster, 2002.

Fuller, Reginald H. *Interpreting the Miracles*. Philadelphia: Westminster, 1963.

Gnilka, Joachim. *Das Evangelium nach Markus*. 2 vols. Evangelisch-katholischer Kommentar zum Neuen Testament 2. Zürich: Benziger; Neukirchen-Vlyun: Neukirchener Verlag, 1978–1979.

Goldworthy, Alan Keith. *The Roman Army at War*. Oxford: Clarendon Press, 1996.

Good, Deirdre J. *Jesus the Meek King*. Harrisburg, Pa.: Trinity Press International, 1999.

Gould, Ezra P. *A Critical and Exegetical Commentary on the Gospel according to St. Mark*. International Critical Commentary. Edinburgh: T & T Clark, 1926.

Graf, Fritz. *Magic in the Ancient World*. Translated by Franklin Philip. Revealing Antiquity 10. Cambridge, Mass.: Harvard University Press, 1997.

Grant, Michael. *The Army of the Caesars*. New York: Scribner, 1974.

Green, Joel B. *Gospel of Luke*. New International Commentary on the New Testament. Grand Rapids: Eerdmanns, 1997.

Grundmann, Walter. *Das Evangelium nach Markus.* 2d ed. Theologischer Handkommentar zum Neuen Testament. Berlin: Evangelische Verlagsanstalt, 1965.

Gundry, Robert H. *Mark: A Commentary on His Apology for the Cross.* Grand Rapids: Eerdmans, 1993.

———. *Matthew: A Commentary on His Literary and Theological Art.* Grand Rapids: Eerdmans, 1982.

Hachlili, Rachel. *Jewish Funerary Customs, Practices and Rites in the Second Temple Period.* Leiden; Boston: Brill, 2005.

Hadas, Moses, and Morton Smith. *Heroes and Gods: Spiritual Biographies in Antiquity.* New York: Harper & Row, 1965.

Haenchen, Ernst. *Der Weg Jesu: Eine Erklärung des Markus-Evangeliums und der kanonischen Parallelen.* 2d ed. Berlin: de Gruyter, 1968.

Hare, Douglas R. A. *Mark.* Westminster Bible Companion. Louisville: Westminster John Knox, 1996.

Harrington, Wilfrid. *Mark.* New Testament Message 4. Wilmington, Del.: Michael Glazier, 1979.

Heil, John Paul. *Jesus Walking on the Sea: Meaning and Gospel Functions of Matt. 14:22–33, Mark 6:45–52, and John 6:15b–21.* Analecta biblica 87. Rome: Biblical Institute Press, 1981.

Held, Heinz Joachim. "Matthew as Interpreter of the Miracle Stories." Pages 165–301 in *Tradition and Interpretation in Matthew.* By Günther Bornkamm, Gerhard Barth, and Heinz Joachim Held. Translated by Percy Scott. Philadelphia: Westminster, 1963.

Helgeland, John. "Roman Army Religion." *ANRW* 16.2:1470–1505. Part 2, *Principat,* 16.2. Edited by H. Temporini and W. Haase. Berlin: de Gruyter, 1978.

Henderson, Tony. "Roman Centurions—at Close Quarters." *The Newcastle Journal,* May, 17, 2007.

Hendrickx, Herman. *The Miracle Stories of the Synoptic Gospels.* Studies in the Synoptic Gospels. San Francisco: Harper & Row, 1987.

Hendriksen, William. *New Testament Commentary: Exposition of the Gospel according to Mark.* Grand Rapids: Baker, 1975.

Hobart, W. K. *The Medical Language of St. Luke.* Dublin: Hodges, Figgis, 1882.

Hoey, Alan S. "Official Policy Towards Oriental Cults in the Roman Army." *Transactions of the American Philological Association* 70 (1939): 456–81.

Hoffman, Birgitta. "The Quarters of Legionary Centurions of the Principate." *Britannia* 26 (1995): 107–51.

Hooker, Morna D. *A Commentary on the Gospel according to St. Mark.* Black's New Testament Commentaries. London: A & C Black, 1991.

Huxley, H. H. "Storm and Shipwreck in Roman Literature." *Greece and Rome* 21 (1952): 117–24.

Jennings, Theodore, Jr., and Tat-Siong Benny Liew. "Mistaken Identities but Model Faith: Rereading the Centurion, the Chap, and the Christ." *Journal of Biblical Literature* 123 (2004): 467–94.

Johnson, Earl S. "Mark 10:46–52." *Catholic Biblical Quarterly* 40 (1978): 191–204.

Johnson, Steven R. *Q 7:1–10: The Centurion's Faith in Jesus' Word.* Documenta Q. Leuven: Peeters, 2002.

Jones, Alexander. *The Gospel according to St. Mark: A Text and Commentary for Students.* New York: Sheed & Ward, 1963.

Kallas, James. *The Significance of the Synoptic Miracles.* London: SPCK, 1961.

Kampen, Natalie. *Image and Status: Roman Working Women in Ostia.* Berlin: Mann, 1981.

Kazmierski, Carl R. "Evangelist and Leper: A Socio-Cultural Study of Mark 1:40–45." *New Testament Studies* 38 (1992): 37–50.

Kee, Howard Clark. "Aretalogy and Gospel." *Journal of Biblical Literature* 92 (1973): 402–22.

———. *Miracle in the Early Christian World: A Study in Sociohistorical Method.* New Haven: Yale University Press, 1983.

Keppie, Lawrence. *The Making of the Roman Army: From Republic to Empire.* Norman: University of Oklahoma Press, 1984.

Kertelge, Karl. *Die Wunder Jesu im Markusevangelium: Eine Redaktionsgeschichtliche Untersuchung.* Studien zum Alten und Neuen Testament 33. Munich: Kösel-Verlag, 1970.

Kloppenborg Verbin, John S. *Excavating Q: The History and Setting of the Sayings Gospel.* Minneapolis: Fortress, 2000.

Klostermann, Erich. *Das Markusevangelium.* 3d ed. HNT 3. Tübingen: Mohr Siebeck, 1936.

Koch, Dietrich-Alex. *Die Bedeutung der Wundererzählungen für die Christologie des Markusevangeliums.* Beihefte zur Zeitschrift für die neutestamentliche Wissenschaft 42. Berlin: de Gruyter, 1975.

Kraus, S. "Das Abdecken des Daches Mc 2:4, Lc 5:19." *Zeitschrift für die neutestamentliche Wissenschaft* 25 (1926): 307–10.

Kuhn, Heinz-Wolfgang. *Ältere Sammlungen im Markusevangelium.* Studien zur Umwelt des Neuen Testaments 8. Göttingen: Vandenhoeck & Ruprecht, 1971.

Lane, William L. *The Gospel according to Mark: The English Text with Introduction, Exposition, and Notes.* New International Commentary on the New Testament. Grand Rapids: Eerdmanns, 1974.

Le Bohec, Yann. *The Roman Imperial Army.* Translated by Raphael Bate. London: Batsford, 1994.

Légasse, Simon. *L'Évangile de Marc.* Lectio divina 5. Paris: Cerf, 1997.

Levine, Amy-Jill. *The Social and Ethnic Dimensions of Matthean Salvation History.* Studies in the Bible and Early Christianity 14. Lewiston, N.Y.: Mellen Press, 1988.

Lightfoot, John. *Horæ Hebraicæ et Talmudicæ: Hebrew and Talmudic Exercitations upon the Gospels, the Acts, Some Chapters of St. Paul's Epistle to the Romans, and the First Epistle to the Corinthians.* Edited by Robert Gandell. 4 vols. Oxford: Oxford University Press, 1859.

Lohmeyer, Ernst. *Das Evangelium des Markus.* 17th ed. Kritisch-exegetischer Kommentar über das Neue Testament 1/2. Göttingen: Vandenhoeck & Ruprecht, 1967.

———. "Und Jesus ging vorüber." *Nieuw Theologisch Tijdschrift* 23 (1934): 206–24.

Lührmann, Dieter. *Das Markusevangelium.* Handbuch zum Neuen Testament 3. Tübingen: Mohr Siebeck, 1987.

MacDonald, Dennis R. *The Homeric Epics and the Gospel of Mark.* New Haven: Yale University Press, 2000.

Mack, Burton L. *A Myth of Innocence: Mark and Christian Origins.* Philadelphia: Fortress, 1988.

Mader, Donald. "The *Entimos Pais* of Matthew 8:5–13 and Luke 7:1–10." Pages 223–35 in *Homosexuality and Religion and Philosophy.* Edited by Wayne R. Dynes and Stephen Donaldson. New York: Garland, 1992.

Marshall, Christopher D. *Faith as a Theme in Mark's Gospel.* Society for New Testament Studies Monograph Series 84. Cambridge: Cambridge University Press, 1990.

Martin, Hubert, Jr. "The Concept of *Philanthrōpia* in Plutarch's *Lives.*" *American Journal of Philology* 82 (1961): 164–75.

———. "The Concept of *Praotes* in Plutarch's *Lives.*" *Greek, Roman, and Byzantine Studies* 3 (1960): 65–73.

McCown, C. C. "Luke's Translation of Semitic into Hellenistic Custom." *Journal of Biblical Literature* 58 (1939): 213–20.

Milgrom, Jacob. *Leviticus 1–16*. Anchor Bible 3. New York: Doubleday, 1964.

Moule, C. F. D. *The Gospel according to Mark*. Cambridge Bible Commentary. Cambridge: Cambridge University Press, 1965.

Neirynck, Frans. *Duality in Mark: Contributions to the Study of the Markan Redaction*. Bibliotheca ephemeridum theologicarum lovaniensium 31. Leuven: Leuven University Press, 1988.

———. "Les expressions double chez Marc et le problème synoptique." *Ephemerides theologicae lovanienses* 59 (1983): 303–30.

———. "The Redactional Text of Mark." *Ephemerides theologicae lovanienses* 57 (1981): 144–62.

Neyrey, Jerome H. "Questions, *Chreiai*, and Challenges to Honor: The Interface of Rhetoric and Culture in Mark's Gospel." *Catholic Biblical Quarterly* 60 (1998): 657–81.

Nineham, Dennis E. *The Gospel of St. Mark*. Pelican Gospel Commentaries. London: A & C Black, 1963.

Painter, John. *Mark's Gospel: Worlds in Conflict*. New Testament Readings. London: Routledge, 1997.

Paulus, Heinrich. *Das Leben Jesu als Grundlage einer reinen Geschichte des Urchristentums*. 2 vols. Heidelberg: C. F. Winter, 1828.

Pesch, Rudolf. *Das Markusevangelium*. 3d ed. 2 vols. Herders theologischer Kommentar zum Neuen Testament. Freiberg: Herder, 1984.

Plummer, Alfred. *A Critical and Exegetical Commentary on the Gospel according to S. Luke*. International Critical Commentary. Edinburgh: T &T Clark, 1896.

Pokorný, Petr. "From Puppy to Child: Problems of Contemporary Biblical Exegesis Demonstrated from Mark 7:24–30/Matt 15:21–28." *New Testament Studies* 41 (1995): 321–37.

Pollard, John. "Divination and Oracles: Greece." Pages 941–50 in vol. 2 of *Civilization of the Ancient Mediterranean: Greece and Rome*. Edited by Michael Grant and Rachel Kitzinger. New York: Scribner, 1988.

Pryke, E. J. *Redactional Style in the Marcan Gospel*. Society for New Testament Studies Monograph Series 33. Cambridge: Cambridge University Press, 1978.

Rawson, Beryl. *Children and Childhood in Roman Italy*. Oxford: Oxford University Press, 2003.

Richardson, Alan. *The Miracle Stories of the Gospels*. 1941. Repr., London: SCM Press, 1963.

Richmond, I. A., et al. "The Agricolan Fort at Fendoch." *Proceedings of the Society of Antiquaries of Scotland* 73 (1938–39): 110–54.

Ringe, Sharon H. "A Gentile Woman's Story, Revisited: Rereading Mark 7:24–31." Pages 79–110 in *A Feminist Companion to Mark*. Edited by Amy-Jill Levine and Marianne Blickenstaff. Feminist Companion to the New Testament and Early Christian Writings 2. Sheffield: Sheffield Academic Press, 2001.

Ritt, Hubert. "Der 'Seewandel Jesu' (Mk 6,45–52 par): Literarische und theologische Aspekte." *Biblische Zeitschrift* 23 (1979): 71–84.

Robbins, Vernon K. "By Land and by Sea: The We-Passages and Ancient Sea Voyages." Pages 215–42 in *Perspectives on Luke-Acts*. Edited by C. H. Talbert. Perspectives in Religious Studies 5. Danville, Va.: Association of Baptist Professors of Religion, 1978.

———. "The Healing of Blind Bartimaeus (Mark 10:46–52) in the Markan Theology." *Journal of Biblical Literature* 92 (1972): 224–43.

———. *Jesus the Teacher: A Socio-Rhetorical Interpretation of Mark*. Philadelphia: Fortress, 1984.

Roloff, Jürgen. *Das Kerygma und der irdische Jesus: Historische Motive in den Jesus-Erzählungen der Evangelien*. Göttingen: Vandehoeck & Ruprecht, 1970.

Saller, Richard. "Anecdotes as Historical Evidence for the Principate." *Greece and Rome*, 2d series, 27, no. 1 (1980): 69–83.

Schenk, Wolfgang. "Tradition und Redaktion in der Epileptiker-Perikope Mk 9:14–29." *Zeitschrift für die neutestamentliche Wissenschaft* 63 (1972): 76–94.

Schenke, Ludger. *Das Markusevangelium*. Kohlhammer Urban-Taschenbücher 405. Stuttgart: Kohlhammer, 1988.

Schlumberger, Sophie. "Le récit de la foi de Bartimée (Marc 10,46–52)." *Études théologiques et religieuses* 68 (1993): 73–81.

Schmithals, Walter. *Das Evangelium nach Markus*. 2 vols. Ökumenischer Taschenbuch-Kommentar. Gütersloh: Mohn, 1979.

Schreiber, Johannes. *Theologie des Vertrauens: Eine redaktionsgeschichtliche Untersuchung des Markusevangeliums*. Hamburg: Furche-Verlag, 1967.

Schürer, Emil. *History of the Jewish People in the Age of Jesus Christ (175 B.C.–A.D. 135)*. Revised and edited by Geza Vermes and F. Millar. Edinburgh: T & T Clark, 1973.

Schweizer, Eduard. *The Good News according to Mark*. Translated by Donald H. Madvig. Richmond: John Knox Press, 1970.

Scroggs, Robin. "Hellenistic Judaism: Pederasty Vilified." Pages 85–98 in *The New Testament and Homosexuality: Contextual Background for Contemporary Debate*. Philadelphia: Fortress, 1983.

———. "Palestinian Judaism: Stern Opposition." Pages 66–84 in *The New Testament and Homosexuality: Contextual Background for Contemporary Debate*. Philadelphia: Fortress, 1983.

Sellew, Philip. "Composition of Didactic Scenes in Mark's Gospel." *Journal of Biblical Literature* 108 (1989): 613–34.

Smith, Jonathan Z. "Good News Is No News: Aretalogy and Gospel." Pages 21–38 in vol. 1 of *Christianity, Judaism and Other Greco-Roman Cults: Studies for Morton Smith at Sixty*. Edited by Jacob Neusner. Studies in Judaism in Late Antiquity 12. Leiden: Brill, 1975.

Smith, Morton. "Prolegomena to a Discussion of Aretalogies, Divine Men, the Gospels and Jesus." *Journal of Biblical Literature* 90 (1971): 174–99.

Speidel, M. P. "The Cult of the Genii in the Roman Army and a New Military Deity." *ANRW* 16.2:1542–55. Part 2, *Principat*, 16.2. Edited by H. Temporini and W. Haase. Berlin: de Gruyter, 1978.

———. "The Roman Army in Judea under the Procurators: The Italian and Augustan Cohort in the Acts of the Apostles." Pages 224–32 in vol. 2 of *Roman Army Studies*. Stuttgart: Franz Steiner, 1992.

———. "The Soldiers' Servants." Pages 342–52 in vol. 2 of *Roman Army Studies*. Stuttgart: Franz Steiner, 1992.

Steinhauser, Michael G. "The Form of the Bartimaeus Narrative." *New Testament Studies* 32 (1986): 583–95.

———. "Part of a Call Story." *Expository Times* 94 (1982–1983): 204–6.

Sterling, Gregory. "Jesus as Exorcist: An Analysis of Matthew 17:14–20; Mark 9:14–29; Luke 9:37–43A." *Catholic Biblical Quarterly* 55 (1993): 467–93.

Stern, Sacha. *Jewish Identity in Early Rabbinic Writings*. Arbeiten zur Geschichte des antiken Judentums und Urchristentums 23. Leiden: Brill, 1994.

Strauss, David Friedrich. *The Life of Jesus*. Translated by George Eliot. 4th ed. London: Swann Sonnenschein, 1906. Repr. 3 vols. Portland, Ore.: Gloger Family Books, 2006.

Struthers, Elizabeth Malbon. *In the Company of Jesus: Characters in Mark's Gospel*. Louisville: Westminster John Knox, 2000.

Tagawa, Kenzo. *Miracles et évangile: la pensée personelle de l'évangéliste Marc*. Études d'histoire et de philosophie religieuses 62. Paris: Presses Universitaires de France, 1966.

Tannehill, Robert C. "The Disciples in Mark: The Function of a Narrative Role." *Journal of Religion* 57 (1977): 386–405.

Taylor, Vincent. *The Formation of the Gospel Tradition.* 2d ed. London: Macmillan, 1949.

———. *The Gospel according to St. Mark: The Greek Text with Introduction, Notes, and Indexes.* London: Macmillan; New York: St. Martin's Press, 1955.

———. *The Life and Ministry of Jesus.* London: Macmillan; New York: St. Martin's Press, 1955.

Theissen, Gerd. *The Gospels in Context: Social and Political History in the Synoptic Tradition.* Translated by Linda M. Maloney. Minneapolis: Fortress, 1991.

———. *The Miracle Stories of the Synoptic Tradition.* Translated by Francis McDonagh. Philadelphia: Fortress, 1983.

Thimmes, Pamela. *Studies in the Biblical Sea-Storm Type-Scene: Convention and Invention.* San Francisco: Mellen Press, 1992.

Tiede, David L. *The Charismatic Figure as Miracle Worker.* Society of Biblical Literature Dissertation Series 1 Missoula, Mont.: Society of Biblical Literature, 1972.

Trocmé, Étienne. *La formation de l'Évangile selon Marc.* Études d'histoire et de philosophie religieuses 57. Paris: Presses Universitaires de France, 1963.

———. *The Formation of the Gospel according to Mark.* Translated by Pamela Gaughan. Philadelphia: Westminster, 1975.

Twelftree, Graham. *Jesus the Exorcist: A Contribution to the Study of the Historical Jesus.* Wissenschaftliche Untersuchungen zum Neuen Testament 2/54. Tübingen: Mohr Siebeck, 1993.

Van der Loos, Hendrik *The Miracles of Jesus.* Supplements to Novum Testamentum 9. Leiden: Brill, 1965.

Wallis, Ian G. *The Faith of Jesus Christ in Early Christian Traditions.* Society for New Testament Studies Monograph Series 84. Cambridge: Cambridge University Press, 1995.

Ward, John. "Military Remains." Pages 38–71 in *Roman Era in Britain.* London: Methuen, 1911.

Webster, Graham. *The Roman Imperial Army of the First and Second Centuries A.D.* London: A & C Black, 1969.

Weinstock, Stefan. *Divus Julius.* Oxford: Clarendon Press, 1971.

Weiss, Johannes. *Das älteste Evangelium: Ein Beitrag zum Verständnis des Markus-Evangeliums und der ältesten evangelischen Überlieferung.* Göttingen: Vandenhoeck & Ruprecht, 1903.

Wellhausen, Julius. *Das Evangelium Marci: Übersetzt und Erklärt.* 2d ed. Berlin: George Reimer, 1909.

Williams, Joel F. *Other Followers of Jesus: Minor Characters as Major Figures in Mark's Gospel.* Journal for the Study of the New Testament: Supplement Series 102. Sheffield: JSOT Press, 1992.

Williamson, Lamar. *Mark.* Interpretation: A Bible Commentary for Teaching and Preaching. Atlanta: John Knox Press, 1983.

Wilmanns, Juliane C. "Der Arzt in der römischen Armee der frühen und hohen Kaiserzeit." Pages 171–87 in vol. 1 of *Ancient Medicine in Its Socio-Cultural Context: Papers Read at the Congress Held at Leiden University, 13–15 April 1992.* Edited by Ph. J. van der Eijk, H. F. J. Horstmanshoff, and P. H. Schrijvers. Clio medica 27. Amsterdam: Rodopi, 1995.

Winter, Bruce. *Roman Wives, Roman Widows: The Appearance of New Women and the Pauline Communities.* Grand Rapids: Eerdmans, 2003.

Witherington, Ben. *The Gospel of Mark: A Socio-Rhetorical Commentary.* Grand Rapids: Eerdmans, 2001.

Wojciechowski, Michal. "The Touching of the Leper (Mark 1:40–45) as a Historical and Symbolic Act of Jesus." *Biblische Zeitschrift* 33 (1989): 114–19.

Woolston, Thomas. *A Fourth Discourse on the Miracles of Our Saviour in View of the Present Controversy between Infidels and Apostates.* 1728. Repr., New York: Garland, 1979.

Index of Names and Subjects

Greeks, 143–45
Green, Joel B., 126n67
Griesbach Hypothesis, 93
Gundry, Robert, 63–64, 66, 87, 131–32,
    158, 165, 167, 183

Hadrian, 159, 190
Haenchen, Ernst, 93, 96
Hansen's disease, 23
hardness of heart, 239
Hare, Douglas, 35, 100
Harrington, Wilfrid, 182
harshness, 150–51, 159
Hazael, 152n36
healing, 49–50, 86, 107, 125, 177, 189
    of Bartimaeus, 42–75, 203
    of blind man of Bethsaida, 236n6
    of demonized boy, 161–91
    of Peter's mother-in-law, 39, 146, 173,
        189
    of the paralytic, 35, 79–105
Hebrew Scriptures, 152, 178, 219
Heil, John Paul, 214
Heliodorus, 213
Hellenism, 240–41
Hellespont, 241, 244, 252
Hendrickx, Herman, 199
hero, 12
Herodians, 80
Herodotus, 73n67, 132, 207n30, 218
Herod the Great, 61, 99, 109–10, 171
Herostratus of Naucratis, 219n69
Hesiod, 69n57
himation (outer garment), 67–70, 74
Hippocrates, 26–27, 28n28, 30, 90
Hobart, W. K., 89
Hoffman, Birgitta, 112n18
Holy Land and the Bible, The (Geikie),
    96
Homer, 59, 69n58, 70n61, 241
homosexuality, 124
Hooker, Morna, 98
Horace, 124n58, 207n30
Huxley, H. H., 207
hygiene, 27–28

Iamblichus, 225–27
identity/identifying, 51, 121, 155, 204,
    228, 250–51, 255
Iliad, 242
illness, 85. *See also* disease

International Q Project, 107
Ishbosheth, 152n36
Isis, 219, 220n69
Italy, 24, 228
"itching disease," 28n28

Jacob, 214n49
Jairus, 91, 129. *See also* raising of Jairus's
    daughter
James (apostle), 45–46, 54, 162, 240
Jennings, Theodore, Jr., 122–24
Jericho, 43–44, 46, 49, 53, 61
Jerusalem, 28
Jesus, 2–3, 7–9, 11–15, 20–23, 25, 29–39,
    41–55, 61–66, 68, 71–72, 74–75,
    79–85, 87–88, 91–93, 101–2, 105–8,
    117, 119–20, 122–23, 125–34, 137–40,
    142, 144, 146, 148–91, 195–99,
    201–7, 210–13, 215–17, 219–24,
    231–40, 246–57
Jewish Scriptures, 212n41
Jewish tradition, 210
Jews, 148, 150–51, 156, 179
Job, 247
John (apostle), 45–46, 54, 162, 240
John of Damascus, 25
Johnson, Earl S., 44, 46
John the Baptist, 122, 171
Jonah, 204–5, 210–11, 220–21, 224, 247
Jones, Alexander, 149
Jones, W. H. S., 24
Joseph, 214n49
Josephus, 61n38, 99, 109–10, 113, 161, 179,
    207n30, 242, 245
Joshua ben Levi (Rabbi), 57
Juda (Jacob's son), 214n49
Julius Caesar, 114n28, 212n40, 224–25,
    228–31
Juvenal, 30, 115, 143, 144n15

Kallas, James, 216
Kazmierski, Carl, 28n29, 33–34
Kelber, Werner, 34
Keppie, Lawrence, 111, 113
Kertelge, Karl, 167
Kingdom of God, 150, 216
Kingdom of Heaven, 3
kissing, 30
kneeling, 31–33, 32n35, 37, 177

Lake of Gennesaret. *See* Sea of Galilee
Lane, William, 87, 100, 181–82

Index of Ancient Sources